W9-AED-805

THE REVOLUTIONARY SPIRIT IN FRANCE AND AMERICA

A study of moral and intellectual relations between France and the United States at the end of the eighteenth century

by
BERNARD FAŸ

Translated by
RAMON GUTHRIE

NEW YORK
HARCOURT, BRACE & COMPANY

Published in France as "L'Esprit Révolutionnaire en France et aux Etats-Unis à la Fin du XVIIIe Siècle"

PRINTED IN THE U. S. A. BY
QUINN & BODEN COMPANY, INC.
RAHWAY, N. J.

Contents

THE REVOLUTIONARY SPIRIT IN FRANCE AND AMERICA

Chapter I

IN SEARCH OF A NEW WORLD

Moral situation of France and England in 1770, pp. 3-8. Rôle and influence of Raynal, pp. 8-13. Deist mysticism in France, pp. 13-17. Controversy on America representing an unknown and admired force, pp. 17-23.

Religious liberty in the new world, pp. 23-26. Quarrel between England and her colonies, pp. 27-33. American opinion and France. Decreasing unpopularity of France, pp. 33-43.

Death of Louis XV. Hopes roused in France and the good will of Louis XVI, pp. 43-45. Desire for a national uplift at home and abroad. The American crisis seems to furnish the opportunity for such a movement. Vergennes wishes to take advantage of it, pp. 45-48. French public opinion seems divided on the question, pp. 48-55. Vergennes' efforts to turn opinion in favor of the Americans. He uses Beaumarchais as a means of persuading Louis XVI, pp. 55-61.

The picture of the intellectual and political world of the times that is presented by the books and newspapers published between 1770 and 1775, is characterized by a contrast: a lull has settled over the earth; the great powers of the West are eyeing each other and seeking to avoid violent conflicts, governments are striving for stability and permanence; and even the great writers seem to be prolonging an age whose most brilliant period has gone by. Yet at the same time, a fever of newness is beginning to spread, an acute and indistinct restlessness prevails throughout the world.

England and France, the two great nations whose diplomats and writers served as models to the world at large, illustrate very clearly the precarious equilibrium between the strength of custom and the desires of men.[1] The state of peace established by the treaty of 1763 was maintained; Louis XV wanted to die without having seen any new wars. England knew this; her newspapers repeated it; but it was also felt that France was undergoing a moral transformation whose results no one could foretell.[2] Together with too feeble efforts at reorganization were seen riots, bankruptcies, and waves of wrath and popular indignation. In 1770 not a month went by without the English papers announcing a revolt in France.[3] And the continental newspapers, although they admired the strength and incontestable political superiority of England, enumerated without pity her quarrels and dissensions, the which were all the more striking and conspicuous since the discussions of the English Parliament were then the only example of the free parliamentary activity.[4]

Peace had facilitated the relations between the philosophers of the various nations, and intellectual collaboration between France and England had developed. At Paris Anglomania went so far that plays and books were written making fun of it, such as the wearying *Anglomane* by Saurin,[5] or attacking it, as did *Le Dictionnaire social et patriotique*. The London newspapers, for their part, were justified in saying that "London is the general clearing-house for French merchandise" (dispatch from London quoted in the *Pennsylvania Gazette* of July 4, 1771).

Unfortunately this cordial intercourse seemed concerned only with futilities, and neither the arts nor the sciences afforded any evidence of its fruitfulness. After the *Encyclopédie*, which was nearing completion; after the great works of Voltaire, the only remaining evidence of whose activity was little clandestine pamphlets; after the famous novels of Rousseau, who was living in retreat, France could offer the world nothing that seemed to be of the same caliber; nor was it Debelloy, Marmontel, or Baculard d'Arnaud who could offset this mediocrity in the eyes of other nations and break this lethargy.

France dozed in her defeat as England in her victory. Louis XV was still called "the Well-Beloved," but he was hated and, even more perhaps, scorned. D'Aiguillon, the Minister of Foreign Affairs, was unpopular; and the Comptroller-General Terray, in spite of his efforts to ameliorate the condition of French finances, found himself both hated for what he did succeed in doing and incapable of realizing sufficient reforms. The exile of the Parliaments had excited against the King and his government both the upper middle class and the writers of the time, and these formed the dominant as well as the most active part of the small group which bore the name of "public opinion." Hatred and scorn reigned everywhere. It was the same in matters of religion. Since the suppression and dispersion of the Jesuits, the philosophic campaign seemed to have died down—although in 1770 Holbach had published his great book, *Le Système de la Nature.* But this book with its materialistic affirmations was rather a *résumé* of already-known theories than a fresh attack. On the contrary, there arose from all sides a call to religious sentiments.[6] Here we have Voltaire building a church, attending communion on Easter Sunday, preaching from the pulpit: here is Rousseau dreaming and finding outlet for his mystic soul in the *Rêveries d'un Promeneur solitaire.* Turgot severs relations with the *Encyclopédistes:* Helvetius,[7] before his death, forms the project of uniting writers and savants into a Masonic lodge for fraternal labors in the search of knowledge and the practice of benevolence. On every hand Freemasonry springs up afresh to create lodges to which are drawn the finest minds and the noblest souls of the century, weary of negation and argument. Whether it be that the lessons of Rousseau are beginning to bring forth fruit, or simply that the French soul is being borne in this direction by the rhythm and the law of its activity, on all sides one hears an appeal to sentiment and a protest against sterility and negation. In religion, in politics, in science, there is a tendency to endow sentiment with power. Odes are written on such subjects as navigation, attacks of fever, etc. The utilitarian rôle of the arts is emphasized and dwelt upon with emotion.[8] People find pleasure in styling themselves patriots; and this term, together with that of Citizen, comes into general usage.[9] This tendency becomes so outstanding as to create a mode: it is fashionable to affect spontaneity. The ascendancy of Madame du Barry over Louis XV was the result of her charm and of a sort of good-fellowship with which she treated him. Thus, underneath the great quarrels of the century—the which were now somewhat appeased—a vast movement, until now obscure and repressed, was sweeping along the younger generations and even laying hold upon their elders, whom it was eventually to sweep away. It is not yet a question of a campaign with a well-defined program and precise aims, as was the *Encyclopédie:* neither is it a group of artists set on the road to success, as in 1660. It seems to be a phenomenon of neither a purely intellectual nor a social order. It is rather a profound modification of the moral being of an entire people and of an entire era. England, no more than France, escaped it. Chatterton and MacPherson were bringing new accents into her poetry. In her political life old Chatham on the brink of death beholds both the amazing corruption of the Court and the violences of the Whigs of Wilkes' following.[10] He lives to see the frenzied people of London carry their radical Lord Mayor in triumph and hail him as a prophet. The old statesman is moved, and his feeble voice takes on an almost religious accent when it foretells his country's trials. Even the far-off colonies in America are inflamed with the fire that the Whigs of Europe have kindled: they are wrought with a fever that no one understands. If one considers the civilizations of France and England as the center of the occidental world of the eighteenth century, it may be said that about 1770 this world was undergoing a religious and sentimental crisis that was impelling nations toward a moral and political ideal differing from the one that was still officially accepted.

After the wave of discussions and criticism, the world was ready to feel, to love and to admire. An urge to worship was making itself felt. But first new objects of worship and new forms were needed.

A study of the most significant intellectual works of the years 1770-1774 ought to show how contemporary writers judged this phenomenon and in what way this mysterious force was working in them.

One of the most remarkable books of the end of the eighteenth century is without question the work which Abbé Raynal published in 1770 under the pompous title, *Histoire philosophique et politique des Etablissements et du Commerce des Européens dans les deux Indes* (Amsterdam, 1770). The concept of the book is an original one. Raynal's intent was not to treat of battles and of kings, but to show how economic considerations dominate nations. He defended, therefore, by the plan of his book and by its very title, a materialistic thesis, which also afforded him an opportunity for criticizing indirectly all the undertakings and all the great enterprises of the European nations during the preceding three centuries. For the splendor of great wars and the glory of valiant kings, he substituted the glamor of far-off discoveries and the prestige, both mysterious and scientific, of the men who found worlds glittering with gold and strange religions. Thus he laid hold upon the imagination, and in a time when books of travel were in such vogue, he furnished in the guise of erudition information at the same time original and picturesque. He afforded a considerable contribution to the effort of the times toward the finding or the creating of a new marvelousness which should be divorced from the childishness of mythology, from conventions and from superstition, and which should be a thing of the living present without losing its emotional appeal. Raynal's talent, bombastic, violent and rationalistic, put vehemence into the most arduous exposition and exploited avidly all the resources of picturesqueness, strangeness and wonder that the New World could offer him, and all this, with a weight and precision well calculated to impress the reader. Given so splendid a subject, he could continue all the attacks of the philosophical eighteenth century against intolerance, superstition, servitude, and the cupidity of the European governments. He could give God a piece of his mind for having permitted so much suffering. A priest himself, he could curse the priests.

This he did. And his book had the most brilliant success of the century; about it rallied all those who felt the irk of discontent and restlessness. In all stations and spheres, hearts and minds were galvanized by it, from young Manon Phlipon,[11] who devoured it, to Monsieur le Chevalier de Chateaubriand, who made it his breviary and drew from it no doubt his desire to set forth in search of Celuta and the Northwest Passage.[12] As was the custom of the time, all the authors who were handling kindred subjects or who were supposedly making new studies of the same one, copied it without troubling to make changes. The Abbé Roubaud[13] in his *Histoire générale de l'Asie, de l'Afrique et de l'Amérique* in fourteen volumes, did little save transcribe the information and statements of Raynal. Hornot, who published in 1776 a *Histoire abrégée des principaux Evénements arrivés dans le Nouveau Monde*, cut out parts of it for the sake of brevity but changed nothing. Thus, up to 1789, hardly a year went by but an imitation of Raynal appeared. His book had been translated into all languages; and in the English colonies in America, who were then in conflict with their motherland, special editions of such chapters of Raynal as dealt with the grounds of this conflict were published. It is, then, by its intention and by its effect, a book of great value.[14] It is surprising how little worth it has from the point of view of exact knowledge. We know that Raynal incorporated into his book items that his friends furnished him and

that he inserted them without verification. These were generally only philosophical dissertations.[15] But he himself did not gather his data with rigorous exactness: to give an idea of the population of Philadelphia he cites the statistics of 1731.[16]

He states that Pennsylvania is on the seacoast, although in reality it is separated from the sea by a distance of more than twenty-five miles. To depict New England and New England life, he inserts a discourse by a poor wench, Polly Baker,[17] who had been accused and convicted of having six illegitimate children. He tells how the court, touched by her frankness and natural virtue, pardoned and released her. And from this he proceeds to draw moving philosophical conclusions. Later Franklin told him the tale of how, when he was a young publisher, he had, for lack of other copy, composed an imaginary discourse which he had attributed to a certain Polly Baker, who was supposed to defend and justify herself for having six illegitimate children. This discourse had had so much success that all the English papers had reprinted it.

Raynal maintained that such an error on his part was a glorious one, and he changed nothing in his book.[18] At any rate, he cannot be accused of having sacrificed exactness merely for the sake of logic. He seems to have felt neither hesitation nor shame at contradicting himself. On page 372 of his Volume VI he bemoans the lot of New England, which he claims has been, for the past fifty

years, falling more and more deeply into decline; and on page 425 of the same volume he declares that soon the colonies will become as densely populated as their mother country and will equal it in power. These errors are particularly unpardonable, for it was quite easy to obtain information concerning the English colonies in America, since they were a constant subject of conversation and had been described in numerous English books. Raynal's inaccuracies were further accentuated by the dogmatic tone with which he spoke on everything and chose to admonish mankind. He undertook to reprimand, with neither modesty nor reserve, the English government, the discontented colonists and the nations of Europe. He regarded all these details as being of relative unimportance to one who possessed the key to the mysteries of life, the true light: a philosophic soul. The information that he furnished was merely a bait. His aim was above all to teach truths of a general nature. Thus the errors in the facts that he furnished generously on Pennsylvania and Boston seemed to him to be abundantly made up for by the great lessons which he drew from the morality of the Quakers, by his predictions of the glorious future of America and by the moral and political applications which he deduced from them.

The most brilliant and affirmative part of his formidable book, in which nothing is spared, is the picture of North America. He executed it with special care and put into it some of his most sonorous pages. In these,

his whole program is revealed, or at least all that he himself knew of his program. It is significant that he inserted them at the end of his sixth and last volume.[19]

It is the thought of the young European peoples, set down in the solitudes of the New World, given to new and simple religions, devoted to liberty and free from corruption, that starts him teaching and prophesying. He sees in them the future masters of the universe, the preceptors of Europe. In doing this he gives concrete expression to ideas that were already in circulation. As early as 1734, Voltaire in his *Lettres sur les Anglais* had given a brilliant picture of the Quakers. He portrays them as primitive men, the only true disciples of Christ, who, like the Quakers, did not baptize, did not partake of communion, and condemned luxury and war (*Œuvres de Voltaire*, Vol. XXII, pp. 82-95). In his *Traité sur la Tolérance* (1763) he lavishes on them the same praises. Indeed, throughout his literary career he used them as a weapon against Catholicism. In his *Essai sur les Mœurs* he devoted entire pages to William Penn and his religious organization in the New World, so simple, so reasonable, and so fraught with virtue. "These primitive beings are of all men the most worthy of respect," he writes. In the *Philosophical Dictionary* the words "baptism," "church," "Quakers," "Hermes," and "tolerance" gave him the opportunity to continue this portrait of the customs and character of the Quakers, with their sane fervor which bore no offense to philosophy and, above all, their altruism. Indeed, one of the most violent attacks against Catholicism about 1770 was the anonymous pamphlet, attributed to Voltaire, *L'Américain sensé par hazard en Europe* (Rome, 1769), in which the Catholic dogmas and the Mass are made the object of ridicule and blasphemy in the name of pure Reason. The custom of using the Quakers as the representatives of wisdom and common sense was so generally accepted that one of the enemies of Voltaire and the philosophers, in refutation of the Sage of Ferney, wrote in 1768 a pamphlet which he entitled *Les Quakers à leur Frère Voltaire*[20] (London, 1768). This little work by Fabry d'Autrey, in which Voltaire is rebuked in concise but measured terms and his violences reproached with firmness, shows the place that, even before Raynal, the Quakers held in religious and philosophic controversy. The principal novelty that Raynal brought into play in treating this subject consisted of the use of a prophetic and impassioned tone instead of the raillery and the indirect allusions of Voltaire.

He describes thus the future of the Quakers: "How may we associate the strictness of the evangelical maxims which govern the Quakers to the letter, with that organization of offensive and defensive force which keeps all Christian peoples in a state of continual warfare? If anything distinguishes favorably the disciples of Jesus from the children of Mohammed, it is the weapons that the former seem to have abandoned to the latter. Was it not persecution and martyrdoms that swelled the ranks of Christianity at its birth? Even so, the Quakers flourished under the hand of the executioner and the conqueror. By patience in prisons and in tortures, they will gain more converts than the gibbets of the wicked can destroy. What would the French or the Spaniards do if they invaded Pennsylvania, weapons in their hands? Unless they slaughtered in a single night or in a single day all the inhabitants of this happy land, they would not stamp out the germ and the posterity of these gentle and charitable men. Violence finds its limitations in its own excesses. It consumes itself and is extinguished like fire in its own ashes. But virtue, when it is directed by an enthusiasm for humanity, by the spirit of fraternity, comes to life again like a tree under the blade of the ax. The wicked need the aid of the multitude to carry out their sanguinary projects. The righteous man, the Quaker, needs only a brother to receive from him or to give him succor. Go, ye warrior peoples, ye peoples of slaves and of tyrants, go to Pennsylvania! There you will find every door open, all possessions unguarded, not a soldier, and many merchants and laborers. But if you torment them or afflict them, they will take flight and leave you their fallow fields, their factories in ruins, their deserted shops. They will push on to cultivate and people a new land, they will circle the world and die along the way rather than slaughter you or obey you. What will you have gained save the hatred of mankind and the execration of centuries to come?" [21] His enthusiasm for this primitive folk leads him to use them as a great lesson to the nations. He exclaims, "Pennsylvania gives the lie to the imposture and the flattery that proclaim with impunity in temples and courts that man has need of gods and kings. The righteous man, the free man, needs only his equals to be happy" (*op. cit.*, Vol. VI, p. 294). Then he depicts the moral decadence of Europe and the progress of America, where agriculture, arts and sciences are to prosper, and which is to bring about a new era for humanity (*idem*, p. 425). He believes that this result is inevitable and does not countenance any attempt of immoral European intrigues to hasten it. He does not even accord the English colonists the right to free themselves by force, so much does he desire their absolute spiritual purity and see in them the apostles of a new moral world. He lays these praises and these heavy responsibilities upon the thirteen colonies, who were then having difficulties with Great Britain, their mother country. In his preaching are mingled the voice of a prophet announcing a God and that of a tutor instructing a pupil. The essential and secret thesis of his book might be recapitulated approximately in this formula: the moral reformation will come about through economic phenomena and through the influence of America; it will be inaugurated by the Anglo-Americans, a people which "enjoys all the happiness compatible with human frailty"; it will follow the lines that human reason and philosophy will trace for it, and therefore it is necessary that proponents of philosophy bring the Philadelphians to understand what their duty is and what their method of accomplishing it should be. Out of this collaboration, to which the former are to contribute their ideas and precepts, the latter their faith and their acts, the reign of wisdom will be born.

His exhortations fell on ready ground. His ideas might seem grotesque because of the daring fashion in which he warped them to his ends. But they could neither surprise nor shock. America and the English colonies were then the center of impassioned discussion, political as well as scientific and philosophical.[22] A certain Abbé De Pauw, a philosopher of the Berlin school, had just published in that city a work which had attained a great success and caused unusual stir. It was entitled *Recherches philosophiques sur les Anglo-Américains.* Abbé De Pauw had discovered that America was a continent of recent formation, that it had hardly finished drying out, or even that it was still just a bit wet. It was therefore in every way inferior to Europe; the plants there were smaller and scentless, the animals were feeble, the men puny, without hair, and, what is still more serious, as inept as they were torpid in the delicate and capital art of reproduction. Abbé De Pauw's book is highly obscene. It is based on most disconcerting scientific lucubrations, as the pages which I have reproduced in Appendix I prove; but it enjoyed great popularity, as much because of its picturesqueness as because of the conclusions of which it was fruitful: the savages are good for nothing, the famous "state of Nature" is a myth; hurrah for luxury and Europe that produced it! As soon as it was published, the book was refuted. A Benedictine, a disciple of Rousseau, Dom Pernetty,[23] showed that De Pauw had misunderstood Lahontan, the principal authority for his calumny of the savages, and that, as a matter of fact, these savages possessed, together with great natural virtue, a degree of strength unknown in our degenerate climes. Dom Pernetty believed in Nature, and Abbé De Pauw, in Progress; both of them based their arguments on inexact data and made more effort to be sensational than to be honest. In this they succeeded, moreover; for in five years De Pauw's book had gone into four editions and Pernetty's into at least three.[24] The whole scientific world was stirred by their quarrel. Buffon went to the trouble of discussing De Pauw and investigating the degree of truth to be found in his work. He concluded that De Pauw had wrongly confused the northern part of America with the southern. It is only in the South that the animals are puny.[25] And even Buffon's conclusion is false, as Jefferson clearly shows in his *Notes on Virginia*.[26] Public opinion, siding with Raynal, preferred to reconcile these two theses: it was agreed that America in itself did not equal Europe, an older and more advanced continent. However, the "state of Nature," which America enjoyed, being in itself good, the

Europeans who had established themselves on that continent and who had improved the soil and the climate united the advantages of both hemispheres, being both carried along by the moral and material progress of Europe and purified by the American "state of Nature."

Such, then, was the double aspect under which these much-discussed colonists were known in France. All the newspapers of the time were united in praising the Quakers for having liberated their slaves and thus given an example to the world.[27] A rather mediocre, but none the less esteemed, writer of the period, Guillard de Beaurieu, dedicated to the inhabitants of Virginia his book, *L'Elève de la Nature*. This book describes a model education as conceived by a disciple of Rousseau. A young man, who has been left to pass his early childhood in complete isolation is then taken, naked, to an almost desert island and left there in order to discover for himself all that man needs to know.[28] Here is an ideal mixture of civilization and nature. And this book is placed under the patronage of the Anglo-Americans and especially of the Virginians; because, says Beaurieu, they have found a means to cultivate their country without having large cities, without luxuries, without crimes, and without infirmities. "You are as Nature would have us all," he cries in an effusion of tenderness.

This testimony of Beaurieu is important, not because of the artistic or philosophical value of the book, but because it expresses the point of view of the followers of Rousseau and the Economists. The latter professed the greatest respect for these transplanted Europeans, who, without becoming corrupted, had been able to base their civilization on agriculture while still practicing the arts. *Le Journal d'Agriculture* and the *Ephémérides du Citoyen*, their two principal organs, spoke continually of this people who had undertaken the destruction of slavery, who so generously defended against England the principles of natural rights, who cultivated their land so well, and who "devoted themselves greatly to education, from which general prosperity for this happy land was expected to spring" (*Ephémérides du Citoyen*, 1771, Vol. XI.[29])

There is also talk of Franklin, the great scholar who had cultivated the sciences and politics and subjugated lightning, while organizing the postal service of Philadelphia. Another object of admiration is the Philosophical Society of Pennsylvania, which had just been founded and whose spirit of philanthropy and utility seemed both to mark the conquest of the solitudes of the New World by European philosophy and to afford in its simple and practical wisdom a lesson to futile and corrupt Europe. The founding of this body was hailed in warm terms addressed to both the society and its organizer, Franklin. Even outside of the Economist group, it was considered a great event: *Les Observations sur la Physique*, *Journal des Savants*, and the publications which copied them mention it.[30] The reason is that

Franklin had come to be known and appreciated. Arriving in France as soon as discussions with England had taken a serious turn, he had previously (on his trip in 1767) made friends with scholars such as Chappe,[31] Father J. E. Berthier and Dalibard, with whom he was already in correspondence. He had seen Quesnay and was in relations with the whole group of Economists, especially with Dupont.[32] From the date of his second visit in 1769, he kept up a very regular correspondence with the scholarly Le Roy[33] and a certain Doctor Barbeu Dubourg, a devout physiocrat, a very worthy man, generous and exceedingly pious, who immediately began to translate Franklin's works.[34] The edition in two thick quarto volumes, very carefully done, appeared in 1773. It was praised and discussed everywhere; for in inventing the lightning-rod, Franklin had made a master stroke: he had hit upon a means of showing himself a benefactor of humanity and of subjugating one of the most mysterious and merciless forces of Nature. People were even more appreciative of the magic of his discovery than of the benefit that it conferred. From 1773 on, he was held up in all the lettered circles in France as the perfect type of a natural man and philosopher. He inspired a pious admiration and a religious respect.

It needed no more than this for public opinion, already restless and in search of emotions, to be roused in favor of the Anglo-Americans. But the persecutions that the English ministry heaped upon these colonists, who had so many good qualities and who had always fought so well for the mother country, redoubled public interest in their favor. Everywhere people took their side. They were carrying on the fight of Liberty, and already they were a matter of legend. The future of this new world of which people dreamed seemed to be in their hands. They were not urged to revolt, for people believed them too righteous to use violence; but it was thought that in them the world would see the first modern martyrs of the true religion.[35] Raynal voiced this impression, the Economists printed it every month in their *Ephémérides*, and the other papers repeated it. Even the official journals acknowledged it; for we find in the *Gazette de France* of April 4, 1774, this truly curious item, which the *Mercure* also published in its number of April, 1774: "Our navigators, who have studied the northern continent well, assert that an innate taste for liberty is inseparable from the soil, the sky, the forests and the lakes which keep this vast and still new country from resembling the other parts of the globe. They are persuaded that any European transported to those climes would contract this peculiar characteristic." Thus public opinion and the leaders of thought in France formed an idea of the Anglo-Americans, which, in the midst of dominant disorder and spiritual restlessness, constituted a sort of moral and social ideal. It was like a Utopia, almost unreal and yet half true. De Pauw's grotesque discussions, Raynal's sensational book, the theories of the Encyclopedists, led people to seek eagerly everything that might come from the colonists and to form the most flattering conception of them as an agricultural, philosophical, tolerant, pious, reasoning, and happy nation.

*
* *

This glowing picture, modeled close to the heart's desire, was in danger of not conforming to reality. The English colonies, it is true, did owe their founding to a need for religious liberty: the Pilgrims, who founded Plymouth, the first New England colony, in 1620, the Puritans who had settled Massachusetts Bay in 1630, had certainly been led to leave England by neither a taste for adventure nor a thirst for riches. One may also believe that George Calvert, Lord Baltimore, the founder of Maryland, sought in the New World only religious liberty for himself and for his Catholic coreligionists. And William Penn, in spite of his political and commercial shrewdness, was clearly guided by his religious faith when he organized his government of Pennsylvania at the end of the seventeenth century; and during this whole century it was indeed religious persecutions that drove the French Huguenots, the Irish Catholics and others of their kind from Europe. But we must not ignore the fact that Virginia, founded by the London Company, as well as the Carolinas, New Jersey, Georgia, Delaware, Connecticut and New Hampshire owe their origins to the spirit of adventure and speculation. As for Rhode Island, although it owed its foundation to religious persecutions, it was to those which the Puritans of Massachusetts visited upon their dissenting brethren. We cannot then deny the religious preoccupations of the Anglo-Americans, but neither can we see in them tolerant and disinterested philosophers. Sometimes they did have these qualities and, taken over a long period, they showed themselves to be liberal on the whole; but throughout New England, the established church was maintained as an exacting and intolerant secular power; and in Virginia, New York, the Carolinas and Maryland, the Church of England occupied a like position, although it held a less tyrannic dogma and displayed a greater degree of complaisance. In 1770-1774 it could be said that, except in Pennsylvania and Rhode Island, absolute tolerance was very little practiced on American soil. Nor was the "state of Nature" in better case. From North to South, all the colonists were united in their hatred of the Indians.[36] They had much more scorn and antipathy for them than the French colonists of Canada had ever felt. Contact and association with these primitive people had not been sufficient to modify the habits of the Anglo-Americans. Concerning the Indians and their ways, they were strangely ignorant. For example, we find the Anglo-Americans who were the most kindly disposed toward the Indians seeing in them one of the Lost Tribes of Israel.[37]

From this point of view, the Jesuits and the French travelers were much ahead of the English. They had, concerning the Indians, a curiosity often mixed with sympathy which enabled them to understand them more thoroughly.[38] Moreover, it must not be thought that the English emigrants to America had kept their customs and civilization just as they were before their emigration. Life in the wilderness, silence and meditation had wrought profound transformations in these people. On the pious, strict and patient men of the North, their surroundings had stamped a new and altogether remarkable character of strength, simplicity and fearlessness. These men had developed pride and individuality at the same time that their entire natures were undergoing simplification. Their instincts had become more direct and more violent. Thanks to the vastness of the territory that they had conquered and the material well-being that they had built up, the inhabitants of New England, coming in direct contact with the soil, were forming a new race in whom, under a strict morality, were hidden faculties for simple and strong delights and whose predominantly pessimistic religion concealed an unlimited optimism. In the South, the cultured class, idle because of slave labor, and delivered, by their remoteness, from many European prejudices, produced, along with typical English gentlemen, some few cultivated minds endowed with curiosity and independence. Since there existed in the South a class of poor whites, whose success was rendered difficult by social conditions and slave labor and who, moreover, were not under the restraint of a strong religious discipline, as was the case in the North, every bold idea and every violent act found fertile soil there. These emigrants, come from Europe to make their fortunes and thrown the more brutally in contact with the wilderness because they had no solid religious bond and strong social instinct to unite them, as did the colonists in the North—these penniless emigrants knew, if not the "state of Nature," at least a state of warfare with Nature in all its might. Among those who did not die of it, the result was a pugnacious, violent and avid temperament. In contrast with such elements, the merchant class of the ports, who carried on commerce with England, enjoyed a cosmopolitan luxury and found time to read, may seem colorless and impotent. But it was this class that furnished staunch citizens and leaders. In vain was it destroyed as Tory; it sprang up again as Federalist. Without its rebellious children, the American Revolution would never have come about. The situation of the Quakers was similar. Even in Pennsylvania, they were in minority. But the pureness of their lives, their commercial shrewdness, their nomadic habits, the advantage that the tolerance which they practiced gave them, and finally, the remarkable development of individual personality which their system produced, all this gave them a prestige and an influence far out of proportion to their number.

These thirteen colonies, each one of whom had its own government with a system of popular representation, a governor named by the king, a very wide autonomy in everything that concerned their internal life, so long as they should show themselves loyal—these thirteen almost independent States were for a long while faithful subjects of England. They were attached to the mother country by their language, by the body of their institutions and customs, and, above all, by a common enemy and peril—the French. For the Anglo-Americans, the great peril had always lain in France. The English and French colonies were founded during the same period. But the French were bolder, penetrated farther, were more adaptable, and more successful in making friends with the savages. If they had been more numerous, with such advantages they would undoubtedly have conquered; but they never came over in sufficient numbers, they were never well enough provisioned; and the French navy was not strong enough to maintain contact between them and France. Thus they were doomed to succumb, but it was not without having fought. When, in 1753, Franklin proposed the union of the English colonies, it was in order to ward off the danger from France. In 1755 the young John Adams thought that the only obstacle that prevented the Anglo-Americans from dominating the world was the French.[39]

The treaty of 1763 did away with this obstacle. England, triumphant, took Canada—for its own advantage and in deference to the wishes of the colonists. These latter, rightfully proud of the part that they had played in the victorious combat, saw opening before them an era of prosperity and growth. In the immense forests, where the English had been beaten, the colonial militia had conquered the French. Young leaders such as Colonel Washington would have done honor even to an old nation. From now on, the danger caused by the Indians allied with the French was to disappear and the peaceful conquest of the West was to be possible. A world had been delivered into the hands of these 1,700,000 colonists. Security and wealth were to grow in proportions that even the most ambitious would not have dared to hope for ten years earlier. This struggle, so gloriously brought to a close, inspired the Americans with a pride and confidence in themselves which prompted them to perfect their social state and to realize their desire for progress. The growth that the thirteen colonies underwent from 1764 to 1774 was both physical and moral.

All this England failed to take into consideration. It was with astonishment that she beheld the colonists demanding rights and prerogatives that heretofore they would not have dreamed of imploring. For two centuries it had been taken for granted that the English Parliament might make laws for the English colonies as well as for the motherland, and there had never been any difficulties on this score. The king was considered to have the same prerogatives in America as in Europe, and Parliament the same power to levy taxes. For two centuries it had been thus. But times had changed. When Lord Bute, later Lord Grenville, the English premier, attempted to make the colonies contribute to the lightening of the heavy debt that England had contracted, the colonists protested. In 1764 James Otis, one of the leaders of New England Whigs, in his stirring pamphlet, *The Rights of the British Colonists Asserted and Proved*, maintained that the English Parliament could make laws for the general good of the colonies, but not tax the property of the Americans nor, consequently, their commerce. He demanded representation in Parliament for his compatriots. His pamphlet was violent. The English government took no notice of it, or considered it only as a bit of empty ranting, and proceeded to pass the Stamp Act. Public opinion in all the colonies was roused, there was a general movement to boycott English goods; the law could not be enforced, and Parliament decided to repeal it in 1765. But the agitation did not cease. In 1767 the English prime minister tried to levy taxes to which the Americans could find no constitutional objection; and, since they had recognized Parliament's right to make laws and regulations for the good of the colonies, so long as these laws in no way concerned their internal administration, he conceived the plan of placing a duty on the tea, glass, paper and lead that was imported into America. He also wished to establish an army in the colonies under the pretext of affording them protection. He was ready to use force and made no attempt to conceal it. The colonists' protest took on a serious tone. Samuel Adams in Massachusetts and John Dickinson in Pennsylvania asserted that these measures violated American liberties, since, by this method of taxing the colonists' imports, Parliament could dominate their commerce entirely. Dickinson asserted, however, that the thought of independence was far from him. But, as one may see, the American controversy had made progress. There were riots, and once more the English government yielded. In 1770 it repealed all duties except the tax on tea but arranged that, even then, tea should be sold cheaper in America than in England.

In spite of this concession, American public opinion was aroused, and it continued to fight for the principle involved. This long quarrel had diminished loyalty to England, strengthened the American Whigs, and given the colonists popular leaders. At Boston in December, 1773, some English ships carrying tea were pillaged. In answer to this, the English government closed the port of Boston, changed the charter of Massachusetts in such a way as to control the administration of this colony and took military measures. Thereat the colonies united, set up a Congress and prepared for resistance.

From this too brief summary it is obvious that the colonists had changed perceptibly since 1763, if not in their disposition, at least in their arguments and their point of view. They had been supported and carried along in this struggle by forces that had taken them far beyond the goal that they had set out to attain. Their effort was the result of the general tendency of the English Whigs toward increasingly democratic concepts. The English Whigs, and especially Pitt, supported them unflaggingly from 1763 to 1773. Thus, this quarrel might seem to be a by-product of the struggle between the English parties. But such an interpretation does not suffice to explain a movement so formidable and so varied in character. As a matter of fact, the American resistance was not purely political and economical. It was also a moral, sentimental and religious crisis. It entailed the revision of the whole system of Anglo-Saxon metaphysical concepts which until then had been tacitly accepted. We find Virginia refusing to receive her Anglican priests from England any longer and abandoning almost entirely the practice of a cult heretofore so strong.[40] The Baptist doctrine was spreading and taking the place of more precise forms of Protestantism.[41] Even New England Congregationalism was dividing into three branches[42] and, under the name of Universalists, a group of pastors and worshipers who refused to believe in damnation was forming. This movement was to go further and further in the direction of liberalism and to lead to Unitarianism. As early as 1773, J. Murray had voiced the desire which the dissident Puritans entertained for a more indulgent church with more vague and consoling dogmas.[43] Moreover, it was between 1760 and

1770 that the first Methodist missionaries traveled through America setting up highly democratic religious associations.[44] Thus in all the Southern colonies, which were originally Anglican, religious practices were dying out; in the Central colonies, where religious tolerance among Protestants prevailed, sects multiplied and became more and more popular, optimistic and anti-dogmatic; and even in New England, the bulwark of Puritanism, a schism was brewing. Men's confidence in their own ability to seek out God, if not to create Him, was apparent and steadily increasing. This attitude was the result of the isolation of the Americans, who, in their simplified life, could not long keep an appreciation of the value of strict and subtle dogmas. It was a result of their effort to free themselves in religion, as in politics, from all foreign domination and to find for themselves codes especially adapted to their own characteristics. In short, it proceeded from this very American sentiment: that the less government there is, the less moral and material restraint there is, the better and happier men are.[45] This was the doctrine of Samuel Adams, one of the most far-seeing among the American leaders. It revealed the influence that Nature and the American soil had exerted on these exiled Englishmen in transforming them and inspiring them with the passionate desire to form an autonomous body with an ideal and a will of its own—a Nation. In 1773, this word had not been pronounced. It was even looked upon with aversion. Nevertheless, it was the inevitable outcome of the struggle that had begun. This nationalism, this religious tension, this urge toward a simple and natural state of society, led toward a new ideal.

This was perceived in France, as we have already noted. But did this discernment—this intuition one might say, for it seems to have been based only on a most vague acquaintance with America—effect the course of the American Revolution? Could the influence of French public opinion and of international philosophy make itself felt in the English colonies from 1760 to 1773?

Many American historians have denied it. Perhaps they have been beguiled by the laudable desire to impute all the merit of this glorious enterprise to the colonists alone. Perhaps they have allowed themselves to be obsessed by the economic causes of the conflict. But the American Revolution was also a moral phenomenon. The English colonies as early as 1763 possessed a powerful, organized and well-informed public opinion. In the years from 1763 to 1773, this public opinion acquired a remarkable degree of coherence and experience. Journalism developed: every town of any importance had its news-sheet. Boston, New York, and Philadelphia had as many as five or six. They were weeklies and often very well edited. They contained a body of news copied from the Whig newspapers of England, local news and letters from other parts of the colony or from the neighboring colonies, numerous advertisements of runaway slaves, stray horses, abducted women, cargoes arriving from Europe, servants, animals or objects for sale, and acts and laws of the colony. Usually one quarter of the space was reserved for letters from the readers discussing political and religious questions. There were also literary extracts. Of course, there were no editorials. Neither the word nor the thing it designates had yet been invented. Such as they were, these newspapers with their modest four pages went everywhere, represented everything, and had a degree of life and activity such as is found in no European newspaper of the same period. Because of the source from which they were taken, the items concerning Europe were numerous and fairly impartial. In addition to the newspapers, all the large cities were beginning to have circulating libraries, such as the Society Library at New York and the Library Company at Philadelphia, Boston and Charleston. One-fifth of the contents of these libraries was non-English. All the people of high society subscribed to them.[46]

The first learned society in the New World was organized at Philadelphia and immediately took its place among the foremost societies of the world. To the already existent colleges—Harvard near Boston, the oldest; William and Mary in Virginia; King's College at New York; the University of Pennsylvania; Princeton in New Jersey—were added others, such as Dartmouth and the College of Rhode Island.[47] They had begun by teaching theology principally, but gradually more profane subjects were mixed with sacred learning. These colleges developed an élite whose moral rôle in the history of the United States was very important.[48] Harvard and Princeton were centers of "enlightenment" and liberalism. These colleges spread European ideas among the younger generations. Moreover, many rich families of New England sent their children to study in England and Switzerland. This custom was even more common in the South. The scions of the first families in Virginia and South Carolina were expected to go to London to study law, and they continued thereafter to make periodic visits to Europe. Many revolutionary leaders had traveled in Europe before 1773; for example, Charles Carroll, Henry Laurens, and especially, Franklin, who in 1767 was humiliated at finding the French so superior to the English in politeness.[49]

What part did France play in the international relations of the colonies? It has often been said that she enjoyed a deep-grounded hatred. And this seems plausible when we consider the years of warfare that had separated the two peoples. It is true that one finds in the American books and newspapers of the period the imprecations that might be expected. Stansbury, in 1771, recalled Crécy, Poitiers and Agincourt and held them up as examples to be repeated.[50] In 1774 John Adams himself asserts that France is too turbulent not to make war.[51] But it is above all the newspapers that furnish a rich harvest of anti-French tirades.

Louis XIV was always held up as the most perfect example of tyranny and intolerance, and the sermons which were constantly being preached against papism never failed to mention France.[52] It was especially in New England, at Boston and Harvard, that the custom of abusing the Pope and, with him, France, his faithful ally, had been preserved.[53] The Puritan pastors also attacked France as irreligious; and Ezra Stiles, the president of Yale University, spoke cruel words on the subject of Voltaire and his spirit of negation in 1771.[54] The aggressive spirit of France was feared: the papers were continually announcing that the French had bought wood to build ships or hemp to make ropes. They also dwelt with harrowing detail on the decadence of France, the revolution that threatened her, the shame of her King and the immorality of her upper classes. From 1770 to 1774, Madame du Barry was mentioned more often than any other European personage.[55] In 1770 a letter signed Marcus Aurelius was published in the *New London Gazette* and reprinted by more than twenty journals throughout the colonies. "Whosoever claims that this nation has the gayest spirit and life is deeply mistaken. For all the gayety there is at Paris, the peasants and villagers are miserably poor. . . . This kingdom, which contains eighteen million of men, has been enslaved by the standing army which the King maintains." [56] And England, to keep this animosity glowing, gave the greatest publicity to the affairs of Corsica. France was shown as the violator of the right of smaller peoples. The colonists, touched to the quick by this propaganda, had formed societies to aid the Corsicans, such as the Knights of Corsica who met in New York in 1770 and 1771.[57]

Thus the animosity against France seems formidable. Nevertheless, on thorough consideration we note that, in most cases, the campaign against France hides in reality a campaign against England. If the *New London Gazette* spoke of a kingdom enslaved by a standing army, it was because the English ministry wanted to establish an army in America. If the Knights of Corsica were so active in New York in 1771, it was because the American patriots were seeking an opportunity to get together and manifest in favor of the rights of smaller peoples.

Often France was taken as a scapegoat rather than directly attacked. Behind her, the real butt of the attacks was Europe, the domination which the Old World was trying to impose upon the New World, and England herself. But these readymade examples and these acknowledged facts were used to bring about the acceptance of a bold conviction. In reality France herself had gained a great deal of prestige in America since 1763. America, thirsting for culture and eager to hold a rank in the world, was beginning to study French. Harvard had begun it in 1732, and the University of Pennsylvania in 1754, under the influence of Franklin. Princeton took up this study in 1768 under the guidance of John Witherspoon, who introduced a new and extensive series of courses.[58] In 1750 Franklin drew up a plan for a university in which French should have a great place. In 1757 he himself took charge of the French education of his daughter. This same condition held in New England.[59] In 1773 Ezra Stiles, the president of Yale College, had his son learn French.[60] In all the cities, schools of French were becoming numerous. We find M. Giraut, a Protestant from Poitou, teaching French and founding a French Night School at New York in 1772. Two years later the Reverend Tétard, pastor of the French Reformed Church of the same city, announced the opening of a French *pension*. M. de Saint Pry, with his courses of French, dancing and deportment, was a competitor. At New York also we find John Haumaid acting as instructor in French to the students of King's College. And in 1774, three Italians established themselves as teachers of dancing, music and French. At Yale a certain Louis Delille from the University of Bordeaux arrived in 1770 and gave lessons in French and history; he was received in the best society. Later he went to Harvard, where he continued to teach—on his own account, it seems—in the shadow of the great university. At Cambridge there was also a M. de Viart, who taught both French and fencing; and in Boston itself M. Regnier, who instructed in both subjects.[61] There were people of this kind everywhere, especially in the ports; but the most curious of them was Francis Daymon, who lived at Philadelphia, where he kept school in a tailor shop and wrote a syntax of French verbs. He claimed to be from Paris and all the newspapers carried his advertisements. He seems to have been successful, for he was engaged as secretary to the first Continental Congress, a post which allowed him to act as sponsor for the French secret envoy, M. de Bonvouloir. It is probable that he himself was already in relations with the French government.[62] Received in households, these teachers went throughout the land and took with them the arts and manners of France. At the age of five, Jefferson was already studying French.[63]

With the spread of the French language, the reading of French books became general. Each month the papers published a list of the books that had arrived from Europe. At New York about a quarter of these books were French. In the other ports the proportion was lower, though never less than one-eighth.

The most popular books were Marmontel's stories, the memoirs of Sully and, above all, Fénelon's *Télémaque* and Rollin's histories, which were in current use in the English colonies and were everywhere praised for their right thinking.[64] Voltaire's *Traité de la Tolérance* enjoyed an extraordinary popularity and more than one correspondence discusses it. Franklin read it in 1764.[65] In lettered circles the French classics were studied, although they were considered scarcely moral—at least such was the opinion of John Adams' wife who, in 1773, declared that "Molière is not moral, for he renders vice ridiculous without exalting virtue." [66]

But the great philosophers were not forgotten. In 1771 and 1772 copies of Rousseau's novels and *Emile* were sold in South Carolina, Pennsylvania, and New York, and even in Virginia.[67] Voltaire's works were also found everywhere, and Montesquieu was even more popular; for he was received in the universities, where Rousseau did not appear and where Voltaire entered only by accident.

It is Montesquieu who is the most frequently quoted. The newspapers speak of Rousseau's behavior and activities,[68] but they give extracts from Montesquieu. On May 3, 1770, *The New York Journal* publishes a letter from a reader who says that the moment predicted by Montesquieu, when the English constitution will be broken down because the legislative branch of the government will be worse than the executive branch, has come. In 1772 *The New London Gazette* prints a tirade against oppression, in which servitude is defined by quoting a page from Montesquieu. In the same year this article was reprinted in Carolina.[69] We find in the next two years many examples of definitions taken from Montesquieu. From Voltaire, philosophic pages which speak of "works that save rather than faith" and such extracts from his letters to Lord Chesterfield as show the servility of England are quoted.[70] In New England, in 1770, his epistle to Frederick, in which he proves to him the necessity of a religion, is reprinted.[71] Raynal likewise is continually praised and sometimes quoted; and even an edition of extracts from his *Histoire des Indes* was published, but care was taken to choose from it only what was positive and to leave out everything negative. For the promulgation of religion everything seems good to the pastors of Philadelphia, who even go so far as to make use of Bossuet.[72]

One might add to these proofs and show that, from the moment of its foundation, the Philosophical Society of Philadelphia was eager to enter into relations with France and to pay homage to Buffon;[73] that during these years the newspapers of South Carolina[74] published articles in French[75] and that French musicians were fêted at Charleston,[76] that De Pauw's and Raynal's books, as soon as they were published, were already being discussed.[77] Every question that impassioned France woke echoes in America. What is more, America was aware of the part that France was to play as arbiter between England and her colonies and felt that a secret complicity linked America and France together in some obscure way. In 1768 *The Boston Gazette* was already appealing to Louis XV.[78] Franklin never ceased to be impressed with the advantages that France would derive from the quarrel between England and her colonies. He felt that it could not be avoided—and this as early as 1764.[79] Could a real hatred exist under such circumstances? Is it not probable that most people of some education shared the opinion of John Adams, then a school-teacher in Massachusetts? "If wc consider everything," he wrote in 1761, "the religion, government, freedom, navy, merchandise, manufactures, policy, arts, sciences, numbers of inhabitants and their virtues, it seems to me that England falls short in more and more important particulars than it exceeds the kingdom of France." [80]

For a long while the English colonies had been the natural enemies of the French, but this was ended now. The French had been beaten and subjugated in the New World, and this victory over a valiant enemy left the colonists with a real pride which was already allaying their hatred. Then too, they had come to consider France as a necessary element of world civilization, an opinion which was common in that day. More and more they saw in her the balance which maintained equilibrium and prevented England from becoming despotic. And this too was the view of the other nations. But they also had a sentiment that belonged to them alone; it was the feeling that, in their moral and political crisis, France was to aid them in finding a solution. They began to seek avidly her support in the field of philosophic innovations, both moral and political.

True, they knew her very slightly. She appeared to them under a threatening and dangerous aspect which differed widely from the idea that Europe held concerning France. But the radicals and the upper classes in America were quite ready to respond to the intense curiosity which was drawing France toward them. The two peoples, with a strange ignorance of each other's most essential characteristics, groped out toward each other and prepared to share the fever that agitated both of them and was to upset the world.

*

* *

On the eve of the first bloodshed in the American conflict, Louis XV died. He had reigned so long and his death was so sudden that public opinion throughout the world was profoundly stirred by it. In France Louis the Well-Beloved had come to be hated and despised; the people were so accustomed to condemning his vices and despotism and decrying the timorous policies of his latter years, that they hailed the new reign as a sort of Golden Age. They could not dissimulate the joy that they felt and the hopes that they held for a future wherein, instead of the good pleasure and the vices of the King, Reason, accompanied by her retinue of virtues and social ameliorations, was to rule. A unanimous enthusiasm drew all hearts toward this young monarch of whom so little was known, but whose pure living, family virtues, zeal and keenness in his work, and finally, whose modesty, indicated that he would understand the wishes of the nation and respond to its appeal by a reorganization of the kingdom. Philosophers as well as officials, commoners, nobles and clergy, impelled by patriotism, the desire for reform and thought for the future—all greeted the new reign with joy; for they believed, even in this happy moment, that it would benefit private, as well as public, interests. The warmth of these sentiments was augmented by the generally accepted impression that the hour was a critical one and that things could not long be left to drift. Abbé Royer expressed this idea in his *Discours sur le Sacre de Louis XVI:* "God will furnish us rules of conduct, as necessary as ever in a time when the seeds of discord sowed by the enemy seem about to bear fruit from the rising to the setting of the sun, from the snows of America to those of Europe," and in the margin he noted: "the English colonies in America", thus indicating clearly the extent of the problem and of the concerns which preoccupied French citizens in 1774.

From Louis XVI, they asked and hoped for a great effort toward liberty. He was called upon to restore parliamentary liberty, liberty of thought and the liberties of the people. And, even more, he was expected to give philosophy the place that the philosophers held to be her due—the direction of the State. The King, for his part, came to the throne with a desire to govern according to the wishes of the people and to repose upon the most enlightened, as well as the most righteous, opinion available. He showed this when he chose as Minister of War the Count de Muy, whose honesty was as famous as his piety. He showed it even more clearly in appointing to his council the old Count de Maurepas and in encouraging by his attitude the compliment that the people paid them both in nicknaming his minister "Mentor." Of weak character, but honest and conscientious, he dreamt of a reign in which he should have no initiatives to take other than those which should be dictated to him by the best minds and the voice of the people. He went so far as to read assiduously the most advanced organs, such as the *Annales* edited by the famous lawyer Linguet; and such reading seems to have fascinated him.[81] He understood that miracles were expected of him, and he counted above all on his good intentions to win the love of his subjects and to realize their desires. Alas, he was called upon simultaneously to free negro slaves, to reëstablish religion, and to be the enlightened despot preached by the philosophers and sought by the Economists!

To satisfy these demands the two primary needs were: first, to reform the internal administration of the kingdom; second, to restore the international importance that it had lost since 1763. There could be no moral unity in France without the complete suppression of injustices and abuses. Public opinion demanded concrete reforms which should be not only a provisional amelioration, but also a proof of a new spirit. Views as to what the nature of these expected reforms should be varied with the individual tendencies and aims. The most definite program was that of the Economists, who held out for a moral as well as a material reform of the kingdom by the encouragement of agriculture, the freedom of trade and the simplification of the administration. All parties emphasized tolerance, *mores*,* a religion and the liberty of discussion. The reëstablishment of French prestige was ardently desired. The peace of 1763 had been humiliating, its consequences had been worse. It was felt that all the nations of the world, even those who looked to her for protection, held France lightly. Compared with England, whose flourishing commerce, naval supremacy and free parliamentary institutions made her an object of both fear and admiration, France seemed a feeble and backward nation, in no condition to impose its will by force or to win respect by its institutions and spirit. This decline was especially apparent in the attitude of the smaller nations, formerly under the protection of France, and who had served her so well and been so greatly succored by her during the preceding century. The French were well aware of this, and the government saw clearly that it would never have prestige in the eyes of the people as long as France remained in this humiliating position, and as long as England held absolute control of international relations. Here was a need that French diplomats, as well as tradesfolk and writers, felt. For the satisfaction of her own citizens, France must regain her moral and material position in the world. A policy of force would not suffice, an intellectual campaign was also called for.[82]

* Whenever the French word "mœurs" is used in this work as part of the philosophic vocabulary of the eighteenth century, I have translated it *mores*. In addition to its usual meaning, "manners and customs," this word implies both "simple living" and, by an extension encouraged by the philosophy of Rousseau and the Encyclopedists, "social and individual morality and virtues."—*Translator's note.*

In the ministry that Louis XVI formed, the two dominant tendencies of opinion were clearly apparent. It was, one might say, a ministry composed of strong men and reformers. Beside Maurepas, the two most notable figures were Turgot, the minister of Finances, and the Count Gravier de Vergennes, ex-minister to Sweden, in which post he had displayed great ability. Turgot, one of the hopes of the Economist group, came into power with definite ideas as to what he intended to, and was expected to, accomplish. He had adopted, with some restrictions and modifications, the program of his friends, and he asked that the King should first of all bend his efforts to the restoration of French credit and finances. Vergennes, who had witnessed the decline of French prestige abroad, intended first of all to remedy that condition. It so happened that the American conflict brought the royal government face to face with the question without leaving it any opportunity to avoid a decision.[83] During these years, 1774 and 1775, circumstances had precipitated the crisis in America.

After the Boston Tea Party (December, 1773) and the severe measures taken by England against Boston and the occupation of the town by a British army under the command of Gage, a common impulse had moved the colonies, and a Continental Congress had assembled at Philadelphia in September, 1774. This body, it seems, dared neither to speak of independence nor even to *think* seriously of it. On the contrary, it proclaimed that the colonies did not wish to separate from England and that they recognized the authority of the King but demanded the exclusive right to make for themselves, subject to the King's veto, such laws as concerned only themselves. They decided to urge the colonies to import nothing further from England. On every hand, the American Whigs organized and armed themselves. Finally, a conflict in which there was bloodshed took place at Lexington, where an English flying detachment, having tried to disperse by force a body of Americans, met with reverses (April 19, 1775). A second Congress assembled at Philadelphia in May, 1775. It addressed a last appeal to the King. But at the same time, it appointed Washington commander-in-chief of the American forces and decided to take up arms. There was still no talk of independence, so strong was the hold of England on these colonies who had so often fought beside the armies which now they were going to fight against. Moreover, who would have dared to raise the standard of revolt against England, when she was known to be so strong and the colonists felt themselves so isolated? As Whigs allied to the English Whigs, the Americans were to hesitate a long while before declaring themselves free, although everything, and above all that deep moral instinct which can not be resisted, urged them to this step.

In these conditions France was called upon to take a definite stand. The conflict placed England in a difficult position and threatened to destroy the finest fruits of her victory in 1763. France could not ignore this opportunity to bring about the revision of that disastrous as well as shameful treaty. This everybody felt; and public opinion was impatient, although its tendencies were still vague and contradictory. This same divergence of opinion prevailed in the King's council, whose two strongest personalities stood in opposition. Turgot, the great reformer, wanted to cure France "from the inside" and scouted anything that smacked of venture, risks, expense and, consequently, of war. The Americans interested him as a curious phenomenon. Their courage and their republicanism enlisted his sympathy. But he opined that they needed neither him nor France and that, moreover, if France was to be saved, the government must allow nothing to distract it. Turgot, it has been said, had a mind as heavy as it was great. He lacked sometimes that fine sensibility which divines the opportune moment and picks its way around difficulties. His colleague, the Count de Vergennes, was a man of another sort. Conscientious, painstaking, of grave countenance, a boring conversationalist, it is said, because of his efforts to be witty, he possessed a fine and quick mind. Hennin, one of his assistants who knew him well, describes him as being of a religious and philosophic turn. "He considered himself to be the minister of the King responsible for the happiness of the world, and he was convinced that his master needed only wisdom and vigilance in order to take the highest place among sovereigns." [84] He knew thoroughly both Europe and the mentality of the times. In his first general report to the King (December 8, 1774), he said: "Opinion, it is said, is the queen of the world. The government that can establish it to its own advantage doubles with the idea of its real strength the consideration and the respect which have been, and ever will be, the reward of a well-directed administration and the most certain guarantee of its tranquillity." In this same document, which is very important since it constitutes a program submitted to the King, he declares himself to be the enemy of all political injustice, "for if might is right," he says, "and convenience a warrant, on what then will the security of states repose?" He wished to have as few wars as possible and refused to countenance a policy of conquest. He believed that the acquisition of colonies was no advantage, for all colonies were difficult to defend and impossible to hold for ever; and European conquests, he concluded, by the moral wrong that they would do France, would harm rather than help her. To win the support of public opinion he conceived to be the King's first need.

It was this that made him decide to take a stand in favor of the Americans immediately. Such a step would be well received in France and could offend nobody in Europe. It would show the smaller nations that the policy of Richelieu was still being followed in France, that the disinterestedness of France was more than a diplomatic formula. Moreover, all that had been done by his predecessors in the Ministry of Foreign Affairs urged him toward this course. It seems certain that in ceding Canada to England, Choiseul had had, if not the intention, at least the consoling hope, that this province might be a bone of contention between the English colonies and their mother country. And why should he not have believed what all the philosophers, his friends, believed at the time: that no state could keep its colonies indefinitely?

It is certain that he kept himself continually informed on American affairs. To mention only a few, and the most illustrious of his agents, it is known that in 1764 he sent M. de Pontleroy to inspect the English colonies in America.[85] Recently there has been found in the archives of the Hydrographic Service the manuscript report of another secret agent, whom he sent to America in 1765 and who saw all the revolutionary leaders: Patrick Henry,[86] Galloway, Charles Carroll, etc. This agent joined to his report maps of the principal American ports and notes indicating how they could be taken.[87] He insisted at length on the sentiment of liberty that existed among the inhabitants. Shortly before his fall in 1768, Choiseul also sent on a similar mission the excellent soldier De Kalb, who visited all the colonies—without great results, however.[88]

Continuing in this tradition in 1775, at the beginning of his ministry, Vergennes sent out Achard de Bonvouloir. This French officer was already well acquainted with

America and succeeded by the intermediary of Francis Daymon in obtaining interviews with the principal American leaders who were concerned with the international questions in Congress, such as John Adams, Samuel Chase and Franklin. Thus Vergennes was following a tradition, although he contributed to it his own high sense of honesty, his concern for public opinion and his comprehension of the moral crisis that the world was passing through.[89]

His task was not easy, for public opinion was far from unanimous. In the ministry itself, M. de Maurepas, old and weary, would have liked to end his career without any new great adventures. Turgot was hostile to the war; and although M. de Saint Germain agreed with Vergennes, his place in the cabinet was not secure, and his successor-to-be, the future minister, Prince de Montbarrey (whose precise motives it is difficult to discern, since he himself seems not to have been too well acquainted with them) was in the opposition. Doubtless he was animated only with a desire to intrigue against a minister of whom he was jealous.[90] But we can not incriminate thus blindly the entire block of public opinion which in 1775 was beginning to come out against America. We read, for example, in the letters of Madame du Deffant, a woman of intelligence and one who knew whereof she spoke, "Lord North is an honest man and I should be sorry if he were to quit the ministry." [91] She declared herself to be a royalist. Mallet du Pan in the *Journal historique et politique* of

Geneva took the same attitude.[92] These people, slightly in arrears of the times, held things English in esteem and could not admit the superiority of the upstart nation. They belonged to the generation of philosophers who had accomplished the great work of criticism and whose religion and hope were summed up in their faith in luxury, the refinements of civilization and enlightenment. Their influence, though considerable, was of no avail against the tide that swept along the younger generation. It is more serious to see such men as Suard, royal censor and editor of a great newspaper, a man up-to-date, modern and constructive, who corresponded with Wilkes in order to be better informed on American affairs, declare that the colonies had a tremendous future from a moral as well as an economic point of view, but that they ought to realize it without breaking away from England.[93] He thought as did Chatham. Thus, many social, literary and intellectual groups resisted the current because of intellectual habits that they had contracted and because of the esteem in which England was held. They felt that it was a question of changing a moral and political ideal, of accepting, and even encouraging, a new nation and an immense and obscure experiment. All those for whom the "state of Nature" had no particular attraction looked on the Americans with antipathy; and this affords a fairly accurate means of measuring the groups into which the doctrines of Rousseau had not penetrated.

Nevertheless, the bulk of public opinion was with

Vergennes. The soldiers longed for a war in order to have a chance to fight; the middle class admired the Americans sincerely and expected much from their revolution. The young nobles were curious concerning these climes and men. And most of the writers continued in the direction that they had already taken and desired this philosophic crusade which might shake the entire world: they supported the Americans in spite of their break with England. All the principal newspapers took the same attitude. In 1775, they published full details concerning the struggle in which the Americans were so deeply engaged. Almost all of them represented the English as the aggressors at Lexington. The most zealous of these sheets were *Le Courrier d'Avignon*, which received its news through Marseilles, and the *Gazette de Leyde*, which, because of religious and commercial bonds, received first-hand information directly from America. Yet, behind praises of these papers, there lurks a certain bewilderment: they are at loss to interpret the future, and a great hesitation seems to reign among them when it comes to saying what ought to, and what will, be done. On the other hand, it is strange to note that the newspapers under the direct control of the government take a clear and affirmative tone. For instance, in 1775 the *Mercure de France* published an article which proclaimed that the discovery and conquest of America by Europe "was the most frightful of the calamities that humanity had suffered at the hands of man." But, this article continues, now that the North American English colonies are rich enough and strong enough to be independent whenever they wish, their independence will be the signal for the liberation of both continents and "the people will labor . . . everything will prosper. Luxuries as well as necessities will abound. All Europe, freed from this expense, will enter into profitable commerce with the whole of America and with prosperity. Then America will be proud to have taken Europeans into her bosom. Then, and only then, will Europe reap the reward for the discovery of America." The *Gazette de France* speaks with quite as much assurance: it praises incessantly the Americans, their leaders and their humaneness in warfare. It was this publication which coined the word "insurgents" which was to have such success. "This is the term," we read, "by which the moderate party designates the Americans, while the others call them traitors and rebels." [94]

Through the pages of these governmental organs we feel the influence of Vergennes. It is he who gives this spirit of decision to the official sheets, while the other papers receive their news only from English sources—Whig, it is true. But even the Whigs were well disposed toward America only as long as she remained English, and they became hostile as soon as she expressed a desire for autonomy. This explains the hesitation of the French papers, eager to praise the colonists but hampered by the very news that they themselves printed, the source of which they could not, however, accuse of being hostile to the insurgents.

This confusion of public opinion and the hesitation of the King hampered Vergennes. Louis XVI was inclined toward peace. He felt that the majority of his ministers was opposed to war and to everything that might bring about war. He wanted to be convinced that to aid the colonies would be honest as well as in accord with both the interests of France and the will of the Nation.[95] Hazard afforded Vergennes the opportunity to convince the King and to stimulate public opinion indirectly.

Caron de Beaumarchais, although of obscure origin, had made a rapid and brilliant conquest of fortune; under the protection of Paris Duverney, he had become rich in a very few years. On the death of his employer, his accounts were subject to suspicion and the heirs of Paris Duverney brought a suit against him which, in spite of liberal bribing of judges, he lost. He got his revenge by publishing libels which made his name famous throughout the world. The following year he produced *The Barber of Seville*, which had marked success. He was then forty-three years old. He was exiled. But since he was known as a clever man and had friends at court, he succeeded in getting the new King to send him to London on a secret mission which called for a discreet, able and wide-awake man. King Louis XV, in the course of his secret correspondence with his emissaries and diplomats, had drawn up a plan for the invasion of England. Unfortunately, this plan, instead of being carefully laid away, had fallen into the hands of the Chevalier d'Eon, whence there had resulted grave annoyance for the French government. The Chevalier d'Eon, diplomat and wit employed in the King's secret service, would have passed on with his century without leaving any more trace than many other wits, if he had not taken it into his head at the age of forty-three to change his sex and become a woman. He had done it, it is true, at the urge of an imperious motive; for, having involved himself in a quarrel with a nobleman who boasted unusual skill with a sword, he was on the edge of being drawn into a duel wherein he might have lost his life. He preferred to lose his sex and proclaimed himself to be a woman. This happened while he was attached to the embassy at London and had Louis XV's plan in his possession. He made use of this circumstance to call upon the French government to provide him with resources sufficient to the needs of a lady of fashion and threatened to sell the plan to England if his demands were not complied with. To settle this complicated affair it was decided to send a skillful agent to discover whether Mademoiselle d'Eon really did belong to the fair sex, whether she could be seduced, and what was the minimum price that must be paid for the documents. Beaumarchais was chosen for this mission because of his physique, his moral and intellectual qualities, and his financial embarrassment, which guaranteed his zeal. He did his best. Unluckily, Mademoiselle d'Eon inspired him with a tender devotion; and she seems not to have shared his sentiment. She even appears to have made use of his affection to dupe him.[96] Beaumarchais was therefore in a sorry situation; but, far from wasting his time, while he was paying court to his enchantress, he cultivated the acquaintance of as many people as possible. Thus he met a certain Arthur Lee, who was the brother of a London alderman and belonged to a powerful Virginia family. Arthur Lee had brothers in both camps, but he was of a very enthusiastic nature and probably favored the Americans. He even acted as their agent at London. He met Beaumarchais and won as much of his heart as was still free. The two men understood each other marvelously. Beaumarchais was suddenly touched with grace. He, who had never been good for anything useful and whose whole life had been one of cynicism and raillery, was filled with faith in the future of America. He was inspired with the idea of being her liberator. And into his letters dealing with the painful d'Eon affair (which dragged out and afforded neither his heart nor his purse the satisfaction that he merited) he insinuated increasingly enthusiastic suggestions that France should aid the Americans and that he himself should be appointed to serve as intermediary. This pleased Vergennes, who showed the letters to the King. They were well written and quick with conviction and intelligence.

This tone, these accents, this comprehension of the intellectual setting and the moral and political situation of the world, were sufficient to weigh down the balance and bring about the eventual decision. Louis XVI saw unmistakably in them the voice of the people. And Vergennes immediately took advantage of his favorable inclination to set about furnishing arms to the insurgents. Beaumarchais was authorized to return to France and to establish a maritime and trading company under the name of Roderigue Hortalez and Company. This firm was to engage in trade with Bermuda and to sell, without thought of profit, everything that the colonists needed to continue their resistance. We must state that Beaumarchais was undoubtedly sincere.[97] His intelligence was too sharp for him to have expected to reap any great profit. He worked for the sake of glory and to have his share in the greatest revolution of the century. He did not manage this enterprise with great wisdom, as we shall see; but he went into it with a great disinterestedness and with a generosity that was rewarded with blackest ingratitude. The adventure—the founding of a new nation in a new world in the name of philosophy and the King of France —was so fascinating and romantic that we may pardon Beaumarchais for having sought to find in it above all an esthetic pleasure. When he went to Le Havre under a false name to tend to the loading of his ships in secret, he could not resist the temptation to attend the theater and even to act in a play there. But, when it was necessary, he did not hesitate to risk his own money, to send his merchant ships into the conflict, and to break his own neck in hurrying to Paris to announce the capture of Burgoyne's army by the Americans. Beaumarchais's love for America was an unhappy one, but now, more than a century later, we must render him justice. He ruined himself for the American cause, and no one would believe it; for it seemed impossible that he had done it in good faith and that he had been so artless as to rob nobody. But the truth is that he did rob nobody and that he died in misery at Paris for having met Arthur Lee and given himself too completely to the American cause.

An ironic destiny had found in him the personage both necessary and sufficient for brushing aside all hesitation and establishing the worship of America. He knew nothing of the New World, and his agreement with Arthur Lee was a wholesale misunderstanding, but he was of service to the nations. His enthusiastic and ill-advised activity was typical of the whole tendency which was drawing France toward America and America toward France without either one knowing anything of the other. This sentiment was only the more acute because of the fact that it was brought about by imaginings so far from reality and because the peoples themselves differed so widely. Thanks to this popular enthusiasm, the decision of Vergennes and the adventurous genius of Beaumarchais brought about French intervention for the liberation of the New World. This act has been represented as a clever wile against England, a machination to regain Canada or Louisiana. But no impartial mind can help being struck by the fact that in Vergennes's reports, Beaumarchais's letters, and the newspapers of the time, there is never any question of acquiring territories nor of ruining England, but of giving the world a new economic law that should fit the needs of all people, and of satisfying public opinion, which demanded a new era, one of justice, liberty and morality.

Chapter II

THE CREATION OF THE UNITED STATES

Obstacles to an understanding between France and the United States, pp. 63-73. Vergennes tries to overcome them; he urges the Americans to declare their independence. The Declaration of Independence and the French government, pp. 73-81. Enthusiasm in France, La Fayette's departure, pp. 81-87. Vergennes continues his propaganda in France to influence the King, the Court and the people, pp. 87-94. He succeeds, thanks to La Fayette, Franklin and Burgoyne's surrender, pp. 94-99. Alliance between France and the United States; integrity of the alliance; its principal aim is, by establishing the United States, to restore the prestige of France, pp. 99-104.

Rejoicing in the United States and in France, pp. 104-108. Vergennes tries to maintain this exaltation at a high pitch and to make use of it. His propaganda in the United States; it encounters hostile forces, pp. 108-115. His energy in carrying on the war. His desire to moderate American ambitions, pp. 115-121. Zeal of the French volunteers for the United States, pp. 121-125. Development of a sympathy with France in the United States and the social transformations resulting from it, pp. 125-132. French secret agents in America are almost entirely successful, pp. 132-138.

France wearied by too long a war; the United States are less popular. Vergennes works to arrest this movement, pp. 138-145. Vergennes's friendship for Franklin, with whom he collaborates without seeing the extent of his influence in France, pp. 145-147. Franklin at Paris: his rôle as a prophet. His secret activities. Masonic, literary and religious organizations growing up about Franklin. Popularity of *Poor Richard*, pp. 147-156. Public opinion in France sees the United States through Franklin and creates the Franklin legend, pp. 156-163.

In 1775 the leading statesmen of both France and America felt a well-defined willingness to work together. The leading spirits of the French ministry, Vergennes and Turgot, felt the necessity of such a movement; and in America Adams, Lee, and Franklin, and all the members of Congress who took thought for the future, turned toward France as toward a natural friend. Reason or instinct had led these far-sighted minds to choose the path toward which public opinion, hungering for a new faith and moral activity, was blindly urging them. But the task of making possible this coöperation was not easy. It involved so complete a change in the traditional thought of the two peoples, so radical a departure in diplomatic policy, that there was no telling where it would lead. Taken as a whole, the French people and the American colonists had no practical knowledge of each other and no means of becoming better acquainted. Their relations lay entirely in the domain of intellect and ideas. Commerce, which is ordinarily the means of establishing relations between people of different nationalities, was prohibited; for England reserved for herself exclusively the rights of importation and exportation in her colonies. It was only a very limited group in each country, composed of travelers, scholars and diplomats, who had any accurate first-hand idea of the nation with which their own land was to link its destinies. In America, where it was necessary to bring into line the majority of the voters, this situation was particularly grave.

The Tories were beginning to perceive it; and out of hatred for France as well as in order to hamper the revolutionary leaders, they revived with a fresh bitterness and zeal all that had formerly been said against France. They depicted France as weak and incapable of opposing a powerful England. They emphasized the danger of allowing France to regain her footing, for then the liberty of the English colonies would be threatened by an ancient and relentless enemy. Their favorite argument, moreover, and the one which they continually repeated in their sermons (for many of these pamphleteers were priests of the Church of England) was that America ran a great risk in allying herself with a "popish" nation.[1] This argument was the more effective since, as we have seen, the American Revolution had a religious side and tended toward a Protestantism increasingly free from all dogma and from all ecclesiastical hierarchy. These pamphlets and these sermons did not fail to impress the people; for, during the year 1775-1776, a goodly number of Frenchmen had gone to America and had not made a favorable impression. In fact, as soon as it was known that hostilities between the colonists and their mother country had begun, every adventurer in the Antilles had come to offer his services to the Americans, with all the air of the greatest generosity—and with an insatiable thirst for commissions, commands and money.[2] Now, there had always been a great many hotheaded and unscrupulous young men in these tropic islands where slavery existed and to which the best families of France were accustomed to send their black sheep. In 1775 and 1776, Congress spent many a weary hour in dickering with these dubious heroes whom the American army had come to hate with utmost sincerity. This was a source of great annoyance to Congress, which was trying to lead the people into an alliance with France and found itself obliged to go about it indirectly.

Vergennes encountered a like difficulty. It was not easy to transfer a zeal for things American from a purely literary plane to one of action. The cult for England still had its devotees, especially in high society. M. de Stormont, the English ambassador at Paris, was a very amiable and popular young man. He was the lion of the drawing-room of many a great lady, young and old. Moreover, he found effective arguments against every pro-American effort on the part of Vergennes. France's hands were tied by the treaty of 1763, which had established between herself and England a peace that she had no plausible pretext for breaking—unless it be this very serious reason: that the treaty of 1763 was brutal, rapacious and insulting. As a further precaution, Stormont fought Vergennes in the field of public opinion. He could not publish books hostile to the Colonies and Vergennes's policy in France because of the censorship which would have immediately suppressed them. But he *could* have them published in Holland. In 1775 and the beginning of 1776, The Hague was flooded with anti-

American pamphlets. They were brought out by merchants with interests at London and by English agents. The Jew, Isaac Pinto, alone signed three of them.[3] These publications were well calculated to have an effect on the French public. They admitted that the course of events must necessarily in time bring about the liberation of the New World, but they denied that the time for this had yet come and that the Americans were in the right. They tried to rouse monarchial sentiment against the rebels. They appealed to the wisdom of European governments, all of whom might well tremble lest the wind of rebellion blow over the entire New World. They tried to employ intimidation and to depict England's strength in glowing colors.

The confusion which reigned amid the French public permitted these pamphlets to win over hesitant minds. As a matter of fact, though everybody in France admired the Americans and expected them to bring about a moral reform, there were few people who had more than very vague notions concerning their present quarrel and their future as a nation. Some people, such as Turgot[4] and most of the physiocrats, considered their victory inevitable and assured even without the aid of France, who had no reason to interfere openly. Others declared that the New World was going to supplant Europe and that its supremacy was the great danger of the future.[5] Others looked down on the insurgents as plebeians and shopkeepers and disparaged this people which was distracting public opinion so much. It was perhaps this sort of jealousy that inspired the pamphleteer Linguet,[6] who was then very popular and was irritated at seeing public attention turn away from him. There were certain shrewd people who looked upon the whole business as only pre-arranged feints between England and her dependencies; high personages such as the Duc de Croÿ belonged to this group.[7] There were also people who, jealous of Vergennes, belittled America for the sake of intrigue, and this was particularly grave since the principal member of this group was the Prince de Montbarrey, the Minister of War.[8] There were adventurers who would have liked to keep participation in American affairs to themselves alone; the Marshal de Broglie furnishes a striking example of this point of view. He believed that America, with her revolution which resembled that of Holland, was in her turn going to need a "stadholder." Now who could aspire to this office if not a European and a great general? He deduced that he himself would be the man, and with this in mind, he encouraged French officers among his friends to emigrate to America. He aided materially the departure of La Fayette;[9] and his own aide-de-camp, De Kalb, went over with the special mission of preparing the way for his stadholdership. Others reflected on the possible establishment of a monarchy in America and sought to aid in bringing it to pass. But the greatest obstacle was the increasingly strong party which, in the name of the ideals of monarchy, refused to countenance the insurgents; great ladies such as Madame du Deffant expressed these views, and in many places the provincial nobility repeated them. They even found echo in the Ministry of Foreign Affairs. This was also the attitude of Favier and of the historian, Moreau. High functionaries like Malouet,[10] commissioner of Santo Domingo, thought that the example of the Americans was dangerous and might lead far afield. Even philosophers, such as D'Alembert, proclaimed that peace was the highest consideration; and, with the greatest theoretical enthusiasm for the colonists, were hostile to an intervention in their favor. D'Alembert wrote to Frederick the Great on February 23, 1776: "Although a war two thousand leagues away concerns me less than did that of 1756, I still fear lest this drop of oil spread till it reach us." [11] In spite of the enthusiasm of the greater part of public opinion, in spite of the enthusiastic articles which the *Gazette de Leyde*, the *Courrier d'Avignon* and the *Journal historique de Genève* published concerning this "people regenerated," there still remained a decisive step to take—and public opinion hesitated.[12]

It was a difficult situation in many ways and Vergennes had more than one reason to be worried. Spain had no sympathy, either as a people or as a government, for this nation in rebellion. Central Europe, where Poland had just been robbed of a third of her territory

(1772), beheld the war between Russia and Turkey scarcely finished before this new war seemed imminent.

It was very natural for a philosophic mind in such circumstances and at a time when so many reforms were urgent in France, to desire above all things to avoid war. This was the attitude of Turgot. Consulted by the King in March, 1776, concerning the policy to be followed with regard to Great Britain, he pronounced himself in favor of peace. He saw three principal reasons for not intervening. First of all, it was useless: the fated course of events would bring about the independence of all the colonies that the various empires, kingdoms and republics of Europe still possessed. "As for colonies integrally united to the mother country," he said, "there can be no more of them. Fortunate and wise will be the nations who renounce their colonies to turn them into allied provinces no longer subject to their rule. Spain must expect to be abandoned by her colonies; she should be preparing for the commercial changes that the new régime will cause. And it is scarcely worth worrying about even if the English should attack our own colonies, since it would be more to our interest to own none at all. What difference does it make to us then whether England subdues her insurgent colonies or not? [13] Subdued, they will keep her so busy with their attempts to be free, that we shall have nothing more to fear from her. If they are freed, the whole commercial system will be changed, and England will have no other preoccupation than that of assuring herself the benefits of the new system by efforts that will be incompatible with war."

Turgot further feared the expense that military operations would entail. He set forth this argument in these terms: "The state of our finances is not so desperate that, if it were absolutely necessary to support a war, we could not find resources—if it were with a probability of such decisive successes as would shorten its duration. But nevertheless, it must be admitted that we ought to avoid it as the greatest of misfortunes, because it would render impossible for a long time, and perhaps forever, a reformation that is absolutely necessary for the prosperity of the state and the relief of the people. In making a premature use of our strength, we should run the risk of making permanent our weakness.

"A third reason ought to make us decide against the project of attacking England; namely, the very great probability that this attack would be the signal for a reconciliation between the mother country and the colonies and would precipitate the very danger which we wish to avoid." Turgot concluded therefore that only measures of precaution would be advisable and only then on condition that they should not commit the government too deeply. "We must do nothing hurriedly but rather wait to have the certitude that England really does intend to attack us. Keeping this in view, however, and on condition of not violating our neutrality and of taking no action directly, let a way be found of furnishing the colonists by means of commerce with the munitions, and even with the money they need." [14]

An attitude so lacking in generosity toward these glorious insurgents seems strange today. To interpret it correctly we must take into consideration both the material circumstances and the intellectual atmosphere of 1776.

Turgot, like Vergennes, wanted a world-wide reformation. He believed that such a reformation was necessary. He hoped that the United States would play a part in it; since, even in 1778, he said of them: "It is impossible not to have hopes that this people will realize all the prosperity for which it is qualified. It is the hope, and can become the model, of humanity at large. It should prove to the world, by actual example, that men *can* be free and orderly and that they *can* get along without the chains of all kinds with which tyrants and charlatans, whatever robe they wear, have tried to shackle them in the name of public welfare.[15] It should furnish the example of political liberty, religious liberty and the liberty of commerce and industry. The refuge which it offers to the oppressed of all countries should comfort the earth. Man's opportunity to avail himself of this refuge in order to flee from the results of bad government, will oblige governments to be just and enlightened: gradually the rest of the world will open its eyes and perceive the emptiness of the illusions with which politicians have deluded themselves." [16] We cannot therefore reproach him with having lacked sympathy for the Americans, but they interested him much less as a people than as the witnesses and martyrs of an ideal. His attachment for them was idealistic, intellectual and exacting. Looking forward to a complete reformation of governments, he joined to a belief in the sovereignty of the people an unshakable faith in popular wisdom. He hoped to see formed purely democratic states wherein the people should wield the power directly by means of a single body of representatives. He insisted that the society of the future should conform to this rule and to the doctrines of the Economists. He wrote to Price, "I am not satisfied, I admit, with the constitutions which have been drawn up thus far in the different American states. You are right in condemning the Constitution of Pennsylvania for the religious oath which is obligatory before one can become a member of the representative body. The others are even worse: there is one, I believe it is that of New Jersey, which obliges one to believe in the divinity of Jesus Christ. I note in the greater part of them purposeless imitations of English usages. Instead of bringing together all authorities into a single one (that of the nation), they establish different bodies, a representative body, a council, a governor—because England has a House of Commons, a House of Lords and a King. They busy themselves with balancing the different powers as if this equilibrium of forces, which was believed necessary to offset the overwhelming preponderance of the royalty, could be of any use in a republic founded on the equality of all its citizens, and as if anything that establishes different bodies were not a source of division." Holding these views, he blamed the Americans for their imperfections. He desired less to lighten their sufferings than to see them attain to true wisdom, and it displeased him that the most democratic nation in the world should be liberated by the most enslaved nation.[17]

While he feared war for France as a *material* disaster, he was alarmed lest French intervention in America should be a *moral* danger for the colonies. And with all his might he struggled against the current that was carrying him along.

But Vergennes, behind an air of moderation, had a bold and ambitious intelligence. He had seen in America a means of restoring the moral credit of France while crushing English pride and winning the favor of a young nation at a time when this was necessary. A real sympathy, which his friends encouraged, impelled him toward the valiant colonists. Instinctively and by the spirit of his profession, he believed in the efficacy of human action on destiny. He believed that America would free herself neither by the action of economic forces nor by her own resources alone, but that she needed aid.

The aid that he gave at first was of a moral nature. By all the means at his disposition, he brought pressure upon the Americans to induce them to think of independence, to talk about it, and to proclaim it. His activities have been underrated and his influence in this decisive phase of the American Revolution has been systematically belittled. He himself later sought to conceal it in order not to be accused of duplicity toward the English. We have seen that in 1775 he sent M. de Bonvouloir to Philadelphia to talk with the members of Congress and to bring them to understand the French attitude. Bonvouloir was to say, "As long as you are subjects of Great Britain, we can not, and must not, do anything for you. The only means that you have of obtaining our support is by declaring yourselves independent." Adams, Franklin, and R. H. Lee had heard this message and had been deeply impressed by it. Moreover, as early as 1775, John Adams and Samuel Chase of Maryland had exposed the necessity of trading with some foreign nation if they were to be in a position to carry on the war for any length of time.[18] Now the French colonies were the nearest, but how were they to negotiate a commercial pact with France without sending her an ambassador, and how were they to send an ambassador without declaring themselves independent? Chase proposed sending a mission to France. Supported by the Adams, he succeeded in passing a motion to choose delegates to negotiate a commercial accord with France. The Tories and the conservatives fought bitterly against this measure which they declared to be the immediate prelude to separation from Great Britain; but they were defeated.[19] This was all that was accomplished in 1775. The time had not yet come. But during the whole winter the patriots did not cease talking it over among themselves. Their newspapers throughout all the colonies spoke continually of the favorable inclinations of France and of the fact that she could not intervene as long as England held sovereignty over America. The *Boston Gazette*, one of the most powerful Whig organs in New England, said on October 28, 1775: "American sailors returning from France all declare that they are well received in the French ports and that the French are waiting only for an American declaration of independence to intervene." It is an ordinary thing to see the most official newspapers continually associating these two terms: independence and alliance with France. It is curious to find Ezra Stiles, the president of Yale College, a fervent patriot but also a fervent Protestant and not over friendly toward France in general, noting in his diary, June 19, 1776, that he had just seen a French merchant and that this man had told him that he had learned from the agent of the Ministry of Foreign Affairs who was in charge of the American section that all the arms and munitions that the Americans needed for their struggle were to be furnished them. France asked only that they declare their independence first.[20] Everything that came from France conveyed the same message; and this impression, thanks to the zeal of the Whig leaders and their newspapers, was spread among the entire population of the colonies.

When the Congress of 1776 opened, so much blood had been shed and things had gone so far that a reconciliation with England seemed very difficult. However, the majority of the delegates had not received from their constituents instructions to render irreparable the break between Great Britain and her former colonies. Certain ardent Whigs, such as John Dickinson, who had fought from the very beginning for the American cause and who held great sway, would have preferred to continue waiting yet a while and to avoid, if possible, any definite steps toward separation from the mother country. The debate was violent and its outcome for a long while remained dubious. The notes which Jefferson took during the discussion and John Adams' autobiography give us an insight as to what took place. Adams and his nationalist friends had drawn up and proposed (June 7, 1776) a resolution couched in these terms: "Resolved, that these united Colonies are and of right ought to be free and independent States, that they are absolved from all allegiance to the British Crown and that all political connection between them and the State of Great Britain is and ought to be totally dissolved. That it is expedient forthwith to take the most effectual measures for forming foreign alliances. That a plan of confederation be prepared and transmitted to the respective Colonies for their consideration and approbation." [21] This text plainly shows the linking up of the two ideas as well as the patriots' effort to win over the conservatives to the idea of independence as an international necessity, a necessary evil—which, however, would be immediately compensated by a new and more worthy relation with great nations. The conservatives argued that France was not ready to intervene and that American opinion did not desire independence.

All that Vergennes had done during the past year furnished ample refutation of this argument. As for the apathy of the American public, it could not be a decisive factor in a moment when circumstances were at so critical a point. The patriots replied that there was no time to be lost, that they must make haste, that they had already waited too long, and that, if they had declared their independence in 1775, they could have already, with the help of France, prevented England from bringing German mercenaries to America. This opinion triumphed. Such is the very great part that France played in the discussion of American independence in 1775 and 1776. Indeed, it seems that she furnished the final and decisive argument. This impression is further confirmed by the disputes in 1777, in the course of which the leaders of the conservatives declare, "You cannot help but see that this declaration of independence was premature, since France has not declared in your favor," while the embarrassed Whig leaders are becoming alarmed at the French government's delay and are beginning to wax indignant about it.[22] We cannot assert that the United States would not have attained independence without the moral influence of France and the activities of Vergennes, but it is evident that the declaration of 1776 would have been impossible at that time and in those particular conditions, without this moral influence and without the steps which the French Ministry of Foreign Affairs had taken during the preceding three years. It was the first great diplomatic success of Louis XVI's government; and it was also, one might say, the first instance of diplomacy through public opinion furnished by this eighteenth century, which was so full of contradictions and, in the course of which, the aspirations of the people, stifled, it seems, by the puissant personalities of great monarchs such as Frederick, Catherine and Maria-Theresa, so seldom made themselves felt.

There has been much discussion to determine the degree to which the Declaration of Independence, considered as an intellectual work, was an American product and how much of it was due to European influences, English or French. Jefferson, who drew it up, was one of the most cultivated minds in Congress, in which there were, however, many men of great ability and high education. Jefferson spoke French and had read the French philosophers—at least the most notable ones, such as Rousseau, Voltaire and Raynal.

At the time of the signing of the Declaration of Independence, an edition of extracts from Rousseau had just been published at Philadelphia.[23] And, although for the most part, Jefferson, belonging as he did to the great Anglo-American Whig party, appears to have taken most of the ideas that the Declaration of Independence contains from Locke, it seems that the idea of an entirely conditional social contract, as well as that of the absolute equality of all men, goes back rather to an inspiration found in Rousseau.[24] But such a discussion would be futile and would lead to nothing save vague hypotheses. Jefferson said that in writing this famous document he had recourse to no other book or pamphlet. The Declaration of Independence was, as far as he was concerned, an outburst of religious and patriotic sentiment. It is this very stamp of fervor and mysticism that is the real innovation. It has often been said that the Declaration of Independence together with the proclamation of rights that it contains was only a *résumé*, a recapitulation of ideas that were already accepted and applied in America. This is not altogether true. The *de facto* liberty which the English colonists enjoyed was as much the result of their isolation as of common-law rights and recognized charters. In short, it was a product of circumstances. Jefferson elevated this liberty, he changed the sense of it, he made it a product of reason and of the will of men. He presented it to the world as an absolute and universal truth, as obligatory and eternal as the truths of religion. He undertakes the expression of it with a conviction, a solemnity and a warmth of spirit that remind us of Rousseau. He hands it down to the world as a universal moral code.

Reread this majestic preamble:

"When in the Course of human events, it becomes necessary for one people to dissolve the political bands which have connected them with another, and to assume among the Powers of the Earth, the separate and equal station to which the Laws of Nature and Nature's God entitle them, a decent respect to the opinions of mankind requires that they should declare the causes which impel them to the separation. We hold these truths to be self-evident, that all men are created equal, that they are endowed by their Creator with certain unalienable Rights, that among these are Life, Liberty and the pursuit of Happiness."

Is it not a profession of faith? It is the fruit of this great movement of philosophic and mystic unrest whose development in France and in America from 1770 to 1776 we have shown. Such is the sentiment that pervaded Jefferson and dictated the Declaration of Independence. This Virginian—philosopher and deist, hostile to the established church, steeped in the worship of Reason, a follower of the doctrines of the physiocrats, filled with a passion for tolerance—formulated the text that was to serve as a standard around which souls in quest of a new faith were to rally. And it was indeed for *them* that he wrote it. Although the ideas that he embodies in it, drawn as they are from Locke and the

French philosophers, are not original, the Declaration of Independence nevertheless remains a document of capital importance in the history of thought. It transfers new and bold ideas from the domain of speculation and polemics into that of popular faith, into the realm of the practical and the sentimental. Is it not just this that Rousseau seems to have been the first to do and that Raynal had tried so brilliantly to accomplish? Is there not ground for believing that, in this also, Jefferson felt unconsciously an influence which came principally from France?

The declaration was well received in France. Few newspapers dared to publish it, because the stir would have been too violent. But it was privately circulated everywhere, and all the papers spoke of it as a moving and sublime act. The *Gazette de France* described the emotion that fired the American troops when the Declaration of Independence was read to them,[25] and in 1777 the same paper published lengthy details concerning the celebrations at Philadelphia and Boston to commemorate July 4, 1776. It described "the enthusiasm that the anniversary of liberty can inspire in republican hearts." [26] In 1777 the *Courrier de l'Europe*, which was subsidized by the French government, published the complete text of the famous document. In February of the same year the *Gazette d'Utrecht* did the same. Both the populace and the upper classes experienced the religious thrill that runs through a nation when a new ideal has just transformed its spiritual life. Participation in this crusade for liberty became the topic of every tongue. At first there was no critical and detailed study of the declaration; this came only gradually and later on. It was accepted as an act of faith, it was lived first and read afterward.

From Stockholm, King Gustave hailed it with enthusiastic applause and wrote to his French friends to tell them that after such a manifestation, this century was undoubtedly going to be "the century of America";[27] while in the streets of Paris a popular refrain all during the autumn of 1776 repeated:

> Vergennes, the ninny,
> Our bungling minister,
> Lets the sullen English
> Beat the insurgents.
> Low and docile valet of all England,
> To George the Third
> He gave his word
> That we should be his friends
> Throughout his ministry.

This effervescence was soon to take a more acute turn; for the Americans at last were going to have a representative who was capable of drawing all Europe into a philosophical crusade.[28]

In March, 1776, Silas Deane, an ex-member of the Congress, had set sail with a commission from this body to procure arms in France and to feel out Vergennes. He was authorized to mention vaguely a possible separation between America and England. Deane was an honest

Connecticut Yankee, fairly well educated, a good business man with a taste for ostentation. He had more zeal than judgment. He was liked in France, where Vergennes received him a few days after the news of the Declaration of Independence had arrived. Vergennes was very kind to him, promised him full liberty and protection in France, refused to enter into a discussion of a possible alliance, but helped him along his way by putting him in contact with Beaumarchais, who was to furnish arms to the colonists, and Gérard, counselor-of-state and the commissioner of the Ministry of Foreign Affairs, who was in charge of maintaining liaison between the colonies and France.[29] From this time forth, Gérard was preparing for the alliance.[30] Deane saw a few people at Paris, but he did not speak French and his magnetism was limited. Luckily for the United States, Congress, immediately after July 4, set about providing itself with diplomatic representation in France. Deane, Franklin and Arthur Lee were chosen as ambassadors to France. The discussion of these measures began on July 18. Franklin sailed October 26 and arrived at Nantes in the early part of December, 1776, after a hard and dangerous crossing. He was instructed to negotiate a treaty of alliance on a footing of equality. He was to promise the King of France no commercial monopoly, to bind him to undertake no conquest on the American continent, and to ask his protection for the American merchant marine, and recognition of American independence, financial aid and arms. He was empowered to offer a convention covering the conquest of English islands and the restitution of the Newfoundland fisheries to France.[31] These terms, which were discussed at length, contained, as one may observe, nothing that might rouse enthusiasm in France. To us today they seem ridiculous. But Franklin's personality was to make up for the insufficiency of the terms that he was instructed to offer. He arrived modestly, with the air of a poor old scholar fleeing from a topsy-turvy world in search of refuge and peace. He seemed so wise and so given to meditation that this pose deceived many—at least among the diplomats and clever people. Simple folk made no such mistake: to them, Franklin was, from the very first, the messenger of America, come to ask for help and to plead the cause of Liberty before an apathetic Europe. In his footsteps, poems, odes and hymns broke into bloom. At Paris the learned made much of him; provincial poets wrote to him; philosophers sent him memoirs; park-bench politicians confided their grandiose schemes to him; and officers of all ranks came to ask him to enroll them in American service. As a matter of fact, most of them wanted to be employed as generals, but they were willing to die for the liberty of the New World. It was an extraordinary outburst of self-sacrifice. In the Antilles there was a movement to raise a French legion to serve under Washington.[32] Congress, a bit weary of the heroism of the Creoles, refused.[33] But they could not refuse all that was offered them. There was at Paris and in the Court in those days a powerful family that has never been forgotten in France, the Noailles family. Together with the La Rochefoucaulds d'Einville, the Noailles formed the most liberal faction of French nobility, and they had taken the American Colonies under their special patronage. Their number, their influence, their social and intellectual prestige were of infinite value to these poor tradesmen of New England whose task it was to negotiate with the most polished court in the world. Now among the Noailles, there was a young man, ambitious, generous, rich and, in the vocabulary of the time, "republican": M. le Marquis de La Fayette, son-in-law of Louis de Noailles, Duc d'Ayen. During this year of 1776, he happened to be attached to the service of the Duc de Broglie at Metz. He met the Duke of Gloucester and heard him praise the Americans and predict the triumph of their cause; he came under the influence of the Duc de Broglie and his dreams. At last, enthusiasm, ambition and the taste for adventure made him decide to join the Americans. Deane and Franklin, deeming that his act would be a signal triumph for the American cause, promised him the rank of General. The Duc de Broglie aided him in every way; and his secretary, M. de Boismartin, was the most active agent in recruiting a group of officers to accompany him, procuring him a ship, and helping him to elude the watchfulness of the Court, which made a pretense at preventing this notorious departure but which, in reality, took no serious measures to stop it.[34] La Fayette set sail with De Kalb and a large detachment of officers.[35] The news was spread about Paris and caused a great sensation. La Fayette was one of the richest nobles of the Court, his uncle, the Duc de Noailles, was French ambassador to the English Court, and he was related to all the first families of France. The unexpectedness and boldness of this sensational escapade delighted everybody. Even the enemies of America had nothing but praise for La Fayette. Madame du Deffant, grown bitter and cheerless, was enchanted. "It is a sheer folly, no doubt," she wrote to Walpole, "but one that in no way dishonors him but, on the contrary, indicates courage and a taste for glory." [36] The contrast between the fine spontaneity of La Fayette and the hesitation and silence of Vergennes roused the indignation of the populace, who attacked the prudent minister vigorously in the song:

> A man of strife he never was,
> For peace he hankers so
> We'll see ourselves well beaten now
> And never strike a blow—
> Thanks to Vergennes.[37]

And the enthusiasm for liberty found a more positive expression in the *Epistle to the Bostonians* by the young poet Parny:

> For my part, it gives me pain
> To see you proclaim in spite of mockery
> This Roman brutality,

Which makes us two thousand years older.
And you, O unjust and rebellious people,
Without pope, king or queen,
Would dance to the clank of the chains
Weighing down the human race;
And upsetting the perfect balance
Of the regular order,
Would have the effrontery to be free
And beard the whole world.[38]

These couplets have already a revolutionary tone. They represent La Fayette's gesture as a crusade and the Declaration of Independence as a message to a suffering and enslaved world. Their wrath is turned against the French government, despotic toward its subjects and timorous toward the outside world. They are imprecations. They come from the people and they represent the people. A new passion was born in the hearts of the French populace.

This attitude was unjust, it is true, in its accusations against Vergennes, for the minister had never ceased to be the propagator of the new ideas and of enthusiasm for America. Patiently and unwearyingly, yet without compromising himself, he worked for realization of a Franco-American treaty; and a large group of his subordinates aided him, supported him, and gave him warm encouragement.[39] There was Hennin, his chief clerk and secretary to the Council of State, who, married to a Protestant, longed for a liberal and tolerant policy in France. There was Gérard de Munster, state councilor, who was of an Alsatian family and was now in charge of American affairs; he was fascinated with the vast prospect that the future of this new nation opened to him. There was Garnier who, because of his intimacy with Franklin and the esteem in which the minister held him, acted as go-between and secret agent both at the French embassy in London and in Paris. He drew up reports, notes and circulars for Vergennes. Finally, there was Genet, the father of Madame Campan, the Queen's chambermaid, and who himself was at the head of the bureau of interpreters, translator for the Minister of Foreign Affairs, and intermediary between this minister and the press. Edme Genet's too great notoriety has made us forget the services that his father rendered the United States. As Minister to Petrograd he could not hold his post, and as Minister to the United States, his blunders would have cost him his head if he had not renounced returning to France forever. His father, a sensible and enterprising man, during the years from 1776 to 1782 busied himself with publishing and reproducing inflammatory pamphlets, which the ministerial censorship had forbidden in the form of brochures, but which the propaganda service brought into France in the guise of magazine articles.[40] Vergennes had to overcome the resistance of M. de Maurepas, who claimed that the Americans were capable of winning their freedom unaided, and who was violently opposed to the idea of having a war at his age. Thus, in the year 1777, we see the Ministry of Foreign Affairs holding to policies of its own, quite distinct from those which the rest of the government followed. In order to force Mentor-Maurepas's hand, Vergennes continued and accentuated his working on public opinion in France and in Europe. All the newspapers that were under the tutelage of the ministry (and in those days the supervision of the principal newspapers was a task that lay in the province of the Ministry of Foreign Affairs) were obliged to print news that was favorable to America. And, from the *Gazette de France* to the *Courrier d'Avignon*, they did it faithfully. The newspapers published abroad, and consequently admitted into France only on authorization from the Ministry of Foreign Affairs, were obliged to adopt the same attitude. And since the papers published in western Germany, where English influence was predominant, did not behave in accordance with these requirements, action was taken against them. The *Courrier d'Europe*, founded at London, was subsidized in order that it should print impartial news concerning the Anglo-American quarrel. The famous Thévenot de Morande and Brissot wrote for it.[41] But they also received money from the English government, which rendered their position a delicate one and caused them to fall into Vergennes's disfavor.[42] Such seems to have been the origin of a most curious sheet of which Genet was the secret director and Franklin the editor-in-chief: *Les Affaires de l'Angleterre et de l'Amérique.* This paper began to appear in 1776; in July of this year, all the decent and "right-thinking" publications, such as the *Mercure de France*, announced its publication in most friendly terms. The importance of this curious magazine, which forms a collection of sixteen volumes, cannot be overestimated. Each volume contains two parts, (1) articles, essays, translations, documents on conditions in England and America, (2) a remarkable *résumé* of current events in these two countries and in France. The prudence of this publication in everything that concerns France, and its boldness in attacking England would be certain enough clews as to its origin.[43] But we also have a correspondence between Genet and Franklin, in which they discuss the best means of working up public opinion. The most audacious move on the part of the *Affaires de l'Angleterre et de l'Amérique* was, without doubt, the reprinting of long extracts from *Common Sense*, Thomas Paine's great revolutionary pamphlet.[44] It is true that the editor of the *Affaires de l'Angleterre et de l'Amérique* takes pains to refute Paine's diatribes against monarchy and inherited privilege, and to show that the American is really a monarchist without being conscious of it. But he praises unstintedly the sentiment of independence with which this book is stamped, as well as its author's patriotism and his zeal for his country's future. The analysis of the Declaration of Independence which this editor publishes and the approbation which he accords it are interesting. He approves especially the principle of the equality of men (which is, he says, a religious principle and the base of all religion) and the idea that legislative authority comes from the people. This concept is recognized by all sensible governments, for they all proclaim that they owe their subjects, above all things, justice. Thus, it is in trying to represent the American program as a religious and moral ideal, a code that corresponds essentially to the deepest needs of man and to the maxims of governments, that this unofficial propaganda is carried on and developed. This periodical did not hesitate to publish Price's *Observations on Civil Liberty*,[45] which the censor of the Ministry of Foreign Affairs had suppressed as containing dangerous views on personal liberty and the extent of human rights.[46] It offered all its subscribers an "American code," thus spreading everywhere the theories from across the sea. We can form an idea of the success of this campaign when we learn that the American constitutions published about 1778-1779 in the *Affaires de l'Angleterre et de l'Amérique* were translated by the Duc de La Rochefoucauld d'Einville.[47]

However, besides M. de Maurepas, it still remained to persuade the one person who alone could decide between peace and war—the King. Louis XVI hesitated between two contradictory desires. He would have liked to cleanse the honor of France from the stain of the last war and to win back the prestige that the crown had enjoyed at the beginning of the century and had lost by the defeats of the Seven Years' War. He would have liked to follow the course mapped out by his Minister of Foreign Affairs, whom he esteemed highly and who showed him the insurgents in a very favorable light. His character led him to fear violence and to despise deception equally. His choice of Maurepas as minister and counselor indicated plainly his desire to live at peace with the world, just as the care he had taken to reorganize his army and navy indicated his ambitions. He left no writings that might allow us to read his thoughts, but such reports of his words as have come down to us show him in this light.

He often expressed the remorse that he felt at supporting the Americans by clandestine aid and secret acts.[48] He read Linguet, whose gazette reflected a monarchial opinion unfavorable to America. And, finally, in Madame Adelaide, whom he was in the habit of consulting on questions of foreign policy, he must have found very little sympathy for a rebellious people. Surely he felt no particular enthusiasm. (Witness the joke which he played on Diane de Polignac, to whom—because she was forever preaching Franklin to him—he sent a certain vessel in which the eye that was traditionally painted on the bottom of such utensils in those days was replaced by a portrait of the hero of the New World.[49]) The English newspapers were acquainted with this attitude and placed their hopes for peace in the King.[50] On the other hand, they accused the Queen of inciting him to war. It is indeed possible that, in 1776, the Queen, under the influence of Choiseul, of whom she was very fond, and the younger members of the Court, who were very warm toward the Americans, may have been well affected toward their cause. But this did not last long; in November, 1776, Maria Theresa wrote to Mercy, "My daughter would do well to show less predilection for the English. I have learned that it has caused some irritation in France." [51] Her interview with Franklin was cold.[52] This was because Vergennes and Louis XVI, far from letting her take part in the diplomatic work of that year, had taken special pains to keep her out of it. She could not favor a policy in which she had had no influence.

Moreover, a doctrinary party had been formed with the purpose of opposing the enthusiasm for America in the name of the sound doctrines of monarchy.[53] The English had taken advantage of this tendency: in the Court and in the city, their agents had set up laments on the blindness of the French monarch. The publications of the *Affaires de l'Angleterre et de l'Amérique* had alarmed the conservative elements in the government. The Declaration of Independence had astonished and dismayed a goodly number of people. The tendency of the day, in making room for faith, had aroused a countercurrent, still feeble and localized, but whose influence was making itself felt, especially among state-functionaries and members of the former Court. It was sufficient to make an impression on the King and to hamper the minister, who claimed to, and wished to, speak in the name of the people.[54]

Haste was necessary: in spite of the secret aid that was being furnished them generously, the Americans were losing ground and their representatives were protesting against the delay in recognizing them. They were beginning to talk of a reconciliation with England. Such information as was obtainable showed them as being animated with a sincere enthusiasm but disagreeing as to means, poorly armed, weakly governed, and the prey of cabals. English propaganda was flooding the world with news affirming the existence of a close accord between France and Great Britain and stating that the French fleet was being dismantled.[55]

Fortunately for the United States, the impression produced by the Declaration of Independence was spreading and becoming more profound: Linguet himself, although he often criticized the insurgents, wrote, toward the end of the year 1777: "It is not this quite fanciful liberty which many look forward to seeing them enjoy [that rouses enthusiasm in France] . . . it is the fact that, while defending only their own interests, it is really our cause that they plead. In calling the English Crown to account, it is the abuses of *all* monarchies that they are attacking. . . . The blind hope of being able perhaps to imitate them some day and even of being aided by them in breaking our own chains, this is what wins the insurgents so many friends among us."[56] The regions far from Paris awoke and gave voice to their sentiments. Even at Marseilles, a club was formed to celebrate every month the victories and the virtues of the Americans and to commemorate their independence and their federal union.[57] Revolutionary sentiment grew, because of the appeal that Jefferson's formula had for all nations. At the same time, revolutionary mysticism became more and more fervent at Paris and built up a veritable worship about Franklin. This "meritorious and handsome old man," this "eagle-creator of America," as the Duc de Croÿ called him, seemed, from his solitude in Passy, where he lived in philosophic retirement, to electrify Paris.[58] People came to see him and consult him; when he went out in society, all the great ladies kissed him. He shared the intimacy of the greatest scholars of France; and the widow of Helvetius, whose salon was so influential, was his agent as well as his intimate friend. He was Turgot's kindred spirit. He moved only in the highest of social circles, but he always kept all of his proud simplicity. In the company of the La Rochefoucaulds, the Noailles, the powerful financier Le Ray de Chaumont, the Maréchale de Mouchy, the Princesse de Tingry, the Marquise de Flamarens—everywhere that Franklin appeared, a religious respect penetrated all those present.[59] At Madame du Deffant's house in a gathering who looked down on the Americans, every tongue was hushed and the conversation took on a grave and calm tone as soon as he appeared. He knew how to retort with moderation, wit and effect.[60] One day at a dinner of wits, some one remarked, "One must admit, sir, that it is a noble and superb spectacle that America presents today." "Yes," he replied modestly, "but the spectators pay no admission." During those months of 1777 when the American cause appeared to be lost, Franklin cloaked himself in a mantle of reserve, ill health and philosophy.[61] He talked very little. But as a comment on the news from America, he had formulated the phrase, "*Ca ira*," a slogan that was to have a long career.[62] He inspired those about him with confidence in this nation with which no one was acquainted but of which they believed him to be the perfect and complete personification. His gravity and moderation impressed the government, the King and the nation. He knew how to hold attention and to show himself as everything that the people expected of him. He knew how to hide away also to allow public imagination the pleasure of perfecting this image which was already so splendid. All the while he was firing the enthusiasts, he seemed so prudent that he reassured the timorous. Everywhere people repeated this Latin verse conceived by Turgot:

Eripuit cælo fulmen, sceptrumque tyrannis.[63]

We shall have occasion to study in detail the extent of his moral influence on the French nation; suffice it to note here that this influence, which was both widespread and profound, was principally consecrated to serving and representing his country. Vergennes, who accepted Franklin's advice and gave him the benefit of his own counsels, made use of his reputation and the legend, which fortified greatly everything that he himself could say to the King regarding the future importance of the United States and their integrity.

The French officers who had gone to America also acted as a powerful stimulant to the portion of the public that loves heroism, the clash of swords, brave display and rapid victories. As a matter of fact, these victories had been neither as complete nor as immediate as the noble adventurers had imagined they would be. But this was not known. There was talk of the Marquis de La Fayette's marvelous deeds in the New World and of the way in which he had become a general at twenty. At home, his young wife, so appealing a figure, showed around letters from the hero, and kind words were spoken for America. "And now," he wrote to her, "as the wife of an American officer, you must study your lesson. People will say, 'They have been defeated.' You will reply, 'It is true, but between two armies of equal strength and in open country, old soldiers always have an advantage over new ones . . . and besides, they lost more men than the Americans.' People will say, 'Philadelphia has been captured.' Answer, 'You are foolish. Philadelphia, an open city, has no importance.' Then, if they insist, send them about their business." This was the kind of propaganda to be found at Madame de La Fayette's house, and it is not so different from that which we ourselves have heard and practiced.[64]

Such zeal found its recompense. The admirable victory of Saratoga, where the American militia captured an English army and the foremost English general, came in time to confirm the words of Madame de La Fayette, Franklin and Vergennes. Songs, comedies and anecdotes sprang up on every side. In the street, one heard sung to the tune of *Femme Sensible* the proclamation of General Burgoyne:[65]

> Now hark to me, ye insurgents,
> Nay, do not weep to hear
> That this poor Burgoyne—
> *Well, what?*
> Has gone to be a monk.

The excitement spread even to Versailles. A farce burlesquing Burgoyne's surrender was played there.[66] The victory was so much the more impressive since the veterans had been beaten by those very untrained troops of whom the English had made such incessant fun. It was indeed the triumph of Mind and Justice over Brute Force. Vergennes profited by the moment. Immediately he opened negotiations with Franklin for the conclusion of a commercial treaty, and then for a defensive alliance. Maurepas, surprised by the insurgents' victory, swayed by public opinion and weary, gave up resisting. The King also was dazzled. His hesitations had been only natural considering the state of the treasury and all the reforms that it was urgent to accomplish in the kingdom, but in the face of this significant omen and popular clamor, he would have considered that he was betraying his trust if he had turned his back on so favorable an opportunity. He yielded gracefully. Moreover, Vergennes had been able to gain his confidence and there was a bond of real friendship between them. Such was the conclusion of a long secret struggle carried on in France by the progressive elements who, since the coronation, had brought pressure on the King to make him accord his policies with the wishes of the nation and restore to France her ancient prestige. To achieve this victory, it had been necessary to shape public opinion, to give it a clear direction and a positive impulse. It had been necessary to accept in general the American ideas and to popularize the American as the type of modern man who was at once the most perfect and the nearest to Nature. Lastly, it had been necessary to accord circumstances with moral needs, to strike a balance between statecraft and generous spontaneity. Vergennes may appear to have been a Utopian, but we cannot deny him the glory of having realized a Utopia that he had long cherished and striven to bring about.

It took both coolness and daring to undertake in 1778 this extraordinary enterprise which consisted in bringing the oldest and most thoroughly traditionalist kingdom in Europe to recognize the youngest republic and the most democratic government in the world. In December the King of Bavaria had died, and the diplomats of all the powers were exchanging notes, while the Prussian and

Austrian armies were preparing for war. France, allied with Austria, was going to have a decision to make. What is more, in this strange adventure she did not even have the support of her principal ally, that great American power, Spain, whom Vergennes had been working in vain for two years to win over. The English navy was intact and had been mistress of the seas since 1763. No European government was showing the least sympathy for the insurgents, not even the King of Prussia, on whom Continental Congress had thought it could count. Frederick found diversion in watching this remote conflict in which one of the strongest powers of the earth was exhausting itself. He saw no reason why any one should fight for what had no bearing on his own interests. The German princelings were selling their soldiers to England and were well satisfied when they failed to return, for in that case, they received a higher price for them. In spite of some few sincere propagandists, Germany was apathetic and cold toward the insurgents.[67] Vienna was hostile. Some interest was felt in Italy, and the inhabitants of the old free cities admired the American example; but Maria Theresa's government was very prosperous. No one made a move. Vergennes's action was courageous and daring. Louis XVI's decision was generous.

True, the King feared that if France did not intervene then, there was danger of a reconciliation between the guilty mother and her emancipated daughter; true, he might well fear for the French colonies in that case. But all that was remote, while the perils to be braved in case of an intervention were immediate. On February 6, the treaties of alliances were signed at Versailles, and Franklin and Deane were presented at the Court. The King immediately had it announced to the English Court that he had recognized the independence of the United States. War was inevitable. Why was France going to fight? To weaken England, it is most frequently answered. To destroy her, it is sometimes said. The treaty of alliance proves that France's only immediate objective was the independence of the United States. In fact, this treaty stipulates that France shall recognize the independence of the United States, that the two nations shall lend each other armed aid for the reciprocal defense of their possessions in the New World. It provides for certain advantages to be accorded to French ships in American ports, but no commercial privileges. The United States are to accord France only the treatment of the most favored nation, but they remain free to accord the same rights to other nations. The two countries engage themselves not to sign a separate peace and not to cease hostilities until the independence of the United States shall be recognized. These terms exchanged between a nation of twenty million inhabitants, provided with a powerful fleet and the first army of Europe, and a diplomatic service that was famous for its superior craft, to say nothing of its past; and a people numbering two millions, half invaded, without commerce or industry, almost without government—these terms in such conditions do honor to Vergennes's spirit of justice. They showed clearly his intentions. The instructions that he gave Gérard when he sent him to be the first French minister plenipotentiary at Philadelphia set forth yet more clearly the minister's views. These instructions, dated March 29, 1778, assign Gérard as his essential objective the maintenance and consolidation of American independence. They order him, to this end, to avoid any separate peace, to work with all his efforts toward cementing the union of the thirteen states. They indicate no territorial ambitions on the part of France and no commercial aim. France desired that this new moral being, the United States, should live. She wanted them to be strong. This, in Vergennes's eyes, was an essential condition for guaranteeing the reëstablishment of the liberty of the seas. But above all, to France it meant the resuming of her rôle as arbiter, and that under particularly brilliant circumstances; for the United States represented an ideal, both spiritual and social, toward which opinion and the enlightened had lifted up their voices these many years.[68] Vergennes's zeal in defending the interests of Spain and his care to safeguard Louisiana for this power have often been blamed. But what reason had he, since he was seeking a success of opinion and influence for his country, to betray an ancient and precious ally? The Family Pact was at that time considered as the kingbolt of the French policy. And beside, who was to have Louisiana if not Spain? To give it to England would have been to give an enemy the key which opened the door both to the Spanish possessions and to the domains of the United States. Give it to the United States? How should he imagine that a group of little republics, spread over an immense and sparsely settled territory, might find any advantage in acquiring the immense continent that was called Louisiana, also, or that they were in any condition to exploit it? The ideal that Vergennes had formed concerning the United States and their philosophic spirit did not allow him to doubt their moderation.[69] There has been an attempt, based on apocryphal memoirs published later, to show that he coveted Louisiana and was scheming to obtain it. This contention is false. Neither Vergennes, nor any of the other French ministers of the day, believed in the permanence of colonies. They were all convinced that the best of colonies were not worth the bloodshed and the money they cost, for they were sure either to free or to ruin themselves.[70] His thoughts were so far from such machinations that he sent word to the Americans to refrain from an expedition into Canada, for fear that the King, who wished neither to betray his one-time subjects nor to take back a domain that he considered useless, should be obliged to adopt an attitude which might offend the Canadians or trouble the Americans.[71] The advantage that Louis XVI and his ministry sought in this treaty and in this war was therefore, above all, of a moral and intellectual nature. It was French civilization that they wanted to see triumph, and whose prestige they wanted to restore by associating it with the most important event of the times. This step had, moreover, an immense material interest, through its repercussion on the other nations, especially the smaller nations, and might well bring about profound changes in the commerce of the entire world.[72]

*
* *

The United States showed themselves worthy of the friendship that was offered them. They received the news with unbounded joy, and the patriots were unanimous in declaring that the alliance guaranteed the safety of the State. Richard Henry Lee wrote to his compatriot Patrick Henry, the great Virginian leader: "I look at the past condition of America as at a dreadful precipice, from which we have escaped by means of the generous French, to whom I will be everlastingly bound by most heartfelt gratitude. . . . Surely Congress will never recede from our French friends. Salvation to America depends upon our holding fast to our attachment to them. . . ." [73] Now, R. H. Lee had been the principal champion of independence and he was later to become the most ambitious and the most sensitive of the American patriots.[74] His colleague in Congress, Samuel Adams, the most uncompromising democrat in America, also wrote under the date of April 20, 1778, that France had dealt generously with America.[75] When the army heard the news, it was fired with the deepest joy and the wildest enthusiasm. Washington felt that France had acted with wisdom and generosity.[76] From one end of the country to the other, the signing of the treaty was celebrated. Boston, the capital of the Puritans and of Protestantism in the New World, set the example. On April 13, a celebration was held at the American Coffee House in honor of the news that had come from France. A toast was drunk to Louis XVI.[77] Articles were published declaring that the war was virtually over in America, since it was going to break out in Europe, and that England would now cease tormenting her one-time colonies.[78] But it is especially in Congress that one may gauge the importance of France's move and the effect which it produced. This body, in which there was so much division and where so many interests were striving for supremacy, was unanimous for accepting the treaty with France and thanking Louis XVI. It is curious and amusing to see shortly afterward the pains that the congressional delegates took in arranging the reception of Gérard when this French minister arrived at Philadelphia. Anxious to show themselves worthy of that French politeness which was so famous throughout the world, and eager to give a good impression of their own station, the members of Congress took council almost every day during two weeks as to the proper etiquette for receiving the

French minister plenipotentiary.[79] The Northern members were in favor of a republican simplicity and feared lest Congress appear servile; the Southern members wanted pomp befitting the occasion of the greatest Republic in the world receiving the representative of the most powerful Monarch of Europe. They debated on the number of horses that should draw the carriages, the number of steps to be climbed and the shape of shirt-frills. But the reception was a great success. In the course of it, Henry Laurens, the presiding officer of Congress, said to Gérard: "The treaties between His Very Catholic Majesty and the United States show so clearly his wisdom and magnaminity that they inspire the respect of all nations." [80] Gérard was delighted. Immediately he wrote to Vergennes that before his arrival there had been factions and dissensions, but that the French alliance had done away with all that. He congratulated himself on seeing all groups equally eager to carry out his wishes and to show him their respect and affection.[81] We cannot help feeling that he was rather easily carried away by effusions. He was chosen as arbiter of mooted questions. Henry Laurens came to consult him and ask his advice on pending business. One side and the other waited on him, and his opinions seemed to settle the decisions of Congress. It was perhaps too good to be true, but he was delighted with it all. We can say without reservation that, for the American people, the alliance with France appeared to be the work of a divine

Providence anxious to save its chosen people. A wave of fraternity ran over the land. It was not to prevent clashes and difficulties, but it rendered possible this fantastic coöperation between two peoples who until then had known each other only through calumnies and wars.

In France a like enthusiasm stirred the nation. One may well say that this was the zenith of Louis XVI's reign. Diplomatic circles, with the exception of the minister's intimates, were surprised.[82] But the nation recognized its own wishes and hopes.[83] There was talk of nothing save enlisting to serve the country, setting out for America as a volunteer, and dying for liberty. This great King in the rôle of the protector of independence was a spectacle that moved every sensitive soul. And in those days every one in France *had* a sensitive soul. The fleet was in excellent shape and well equipped (twelve years after a most humiliating peace it could still meet the English fleet on an equal footing). The French enjoyed the astonishment of Europe, they were amused at the rage and surprise of England, but above all, they savored the new and philosophic sentiment of having, beyond the seas, a brother-people, so noble, so courageous, so steadfast, whom they loved so well and knew so little. In France, these months were to mark the apotheosis of Philosophy, at last triumphant and creative. Voltaire, old and laden with glory, came to pluck the last laurels that his gnarled hand was to gather. At the Comédie Française he was crowned. At the Academy of Sciences, Franklin brought forward his grandson to receive Voltaire's blessing, and the dying poet pronounced over the young man's head the words, "God, Liberty," which caused a thrill of mystic enthusiasm to run over the throng, while the apostle of tolerance and the liberator of the New World embraced.[84] Their glory seemed for an instant to blend together, and the spectators understood then the identity of their work; there was no mistaking the significance of this ceremony. Philosophy, too long the slave of abstract reasoning, entered into all hearts and brought forth at last tangible manifestations and contributions. People wept for joy and knelt in worship of human wisdom, now grown so powerful that it could engender life, guide the soul, and enrapture hearts with ecstasy. Mind, satisfied with its triumphs, rested on the magnificent spectacle of liberty conquering a world, creating an ideal, producing a saint, and converting the great ones of the earth.

Whether or not he shared it himself, Vergennes was obliged to sustain public opinion at this high pitch of enthusiasm, or at least to be able to show the world the spectacle of this young nation, free and natural, prospering through the aid and friendship of France. It was necessary that public interest should be held and that a union of purpose, desire and ideal should reign between the two allies. It was hoped that the war would be a brief one and that England would avail herself of facilities for yielding gracefully.[85] Neither the minister nor the public felt any hatred toward her. They were glad to have a chance to teach her a lesson, but they admired her civilization and knew that she was necessary to the equilibrium of Europe. One might say that the relations between the two countries never ceased to be courteous, or even that they were more courteous after the beginning of hostilities than before. Admiral Rodney, who was in France at the time, was allowed to return to England. It was not a question of war to the death, but of a struggle for prestige and influence. French plans for an invasion of England were never carried very far, and England never attacked France on the continent. It was in the New World that the war waxed bitter, and it was waged as much in the minds of the people as on the fields of battle. The English left no stone unturned to regain by force, fraud and persuasion, the domination that was slipping away from them. Vergennes on his part made use of all his resources to aid the Americans and to guide them. The primary result of the war was to be the creation of the United States; the problem was therefore not solely a diplomatic and military one.

First of all, it was necessary that the United States should consolidate their national life. Now during the period of struggle and suffering that extends from the moment of the French intervention to the capitulation at Yorktown, Congress showed particular weakness and sluggishness. The people, weary of a war too long drawn-out, did not furnish enough volunteers, and finances were in a bad way, for taxes were not coming in. All these difficulties encouraged the royalists and engendered factional quarrels. Congress turned continually toward France, their powerful ally, who was so rich and so strong, and whose aid should have made success so easy. The Tories exploited this tendency. In their pamphlets they repeated that France had deceived the insurgents in not sending them sufficient assistance.[86] In their verses, in the countless popular songs which they spread throughout the country, they dwelt on the desperate slowness of the war, due to the indolence and blundering of France, or on the indemnities which would be a consequence of pretended French generosity.[87] Their newspapers, which the patriotic sheets quoted, claimed that the French people, thoroughly devoted to monarchy, would have refused to fight for the United States if the Pope had not given the French King the right to invest the entire North American continent.[88] One of these papers, edited by a man of learning who was, at once, a cunning pamphleteer, a good editor and a clever spy, a certain Rivington, conducted a campaign against France that was as patient as it was violent. He made use of calumnies concerning the stupidity of the King, the frivolity of the Queen, the bad condition of French finances, the wrath of the people; he printed fables threatening the Americans with a fate similar to that of the frogs who wanted a king.[89] But, above all, he published exact and disheartening details concerning all that was happening and was going to happen in France. The accuracy of his information is remarkable, and it could not fail of its effect.[90] As early as May 17, 1780, Rivington announced that La Fayette had persuaded Louis XVI to send an army commanded by Rochambeau to America, and he furnished a number of curious details on this subject.[91] But his principal effort was directed against Franklin and the French alliance.[92] When, in March, 1780, *Americanus* claimed that Franklin had delivered the colonies over to the King of France on the sole condition that they should be free from English domination, should have the privileges of free French citizens and the certitude of escaping Purgatory, thanks to the intervention of the Pope, it had little weight, although these pleasantries did not fail to amuse even the Whigs; but when, among letters seized by English cruisers, Rivington published extracts from the correspondence of Beaumarchais, Barbé-Marbois, etc., tending to prove that France, far from being disinterested, had territorial ambitions, he touched a sensitive spot; for this had direct bearing on the results of the war.[93]

In 1778, England, her first lunge having failed, could no longer hope to regain her colonies. She was prevented from this by her internal situation and by international developments. The Tories, angered against the Americans and their democratic spirit, were unwilling to see a reconciliation effected otherwise than by force and thus rendered any peaceable adjustment impossible. The

Whigs, who had always supported their brothers across the sea, could not abandon them in the hour of greatest danger. They therefore carried on an intense liberal and revolutionary propaganda, of which the campaigns of the famous Wilkes are the most conspicuous example. But they hated despotic and catholic France. She had always appeared to them, and still appeared to them, as the most implacable enemy of philosophic ideas and of liberty. They could not allow her to triumph. Thus opinion was irreparably divided, and the ministry was in no condition to maneuver skillfully to obtain a peace without dishonor. It was obliged to fight. Unfortunately the strength of France, the heroism of the American patriots, and the hostile indifference of Europe rendered a military triumph impossible. England could no longer reasonably hope to see a royal government reëstablished in America and the loyalists reseated in power; but she could hope to wear out France, divide the insurgents and regain a foothold among them. She did not cease to work with these results in view, and it may be said that she did not fail entirely.

After Gérard's arrival quarrels and parties seemed to have disappeared in Congress. But such admirable harmony was not to last long. Subjects for dissensions were not lacking in Congress. There was the natural rivalry between the big states, such as Massachusetts and Virginia, and the little states, such as Delaware and New Jersey; then there was the opposition of interests and temperaments that divided the North from the South. There were the aspirations of every state that wanted to expand toward the West and demanded its share of these lands, for which it was so difficult to show valid titles (for the only legitimate proprietors were the Indians, and *they* had no titles). Also there were private questions and rivalries, struggles for influence and power between men endowed with a strong combative spirit, a high sense of their rights and a mystic enthusiasm for their works. The question of embassies and missions in Europe was a most ticklish one; for almost all these men, who drew no salary as delegates to Congress, were tradesmen; and a trip to Europe in a time like this might mean considerable profit to them. This question was the apple of discord. Jealousy led the Lees of Virginia, who had a strong following in Congress, to accuse Deane, and indirectly Franklin, of having arranged with Beaumarchais to make Congress pay for provisions and equipment which, the Lees said, were a gift from the King of France. Deane, angered at this injustice, flew into a rage and ruined everything. Beaumarchais tried to prove that he had really paid for the merchandise sent to America and he could not do it; because, though he had indeed paid for it, he had nevertheless drawn it from the arsenals of the King, who was still at peace with England.[94] Gérard wanted to defend the honor of the King, who was thus indirectly accused of having aided the United States secretly while he was still at peace with

England. He wanted to put an end to the quarrel and seemed thus to be siding with Deane. The Lees turned in wrath against him. Thomas Paine, then secretary of the Committee on Foreign Affairs in Congress, sided against Deane for some unknown reason (for it has not been proved that he had received money from the Lees, though it is certain that he was entirely ignorant of the facts of the affair). Beaumarchais and Gérard alone could reveal the origin of the goods, but reasons of state prevented them from bringing forward anything save affirmations. Thus the case turned out very badly. Beaumarchais, whom Congress, prudent in case of doubt, refused to pay, went to his ruin and disgrace.[95] Deane ruined himself in seeking justice and, mad with rage, revolted against Congress and France, the cause of his misfortunes, and became a traitor without salary in the service of England, for whose benefit he filled gazettes with recriminations against Congressional stupidity and French duplicity.[96] Led on by this controversy, the Lees had formed in Congress a compact group which henceforth regarded Gérard with such suspicion that the unhappy minister chose to fall ill and return to France. He was regretted by Congress, for whom he had gone to infinite pains and whom he had loved sincerely. They had been grateful to him for having been so worthy, so distinguished, so well informed on all subjects and so obliging. But he had committed one grave error in the course of his embassy. He had come to America as to a land that lay very close to the state of Nature. He had behaved according to the dictates of sentiment, had been warm-hearted, always ready to give his time, efforts and advice. In spite of his great intelligence, he had chosen the wrong road.[97] The effusions of April, 1778, were not to be confused with everyday life, and the all-embracing benevolence of Franklin was not to be attributed to a deliberative assembly. He left a Congress seriously divided against itself and suspicious of France; already a separation into parties was beginning to manifest itself in its ranks. The Lees, irritated against Gérard, gathered around them all those who were partisans of an absolute and uncompromising independence, a far-spread development of the country and the establishment of a balance between France and England.[98] To them, America's mission seemed to be of such a nature that it allowed of no collaboration, unless it were of a temporary nature. On the other hand, their opponents still stood out for the benign and philosophic solution which was Franklin's aim; the union of the freest nation in the world with the most enlightened nation in the world to assure peace and the prudent and regulated development of the United States. These two parties differed essentially on one capital point: the reliance that could be placed on the moral integrity of France. The former were inclined to survey it continually and doubted its genuineness. The latter trusted France and saw her as their sister-nation.

The predominance of the latter group had to be

assured at any price. Vergennes, through his ministers, his manner of conducting the war, in short, through his entire official position, strove toward this end and brought a veritable propaganda to play on public opinion in order to accomplish it.

In place of Gérard, he took care to send a cautious and prudent man; he warned him against excesses of zeal and against sentimental indiscretions. The Count de La Luzerne was fat, red-faced, myopic, and had rather fine manners. He was highly cultured and had a deep knowledge of his profession. The Americans found him punctilious and a bit of a routinist. He did not give the impression of being a strong personality, and this was no doubt for the best.[99] He had with him as Consul-General, M. de Barbé-Marbois, quick-witted, curious, learned and a bit restless, a man who had the art of both pleasing and displeasing the Americans sovereignly. Marbois did not content himself with living at Philadelphia and there attending to such business as was confided to his cares; he took great pains to become acquainted with the country; its inhabitants and their genius. Often in La Luzerne's absence, he exercised the functions of chargé-d'affaires and succeeded fairly well, although his rather meddling activity often annoyed the Americans. La Luzerne arrived in America in the midst of the quarrels stirred up by the Deane affair. He took pains not to involve himself in it in any way and thus succeeded in appeasing somewhat the partisans of the Lees. The critical situation of affairs in the winter of 1779-1780 gave France an opportunity to prove her intentions and the sincerity of her friendship. Already the French fleet had twice been sent to aid the insurgents. Vergennes went further than this; it was decided to send an army of two divisions to the American continent and to place this army under Washington's orders. It was this army that was to render such effective aid in bringing about the surrender at Yorktown (October, 1781), which finally decided the destiny of America. In addition to this, two French fleets were to lend their support to the Americans, and the great fleet commanded by M. de Grasse was to assure the naval superiority of the allies in the waters of the New World. These good offices were not confined to the field of military operations. France, through the medium and at the instance of Vergennes, during these years made a gift to America of ten million livres Tournois and lent them forty-seven million.[100] At a period when the treasury was empty and when financial reforms were so urgent, this constituted a veritable proof of affection. Moreover, in all questions and in all diplomatic circles, Vergennes acted as agent for the Americans. It was through his influence that Spain came into the war despite her antipathy for the Americans and the uneasiness with which they inspired her. This feeling was so strong in Spain that the King could never be persuaded to sign a treaty or an article of alliance with the Americans. In vain did the French ambassador, M. de Montmorin, try to persuade the Court of Madrid. M. de la Vauguyon was more successful at The Hague, where, with his assistance, John Adams succeeded in inducing the Dutch government to declare in favor of America.[101] We find Vergennes being of as much service as possible to the American ambassadors in the posts that they occupy in Europe and lavishing on them such counsels as he deems prudent to prevent them from going about begging for alliances sure to be refused.[102] Arthur Lee and Ralph Izard scorned his advices but had reason to regret having done so.[103]

While France was doing so much, one would be inclined to think that La Luzerne's position must have been an easy one. Much to the contrary, every month that went by rendered it more difficult. Their reverses and the sufferings that an interminable war inflicted on a people who were naturally peaceful, embittered the Americans. They laid the blame on France. Congress was proving unreasonable in its demands.[104] Between their constituents, who were already exhausted with sacrifices and who were going to be called upon to reëlect them, and the King of France, who was so wealthy, the delegates preferred to have recourse to the latter; and if La Luzerne seemed inclined to deny them, they sadly voiced fears that they might be obliged to treat with England if the war did not end soon.

Congress dealt fairly. It kept up no clandestine relations with England and it made no attempt at a reconciliation. But all of its members did not entertain an equal affection for France, and more than one of them longed for the easy commercial relations of the old days with people of the same blood and tongue. La Luzerne felt this very clearly when he was obliged to resume an irritating discussion that Gérard had rather clumsily stirred up in Congress. It was the matter of deciding what peace conditions should be imposed on England and what conditions should be accepted from her. Vergennes, anxious to get through with it, and persuaded that a favorable turn of events, properly handled, would bring a solution of the problem quite as well as military successes, wanted to know in advance the intentions of the United States and the minimum of their demands. The discussion began in 1778, and it was still going on when the preliminaries were signed.[105] It had done more to cause coolness between France and the United States than any other incident. France and Vergennes admired the United States and judged them to be intelligent and philosophical, but still weak and badly organized. Vergennes judged that after the war they would need time and quiet to work out a stable government and to regain their prosperity. He wished sincerely to see them happy. He did not imagine them at all as conquerors or imperialists, but thought that their immense territory and abundant resources would suffice them. He hoped that they would continue to set the world an example of moderation and prudence. He had to take into account the fears expressed by many people in high situations, that too much encouragement might render them aggressive and thus create a new danger for Europe.[106] Nothing could persuade him to set them up as rivals to Spain, the ancient ally of France, and to allot them the territory of Louisiana, which the French had discovered and colonized. Nor could anything persuade him to sacrifice to the Americans the one right and privilege of long standing that France had succeeded in preserving from England in 1763, the fishing rights of Newfoundland. In 1778, very few Americans would have protested strongly against this point of view. The most prudent of them, Gouverneur Morris, for example, declared: "In general, we feel the disadvantages of expanding toward the South." But the irritation which smoldered in a certain Congressional party against Gérard led some politicians not to accept the French suggestions without opposition. Adams, in the name of the New England fishermen, demanded imperiously fishing rights along the entire bank of Newfoundland, and he united all the Northern states in a bloc that had every appearance of hostility toward France. Some of these violent patriots may have feared too prompt an end to the war and consequently held out for conditions that would not be easy to obtain. They demanded, as fundamental peace terms, navigation privileges on the Mississippi and the Newfoundland fishing rights; and they urged the conquest of Canada. This greed shocked and surprised Vergennes.

La Luzerne, ordinarily prudent and silent, pled so well that he rallied and kept a majority on his side and that Congress, trusting in Vergennes, concluded by leaving him to judge the peace terms. But all this discussion, all this haggling, had done real harm to French prestige. It left a goodly number of the delegates irritated and excited. The eventual solution was both courteous to the King of France and flattering to his minister; but suspicions had been awakened and a spirit had been stirred up in Congress which was to incite this body to free itself of every vestige of French tutelage as soon as it was possible. This feeling did not amount to hatred save in the case of one or two members; it was not even animosity, for it did not entirely exclude gratitude; but it was a sympathy mixed with reserve, fear and doubt. It did not extend to all the members of Congress, or perhaps even to a majority; but it influenced Congress as a body, and it was not able to overlook it. This conflict is a grave one, for it has definite bearing on the mission and moral rôle of the United States in the world.[107]

France was not represented in the United States by its diplomatic agents alone. She had other envoys who were more apt to reach the hearts of a young and generous people. The officers who, from 1776 on, had flocked to serve Liberty on the battlefields of the New World were not all spotless heroes, but almost all of them were men of courage, and some of them gave proof of a loyalty and generosity that were worthy of the people to whom they were devoted. After a stormy youth, the Marquis de la Rouërie,[108] a very wealthy young nobleman from Brittany, had decided to finish his life in a monastery, but he suddenly caught the enthusiasm for America and, crossing the water, renouncing his title and his name and spending his fortune unstintedly to equip a cavalry corps, he won a place among the foremost combatants of the war. He was in a continual wrangle with Congress, who refused to make him a general but sent him horses which were killed under him. He was always threatening to abandon the whole adventure, but when he did leave for Europe it was only to return with arms, money and provisions for his beloved companions in arms. He was not killed in action, but he displayed thoroughly his Breton pride and courage. We must also mention all those officers of Pulawski's Legion who went to their death so nobly along with him. Nor would it do to pass over the magnificent zeal of those who with Steuben and Du Portail built up the engineering corps of the American army and brought to a victorious end the glorious operations of the siege of Yorktown. It may be said that the military science of the Americans came from France. All the books that were printed for the instruction of officers, artillerymen and engineers, were translations from the French.[109] It would take many pages to give the Marquis de La Fayette all the credit that he deserves. He was patient, modest, courageous and able during his whole stay in America. He was unassuming enough to accept a modest situation in 1777, and he won to his rank by his courage. Wounded in the first battle in which he took part, he then accepted the dangerous mission of making an expedition into Canada; and when Congress gave up this plan, La Fayette returned to his subaltern rank. He served as Washington's lieutenant in the hardest battles of 1778. When d'Estaing and his expeditionary force were beaten off Rhode Island, he was strong enough and calm enough to stand between the irate Americans and the French, who were indignant at the injustice done them. When he returned to France to offer his services to the King against England, he did not forget the Americans; and it was his entreaties that opened Vergennes's eyes and made him decide to send an expeditionary force to Washington's aid. La Fayette had had reason to hope to be chosen for this command, and to desire that the leadership of these superb divisions might be accorded to him even unofficially. Yet he was able to become a devoted friend to Rochambeau, as he had been to Washington. The end of the Virginia campaign is largely due to the consummate skill which he displayed in drawing Cornwallis into the trap that was laid for him at Yorktown. La Fayette was spirited, gracious, well-dressed, generous, and truly a young hero.

In a material way he did much for the Franco-American cause. He did even more by his example, his attitude and his enthusiasm. In America his name was on every tongue. Every heart beat with gratitude to him. "The

Marquis" meant La Fayette. And this name was blessed. Many others had come before him, of whom some were even more courageous, more devoted or more learned in military arts. Many came after him who were still more brilliant: there was the Duc de Lauzun with his legion that was to be found everywhere where there was danger or pretty women; there was the Chevalier de Chastellux with his halo of philosophy and his charming manners; there was the Count de Damas,[110] the Viscount de Noailles, the Count de Charlus, the Count de Broglie—all handsome, noble and wealthy. There were the six thousand soldiers, the finest of the French army, whose fine build, discipline and courage won all hearts. It is true that the people admired them, that they were astonished to find them so different from what the English had said of them, so polite and reserved, so strict against pillage. It is true that they flocked out to welcome them and that afterward they talked of their admirable conduct, but still "the Marquis" was chosen as the type for all the rest.[111] He alone stood out as a definite personality for the mass of the American people. And this image did more than everything else to facilitate the relations between the French and the Americans in the New World. The mind needs an image in order to love and understand. La Fayette was this image. Whatever there was of incomplete, immature and superficial about him, far from hurting him in their eyes, was accepted by the mass as a mark of youth; and he fired this young nation with enthusiasm. La Fayette was made to be a young hero. It was only in America that he fulfilled his destiny. The passing years, which brought him heaviness, did not bring him maturity. But at twenty, lithe, energetic, generous and filled with a patriotic faith, he was a fine example of a being to whom philosophy was a religion, without pedantry, platitude or pettiness. All the newspapers in America related his exploits. People in all parts of the country, at Boston, Philadelphia, Richmond and Baltimore, had a chance to see him. He never came into conflict with Congress. In the army he kept aloof from juntas and remained faithful to Washington.[112] The only relations that any one had with him were personal. And this was why he was loved. Even with his soldiers he was never anything but a gentleman to whom a military command had been confided. And this was his salvation. Even the regions that were most refractory to French influence, such as New England, sang his praises.

He was seen everywhere. All the highest and wealthiest social circles were open to the French officers. And these were also intellectual circles. It is evident that this fusion was not without influence on the spiritual life of the United States; so much the more so, since at the same time French merchants were establishing themselves in all the ports. As a matter of fact, most of these latter were badly adapted to the United States. Some of them, however, succeeded; and those who did not, remained in the cities and taught French for a living. There were also some few penniless officers who did the same.[113]

Under these combined influences, various currents developed in America. The most elementary one consisted of a refining of manners. The newspapers published articles protesting against such boorish usages as toasts which every one around the table drank out of the same bowl, drinking-bees, etc. They proudly published the list of the names of the most elegant French officers who had come over the sea, and it is easy to perceive that their minds were on France and that they were observing her intently.[114] In 1777, Washington wrote to Congress that they must receive La Fayette well because of his high social position, and among his papers we find a list of the most distinguished nobles of the French army, which he had requested La Fayette to draw up for him in 1780.[115] Washington thought it wise to seek the support of this class of society and to study their politeness, which was renowned throughout the world.[116]

This influence, though it is incontestable, is subtle and difficult to analyze. We may indicate its presence, but any attempt to trace its manifestations would be futile. It is easier to show how the French officers and professors rendered American education more artistic and intellectual.

Frenchmen settled in all the cities, even those that were occupied by the English. Advertisements of French professors appeared in the papers at Baltimore, Boston, New

York, Richmond and, above all, at Philadelphia, where there were as many as three of them, of whom one was a certain M. Robin of Paris, who said that he was a professor for adults and refused to take children as pupils; another was M. Quesnay, the son of Louis XV's physician; and the third was a M. Brival de la Broderie, who taught Latin, English and French, especially to ladies.[117]

> Fair sex, in you I do confide.
> Choose me and make no error;
> Beneath the wings of such a guide
> The hawk inspires no terror,

his advertisement read.

Thus the study of French was spreading among already mature people who wished to perfect their education. It is significant to see the large universities including French in their curriculums. From Paris, Deane had written to Stiles, the president of Yale, to propose founding a chair of French and a French library at Yale. He prided himself on having interested a number of his wealthy French friends in this project and on being able to raise the money easily. Stiles was perplexed; the idea pleased him, but he did not dare carry it out, for Yale was the center of orthodox Puritanism. He consulted his friends: the preachers were of the opinion that it would be very dangerous because of "popery" and that the offer should be refused; the judges saw no danger in it and wanted him to accept the offer; the Governor was consulted and he also urged Stiles to accept. Finally, the

Corporation which directed the college ratified the measure. But Deane could no longer make good his offers. Harvard showed itself more liberal.[118] In 1779, an instructor was chosen to teach French outside of the college. The first of these instructors was Vandal in 1779. In 1780, Poullin was given the appointment and, in 1782, Albert Gallatin, a young immigrant from Geneva, who was to become one of the most remarkable Secretaries of the Treasury that the United States ever had, after having been a violent democrat.[119] In 1780, French had become a regular, though not an obligatory, part of the instruction at Harvard.[120] In 1782, freshmen and sophomores were allowed to study it in place of Hebrew. This is a very significant fact and one that marks clearly the growth of what might be called secular learning in this old Puritan university. Moreover, Franklin was having sent from France to Harvard profane books of a decidedly deistic tendency, such as *Le Monde primitif* by Court de Gébelin, which same Gébelin was in regular correspondence with Professor Sewall.[121] And Harvard paid its court to her country's allies by awarding doctorates *honoris causa* to M. de La Luzerne, M. de Marbois and M. de Valnais, the French consul at Boston.[122] We find the same attitude at William and Mary College, the oldest and most famous institution of the South and one which in those days rivaled Harvard. In 1779, Jefferson, as governor of Virginia and "visitor" of William and Mary, had a chair of French created and gave it to

Charles Bellini. This was the first professorial chair to be established in the New World for the teaching of a modern language.[123] But in 1782, Rhode Island College wrote to the King of France requesting him to found a chair of French and a French library in their institution.[124] Dartmouth College sent its president to Europe for the same purpose.[125] And the legislators of Massachusetts inserted in their constitution a clause relative to education and the arts which was inspired, John Adams says, by a desire to follow the example of France in encouraging the sciences. From this resulted the foundation of the Academy of Arts and Sciences at Boston, which resembled the French Academy.[126]

The spirit of philosophy penetrated along with French books. The bookshops advertised an ever-increasing proportion of French works, and even the towns that the English occupied were touched by this movement. Thus, at New York in 1782, Rivington published a new edition of Raynal's great work.[127] In various parts of the United States, the newspapers published translations of Raynal's book on the American Revolution or of his other works.[128] It is above all Virginia, where the established church was broken down and where great religious confusion seems to have reigned, that furnishes examples of this kind.[129] Jefferson, who is a good representative both of the culture and the intellectual attitude of the highest class in Virginia, was writing about this time, at the request of Barbé-Marbois, his *Notes on Virginia*, which are so pervaded by the doctrine of the Economists and so fired with philosophic zeal for the freeing of negro slaves and for tolerance.[130]

In these *Notes*, he refutes with indignation and respect Abbé De Pauw's calumnies against America. He quotes Buffon, Daubenton and all the great French scientists of the period. He turns toward them as his instructors. One feels his eagerness to seize their spirit. It is also during this period that, in the discussions of Congress, Benjamin Rush uses examples from Raynal and Montesquieu to combat a project for having each state cast a uniform vote.[131] John Adams, setting out for Europe and having decided to become a great diplomat, bought all the French treatises on diplomacy that he could find.[132] In short, the leaders of American thought are suddenly becoming disciples of this civilization with which they are so unfamiliar. They select from it whatever best completes their own personalities and responds to their own instincts and desires. Thus formal refinement and the philosophic spirit are the two contrasting aspects that French influence takes on. Even La Luzerne becomes a propagator of philosophy and tolerance. It was he who brought Congress to listen for the first and only time to a sermon preached by a Catholic priest in a Catholic chapel. The good Abbé Bandole, chaplain of the French embassy, had the honor after the siege of Yorktown of congratulating Congress in the name of God in the following terms: "You offer the universe the admirable spectacle of a society which, founded on the principles of equality and justice and now arriving at its perfection, can insure to the individuals who compose it all the happiness of which human institutions are capable." [133] It was he and Gérard who acted as intermediaries between Congress and the Quakers.[134] Their great apostle, Benezet, became so intimate a friend to Gérard that he was in the habit of writing letters to him to explain his duties and those of the King of France. As a matter of fact, Louis XVI, or rather Vergennes, was anxious to be in the good graces of this estimable sect and to reconcile them as much as possible with Congress.[135] Under French influence, the harshness of Puritanism thawed to such an extent that Quesnay played Beaumarchais' *Eugénie* at Philadelphia at a time when all theatrical productions were forbidden by Congress. This was the first French play given in the United States. A tempering of too bleak a morality, an easing of social and political bonds, a moderate sentimentality and, on the whole, a tendency to rely on men and instincts rather than on governments—these are the characteristics that we find among the Americans who came under the influence of French philosophy about 1780; and they were the best minds of the country. The Constitution of Pennsylvania is an example of the work of faithful readers of Turgot: in order to give the people absolute control of public acts, they provided for a single house, elected for short terms and under the continual supervision of the voters. Here the blind enthusiasm that

France had received from America comes back to it. It is a curious case of a people imitating itself by taking as a model a concept that another people has formed of it.

Alarmed at seeing America open itself to such diverse and opposed doctrines, Gérard, and later La Luzerne, had sought to exercise a more methodic influence on the country through its best newspapers and preachers. They wanted to obey the instructions of Vergennes, who had ordered them to do everything in their power to consolidate the national union of the United States; and they had recognized, as had their superior at Paris, that only public opinion could impose this discipline. Many American writers and journalists offered Gérard their services.[136] But he had judgment enough to prefer to choose his men.[137] He had a man to do the heavy work such as pamphlets and daily articles. For a long time this writer signed his work Leonidas. His task was to bring people to appreciate the value of liberty and independence and to see what an excellent thing was the French alliance. All this was nothing but the truth. Leonidas expressed it well but not brilliantly. Gérard found a better man. The celebrated pamphleteer Thomas Paine had had difficulties with Congress over certain indiscretions committed in the exercise of his functions as secretary of the Committee on Foreign Affairs. Since Gérard believed himself to have been the original cause of Paine's having lost his place, and since Paine was both impecunious and willing, Gérard offered to facilitate his work. He asked nothing of him save that he continue to publish his courageous and patriotic works as he was in the habit of doing.[138] He was requested not to attack France. It was under these conditions that Paine wrote his *Crisis*. He had even the politeness to bring La Luzerne the draft of the pamphlet for corrections, and some of the most stirring passages of this republican pamphlet were gone over by the French minister to the United States. His work was so satisfactory that he was requested to write a history of the war. The archives of the French consulates and of the embassy to the United States would have been placed at his disposition; but Paine was indolent, and the history of the American Revolution never saw day, to the great regret of La Luzerne.[139] There was also a clergyman from Boston, Samuel Cooper, an excellent man, cultivated and pious, and who for the past twenty years had devoted himself to the Whig cause in Massachusetts. He was a preacher with a very open and philosophic mind. He had seen that, without France, the United States would probably not be able to hold out to the end. He had viewed with alarm the hostility of the Bostonians and all the Congregational clergy toward France, and he had set himself courageously to battle against this current.[140] His resources did not allow him to do much. He accepted the aid of the King of France, who gave him, as he did Paine, a thousand dollars a year to allow him to hire a secretary or an assistant. It would be unjust to accuse these men, and presumptious to seek to defend them. In a critical moment for their country, their country's most faithful friend asked them to help her to unite the spiritual forces of the United States into a desperate resistance against the invader. Nothing was demanded of them except that they should devote themselves to the service of the common cause. Vergennes had clearly specified this to Gérard and he repeated it to La Luzerne, and both these ministers obeyed his instructions. Such good words as the writers who were in relations with La Luzerne had to say for France were rather less emphatic than those voiced by other writers, but they were more accurate. It is meet that the King of France should have given a pension to the most brilliant pamphleteer and the most prominent republican in America, the man who was later to become one of the principal agents of the republican Revolution in France and who was to risk his life to save that of the King who had fed him, and whom he had flattered, combated and dethroned. Such was the destiny of Thomas Paine. That of the Boston preacher was simpler; after three years of patient and fruitful work, he was taken ill. He had succeeded in gathering about him both Frenchmen and Americans and in bringing them to understand each other and discuss things intelligently. His sermons had made the pretty, slender Colonial churches ring with the name of the King of France; and Puritan congregations had prayed for His Very Christian Majesty. He died and his work, like the friendships that he had built, lived after him.[141]

For General Sullivan I have less esteem. He kept La Luzerne informed concerning the intentions of Congress. The French were obliged to pension him to prevent the English from doing it. His servile attitude toward La Luzerne is painful; he was an employee rather than a discreet friend.[142]

These methods succeeded. The American papers, inclined to take over integrally news items and articles from the English Whig papers, were provided with original articles and discussions. They heard of France and its heroes and sometimes of its philosophers. It was especially at Boston and Philadelphia, the two intellectual and religious capitals of the country, that this effort made itself felt. The bulk of the American people was admirable human raw-material, shaped by the civilizations of Europe, but renewed by Nature and rich in a vast future.[143] It was capable of creating an absolutely new motherland and of feeling for a far-off people, foreign in race and culture, a spontaneous and generous fraternity. The American people turned toward France deliberately and gave her their affection. The proofs of this are innumerable. In the popular comedies, we find Tories cursing the French intervention as the principal cause of American independence; in treatises on political economy, we find apostrophes addressed to the public saying: Should we not be ashamed to ask France for money to spend on ourselves instead of paying our taxes?[144] And the newspapers repeat: The fine thing about the Franco-American alliance is that it is equally favorable to both nations and that the French people desire it.[145] It is also recalled that, even before their entering the war, the French were favorable to the Americans, that they received them in a friendly way, that prayers were offered up in the convents for an American victory, and that the women had favored them. Louis was compared to Abel and George to Cain. There was resentment against the members of Congress who were unwilling to show confidence in France. In Virginia, the Lees found themselves the butt of a veritable popular indignation. Even Adams was an object of disapproval. A warm sympathy guided the American people.[146] Here and there a group resisted. At Yale, the students from old Puritan families discussed in their clubs the dangers of the French alliance.[147] At Boston, merchants who had kept up English affiliations battled stoutly against public opinion. At Philadelphia the surliest of the Quakers might well consider these impudent foreigners as Moloch in person; all this was merely local opposition and without influence. For the United States at war, the French alliance was truly an unmitigated blessing and a full satisfaction. It was only Congress as a body that reacted in a certain measure against the general current. This was because it did not accept the moral and philosophical ideal with which Vergennes was imbued and which the French thought might rightly be attributed to the Americans as a nation. Congress felt that this land was called to a great destiny, but it did not foresee the decisive influence that the American Revolution would have on Europe. It took more thought for worldly greatness and material power. However, its opposition remained vague and was mitigated by respect for Vergennes and the ideal that he had formed of the United States.[148] As for the people, they had accepted whole-heartedly the friendship that the greatest European nation held out to them. They were willing to share their enthusiasm and to hold in common the great aspirations which impelled them toward a spiritual life that should be at once humane, concerned with utility, preoccupied with the mysteries of sciences and directed by a great and vague love for their fellow men. The blending of these two races permitted the sentiment of equality to develop to an extraordinary degree, for it brought together men from the two extremes of society. The brotherhood of camps was a bond between them. In short, this period of tumult and effusions afforded every one a vision of Liberty that was not to be forgotten. The ardent curiosity and zeal of the French hastened and shaped the development of the United States into a nation and woke in the Americans an eagerness to know themselves and to define and realize their potentialities. And this same influence that inspired them with an international and universal genius also roused their national spirit. Vergennes did more than any one else to group the Americans behind Congress and to make them feel the brotherhood of nations.

*
* *

In Europe, he had to combat the discouragement that too long a war engendered. It was not always easy to maintain harmony between French and American opinion. When the French fleet was beaten off Rhode Island, when d'Estaing lost the battle before Savannah, when it was learned that the English had taken Charleston and reconquered the whole of Georgia, the people were irritated at seeing a war that should have been ended quickly drawn out to such length. Naval officers were beginning to attack d'Estaing and to criticize the Americans.[149] The French sailors, accustomed for centuries to fighting the English, could not associate with the New England sailors, who had so often engaged in privateering against France, without brawls breaking out between them. We find evidence of this friction in a book published in 1780, entitled *Le Journal d'un Officier de la Flotte de M. le Comte d'Estaing*. These naval reverses also had the disadvantage of causing enormous losses to French commerce and of bringing French merchants, who heretofore had been in favor of the American cause, to wish for peace. John Adams was impressed with this attitude on the part of French middle-class society in 1779.[150] The depreciation of continental money and the attempt that Congress made to fix the value of paper money at one-fortieth of its original value contributed to disrupting commerce and ruining many French firms who were engaged in exporting to America. Such measures gave the impression that America was completely exhausted.[151] This view was whispered about at Versailles. And in 1779, there were to be heard on the streets the following couplets deriding Raynal, "whose mistakes had been cut out of whole cloth," and the United States:

> I have seen the various refuges
> Of this nation still in infancy.
> Its pride, its independence,
> Are unknowingly preparing its chains.
> It is frugal because of indolence
> And the liberty it worships
> Is only a hatred of duty.[152]

The return of a large group of French officers, whom Congress had refused to commission as generals, helped to spread this discontent.[153] The English propaganda made use of these divers incidents and the favorable atmosphere. The *Mémoire justificatif de la Cour de Londres sur la présente guerre* brings out the duplicity of Louis XVI in inciting the Americans to revolt, aiding them secretly, and, having thus broken his pledge, trying to make it appear that he had gone into the war only because he was forced into it by armed aggression. This document appeals to monarchial sentiment. The writings of Tucker and Pownall were even more artful and effective.[154] They set forth the fact that, as soon as the war was finished, Great Britain would resume her commerce with the United States, and thus France would have given her time, money, enthusiasm and men for nothing. Ignoble pamphlets attacking Vergennes, Sartines and Franklin, "the octogenarian chameleon," were secretly circulated. The most notorious works of this kind were *La Cassette verte de M. de Sartines*, which appeared in 1779, and *L'Histoire d'un Pou français*, which was published in 1781. They relate, in the guise of court gossip, everything that could be gathered together concerning the weakness of the Americans, their impudent way of asking for money and the annoyance that this caused the King. They consisted mainly of statistics on amounts that France had already advanced to the insurgents, and of anecdotes showing the Queen's irritation against America.[155] They made mock of Franklin's noble simplicity and described him as a dull bourgeois; they appealed to every prejudice of caste and station to poke ridicule at both Franklin and, especially, those whom he represented—the Quakers, "whose arrogance sticks through their cloaks," as a song of the time said of them. This propaganda slipped in with everything that came to France from England (for relations between the two countries were never suspended) and also with everything that was allowed to come in from Germany. Hanover and all the adjacent regions, and in general all the official circles throughout Germany, were at this time entirely under the control of English newspapers and the English Court. In 1780, when Prince Max de Deux Ponts (Zweibrücken) and his regiment the Royal Deux Ponts were fighting in America in Rochambeau's division, the *Gazette de Deux Ponts* announced that, to its great regret, it could not publish in its columns a letter from a young French sailor who was filled with enthusiasm for the United States, "because," it went on, "there is still in the minds of the German people a certain admiration for the English which prevents them from taking kindly to anything that is detrimental to England." [156]

There was therefore a secret fermentation that could not be checked by force and which was all the more dangerous because Necker, like Turgot, did not believe in the necessity of the war and because, except for the independence of the United States, the French people could see no definite reason for fighting nor any immediate end to be gained by all this bloodshed. The cabal that was working against Vergennes, his policies and the United States, had every opportunity during these hard years for sowing discord and shaking the confidence of those who had faith in the future, France's moral rôle and the Americans. All the cynicism, sarcasm and jealousy of the Court was banded together against Vergennes. He defended himself as best he could. He kept a close watch over the newspapers and punished those of them who behaved badly or attacked the Americans. His faithful Genet [157] continued to insert in their columns everything he could find that was encouraging for the future of the alliance. The *Mercure*, the *Journal des Savants*, the *Affaires de l'Angleterre et de l'Amérique* continued their work and redoubled their activities.

In 1779 and 1780, Vergennes published or circulated a series of pamphlets designed to dissipate the unfavorable impressions that were spread among the masses and to defend the American cause. There was Favier, who grudgingly rendered him the service of writing *Les Lettres du Comte d'Albany au Lord Bute*, in which it is stated that the King of France had the right to recognize the United States, since all the powers recognized without hesitation the Barbary States. Favier, hostile in his heart to the recognition of the United States, but anxious to win Vergennes's favor, accepted this way of doing it.[158] His controversy with the minister on this subject is so curious and sets forth so clearly the point of view of both of these men that I have thought it well to give it in extenso in my Appendix II. Among these pamphlets, we also find one by Beaumarchais, *Observations sur le Mémoire justificatif de la Cour de Londres*, in which the author boldly declares that he had done everything on his own initiative and despite the King's wishes and cites, by way of proof, the fact that he had ruined himself thereby. Shrewd and thoroughly familiar with the current of public opinion, he asserted that, if Congress had rejected the services of French officers, it showed clearly that the King had not sent them and that Congress "through republican pride, was not willing to share the glory of their victory!" There were also the *Lettres de M. R. au Lord D. touchant le Traité de Commerce conclu entre la France et les Etats-Unis* written by an anonymous author who knew what ought to be said. He maintained that the aim of the war was the freedom of the seas and that it was therefore a just one. He refused to discuss the question as to whether or not a people had the right of insurrection, and he affirms that, in any case, this right does not exist in an absolute monarchy such as France. We must also mention *Les Lettres d'un Membre du Congrès américain*, *Le Pamphlet programmatique*, *Le Procès des trois Rois*, *Les Observations sur le Traité de Paix de 1763* by the Baron de Sainte-Croix, *Le Destin de l'Amérique* by Cerisier, *Les Réflexions impartiales sur l'Amérique*, and *L'Américain aux Anglais*. All these pamphlets undertook to prove that the Americans had revolted because of English injustice, which violated the British constitution. They were therefore in the right and their revolution, by opening up a new commerce to Europe, would bring back peace and prosperity and moderation to the world. All these pamphlets argue the good faith of the King of France, the utility of the war, and the brilliant future of the United States. They are well worded but monotonous and rather colorless. Were they sufficient to stir public opinion and to silence criticisms? This is all the less probable since good reasons have never soothed any irritation, no matter how unjust it may have been. The movements of public opinion which were then going on in France, and which by their violence should have foretold other troubles to come, could be appeased only by means of the same nature. This is why we find Vergennes making as much use as possible of imagination and sentiment.[159] He tried to engrave on all hearts the image of Washington, whom he held in unbounded esteem and whom he would like to have seen made dictator of America. Having felt the influence that this great man exerted on those about him, he wanted to make him appear still greater and he did everything in his power to increase his prestige. He took as a basis the legend that was beginning to grow up about this name—Washington, the Fabius of the New World, as great as a Roman, and as calm as they, like them a citizen and more enlightened and modest than they, Washington, whom people were beginning to admire as the hero of a war without victories but full of sacrifices, Washington, who was nothing except by the will of the people, and who professed a religious respect for the people's will. Here was a new type of hero, one who, thanks to his virtues and his remoteness, entered into, and established himself in, the popular imagination. Along with Washington went the image of William Penn and the legend of the Quakers, a people so pious without priests or churches, so virtuous without dogmas. This legend already existed for a group of intellectuals and philosophers, but it became popular especially through Franklin, whose simple manners and modest dignity were taken for Quakerisms. Franklin was the prototype in accord with which all other images were formed. People saw in him and Penn the deist sage, and in Washington the prudent and heroic patriot. Franklin's personality and his stay in France are the source of most of the visions and hopes that were the immediate preparation for the French Revolution. His importance is primordial, and Vergennes knew it; and for this reason their co-operation was at once of a personal, philosophic and political nature.[160] Without Franklin's presence at Paris from 1776 to 1783, Vergennes's politics would have been powerless to guide public opinion.

There was a great friendship between these two men. In the crucial hours, Franklin went to comfort Vergennes. He pointed out victory as being inevitable, the Americans as being resolved to fight to the bitter end, and England as weakened.[161] He set forth frankly his own views and the demands that the situation of the United States obliged him to transmit to the French Court, but he also let him see that the alliance had in him a resolute defender. Although the partisans of the Lees, jealous of Franklin's success and uneasy at the harmony that existed between him and Vergennes, repeatedly urged Congress to recall Franklin and to hold an investigation of his activities, these offensive measures were never taken; and, without having any such dazzling popularity in the New World as he enjoyed in Europe, the "modern Lycurgus" was nevertheless able to do much to calm American skittishness and to encourage a feeling of friendship for France.[162] Invariably he wrote to his friends, even those who were tainted with Toryism, that the alliance with France alone could save America, that the welcome which the French tendered to the Americans was both moving and marked with a splendid generosity, and finally, that the King and his ministers had no aims other than the independence of the United States and the peace of the world.[163] Thus the sincerity and loyalty of Franklin, during this long mission in France, afforded one of the finest examples of moral diplomacy to be found in those days, or since. The only guile that he deigned to use was that affectation of weariness and decrepitude which permitted him to give counsel, advice and warnings to Vergennes, like a grandsire on his death-bed bidding a last farewell to his tearful grandchildren. The French Court, which appreciated his intelligence, his zeal and his uprightness and wanted to keep him at any price, was always impressed by this tone—which, by the way, brought more than a little money into the depleted American treasury. But this pose, sincere without doubt, but in any case philosophic, pleased the French so much and was so in keeping with the conception which they had formed of their idol, that we cannot blame Franklin for having responded in this way to the encouragement of popular fervor.

A more serious difference than either of them was clearly aware of separated Franklin from Vergennes.

Both of them were philosophers and what we should call *esprits libres*. Both of them dreamed of a world in which men should be more righteous, happier and less oppressed. Both of them saw in the American war a means of bringing closer this happy era. They both yearned for a new ideal of brotherhood and justice to reign over the nations. But for Vergennes, this ideal had a Catholic and monarchial basis, while Franklin's concept was that of a mind formed by his heredity and the democratic and Protestant education of Boston. While they thought that they were collaborating in the same work, in reality Vergennes and Franklin were headed in diverging directions.[164] Vergennes aspired to a moral ideal which should supplement the traditions and dogmas of Catholicism without destroying them. Franklin, without desiring a social and political revolution nor brutal overthrowing of religion, envisaged a moral religion which should destroy dogmas and finally reign alone. He could not help favoring certain manifestations in France which alarmed the orthodoxy of Vergennes; and he went much further in this direction than Vergennes suspected, much further than it is ordinarily believed even today.

From 1777 to 1784, Franklin had a considerable social influence in Paris; he was one of the most elegant figures, and probably the most sought-after man in the capital. His glorious situation, his illustrious friends, his fascinating personality—all this led the most fashionable hostesses to seek to draw him to their salons; and he could not always refuse gracefully. Popularity is an extraordinarily capricious pet: to keep it from running away one must feed it and caress it continually. Franklin nursed his public along. He appeared in their drawing-rooms modestly dressed, without a wig, but with the halo of his magnificent white hair. Knowing the prejudices and gossip that were stirred up by his frequent requests on the behalf of the United States for money, he observed the greatest simplicity. His grandsons, who lacked the good sense to follow his example, became the object of unfavorable comment. Franklin kept an air of silence and reserve, as much by inclination as for the sake of dignity and to discourage calumnies which would have made him out to be a clever propagator of subversive theories. His intelligent silence delighted Paris. He talked freely only in the houses of some few of his friends: Madame Helvetius, whom he thought of marrying and in whose *salon* all the philosophers and influential Freemasons of the time used to gather; Madame Brillon, the wife of a *fermier-général*, and Turgot. He was less restrained with his colleagues at the Academy of Sciences.[165] Le Veillard, Le Roy and Dalibard were old friends of his, and conversations with them presented neither dangers nor drawbacks. He was therefore assiduous in his attendance at the Academy, and this exemplary regularity was still another source of popularity. The same good sense that had made him decide to live in Passy and to stay there in spite of the hardship that it entailed when he wanted to go to Paris or Versailles, had led him to furnish his house modestly and to manage it with frugality. He had few visitors; and he had leisure for work, for carrying on secret negotiations and even for printing in secret, for he had installed a printing-press in his house.[166] His only luxury was a carriage, which shocked John Adams, but was indispensable.[167] He entertained well, however, and knew how to spend money when it was necessary; but in his home he had the art of giving always the impression that his life, his habits and his person were strange and foreign. By this means, he kept both curiosity and public interest unflagging and always remained for the French something new, original and different. He knew and understood his surroundings so well that he adapted himself to them without losing anything of his own personality. Thus he proved the possibility of reconciling a friendship for France with fidelity to American virtues. Nothing could have done more to dispose the intelligent public, and even the masses, in favor of his far-off country than this man who understood them so well, loved them so intelligently and imitated them so little. The memory of Franklin lasted for half a century.

The public still admired this great man obscurely and imagined his activities as having something mysterious about them. Though it was not definitely known, it was suspected that the three editions of the American constitutions published at Paris in 1778 and 1783 had been brought out through his efforts.[168] He had succeeded in having them translated by the Duc de La Rochefoucauld d'Einville, and had obtained from Vergennes the promise that the censorship, without formally approving them, would allow them to circulate and would do nothing to hinder their sale, which officially was secret.[169] He put the Articles of Confederation into circulation in the same way. Moreover, the *Affaires de l'Angleterre et de l'Amérique*, in which he played a not unimportant part, was free to print whatever it wished, and it took full advantage of this privilege. Beside this, Franklin procured here and there pamphlets which he proceeded to turn to good use. It is thus that the *Letter to the Hessians* by Mirabeau, published through Franklin's offices and perhaps written at his request, was for a long while attributed to him. He also gave the public translations of such letters as had been seized at sea when they happened to contain messages from Clinton to his government and were encouraging to the American cause.[170] He read the American papers carefully and had reprinted everything that gave a favorable impression of the courage of the insurgents, their morale, their kindness and their enthusiasm for the French alliance.

To these discreet labors, which Vergennes encouraged, he joined another activity. Franklin had become the center of Masonic activities in Paris. Before leaving the United States, he had been a high dignitary in American Freemasonry. During his stay in France, he took part in the great effort to strengthen and spread Freemasonry, which began about 1775 and lasted until 1789.[171] The establishing of the first Grand Orient in France dates from 1773. All throughout the country at this time, secret societies were being formed directly or indirectly under the influence of Freemasonry. Some of these had special aims, such as the Society of the Wooden Sword which united the young nobles of the Court about 1772-1774. Several clubs had the purpose of aiding the Americans and spreading their ideas.[172] We have already mentioned the existence of one or two of these at Marseilles. At Paris there were others, of which the most important had as their center the Palais Royal and the foyer of the Opera. Many of the Economists and many of Franklin's learned friends were Masons, and his great friend, Madame Helvetius, was somewhat the Egeria of the association.[173] She and her husband had tried to create a lodge of a new kind, one which should group all the most prominent artists and writers of the period. Helvetius thought, and not illogically, that since Freemasonry envisaged the reform of society by means of enlightenment and philosophic benevolence, it was essential to interest philosophers and writers in it. This project was realized about 1769 through the initiative of Lalande, who was very influential in Freemasonry, and Madame Helvetius, who recruited members for the new lodge, which was called the Lodge of the Nine Sisters. Among the first to be received were the president Dupaty, Condorcet, Cailhava d'Estandoux, Fallet, the secretary of the *Gazette de France*, Garnier, the elder Parny, Dorat Cubières—and then, after 1778, Romme, Court de Gébelin, Grouvelle, Mercier, de Sèze, Comte Turpin de Crissé, Piccini, François de Neufchâteau, Fontanes, Chamfort, Demeusnier, Voltaire, Roucher, Prince C. de Rohan, the younger Parny, Prince E. de Salm-Salm, Vernet, Lacépède, Houdon, Berthelot, Lemierre, Imbert, and Flins des Oliviers. It is also said that La Métherie, Brissot, Bailly, Cérutti, Danton, Chénier, Péthion, Rabaut Saint-Etienne, Fauchet, Bonneville, Florian and Berquin belonged to it after 1783. This lodge was very prominent for the caliber of its members. Its beginnings were propitious. In 1778 it admitted Voltaire, who was proposed by Court de Gébelin and Franklin. On November 28, 1778, in spite of the prohibitions of the government, who did not want any further notoriety to be given this philosopher, the lodge held a great session to celebrate the apotheosis of Voltaire. In the course of the ceremony, hopes for the success of the Americans were expressed. In spite of the government, the lodge continued its activities, which consisted in directing lectures, literary studies and artistic expositions, and aiding the poor.[174] Encouraged by the favor of the public, it decided to create an auxiliary lodge composed of women. The formal affiliation took place on March 9, 1779. It occasioned a scandal which shows clearly the nature and the boldness of the Lodge of the Nine Sisters. In the usual discourse, instead of having the serpent speak to Eve, Cupid was substituted. The ladies objected. There was a riot, which was both disreputable and scandalous. The Grand Orient was informed of it (Louis XVI himself saw to it, it is said), but Lalande warded off the danger; and to assure itself against prosecution by the authorities and the Grand Orient, the lodge chose Franklin as "Venerable" in 1779. He was already an assiduous member and attended all the meetings and assisted such poor as were assigned him. He became the protector of the lodge and saved it. While he was occupying the office of "Venerable," a celebration was held in his honor (May 1, 1780) and the lodge made considerable gains in membership. It also founded, under the name of the Museé de Paris, a sort of free university, where the public was offered a higher education that was at once modern, scientific and philosophic. This institution had great success. It established branches, the most flourishing of which was known under the name of the Lycée de Paris. There La Salle, Milly, Dupaty, E. de Beaumont, Pastoret and La Harpe gave lectures that won great favor with the public and attracted much attention. The promoters of the idea, Court de Gébelin, the Abbé Cordier de Saint-Firmin, La Dixmerie, and Fontanes had leaned continually on Franklin for the realization of their project whose original initiative may well have been Franklin's.[175] The Musée was loyal to the United States.[176] On November 22, 1782, it held a celebration in their honor; and it was at the Lycée that

Hilliard d'Auberteuil first introduced his book on the United States, the first French work to be consecrated to the history of that nation.[177] The activities of the Lodge of the Nine Sisters had therefore an aim that was both political, literary and moral.[178] But, in the last analysis, it was the religious and moral side that most impressed its contemporaries; and it is in this that Franklin was of special value to the lodge. As a matter of fact, he attended the meetings of many other lodges and literary societies, but none of them interested him as much as the Lodge of the Nine Sisters, where his position as patriarch was recognized and utilized. For instance, we find him going to the "Assemblée des Savants et Artistes," directed by Pahin de Champlain de la Blancherie, who hoped to organize a vast international collaboration of all savants in the service of science and fraternity.[179] In Franklin's papers, we find many invitations to the meetings of other lodges, which he seems to have attended, but he gave all his devotion only to the Lodge of the Nine Sisters.[180] And it is this lodge, more than any other organized body, that made him the "holy philosopher and saint" that he so long remained in the eyes of France. The Lodge of the Nine Sisters, with its great religious and symbolic ceremonies in which the Supreme Being and Wisdom were worshiped, is a forerunner of things to come. It was aided in its work by a little book by Franklin, which had just been newly translated and published in France and had achieved a considerable success

—*Poor Richard's Almanac.* In 1773 Barbeu-Dubourg had published a French translation of it in his *Œuvres complètes de Franklin*, but these two thick *in quarto* volumes were too cumbersome to sell well and circulate among the people. In 1777 was published a new translation in an *octavo* volume, which had at least one edition in 1777 and five in 1778. All the newspapers spoke of it. Here we must mention the great career that this little book had in France from 1771 to 1800. In December, 1777, Grimm's *Correspondance littéraire* says of it: "The morality of this book is set forth in a series of maxims full of good sense, energy and clearness. Nothing except the eternal repetition of the phrase, 'as Poor Richard says,' makes this little patriotic catechism wearying to read. Yet we know of no book that is more worthy of being placed in the hands of all readers." [181] The book was circulated in the provinces. The *Feuille hebdomadaire de la Généralité de Limoges* declares on January 28, 1778: "We exhort country priests and school-masters to procure this work and to have their scholars learn it by heart." It scored a popular success and was sold in the streets for four sous.[182] A legend was growing up about Franklin. All the portraits of the time picture him taming the lightning and conquering tyrants. This twofold victory is constantly recalled.[183] The Constitution of Pennsylvania, the most democratic in the world, and the Declaration of Independence were also attributed to him. It was said, and believed, that he, Samuel Adams and

Washington between them had *made* the American Revolution.

He united all the qualities necessary to give him a great religious influence in this eighteenth century, so restless and hungry for faith. His brilliant career, starting from such a humble beginning, his scientific discoveries, which revealed new and unknown forces and even gave the impression of having subdued and enchained them, his courageous position as an American patriot, which made him appear to all eyes as the sponsor of independence, his moral writings, his goodness, his intelligence, the mixture of intellectual simplicity and penetration and, lastly, his marvelous ability to reduce things to their simplest terms and to make the masses understand them—all this tended to make him a sort of high priest of Philosophy. When Voltaire died, he stood unquestioned in this position. His correspondence testifies to the place that he held in all hearts. Here we find a letter from an officer who desires to go to America. Here is the son of a wool merchant, dissatisfied with his life in his father's house, who writes to ask him for advice. Here an Irish exile implores his aid. A Benedictine writes to ask him to pay his debts and promises him his prayers in exchange. Condorcet asks for information regarding the fitness of the negroes for liberty. Mably seeks details concerning the laws of the United States. A village school-master sends him the text of a federal and Masonic pact to be proposed to all the sovereigns of the world in order to assure perpetual peace. Now a Utopian sends him a tract on the reform of France to be transmitted to Vergennes. The Cardinal de Rohan invites him to dinner, and Marat takes him to see experiments in physics.[184] M. de Montlosier consults him as to means of earning money, and Brissot seeks information on the New World. Dozens of odes on peace and America are sent to him. Madame d'Houdetot gives a garden-party in his honor, at which is sung:

> He restores to human nature its due.
> In order to free it he strove to enlighten it.
> Virtue herself to win fresh adoration
> Has borrowed the form of Benjamin.[185]

Preachers quote him from the pulpit,[186] and Robespierre dedicates to him his first great speech, in defense of a burgher of St. Omer who insisted, despite the terror of his fellow-citizens, on maintaining a lightning-rod on his house.[187] The past and the future of France join in the worship of Franklin. The entire group of future revolutionary leaders are already gathered about him; among them are Brissot, Robespierre, Danton, La Fayette, Marat, Bailly, Target, Duval d'Esprémesnil, Péthion, Abbé Fauchet, La Rochefoucauld Liancourt, the Duke of Orléans, etc. They are drawn to him as the annunciator of a new faith that they were seeking and that they bore in their hearts. It is no exaggeration to consider him as the prophet and saint of a new religion; for all the mystic elements ordinarily attributed to a saint are found in his legend—humility, an almost supernatural power capable of performing miracles and of controlling the forces of Nature, goodness, suffering and piety. He points the way to all the eager and restless souls who feel the need of a new faith, rational and, at the same time, practical. This is what Vergennes did not perceive, and it is the gravest deception that Franklin, quite unintentionally, practiced on his friend.

The literature of the time bears witness to all this. It is mediocre and swamped with books on the Americans —as seen through Franklin. There is no first-hand knowledge of the subject, no serious documentation, but quantities of enthusiasm and of moralization. There was a swarm of curious mystic pamphlets which, in the form of prophecy and in the style of the Apocalypse, predict the victory of the insurgents, the rise of America and the decline of Europe.[188] Such books as had serious pretensions were usually worth scarcely more. Dubuisson, a Creole from Santo Domingo, published in 1778 a work entitled *Abrégé de la Révolution de l'Amérique anglaise*. It was not without a certain facility of style, but it had no other value. In his documentation, taken entirely from English newspapers and periodicals, the author ignores both official papers and secret documents. He had had personal contact with none of the great men who directed or opposed the Revolution. He wrote his book to be agreeable to the public by praising the Americans and to please the minister by showing that the Americans were not rebels, but poor people whom England had tormented and driven to violence. He paints a sublime and vague picture of Washington. *Les Essais historiques et politiques sur les Anglo-Américains* by Hilliard d'Auberteuil, in spite of his title, is quite as bad. Hilliard, also, conceived the idea of writing his book when he was in Santo Domingo. He was pensioned by M. de Sartines and wrote for him.[189] His work, in two thick quarto volumes, does not seem to have cost him much effort. It is merely a jumble of irrelevant detail taken from newspapers of various localities and put together without criticism and with no other aim than the picturesque and sentimental. Since the book is made up of material taken from English papers and was written with the intent of pleasing the French public and government, it is particularly faulty. It is an account, in chronological order and with many errors, of the American war. It is illuminated with flowers of rhetoric, such as the description of the burning of New York by the despairing patriots, or the story of George and Molly, slain by the English soldiers at the height of their wedding feast. Here is the picture that Hilliard gives of Congress in 1776: "The most illustrious and the wisest men among the Americans met in all the provinces. They opened the books where the ancient charters which had been granted to the colonies and the general assemblies were preserved. The people were struck with respect on seeing a gathering of old men whom age had rendered venerable without sapping the vigor of their minds." His description of the Anglo-Americans is not less imaginary. He takes the only precise details that he furnishes from the famous Abbé de Pauw: "Although the Anglo-Americans are less robust than most of the European peoples, although the humidity of their climate seems to weaken them, yet they have more temerity and are less sensitive to wounds than the Europeans, and in general they recover more easily." He describes Franklin thus: "Everything about him announces the simplicity and innocence of the manners and customs of the ancients. . . . He had stripped off borrowed hair. . . ." By which he means that Franklin did not wear a wig. Such is the literary and historical value of Hilliard d'Auberteuil, whose work enjoyed the high patronage of M. de Sartines, was paid for by the ministry, received with favor by the philosophic public, and turned to derision only by the paltry handful of people who knew something of the subject. Hilliard had given his book some slight interest by publishing at the end of it the constitutions of the various American states. The only clear and accurate idea that Franklin had been able to put into his head was that of the future greatness of the United States and the necessity of opening commerce with the French colonies to them. The only impression that this rubbish left on the public was one of admiration for certain great men and of religious respect for the United States. As for the subtle distinctions with which he attempts to prove that the Americans have, through their charters, certain rights that the French, as subjects of an absolute monarchy, will never have, no one took them seriously. They merely reveal certain fears that the French government felt at that time and the secret difference between official opinion and real opinion.

Thus the war did not continue in the conditions under which it had begun. Between malcontents and enthusiasts, the minister's position was becoming difficult; and, probably without wishing it, Franklin was the principal cause of this trouble. In 1782 nobody perceived this, for then the important fact was still that France had helped the Anglo-Americans to found a nation with a new ideal about which the partisans of progress were to rally and which was to be the basis of new alignments of power in the political and moral world. Both the French and the Americans, when they heard the news of the surrender at Yorktown, where the finest English army in the New World had been captured by a combined French and American army, experienced emotions very like those called forth by the Declaration of Independence and the alliance. Here again was a triumph for Franklin and Vergennes.

But behind this apparent result, a movement as yet obscure was developing. All these men who had united for a crusade against England the oppressor, and who had succeeded in breaking down both her domination in the New World and her supremacy of the sea, all these men who, drawn together by great ideas and a great hope, had read the Declaration of Independence with such enthusiasm and had adored Franklin, now found themselves carried further than they had intended. For Vergennes, there seemed to be nothing further to do except to apply this victorious policy of justice to interior reforms that should be in accord with this new spirit while still respecting the ancient institutions of France and the political and religious dogmas of which they were the expression. For the disciples of Franklin, there loomed the necessity of bringing to its full realization this religion, which as yet existed only in promise, but which was to become a thing apart, to complete the ancient forms of worship and to overthrow them. They wanted to keep the United States as a rallying-point; they understood that the new nation had risen on the political and intellectual horizon only by the assistance of France; but they refused to admit that the reformation of France could be limited to a mere readjusting. Between them and Vergennes, there seemed to be only a difference of degree; but already there was all the distance that separates 1788 from 1789 between them, all the distance that lies between the Assembly of the Notables and the night of August 4th.

Once more France had shown her adaptability and the versatility of her culture. Out of her Latin and Catholic civilization, out of her monarchial society, she had drawn elements capable of winning over, enchanting and aiding infinitely this young Anglo-Saxon, Protestant and democratic people. The two nations had been a marvelous stimulant for each other. They had furnished an admirable example of spontaneous friendship. France had done much to give the United States more order, stability, national consciousness and culture and, at the same time, an international consciousness. And the United States had stirred up in France an intellectual and sentimental tide whose might was to overthrow an entire world established for three centuries.

Chapter III

ESSAYS IN FRATERNITY

The end of the war separates France and the United States instead of drawing them together. Coldness between Vergennes and Congress, pp. 164-173. This is not, however, a break between them, pp. 173-175. The United States are still popular with the Frenchmen who have been in America, priests, officers and writers, pp. 175-184. An entire literature grows up about the United States, pp. 184-190. La Fayette is the center of the movement in favor of the United States, pp. 190-193. The French philosophers consider the United States as a field of experiment for the world; Raynal and Mably, pp. 193-203. Mirabeau, pp. 203-206.

In America France as a nation becomes more and more popular, although her moral corruption is feared. French ideas penetrate the colleges, society, literature, religion and politics, pp. 206-223. Example of the Constitutional Convention, pp. 223-229.

In France a revolutionary group forms about La Fayette, among the nobles, and Brissot, among the middle classes, the which, with the support of the republican and moral ideas from America, tries to undertake the reform of France and of the world. This is the Patriot's party, pp. 229-251.

THE TREATY OF 1783 MARKED THE TRIUMPH OF THE Allies but also divided them irreparably. Indeed it was rather an outline for reconciliation between England and America than a consecration of the Franco-American alliance. In spite of the efforts of Vergennes and Franklin, this treaty, which was to have been the basis of a close collaboration between France and the United States, ruined all hope of an intimate political accord between the two countries.

In fact, from 1781 the irreconcilables in America had succeeded in imposing one of their leaders, John Adams, as a member of the Peace Commission. John Jay, who was chosen along with Adams to represent the United States in the negotiations, was supposed to be very favorable to France. In Congress he had shown himself as moderate and very friendly to La Luzerne. He was descended from a French family which had emigrated for religious reasons and settled in New York. In this family there still smoldered a warm indignation against the royal Government of France and the Catholics. But John Jay, with great self-control, had never let any of this show before the French Minister. Nevertheless, when he was sent to Madrid to prepare an alliance with Spain, and saw himself scorned and ignored, he felt wrath rising in him against his Catholic Majesty and Courts in general. Shortly after he was ordered to Paris where peace negotiations were beginning between Vergennes and Franklin on one side and Oswald on the other.[1] The American delegates were instructed to demand the unconditional recognition of American independence, the integrity of their territory and the fishing rights and the navigation of the Mississippi; but they were to follow in every respect Vergennes's opinion and to decide nothing without him. The French Minister had brought England to accept all the American demands and those of

Spain, France's old ally, who wanted Florida, which she had conquered, and Gibraltar, which she had not been able to take in spite of violent efforts and great sacrifices.[2] For herself, France asked only the restitution of Senegal, the right to fortify Dunkirk, the fishing rights of Newfoundland and *status quo* in the Antilles. Vergennes was anxious to furnish an example of a just and generous peace. Oswald, the English delegate, proved amenable. He had promised that his Court would recognize the United States and cede them a portion of Canada; and he seemed ready to make peace at any price. One point remained difficult to solve: Gibraltar, which the English did not wish to give up and which the Spanish demanded. Vergennes sent Rayneval to London to see if the English Ministry could not be persuaded to give in. Just then Jay arrived at Paris. Rayneval's mission seemed suspicious to him; he thought that Vergennes was making a pawn of the United States. Oswald saw this and took advantage of it. He showed Jay a letter which had just been seized at sea in which Barbé-Marbois, the French chargé d'affaires at Philadelphia, protested to Vergennes against the territorial ambitions of the Americans and especially against their designs on the Mississippi. Jay allowed himself to be convinced that Vergennes shared his agent's views, and wanted to betray the United States. He believed it; and he easily won over John Adams to his views, and both of them forced the hand of Franklin, who refused to admit Vergennes's duplicity. The American delegates therefore had secret conferences with Oswald. They found him well disposed and obtained everything they desired except Canada. When they had come to an agreement and had signed the preliminary articles, they delegated Franklin to inform Vergennes of it. Thus they had violated their instructions, abandoned an ally against whom they had no evidence, except such as was furnished by the common enemy, and they deserted Vergennes, whose task it was to defend the interests of France and of Spain against England and failed to give him any support. Now, the question of Gibraltar was still pending, and the English Minister who, before the signature of the preliminary articles with the Americans, would perhaps have yielded, now refused, feeling that it was certain that France would now find it decidedly awkward to continue alone with Spain this war which she had begun with the purpose of aiding the United States. As a matter of fact, the American delegates had added to their treaty a clause specifying that it should be valid only from the moment when France and England should come to an agreement. Thus they did not violate the pact of alliance with France—or at least the letter of it. But they felt that their action was open to criticism; they hastened to justify themselves before Congress, and they brandished Marbois's letter. Congress, much agitated by the event, deliberated for a week (November 23-30, 1782). In the end it condemned its ambassadors—and at the same time ratified their treaty; but it did proclaim that it would not lay down arms without France. Thereupon Spain, worn out, renounced Gibraltar and peace was signed.[3]

Vergennes had been indignant when he had learned of the secret and direct negotiations of the Americans with the English. The harm done to the Allied cause had seemed to him the more grave, and the Americans the more culpable, because at that very moment Congress was making urgent requests for further financial aid. He was angry, not at seeing the advantageous terms obtained by the Americans, but at discovering duplicity in them in place of the candor that he had expected. In all these negotiations, he had had in view not the ambitions of France or of her Allies, but the balance of power. He found it insulting and bitter to be so misunderstood. France, and himself in her name, had shown conclusively that she did not seek any territorial acquisitions or any exclusive commercial privilege. He had aided the United States to make of them a free and happy nation, but he had not had the least intention of making them the great conquering nation of the New World; and he did not conceive that the Americans, already masters of a territory that was scarcely settled, should feel the need of increasing this immense domain.[4] He thought that the majority of the Americans were with him in these "moderate" views. His error was therefore of an intellectual order. What would have happened if the delegates of the United States had had confidence in him? It is hard to say; but it seems, judging from all he had done for Franklin, that the latter would have been able to convince him and to persuade him to defend whole-heartedly the demands of Congress.

Vergennes was too prudent to break off everything in a moment of impatience. He was too deeply involved with the United States to retreat gracefully in the eyes of the world. He could not thus lightly abandon what was considered as his great life work. He remained silent. It was with satisfaction that he saw Congress condemn its delegates. He was glad to be able to conclude the work of peace satisfactorily in spite of this incident. He gave the money that was asked of him. But he did not forget the lesson that he had received.[5] A member of Congress had asked Barbé-Marbois if the French king would complain. "A great nation never complains, sir," replied Marbois, "but it feels the injury and does not forget."[6] There was less chance of Vergennes's forgetting since the enemies of France and America never gave him an opportunity. Congress, more and more dominated by the irreconcilables, appointed John Jay as Secretary of State. As far as France was concerned, this amounted to a justification of those who had attacked her in 1783. It meant that the control of external politics was placed in the hands of an enemy of the alliance. Jay considered that France had already benefited more by the alliance than the United States. He felt that the States should immediately set about isolating themselves. He distrusted all of Europe, but he was inclined to feel some sympathy for England since she was a Protestant power. He was too clever to attack Vergennes openly, but he took advantage of every opportunity to lessen political relations between France and the United States. He succeeded in preventing the signing of a consular convention between the two countries. In 1788, when Vergennes, whose personal prestige in America was considerable, died, Jay informed Montmorin, who was then French Minister of Foreign Affairs, that he considered that in the alliance of 1778 the King of France had had in view only the independence of the United States and that, since this independence was now recognized and assured, he considered the alliance terminated. Montmorin protested indignantly in the name of the King.[7] Jay was aided in his work by the English propaganda which had been revived since 1783 and was being carried on actively. The English had newspapers devoted to attacking France. Indeed, the first newspaper printed in French in the United States seems to have been one of these. This organ named *Le Courrier de l'Amérique* was published at Philadelphia from July to October, 1784. It was edited and published by Boinod and Gaillard, two Dutchmen of French descent, who hated France cordially. Their work consisted in slandering the French Minister and his agents; they laid stress on all the causes of discord between France and America and dwelt on the persecutions that France had made the Huguenots suffer. They published a list of illustrious Americans whose families had been obliged to leave France because of the repeal of the Edict of Nantes, and among them there was of course John Jay. Their paper praised Raynal and quoted him continually. These tirades were too violent; they did not succeed, and the American Post Office Department, in accord with the French Minister, refused to admit the paper to the mails, which brought about its fall.[8] The most serious thing in this affair had been that the paper aimed not only at being sold in America, but also at coming into France and there carrying on a campaign against the Government.[9]

The Independent Gazetteer of Boston took its place in attacking France;[10] but even the loyal and moderate newspapers were open to English propaganda, for they had no French translators and made up their columns from those of the London newspapers. Thus the Court of Great Britain always succeeded in circulating news items announcing both that France held the United States under a humiliating tutelage and that Vergennes was thinking of taking over a part of the American continent.[11] This went so far that in 1787 Vergennes issued an official denial of these rumors. There was nothing to make them plausible, but they were repeated incessantly, and, what is more, are still running on. This secret campaign had some influence on Congress, which had been impressed by the incidents of 1783. The aristocracy of New England, very religious and anti-Catholic, listened favorably to it. Many a sermon of this period contains pious exhortations to the Americans to turn away from dangerous and corrupt Europe. For a while these criticisms endangered the popularity of Franklin, who was accused of blind devotion to France.[12] In self-defense, he was obliged to ask John Jay to give him a certificate of loyal services. Jay very grudgingly gave him one, but couched it in very curt terms.[13]

Vergennes observed this campaign. It no longer surprised him. But it wearied him and kept him from feeling the warm interest in the United States that he had felt heretofore. Besides, the Court was frankly hostile to Americans. The Queen refused to receive Monsieur de Moustier,[14] who was sailing as Minister to the United States in 1788, for "she had nothing to say to a people among whom the name of the King and that of the Queen must be hated." [15] Many of the philosophers and writers condemned the peace of 1783, not that they wanted conquests, but there was a desire for reparations for all the financial losses that this long war had entailed, and there had been no provision for these. Certain newspapers began to complain and to criticize America sharply.[16] The French merchants and fishermen were in favor of an act forbidding the importation of American merchandise into the French West Indies.[17] Moreover, since there was seldom any mail directly from the United States and all the news came through England (which meant that it was very much blackened), it was very difficult for any one to form a favorable opinion of the young nation. As a consequence of England's skill in reëstablishing herself in the United States, American commerce had fallen back almost entirely into the hands of those who had held it before 1774; and this did nothing to smooth the course of Franco-American relations.

Vergennes, therefore, ceased to feel unlimited good will towards the United States. He held their fickleness and their distrust against them. His instructions to the French Ambassadors in the United States were limited to this: "No more propaganda, no more expense; let us maintain simply the alliance, and let us be on our guard. Let us refrain from meddling in American internal affairs." His policy bore no trace of resentment. He sought to please the Americans by opening up to them, as much as the ideas of the time allowed, commerce with the French Antilles, in giving them a free port in France and in showing friendship for them in many ways.[18] La Luzerne, who was Minister until 1784, had become attached to the American people, and, without having much use for their Government, thought well of the nation. Therefore he went about putting in effect Vergennes' orders only by delicate degrees.[19] He ceased paying salaries to members of Congress, cut off Paine's pension, it seems, in 1784, and took no other journalists either in Massachusetts or Philadelphia into his employ. He had thought of having Paine write a history of the war in America, and finding him too lazy, he contented himself with going over with Ramsay every page of his book on the revolution in South Carolina. More than a hundred passages in this book, which is still one of the best histories of the war in America, were changed according to the instructions of the French Minister.[20] La Luzerne, Marbois, who took this Minister's place, and Otto,[21] who replaced Marbois, made a point of keeping in close touch with the Universities and the learned bodies.[22] The French Ministers were fond of frequenting the American Philosophical Society. In short, although they gave up all intense and precise propaganda, they continued to be interested in the intellectual and moral destiny of the United States.[23] They watched over this country with passion and curiosity. They kept up a constant solicitude mingled with reserve. Such was the attitude that Vergennes had also adopted and that he deemed becoming to France. He made the newspapers under his control take up the same line. The *Gazette de France*, for example, said nothing against the United States; it mentioned them much less often, but it avoided laying stress on their troubles and their difficulties. He had kept his friendship for Franklin, who mourned him sincerely when he died. After his death, a similar line of conduct was followed until 1789. Monsieur de Montmorin had indeed some new ideas, but these already belonged to the French Revolution. Vergennes and the group of agents who surrounded him had remained faithful to the people of the United States out of dignity and sentimental sympathy. But, alarmed by the tendencies of their politicians, he had avoided keeping up relations with them. In accord with Calonne, they had opened French ports to the Nantucket whalers whom the new situation and the taxes levied by England were starving. Many American families settled therefore at Dunkirk.[24] A considerable portion of the public followed the Government in its attitude. Peace had appeared to be an honorific victory for France, and it was felt that the United States, having overcome their difficulties, no longer needed French aid. People of conservative opinion had adopted this opinion, which, as far as Vergennes was concerned, cloaked but partially a sad disillusionment and almost a moral bewilderment.

The people of the two nations did not perceive the difficulties under which the Franco-American alliance was operating.[25] It is true that the friendly relations which they still kept up underwent a change of character, but there was a strong sympathy on both sides. It even increased. In spite of the ill repute that American finances had in Europe, in spite of the jealousy of the French merchants, who feared American competition in the markets of the Antilles and even in France, the middle classes and the small tradesmen were more and more interested in what was going on across the seas and more and more willing to undertake the voyage.

The officers who had come back from the United

States with Rochambeau had given enthusiastic accounts of their stay in America. The impression that they had received, like that which they had left behind them, was one of the principal bases of Franco-American harmony. They had all come back filled with zeal for the young nation. The most enthusiastic of all were, perhaps, the priests who accompanied the army. We have already spoken of Abbé Bandole, chaplain to the Embassy of France, who preached before Congress in honor of the surrender at Yorktown and delivered such a fine republican sermon. We must also mention Abbé Colin de Sepvigny, who before leaving the United States wrote to Ezra Stiles, "In gremio ecclesiae romanae ossa mea requiescent. Sed usque ad ultimum vitae meoe finem, in veneratione Americanorum delectata erit anima mea."[26] But the most noteworthy of the Americanizing priests was the Abbé Robin. This righteous ecclesiastic was already known for his Masonic activity; he belonged to the group which had founded the Lodge of the Nine Sisters. On Franklin's recommendation, he was attached to Rochambeau's army as chaplain and followed particularly the Vicomte de Noailles and his regiment, where he established a sort of welfare center to keep the officers from becoming restless, drinking or indulging in any of the other distractions that were better avoided in a country where it was necessary to inspire respect and sympathy. This work, both pious and social, had drawn attention to Abbé Robin. Soon it was announced that he was going to publish a book on his campaigns, and the *Nouveau Voyage* by Abbé Robin (1782) was the first public testimony to the enthusiasm which the expeditionary force felt for the Americans.[27] This little book is rather ridiculous and very dull. The style has neither sparkle nor vivacity. It is both unctuous and in bad taste. Nevertheless, a certain simplicity as to both form and subject matter pleased the public and won the chaplain its favor. Robin begins by describing his troubles aboard the frigate which took him to America over stormy seas.[28] He embroiders on the old tales of the Abbé De Pauw and Raynal; he depicts with care the American women, who are so pretty at twenty, but whom the humidity of the climate ages prematurely, and the men, who are so robust, but whom the same condition renders indolent. He asserts that the natural virtues of this people go so far that mothers are in the habit of putting their virgin daughters to bed with transient guests as an expression of confidence and to keep them warm. "And nothing immodest ever happens," says the good Abbé, who had found this account in the works of English travelers who in turn had taken it from the works of other travelers of the seventeenth century and of limited veracity. The Abbé Robin admires Boston with its pretty little wooden houses and its wealthy peasants. He praises Washington, the hero of the modern world, who commands like a citizen and serves like a nobleman. He exalts the future of the United States, which have already gone so far but which will become rich, powerful and enlightened. The most curious thing in this book is his religious concept. He has a deep admiration for the Quakers, whom he defends and is to defend on every occasion. He is but little concerned with dogma, but he condemns "unlimited tolerance." "The more enlightened a religion is," he says, "the more intolerant it is." The United States will be obliged to impose a unified faith, for without it there can be no national unity. Thus in the United States, Robin acquired a great sympathy for the Americans' liberty and equality. He expects from them a veritable revelation, but he had beheld them without losing his philosophical tendencies which inclined him to accord the State excessive powers and influence. He was in favor of intolerance, not as a Catholic, but as a philosopher who wanted to reorganize the world on a new plan, and desired that this reform should be accomplished by the Government under the direction of enlightened minds.

One may trace the diffusion of these doctrines and of this moral and social faith throughout the French clergy. One of the most curious examples of it without doubt is the sermon which the Abbé Racine pronounced at Toulouse, January 11, 1784, in praise of Louis XVI and America. He describes the enthusiasm for liberty to which he attributes the tenacity of the Americans. It is this enthusiasm that gave badly armed militia the victory over picked soldiers. In this sermon Franklin and

Washington are held up as great moral reformers. A large portion of the lower and middle clergy was imbued with this American sentiment which led them to believe in the coming of a new world, which should be organized according to religious principles, benevolent, rational and universal.

It is an acknowledged fact that the officers of the French army in America came back to France enthusiastic for the new country and filled with subversive ideas. Enough distinction is not made between these officers, for it is hardly probable that all of them held the same opinion and had the same experience. We must not confuse the officers who went to America before the alliance and those who followed Rochambeau. Almost all the officers who went before 1778 and who came back to France were hostile to the United States for not having given them enough decorations, enough glory or enough money.[29] Those who were satisfied and remained to the end had a chance to know the Americans and became attached to them without greatly admiring their political forms, which during this war had shown themselves as very lax and impotent.[30] La Fayette was almost the only one who was a faithful admirer of American political institutions and even he wrote in 1780 that Washington was going to be appointed dictator of the United States and that it was a very good thing.[31]

In Rochambeau's army, which was mostly composed of volunteers, and which had only social relations with the Americans, the officers were greatly in favor of the customs and ideas of the New World. They came as saviors. They were received everywhere as honored guests, and the women admired them. Now, the women of the United States, then as now, were very beautiful. The French officers were struck by this, and it disposed them immediately in favor of liberty. Since their beautiful hostesses were as virtuous as they were charming and simple, this roused in them a flood of images inspired by Rousseau and their best instincts. They described the pretty Quakeresses of Philadelphia or the beautiful Puritans of Newport so vividly that they built up a veritable legend. It must be said to the glory of France that the foreign officers in the King's pay proved much more surly and much less susceptible to the qualities of the fair sex. The only discordant notes in the concert of praise which the field journals of the French officers in America contained are found in the accounts and letters of the Swede Fersen and the Rhinelander Deux Ponts. Except for these two (and the Duc de Lauzun) they all praised the virtues and beauty of America and of the American women.[32]

They brought back an unforgettable impression of Washington. This hero had received them with a simple grandeur in which there had been nothing provincial or servile. He had spoken with frankness and dignity; he had discussed questions with courtesy and, except for a moment of temper, which had been quickly pardoned, his conduct had merited nothing but praise.[33] And praise him they did, and fervently. Every diary kept by a member of the French forces contains a physical and moral portrait of the American Commander-in-Chief. The best known of these is the one which was written by the Chevalier de Chastellux, Orderly-Officer to Rochambeau, "If some one shows you medallions of Caesar, Trajan or Alexander, you may, on seeing their features, still ask what was their stature and their build. But if you discover among the ruins the head or a bit of marble from an antique Apollo, give no thought to the other parts of the statue but be assured that they are worthy of a god. . . . I desire only to express the impression made on me by General Washington, the concept of a perfect ensemble which cannot be reproduced by enthusiasm, which would rather reject it, since the effect of proportion is to diminish the idea of size." [34] This encomium is typical, for although Monsieur de Rochambeau was the military leader of the French army in America, and although his prudence, his philosophic mind and public spirit were able to win everybody's support and to facilitate relations with Washington and his staff, Monsieur de Chastellux, member of the French Academy, champion of the idea of progress in France, and intimate friend of the house of Orléans, was truly the spiritual leader of the expedition. He made a point of visiting all the famous places and people of America, and the account of his travels is a very diverting picture of the United States in 1780. Its style is facile and pungent, too much so perhaps, for it shocked many people when it was published; they could not understand how M. de Chastellux could have chosen to be witty on so great and religious a subject. What especially spoils Chastellux's style for the modern reader is an affectation of Anglicisms that is neither natural nor amusing. However, he reports conversations, and he describes personages in an exact and living way. He was very happy in the United States, but he enjoyed especially the prestige that he derived from his name, his title and his glory. He admired the Americans and he loved them; he found in them a rare example of virtue, but he poked fun at the Quakers. He expressed doubts concerning equality and protested in the name of the Arts which the United States were neglecting too much. His book was admired especially for the portraits it contained and the accounts of military operations, which he described at length.

He brought back from this New World an agreeable impression and an inclination towards enthusiasm. He had talked a great deal with Jefferson about Ossian, liberty and religion, and almost always they had come to agree. The Virginian sage therefore seemed to him the perfect type of the philosopher. Both of them felt the same need of an entirely interior religion which should have an application to social and rational life. Altogether, this is the most precious memory that Monsieur de Chastellux brought back from America; and in spite of his care to say nothing which should be subversive or might encourage revolution, through his admiration for Washington, his friendship with Jefferson and his religious aspirations, Chastellux exerted an influence favorable to the United States and the new ideas.[35]

There were very few of these officers who did not hold a like attitude. We can feel various tendencies among them. Some of them caught simply a taste for an adventurous life and saw nothing in America that they thought France should imitate. The Vicomte de Mirabeau is a notable example of these.[36] Others were overcome with admiration; they felt a sort of vague and mystic worship scarcely apt to make for action, but which prepared them to expect great commotions.[37] But most of them had admired, compared and discussed, and these had come back home with their heads full of ideas for reforms, at first obscure, but which became more definite and acquired more and more a general direction as the years went by and as their memories became classified. In general, their concept is one that derives from Rousseau, but the image that they formed of the "state of Nature" is less vague and less abstract.[38] It leads more directly to action and to a religious sentiment. It has come out of the domain of literature into that of deeds and immediate desires. They dream of a revolution without persecutions like that of America, of equality without jealousy, of natural righteousness without imperative dogmas and of a religious faith without clergy or mysteries.

It is difficult to know what the common soldiers thought and said on their return. If one might judge by modern times, they must have described the taverns, the wine, the tobacco and the beds and decided in favor of their own country. But this is perhaps unjust. The only two texts which represent the middle-class opinions at this period are not less enthusiastic than the writings of the young nobles. A letter from a young French sailor which was published in the *Gazette des Deux Ponts* of January, 1781, describes with rapture the United States and declares that a nation made up of such citizens can not be vanquished. And in 1782 a young French merchant, Joseph Mandrillon, published *Le Voyageur américain*, a book of information concerning the trade, the life and the resources of the United States. Mandrillon copied from English books all such details as are accurate, and from Raynal all those that are false. But where it is a question of judgment and conclusions, he listened only to his heart. "The virtues of the Americans, drawn from nature and from the simplicity of their habits, are not as with us, the product of hypocrisy or of pride; it is virtue unmixed and unornamented." [39]

A knowledge of the United States was disseminated among the public during the years from 1783 to 1789 by accounts and diaries published by returning officers. In general, they were taken as a basis for opinions concerning the United States. But it is also necessary to take into account the modifications of opinion which were accomplished by the numerous translations of English works on the United States that appeared at this time.[40] Among these were Carver's *Travels* (1784) [41] with his amusing and fantastic stories of the Indians, Burnaby's account which is full of praise of Washington and confidence in the future of the United States. There is also John Filson's book (1785) with its curious accounts of the mysterious river in Kentucky where the Europeans and the Indians lived side by side and amused themselves by massacring each other.[42] Finally, we have the *History of the American Revolution in South Carolina* (1787) by David Ramsay, a reliable work, well written and well translated. Ramsay is the first real historian to write an exact account of the events which took place between 1770 and 1783. What is more, his book is clear and entertaining. This series of books might have sufficed to instruct the French public and to prevent it from making serious errors, but it seems as if nothing could prevent popular imagination from creating for itself a sentimental and philosophic America. Even while these translations and memoirs were being published, the "historians" who gathered these documents and wrote the histories sought only to rouse emotion. Hilliard d'Auberteuil dared to republish under new titles his voluminous work of 1782 which contained such a lovely jumble of errors and sentiments. A certain Abbé Pierre de Longchamps gave the public an *Histoire impartiale des Evènements militaires et politiques de la dernière Guerre*

(1785) in three volumes. This work went into three editions. It included a sketch of the English Colonies in 1775, copied from Raynal, and a sort of calendar of military operations taken from English publications. In his preface Abbé de Longchamps set forth and adopted as his own the French ministerial thesis of 1778: Great Britain had violated the contract that she had granted to her people; the Americans were therefore within their right, and Louis XVI, in aiding them, had only followed the tradition of the Kings of France who had always defended the weak and the oppressed. He predicted that the Revolution of English America would spread into South America and "there develop talents and lights which until now had been smothered by the European despotism." In 1787 two other historical works on the late war were published in Paris: *L'Histoire de la dernière Guerre* by Julien Leboucher, which gave an accurate account of the military operations almost without alluding to political events, and *L'Histoire des Troubles de l'Amérique anglaise* by François Soulès. These two authors took almost everything they said from documents published by the English Government, Leboucher with greater insight, Soulès with greater imagination. Soulès set forth all the arguments most favorable to the Americans, and he proclaims the right of nations to self-determination. He praises the United States but believes it his duty to remind them that they are made for virtue and that without virtue they will fall and that the greatness of nations comes from such *mores* as strengthen a government. In these works there is no trace of personal research, no original philosophic view, no serious intent, only a perpetual scramble to enhance the heroes—Penn, Washington and Franklin, and a philosophic concern for giving good advice to the Americans, who seemed to be the pampered darlings of humanity. The compilers who handled the same subjects followed this same method in order to bring them within the understanding of the great public, but they took even less pains. Monsieur Poncelin de la Roche Tilhac, Counselor of the Marble Table, in spite of his pompous name and his fine title, published a sorry little *Almanach américain* in 1783, which gives a sketch of America taken from Raynal, whose mistakes he religiously preserves. In 1784, J. Mandrillon brought out a new edition of his book under the title of *Le Spectateur américain*, but he had done nothing save to add encomiums of Washington and moral counsels to the Americans.[43] He says in this book: "To break the chains of despotism in the sacred name of liberty is the most righteous and the worthiest act of man." Mandrillon is especially anxious that the Americans preserve their virtue in order to continue their sublime work. To this end he advises them to set up in their temples images of their great men and to have a political and religious calendar in which each day shall be marked with the name of one of these heroes. "What glory for you and what joy for your descendants to read some day with holy respect these precious names!" he says. This extraordinary need for morality and religious sentiment came over every one who had to do with the United States. We find an epic poem on America Delivered published at Antwerp in 1783 by a French refugee who was trying to curry favor. In this incredible conglomeration of verses and notes, which fills no less than two volumes, the author seems sincere only when he speaks of liberty and tolerance:

> Great liberty, the highest happiness!
> The only true blessing of mankind! [44]

The rest is a jumble of personifications, allegories, platitudes and flatteries.

Several novels contribute to this glorification of the virtues and greatness of the American heroes. An entire literature turns around Asgill, the young English officer who, taken prisoner by the Americans, was to have been put to death to avenge the brutal execution of an American Major, but whom the intervention of the Queen of France saved. Monsieur de Mayer began by publishing a novel about this unhappy young man in the *Collection des Romans;* then he brought out a second and more complete version of the story in which he describes the anxiety of Mrs. Asgill while waiting for her son to be put to death and Washington's grief at being obliged to refuse him mercy. In 1785 J. L. Lebarbier Le Jeune published a play on the same subject; it was badly constructed in the conventional style with no psychology other than that of effusion, but it shows the Americans and the French so brimming over with brotherly feeling and devotion to the commonweal that the audience is deeply touched. And this is only the beginning of a series. Even Hilliard d'Auberteuil recovered his loquacity and described the unhappy lot of Miss MacRea, a young American girl, in love with an English officer, who was killed by the savages while she was trying to reach Burgoyne's army. This little book is interesting, for it is made up of sentimental and picturesque elements taken from Chastellux. Hilliard lays stress upon the Biblical character of the United States. The whole novel is flooded with a light of piety, nature and sorrow. It belongs to the series of works which paved the way for romanticism and which themselves struck the romantic note. It is interesting to note that Baculard d'Arnauld, one of the authors who exploited this vein the most thoroughly, during the eighteenth century devotes a long story to a similar episode. His novel *Amélie* seems to have been inspired by Hilliard's Miss MacRea.[45] A little later it became fashionable to use the United States as a background for any novel in which the author wished to portray true virtue. Loszwinski, the worthy and kindly hero of *Faublas* by Louvet, has served with Washington and La Fayette: he remembers it with pride.[46] Ducray Duminil in *Lolotte et Fanfan* (1788) describes Boston and New England; then he skips to Charleston and gives a new description.

Against this background he deploys a most moving story of unrewarded virtue and miraculous adventures.

Thus, books were continually presenting to the public the romantic, sentimental and religious legend which, through the efforts of travelers and authors, the United States had become. But this legend was symbolized and illustrated most perfectly by the Marquis de La Fayette. After his return to France, M. de La Fayette had not lost sight of his adopted country, which he visited in 1784 to be overwhelmed by ovations in all the cities through which he passed. He kept up the closest friendship with General Washington, and during his whole political career he was always glad to accept advice from the American Fabius. He let it be seen and known that Washington was his ideal morally as well as politically. He encouraged the consequent linking of their names which writers had adopted since 1778. Reposing on this friendship and on the popularity that he enjoyed throughout the United States, La Fayette had set himself up as the protector of the Americans in France.[47] Besides the Minister, who for his part had wisdom and perception enough to keep up cordial and intimate relations with him, La Fayette played a diplomatic part, less discreet than he seems to have believed, but still very efficacious.[48] When Jay tried to obtain facilities for American commerce in the French West Indies and in Europe, he made use of La Fayette, who through his great prestige, his family's position and Vergennes's favor, could obtain anything that his friends desired.[49] Every Monday he invited the principal members of the American colony of Paris to dinner, and he was their intercessor at the Court.[50] It is he who persuaded Calonne to have the Nantucket fishermen, whom the English attitude had deprived of their means of livelihood, come to France.[51] The most brilliant part of his activities consisted in being to some degree the intellectual ambassador of the United States. While the Minister of the United States could do nothing except represent his Government and defend its political and commercial interests, La Fayette, whom every one considered as an American, and as the most perfect representative of America, defended and propagated the ideas that were then held to be essentially American: tolerance, the suppression of slavery, the liberty of the press, and parliamentary government.[52] La Fayette was American and not English because he considered as essential a zeal for Liberty rather than the subtle combinations of constitutions. His public activity was greatly aided by the secret and energetic support that Vergennes always lent him. It was through him that he was able to bring to a successful end his campaign in favor of the Protestants. Vergennes was a partisan of tolerance.[53] He defended it before the King, and one may believe that the memorandums that the Quaker Benezet sent him in 1781 to point out to him the necessity of liberating the French Protestants made an impression upon him; for in 1786 the French Quakers and the Nantucket fishermen living at Dunkirk wrote to him to obtain recognition of their rights to practice their religion freely. Vergennes obtained the liberty of the Quaker cult in France in spite of the opposition of certain Catholic bishops and the other Reformed churches.[54] But no one knew this at the time, and La Fayette profited by the discretion of his illustrious friend. He gained another brilliant victory for humanity and for his own glory when, at his own expense, he had all the slaves in Guiana set free.[55] At the Assembly of the Notables, his solemn protest in the name of the Protestants and his appeal to the States-General, the first that had ever been made, spread his renown everywhere. There were jealous people who accused him of being a free thinker and of seeking notoriety, but he gathered behind him the group of young men who were full of ideals of progress and generosity.[56]

Occupying a prominent place in the public eye and taking care to remain there, La Fayette did not allow France to forget the United States and their teachings. He failed perhaps to show the real conditions of life in the New World, and he did not give a very exact idea of what American character and liberty were; but he was an admirable living legend. With all the newspapers, even the most favorably inclined printing English news concerning the United States, he was the most positive and the most shining refutation of the calumny which condemned all the free Americans as a nation of beggars and boors. Gradually all his former companions in arms grouped around him, and a sort of a party was formed, American in name and tendency, although they knew this far-off country very imperfectly.

The philosophers, who were not less eager for influence and power, also sought to utilize the United States. This new country interested them greatly and aroused their imagination as well as their curiosity—the former, without doubt, more than the latter. This virgin continent where everything remained to be done and which lay plastic and malleable in the hand of the legislator, was for these impassioned legislators as fascinating a spectacle as a superb block of marble is to a sculptor. They were but little interested in becoming acquainted with this people and its country, for they considered it unformed and sincerely hoped that it was not *too* well formed, for this would have deprived them of a chance to exercise their talents. Moreover, they admired it infinitely for this very quality and were ready to concede it the best of instincts and the noblest of dispositions on condition that they be asked to concede nothing else. It was an unlimited possibility, a field of experiment for Europe wherein philosophy would realize all its dreams and create its Eden.

We find this attitude among the most illustrious as well as among the most humble—Mably, Raynal, Target, Dupaty, Mirabeau, Mazzéi,[57] Abbé Genty, the royal censor, Condorcet and the philosopher Gargaz, who was a school-teacher in Provence and an ex-convict. Not a book on America was printed between 1775 and 1790 but ended with a sort of homily. There were very few visionaries of the time who could pass by this opportunity to aid the insurgents at least by their advice. In 1784 Target sent a long letter to the newspapers of New York, whence it was copied by all the American newspapers. This worthy parliamentarian reminded the Americans that the eyes of Europe were fixed on them, that they were obliged to make a success of their Constitution. He recommended good *mores* as being indispensable to the happiness of nations. He recognized that the Americans already had good *mores;* but if they did not encourage them sufficiently, they might disappear. "Develop national education, outlaw riches and conquests, hold brotherly feasts and, above all, have passions—virtuous ones it goes without saying, for without passion a people is nothing." [58] They were so determined to enlighten the New World that Monsieur Pollier, a magistrate of Lausanne, begged Franklin to send Congress the copies of his book on government and *mores* which he had intended for this august body.[59] But, compared with Abbé Raynal, all the others are mere schoolboys.

Towards the end of the American war, Raynal took two initiatives which were to have a great influence on contemporary thought. He published a book to enlighten the United States concerning themselves (1781) and established at the Academy of Lyons [60] a literary contest to determine whether the discovery of the New World had been a blessing or a curse, and how the sufferings that it had brought about could be remedied. Raynal's book is a clear and luminous production, but it is full of contradictions and errors. Raynal wants to praise the Americans, but he wants to make them understand that their task is not yet finished—nay, that it is scarcely begun. In an emphatic and religious tone, he admonishes them. "People of septentrional America, may the example of all the nations that have preceded you, and especially that of your mother country, instruct you. Beware of the affluence of gold!" Moved by a desire to be impartial and to show how completely he has his subject in hand, he places himself at all possible points of view. The result is comic. He reproaches France for having made an unnatural alliance and one which surely hides ulterior motives. He rebukes France for this and then concludes that it would have been more seemly to have kept a high hand over the insurgents instead of according them a treaty which gave them rights over France. He praises the heroism of the Americans for defending the glorious cause of liberty, and he adds: "However, their soldiers are not very courageous; and this is because the Revolution came about without the Americans having had any serious reason for complaint and without their having suffered any grave wrong at the hands of England." He concludes that "the Americans will free the New World, but it is to be hoped that a rival power will spring up against them, for without danger republics could not conserve that virtue which is the soul of liberty. After the war," he went on, "the United States will undoubtedly become a refuge for all the scum of Europe"; and this worried him, but he ended up superbly: "Heroic country, my advanced age does not permit me to visit thee. Never shall I find myself in the midst of the worthy personages of thine Areopagus. Never shall I attend the deliberations of thy Congress. I shall die without having seen the abode of tolerance, of *mores*, of laws, of virtue and of liberty. A free and sacred earth will not receive my ashes, but I shall have yearned for it, and my last words will be prayers to Heaven for thy prosperity." [61] It is, and it was, easy to criticize this generous outburst, to show in all these fine sentiments which follow and contradict each other an effort toward an emotion that the heart does not feel, in all these conflicting counsels and prophecies an attempt to be very wise ending up in sheer nonsense, and finally, in this criticism of the Franco-American alliance an exaggerated respect for England mixed with an exaggerated scorn for France. Thomas Paine, at the instigation of the French Minister in Philadelphia, from whom he was receiving a pension, wrote a sharp reply to Raynal. He denounced his errors in facts and his faults of logic and refuted the absurd claim that the Franco-American alliance was contrary to nature, by showing that this alliance had benefited and would benefit both nations.[62] He held Raynal up to ridicule, but the

Abbé kept his prestige and the influence of his book was prodigious. He was credited with great wisdom. To live up to his reputation he founded at the Academy of Lyons a literary prize consisting of a sum of 1200 livres. The subject of the contest was the following: "Has the discovery of America been useful or harmful to mankind? If benefits have resulted from it, by what means may they be preserved and augmented? If it has produced evils, by what means may they be remedied?" The prize was to have been awarded in 1783; it never was awarded. No satisfactory reply was submitted, and the prize was carried over from year to year, until in 1789 the Academy of Lyons, in accord with Raynal, decided that the sum should be devoted to other purposes.[63] Of the numerous essays which were submitted, four have come down to us. One of them is by Condorcet and another by Chastellux; Abbé Genty, the royal censor, is the author of the third; as to the fourth, it has come down to us without the author's name. These four essays are unanimous in declaring that the discovery of America was a misfortune, since it spread intolerance and slavery, but that the American Revolution is the remedy to the evil, since it opens a new era for humanity. "O country of Franklin, of Washington, of Hancock, and Adams, who could wish that you had not existed both for them and for us?" exclaims Chastellux. "The independence of the Anglo-Americans is the event the most apt to hasten the coming of the Revolution which should bring happiness to the world. In the bosom of this newborn Republic lie the true treasures which will enrich the world," says Genty. As for Condorcet, he goes even further; writing under the pseudonym of Godard, he shows that in developing the population of the world, in making commerce free, and above all, in giving the world a new and unique example of the respect that is due to the rights of man, North America is laying the foundation for a renovation of the world, which at last beholds the triumph of the true principles. The anonymous author takes the same stand and declares that, in affording the nations a model of a pure and free nation, the United States have forced governments to become moderate and peoples to take stock of themselves. We see toward what doctrines Raynal had led his compatriots, thanks to the United States. It is also to be noted that the Académie des Jeux Floraux of Toulouse had had the same idea as Raynal and had established a prize for dissertations on the greatness and the importance of the American Revolution in 1784. The two essays submitted for this prize which have come down to us have less value than those submitted for the prize that Raynal offered. They were composed by a lawyer in the Parliament of Toulouse and a captain in the Regiment of Brittany. Both of them are enthusiastic; but the lawyer extols the Americans rather in the name of Reason, and the captain in the name of Nature, for he was a disciple of Rousseau. Both of them set forth the utility of the American Revolution in holding up an example for the world at large to follow. Both of them, but especially the captain, put in a good word for virtue and lay stress on conjugal virtue as being of the greatest value to newly formed societies.

While this group of philosophers were preaching good *mores* to the Americans and, at the same time, lauding American doctrines to the rest of the world, Abbé Mably, just and severe, was making a thorough study of the new and much-vaunted constitutions; and when John Adams questioned him, he confessed to grave misgivings as to this experiment on the part of so virtuous a people.[64] How should all their noble qualities escape from the corruption that penetrates everywhere through laws? Alas —"the legislator will take steps to guard them; he will feel sure of realizing his hopes; but his work will serve only as a spur to ungoverned passions which will precipitate the Republic either into anarchy or into oligarchy," he says on page 5 of his book. The thought that a nation is made up of men dismays him: "How shall one view without alarm the mass of men who make up society? All of them have active and differing passions. Some of them are incapable of thinking. And these are the greater, and even the greatest number." With such an opinion of men and their faculties, it is easy to imagine what must have been the misgivings of the good Abbé Mably, who was, moreover, enamored of perfection, virtue and ideal legislation, and who felt the deepest sympathy for the Americans. He praises them for being the only republic wherein the citizens are not treated like cattle. He made a study of their constitutions one by one, and in a very confused book, he points out their shortcomings. He takes up the text of each constitution without knowing or stopping to consider its application, then he proceeds to praise or condemn it. When he finds defects, he considers them as the germ of immediate disaster. When there are no defects to be found, he is even more alarmed, for there is nothing more deceptive than an appearance of perfect health. He sees in everything the signs of a nascent aristocracy; but he seems however to look forward to it, though he regrets that a perfect democracy should be impossible to realize. He emphasizes the Americans' duty to encourage good *mores*. The liberty of the press and tolerance are bad, for they bring about laxness and open too clear a field to the vices. He fears lest the United States end up in atheism and would like Congress to draw up a "moral and political catechism" which all the Americans should be obliged to accept. He remarks that the Greeks and the Romans, although they were so strong for liberty, would never have tolerated the absolute freedom of the press. He is in favor of suppressing commerce and luxury because they undermine *mores*. To maintain these *mores*, he advises that Congress be strengthened, that a more durable executive branch be created and that great celebrations be held every year to commemorate the anniversary of independence. He warns the Americans that they must make haste, for vices creep in rapidly and become habits. But he concludes sadly: Do all this; it will undoubtedly be in vain, but at least you will have nothing for which to reproach yourselves.

This attitude of an idealist reformer whom nothing here below could satisfy, but who would like at least to save from disaster the only people in whom he finds a tendency toward perfection, was much appreciated at the time. Mably was frequently copied and imitated. This afforded writers the opportunity to speak of free constitutions and, under the guise of condemning them, to admire them at heart and to lavish on them from time to time compliments which more than made up for criticisms. A certain Demeusnier, who was commissioned by the *Encyclopédie méthodique* to write the article on the United States, put so much philosophic zeal into it that he almost drove Jefferson to distraction. Since he was favorable to the United States and anxious to speak well of them, he begged the American minister at Paris to draw up a *résumé* of the American constitutions for him. Jefferson sent him an article, which Demeusnier altered and then sent back to Jefferson, who corrected the errors. Demeusnier invented fresh ones and then sent his article to Jefferson and Humphreys, and later to La Fayette. After this final correction, Demeusnier retouched his work and, in so doing, recast the whole article, much to the detriment of accuracy. The result was an essay of which one half was taken from Raynal, while the other half was made up of inaccurate commentaries from Mably on a few exact bits of information which Jefferson furnished. It laid stress, however, on the part that Jefferson had played in spreading tolerance and the victory that he had won in Virginia.[65] As a general thing, this is the only clear point brought out in the studies of America of this period.

At any rate, this emphatic and, one might say, apocalyptic tone annoyed the Americans greatly. They would have liked people to know their country and not its shadow, their life and not the dreams of the reformers who talked about it. They felt, wrongly perhaps, that a real knowledge of the United States would spread their influence and make it a more fortunate one. Jefferson did his best to fight against the mania for dissertation without documentation. We have seen what pains he took with Demeusnier and for what little results. He did even more than this. He published his *Notes on Virginia*, which he had formerly prepared in order to refute De Pauw and Raynal. He made them more complete and furnished concrete information on the United States and their products to prove that they are in no way inferior to those of Europe. His book, ponderous and without literary value, would not have been read if it had not contained some chapters in favor of the freedom of the negro slaves. It was not until 1788 that a book was published which gave a clear idea of the United States. In that year, Mazzéi published his *Recherches historiques et politiques sur les Etats-Unis*, of which one volume is devoted to pointing out Raynal's errors, another to Mably's absurdities, and many pages to the various other stupidities written about the Americans. His work is well done, but it is almost unreadable because of the accumulation of details and the confusion of discussions. It was not widely read, although it furnished for the first time an exact *résumé* of the founding of the thirteen colonies and a truthful exposition of the economic difficulties which led to a break between England and her colonies. His fourth volume, devoted to a study of the contemporary United States, is very interesting. He paints them with optimism and shows the eminent qualities of the savages and negroes. He tells how much the example of the Americans in bringing over the doctrines of liberty from theory into practice, had aided and would aid the European nations. His democratic and anti-religious zeal led him to attack the Quakers as sectarians. Mazzéi was undoubtedly right in trying to make the worship for the United States that was in vogue in France more precise and nearer to reality; but he did not employ a tone that could win favor. People did not ask to be convinced of the virtues of the Americans, but to be thrilled and moved by them. Pamphlets like those of Turgot and Mirabeau, with all their prejudice and sententiousness, even when they contained reproaches against the United States, did more to make them popular than the most serious studies could as long as they remained unimpassioned and cold. Turgot's little book, which was published in 1784 (as were Mirabeau's *Considérations sur l'Ordre de Cincinnatus*), had been written in 1778 as a reply to Price, who had just published a tract in favor of the United States. Turgot informed him that, in his opinion, the United States were indeed "the hope of mankind . . . and especially of the enlightened; all the friends of humanity should at this time join their lights and add the fruit of their reflections to that of the American sages to aid them in the great work of their legislation." He condemned their attempt to set up a balance of the powers of government, which he considered to be an illusion and a serious drawback to liberty. He blamed the American tendency to mix religion and civil government. He was in favor of as little government as possible and absolute tolerance; in short, he asked that the Americans be themselves completely and without restriction. There is something pathetic in the worried and solicitous tone with which he says all this. But his pages are pale beside those of Mirabeau. This latter writer had taken up arms with fury against an institution which the American officers had decided to create to perpetuate the memory of their efforts and their victory—the Order of the Cincinnati. This society was also to have a treasury in order to assist such members or such of their families as might be in need. The officers who had fought in the war and their direct descendants were to have the right to belong to it. The idea of a military league at once aroused violent opposition in America, and particular indignation was felt against the clause which provided for hereditary transmission of the right of membership.

A magistrate from South Carolina wrote a virulent pamphlet denouncing this autocratic and military conspiracy against which there was soon a strong opposition. Washington, who was elected President of the Order, yielded to the extent of repealing the hereditary clause, but he maintained the Order, saying that to dissolve it now would be an insult to the French officers who had consented to belong to it. Certain enemies of the Order of Cincinnatus, and among them Franklin, suggested to Mirabeau that he take up the controversy and attack the Order in the name of France. Mirabeau hastened to follow this counsel. In 1784, he published one of the most daring works of the times. He had translated and abridged the American pamphlet. He had added to it a violent attack against nobility on the pretext that, in the only country that was happy enough to be free of this scourge, the Order of the Cincinnati could lead to no other end than the creation of a patrician order. He exclaimed, "The idea of a man being born a magistrate, a legislator or a judge is absurd and contrary to nature!" There is no truth in the claims of the nobles who say that virtues are transmitted along with blood. "How much of the original blood remains after ten generations, and are not the proudest families those that go back the furthest?" To the Americans he said, "America can, and is even going to, determine with certainty whether mankind is destined by its nature to liberty or to slavery." [66] It was therefore easy to see that if the violent blame seemed to fall on the Americans, in truth, it was not they who bore the brunt of these accusations. On the contrary, they were held up as the enviable model for those who have yet to set themselves free. Mirabeau employed, but with more daring and precision, the method that Mably and Raynal had used, and, following their example, he utilized the United States as the model for other nations, the concrete form of their moral ideal.

*
* *

These methods annoyed certain Americans who did not feel attracted by the vocation of Messiah-nation; but, on the whole the people were flattered, and the bolder spirits across the sea read eagerly these polemics in which the name of the United States recurred frequently as the emblem of Liberty and moral perfection. In spite of the hostility of the American government, who feared the guile of the French King and the corrupting spirit of the French pamphleteers, the American people kept up its sympathy for those who had helped them so much in working out their salvation.[67] In this critical period for the American nation, when it had to rally about a new government and resist tendencies toward demagogy and all the other dangers which assail a new people, its newspapers found space to print long dispatches on happenings in France. Most of these dispatches came from London, and although the American journalists avoided printing anything that was too unfavorable to France, a good many insinuating details slipped into their columns. The English government took care to have it announced from time to time that France was going to retake Louisiana or Florida or Canada, or that she had been obliged to give up Corsica because she could no longer govern it. Letters were printed whose burden was that America ought not to allow theatrical productions, since it was because of the theater and the vices that it fostered that France had been able to subjugate virtuous Geneva.[68] But, in as much as it was possible, the American papers fought against English propaganda, and their columns are a striking testimony to the vitality of popular sympathy with France. They reprinted the articles by the great philosophers on the United States and usually praised the wise counsels that their ardent writings contained. They gave news of the French officers who had served in America,[69] of La Fayette especially, but also of La Rouërie, whom they declared was a great friend of the United States.[70] The prizes that the provincial academies were founding in France were announced; and in each number we find professors, merchants, dressmakers and importers of French wines appealing to the public, which seems to have treated them well. Their advertisements were printed in French and in English. The newspapers in the large ports especially, such as Baltimore, Philadelphia, New York and Boston, prided themselves on understanding France and doing her justice. They went so far as to publish notes affirming that the French press was not as completely gagged as the English would have it believed, that France was ceasing to be bigoted and was breaking away from Catholicism. Certain pamphleteers, to shame the United States for their slowness in reorganizing their finances, recalled the generosity of Louis XVI; and this prince was continually held up as the great benefactor of the United States. On the death of Vergennes, the papers gratefully enumerated all that he had done for the United States and for humanity.[71] Lastly, a new sentiment was becoming more and more evident every year in the American papers, national pride and pleasure at seeing France, who was their great and generous friend, beginning to be fired by their ideas and to imitate them. During the year 1788, there was not a single American town in which this sentiment was not expressed. The spiritual partnership between the two nations and the moral rôle of the United States was becoming a matter of popular interest.[72] Undoubtedly one of the most interesting examples of this was the mayor of New Haven's decision to appoint as citizens of the town a number of illustrious Frenchmen, among whom were Target, La Rochefoucauld, Condorcet, etc.[73]

Education had a tendency to adopt itself to these new

interests. Everywhere colleges and schools were being founded, and educational problems were being discussed with great ardor. In a curious article in the *New York Daily Advertiser*, Benevolus asserts that the Americans ought to have an education of their own, for, he says, the system of education conceived by Rousseau is fitting only for a Swiss bourgeois and Fénelon's system is becoming to a French prince.[74] The best models would be Leyden or Edinburgh, but what is needed is a more practical education and one which would not oblige our young men to go abroad. This was the general opinion. Even the most educated Americans and those who knew Europe best, such as Adams and Jefferson, recommended that young men should study in America and go to Europe only to finish up their education.[75] All of them feared lest the young men acquire aristocratic habits, and only a few rich merchants like Robert Morris [76] saw an advantage in sending their sons to study in the Old World. The Americans were anxious to develop their national characteristics and to impose their ideals on the growing generation. However, they considered a knowledge of French as indispensable to a cultivated man. In 1786, the Maryland newspapers published at length discussions as to whether a college should be established in the state and on what system; and every one agreed that such a college should teach French, since it was the language most in use in good society. It should be remembered that, in the minds of its founders, the University of Maryland was not to be established for the education of an intellectual élite, but for young men of the middle classes.[77] Every one admitted that for girls French was a necessary ornament like music and dancing.[78] Thus, while French was gaining rather slowly in the colleges, we find professors of French in great number in all of the important cities and especially in the ports. At Philadelphia in 1785, there seem to have been at least five French professors, of whom two were for women: at New York there were three, at Baltimore eight, at Annapolis one, at Portsmouth, Virginia, one, at Augusta four, of whom two also taught music, at New Rochelle one, at Providence one, and at Boston two or three.[79] It is to be noted in passing that the South, where individual luxury is more developed in the upper classes, seems to have attracted the most professors of French. Beside, it was easier to come over from Santo Domingo to Baltimore or Portsmouth than to Boston. And most of these professors came from the French West Indies.[80]

In the colleges, French was considered as both useful and dangerous. It was feared that this language might serve as a vehicle for new and subversive ideas. Now most of the American colleges were situated in New England and were dominated by the clergy. At Yale, for example, Ezra Stiles, a clergyman himself, but cultured and a philosopher as well as pious, was unable to install a French professor—even a Protestant one. He did however introduce Montesquieu's *Esprit des Lois* as a text-book and taught it himself to seniors.[81] Harvard, which was under the control of a more liberal clergy, had been bolder and continued so. Indeed there seem to have been as many as two instructors in French there at once, and French was a regular part of the curriculum for sophomores and juniors. It was accepted as a substitute for Hebrew, the old religious tongue in such repute among the Puritan clergymen. In 1787, a new French professor, M. de Nancrède, a very likable and brilliant man, had been appointed by the University and was to exert a real influence on the students.[82] When the School of Medicine was founded, the French consul was present at the ceremony; and this school showed more French influence than any other part of the University. In fact, J. Warren, the director of the school and the brother of the hero who was killed at Bunker Hill, had been impressed by the methods employed by the French surgeons in the last campaign, in which he himself had served as a military surgeon. He had therefore adopted French methods in many particulars. In chemistry, the text-book used was Fourcroy.[83] Through Crèvecœur, the French consul at New York, the University, as well as the principal American physicians, received free the *Journal des Médecins militaires français*,[84] and French representatives endeavored to gain publicity in America for the *Observations sur la Physique*, the best French scientific review.[85] The King had given to Harvard a collection of seeds with which to start a botanical garden. He had also given books to Harvard, William and Mary and the University of Pennsylvania. The Academy of Sciences at Paris sent its publications to Harvard, and French travelers sent it their works. Thus we find a letter from Harvard thanking Brissot for the gift of his *Voyage en Amérique*. At Princeton, Witherspoon, an intelligent, erudite and pious president, paid tribute to French as a language. He often quoted the French theologians, the Jansenists and even Bossuet.[86] He carried on a systematic campaign against the Libertines and preached against Rousseau, although he himself had advanced and liberal views. In short, he inspired a desire to know French, but he did not judge it prudent to do more.[87] It was this question of philosophy in general that governed the spread of French. In the West, where there must have been much less need of it, it was nevertheless introduced very early (in 1783), for the clergy had almost no influence in this region.[88] French was ordinarily offered to the wealthier students who went to boarding-schools before going to college.[89] Law students were also urged to take up French because of the great prestige that Montesquieu enjoyed, and because a desire was felt to liberate America from English law.[90] In art and in all higher education, France was considered as the best school.[91] Students were sent to see the Louvre and David's studio.[92] It was this that inspired the project of Quesnay de Beaurepaire, who in 1786-1788 tried to found a Franco-American University at Richmond and almost succeeded. After having been an officer in the French army, he resigned his commission in order to serve in America, where he fell ill and was taken in by a Virginian family. After the war Quesnay tried to earn a living in the New World. He had tried to establish a French school at Philadelphia or New York, but he had found Virginia more propitious. There, thanks to the support of high society and of Masonic lodges, of which he was a faithful member, he was enabled to build a college. His project was to make it a school of higher learning especially designed to fit the needs of young men who were planning to become architects, painters, etc. He even offered scholarships for students who should show themselves to be gifted and promised to send them to Europe to complete their artistic education. He wanted his college to be international. He asked the French Academy to take it under their patronage and to choose professors for it. He had formed a European committee to launch his work. He also wanted to obtain the support of the Academy of Sciences of London, to which he made some advances. In exchange for this patronage, he promised the European Academies to carry on such research, studies or experiments as they might desire. The Academy of Sciences of Paris accorded him the support that he asked.[93] He began collecting funds. All the great friends of America and of the new ideas in France were behind him. He was presented to King Louis XVI in October, 1788.[94]

The movement of intellectual collaboration was encouraged by the learned societies of France and America, guided usually by partisans of progress and reform. A degree of intimacy had grown up between the French Academies and those of America, especially that of Philadelphia, which in 1786 had elected as members Vergennes, the Marquis d'Angeville, Barbeu-Dubourg, Chastellux, Coste, Daubenton, La Fayette, D'Annemours, the French Consul, Abbé Fontant, the Comte de Guichen, La Luzerne, Lavoisier, Barbé-Marbois, who even held the post of Counselor, Raynal, the Abbé Rozier, the Duc de La Rochefoucauld, Condorcet, Cabanis, the aeronaut Charles, and was to elect in 1787, Otto, Cadet de Vaux, etc.—altogether twenty-one Frenchmen out of fifty-five members. Every year it received the best scientific works published in France. It discussed the subjects in which Paris was most deeply interested, such as aerial navigation and animal magnetism. The Academy of Sciences of Paris sent it a fine electric apparatus; and Rittenhouse, one of its members, constructed at his own expense a superb astronomical machine for the King of France. The King showed his satisfaction by gifts and friendly letters.[95]

This whole movement had been started by Franklin, who had the gift of circulating knowledge of every kind and of stirring intellectual activity in all those who came in contact with him. He was in the habit of sending his friends the best books that came out in France, and Jefferson followed his example. He sent books on mathematics to his young friends, the *Gazette de Leyde* and the *Gazette de France* to all those who wanted to keep up with European affairs, and, to give him an idea of the political situation and of coming reforms, he sent Madison the works of Mably, the *Tableau de Paris*, *L'Espion anglais*, and the pamphlets of Dupont and Condorcet.[96]

This philosophic literature was to be found everywhere. The catalogues of the libraries and those of the reading-rooms show that, despite a marked fidelity to Fénelon and Rollin, both of whom remained as classics in education, there was an invasion of Montesquieu, who was being read more and more, and of Rousseau, whose *Confessions* and *Nouvelle Héloise* were often mentioned. But it is Voltaire and Raynal especially who seem to have gained in favor with the public at large. The newspapers frequently printed extracts from Voltaire, particularly the pages concerning tolerance and his relations with Frederick the Great. They often printed Raynal's exhortations inciting the Americans to continue in their virtues. About 1788, more interesting reviews were beginning to be published, especially at Boston and Philadelphia.[97] From the start they gave a great deal of space to things French. One of them went so far as to publish long extracts from the *Code de la Nature*,[98] and one feels that this kind of sensibility had gained considerable ground. We find many selections of this nature: moving and sentimental stories and encomiums of Nature and tolerance, which were sought in French literature. These were read eagerly and were used as weapons in the political struggles that were then going on. Saint Jean de Crèvecœur's moving book which dealt with the experiences of a French colonist in the West persecuted by the Indians, had a wide success; and the saddest and most picturesque episodes of his work were reprinted many times in America from 1782 to 1788.[99] This book glorified the free and enlightened man, living in the midst of virgin nature as it existed in the frontier posts and the great forests along the Mississippi. This ideal was also that which the poets, the historians and the novelists sought. David Ramsay's history, written with the assistance of La Luzerne, professed a sincere and naïve respect for France and represented the Franco-American alliance as being beneficial and generous to America. But this history kept within the bounds of prudence. The two great poets of the American Revolution, Freneau and Joel Barlow, on the contrary, dared to speak out. In American poetry, which was then very abundant, there was constant reference to the revolutionary spirit of the French and of their philosophers. David Humphreys, who had been orderly-officer to Washington, dedicated his collected poems to one of them, the Duc de La Rochefoucauld. He spoke of the King of France and his subjects as

> Sublimely good, magnanimously great,
> Protector of the rights of human kind.[100]

Barlow published at Hartford in 1787 the first and the finest epic poem that America has produced: *The Vision of Columbus.*[101] This poem was to have been part of a more voluminous work. The author imagines Columbus receiving in a dream a revelation of the sublime future that awaits the United States. This method, which seems to have been inspired by Voltaire's *Henriade*, permits him to burst forth into lyric praise of the Bourbons and France. He hails Louis XVI as the "pride of Kings" and praises him for the generosity that he had shown in intervening in favor of the United States without seeking any selfish end and with the sole purpose of aiding an unhappy people and responding to the enthusiasm of his subjects. After having extolled French soldiers and their generals, Barlow, in a style that has both amplitude and strength, goes on to describe Columbus' vision of universal peace. The destiny of America was to lead all the nations to unite in one vast democratic league. A religious fervor suffuses the soul of the poet. Later he was to become one of the leaders of the democratic party and to carry on a widespread propaganda in favor of the French alliance. Freneau had a like destiny and we shall find him at the head of the Jacobin pamphleteers in 1790. Between 1783 and 1788 he wrote excellent poetry. He had composed a prologue for Beaumarchais's *Eugénie* when Quesnay had produced it at Philadelphia in 1780; and in all his work, he expressed an intense enthusiasm for liberty—a sentiment that Witherspoon may perhaps have communicated to him when he was a student at Princeton. Freneau was a very gifted poet. He loved nature and especially the sea, on which he passed many years of his life. He was in advance of his times, and sometimes his work has a violent and desperate accent that since the beginning of the nineteenth century has been called Romanticism. He is the only one of his generation in America who has this quality. His satiric poems breathe an ardent hatred of despotism, and he had the art of carrying bitterness to such lengths as were permissible in those days—which is to say, further than we should consider proper today. He carried on a vigorous campaign in favor of the alliance with France and praised Louis XVI as the greatest monarch that the centuries had known. Everything that came from France roused his enthusiasm: in the Montgolfiers, he saw the promise of a new age, scientific and happy. Behind the French monarchy he divined and sought eagerly for the France of the Revolution, which already filled him with rapture.[102] The conflict between the conservative elements, who were religious and Anglophile, and the Francophiles, who were partisans of philosophy and tended toward deism, is illustrated by the resistance with which a group of Connecticut poets called the "Hartford Wits" met the propagation of French ideas. In 1786 they collaborated in publishing an epic poem entitled *The Anarchiad*.[103]

This poem is amusing and brutal. Its young authors wrote it to express their scorn for all these windy, ignorant and impractical French philosophers who dared to condemn the United States and to give them advice while they themselves were living under a despotism. They depicted De Pauw as being puffed with pride at having discovered a telescope which diminished objects in proportion to their remoteness. Thanks to this fine instrument, one could see everything that grew and lived in America as infinitely smaller than the products and men of Europe. Target, Raynal, Mably and Hilliard d'Auberteuil were also assailed. But it was especially against Mirabeau, his immorality and violent theories, that the authors turned their wrath.

Throughout the United States, a religious restlessness was making itself felt. The people as a whole were touched with a disaffection toward priests and churches. There was difficulty in the South in reorganizing the Church of England, which had now become the Episcopal Church. In Maryland the newspapers were agitating for the most complete tolerance. The Baptists, who were to make so much progress, were still in a preparatory phase. Their democratic spirit and manners destined them to become the most flourishing sect during these troubled years. The Lutheran Church was going through the most trying crisis that she had ever been subject to in the New World.

The credo was becoming vague, especially among the pastors; and the members of the congregations were refusing to pay for the maintenance of the parishes, many of which disappeared. Even in New England, a region so pious and so faithful to traditions, the spirit of tolerance and indifference was spreading together with deism.[104] A Catholic funeral was held at Philadelphia for the first time since the foundation of the city when Don Juan de Miralles died and a great ceremony was held in his honor. The spectators were even somewhat surprised at the piety and edifying deportment of the Papists.[105] In 1785, when John Thayer's conversion to Catholicism was known, people were a little surprised and shocked; but, when in 1788 a French priest came to settle in Boston, founded a church there and asked for Protestant help to finish paying for it, it called forth either indignation or enthusiasm. Certain newspapers made use of the occasion to speak of Catholicism and to come out in favor of tolerance.[106] *The Massachusetts Sentinel* for June 21, 1788, said: "Most of these happy results may be attributed to our independence and our alliance with our great and good ally, Louis of France, the protector of the rights of humanity against tyranny." The edict which gave full liberty to the Protestants in France and the various other liberal decisions of Louis XVI had caused great stir in America. Pastors had spoken of them in the pulpit. They began to quote Montesquieu and to discuss La Rochefoucauld in their sermons. They preached the generosity of the King of France and, in general, were favorable to the alliance, although it caused them some uneasiness. They admired the fine manners of the Frenchmen, the refinement that they had brought into vogue; but, as ministers of the gospel, they condemned this superficial elegance and beauty which are only external and constitute a kind of hypocrisy.[107] The gravest manifestation—for this time it was not mere corrupt living nor a mild tendency toward tolerance—came from Colonel Ethan Allen, the hero of Ticonderoga. In 1784, he published a book entitled *Reason, the Only Oracle of Man*, in which he set forth for the benefit of Vermont farmers the most cynical theories of the deists. He denied the divinity of Christ, the veracity of the Scriptures, the miracles and revelations. He demanded a traditional cult and a practical morality. His style, simple and even dull, and his direct arguments, rendered the work even more effective and shocking.

This restlessness was not to limit itself to remaining abstract and intellectual. It was to engender material disorders, the most famous of which were the riots in Massachusetts known as Shays' Rebellion, because Shays was the principal leader of the rebels.[108] These riots resembled those which took place in Rome when the plebeians refused to pay their debts. In truth, causes for dissatisfaction were not lacking in America during 1786 and 1787. Taxes were heavy, trade was far from flourishing, and many people had contracted debts during the war. The creditors wanted to recover their money, the debtors clamored for governmental aid; and when they did not get it, they had recourse to violence.

This revolt, which was accompanied by bloodshed and of which English propaganda made abundant use against the United States, was variously received. Some people were alarmed by it and thought that it would be necessary to modify the Constitution. Others felt that it was only natural and, on the whole, rather wholesome and beneficial, because it kept up the taste for liberty and the sense of independence alive in the nation. Jefferson was one of the latter; and one can see in his attitude a trace of the intellectual habits that he had contracted, undoubtedly from frequenting the French philosophers. Jefferson and his friends, Madison and Monroe, all the group of liberal politicians and patriots from Virginia, found in the French philosophers two inspirations which seem to be contradictory: the cult for the United States as the chosen nation which was responsible for the salvation of the world and for its reformation, and the desire to have as weak a government as possible.[109] These two tendencies, one of which seems to lead to a narrow and haughty nationalism, the other toward a weak and impotent and very individualistic democracy, are reconciled, as the reader will recall, only by the French philosophers from whom Jefferson and his group drew their ideas. According to them *mores* are the important bond which makes nations strong. The state should be weak, but there should be a strong and active public spirit. It was necessary to be ready at all times to modify the laws in order to fit them to circumstances and temperaments. The important thing was the creation of a national character and of a popular ideal, to which everything else should, if necessary, be sacrificed. They were therefore only mildly concerned over the uprising. Their great hope was to succeed in infusing their fellow citizens with the ideal that was to remodel the world. Meanwhile other groups were alarmed at seeing the disorder gaining ground and menacing private property as well as the property of the State. They were so disturbed that there were even murmurs in favor of a monarchy.[110] The merchants in the ports, the New England clergymen, dismayed at seeing their prestige diminish, and, in general, all men of wealth and position wished for a transformation of the Constitution. The inaction and weakness of Congress was visible evidence of the need for a change. Something resembling harmony was established between the democrats and the conservatives: the former saw that now was the time to act if their dream of creating a model nation was not to have been a vain illusion and the United States to lose their prestige; the latter were anxious to build up a strong central government. The masses awaited the outcome, once more curious and divided.[111]

In May, 1787, a convention composed of the leading spirits and the best citizens of America met at Philadelphia to work out the basis of a new constitution. All the states were represented. Washington, Franklin, Jay, Hamilton, Madison, Gouverneur Morris, Charles Pinckney, Rufus King and the famous jurist Wilson were present, together with many others. A battle immediately broke out between the little states and the large ones, both parties holding out for statutes that would accord them a more important part in the future federation. The smaller states feared that they would be oppressed by the larger ones and did not want a constitution which would bind them too closely and give the central government too much power. The larger states were in favor of a confederation whose bonds should be solid and whose government strong. One can easily imagine how involved the debate must have been in view of this opposition between the two constituent elements of the Union as well as the latent conflict between temperaments and political ideals. This latter conflict led a democrat like Madison, because he represented the interests of a large state, to support the contentions of a Northerner, a conservative and a partisan of a strong central power, like Rufus King or the illustrious Alexander Hamilton. Therefore, from an intellectual, as well as a political, point of view, this famous constitution, which for more than a century seems to have assured the happiness and prosperity of the United States, must be considered as a series of compromises. From an intellectual point of view, the discussion was very confused.

From 1783 on, the great authority in matters of law and political theories was Montesquieu. He was continually quoted and sometimes read, for the newspapers and magazines published extracts from his works. But this brilliant and subtle mind, so full of devious turnings, had not left a clear impression on all intelligences. Therefore we find everybody citing this authority during the Constitutional Convention and making use of him to defend contradictory theses.[112] The patriots in general agreed as to adopting Montesquieu's idea of the three powers, as they applied it, and his concept of a strong government founded on the balancing of these powers. During the Philadelphia convention, the partisans of a strong government, who in reality considered monarchy as the best form of government and the English monarchy as the most perfect type of monarchy, abandoned hope of imposing this view and, fearing public opinion, scarcely mentioned the idea of royal government.[113] Alexander Hamilton was one of this group, and probably John Jay also. It is possible that the almost religious cult for democracy which had spread at an equal pace in France and in America, each country influencing the other, had something to do with this discretion on their part.[114] This hypothesis is the more reasonable since Hamilton and Jay were both anxious to establish a form of government which should resemble as much as possible the English government as seen through Montesquieu.[115]

The democrats, for their part, remained moderate. Franklin made a motion, which from an intellectual point of view was a most important one, that the two houses be replaced by a single house and that the system of checks and balances modeled on Montesquieu's English doctrine be replaced by a purely democratic system which would have given the people as much direct exercise of power as possible. This was the concept of Turgot and of the French democrats who had served in the American Revolution. Franklin failed in this project. He next tried to provide that the chief magistrate should not be paid, thinking thus to avoid intriguing for the place and to safeguard social morality. He cited the example of the members of the French parliament but without success; but in the course of this discussion he had several times the opportunity to speak of monarchy, and this he did in no uncertain terms.[116] At the critical moment when slavery and its suppression were being discussed, Dickinson, who was in favor of abolishing it, held up the example of France, who had forbidden the keeping of slaves in her territory.[117] In these divers discussions, Franklin and his friends yielded, because they did not attach much importance to a written constitution, which it had been promised, moreover, would be revised. They deemed that the important thing was to establish harmony, to form a solid body as a nation and to maintain the democratic spirit. They said that this text, mediocre as it was, would be a good basis for discussions and changes in the years that were to come. Various elements were involved in the controversies which then took place in order to get the various states to accept the Constitution. First of all, it cannot be denied that a strong impulse was leading the colonies toward a union. For a long time the Americans had dreamed of a federation. But it is interesting to note that the example most often cited as an example of a federation is the one which Henry IV had hoped to establish among the European countries.[118] This example had certainly a strong appeal in religious and liberal circles in the United States. On the other hand, the enemies of the new Constitution seized on everything that Montesquieu says against large republics, while the partisans of the Constitution replied that the only way to avoid meriting the just condemnations which Montesquieu directs at large republics was to unite in a federation, a form of government that Montesquieu praises positively.[119] The Anti-Federalists turned to Turgot and laid stress on his criticisms of the system of two houses. In the great and splendid pamphlet which Hamilton, Jay and Madison[120] published in defense of the work of the Constitutional Convention, all three of them cited the example of France and the works of French authors, each according to his personal tendencies; Jay used such references to show the dangers that foreign interventions and intrigues held for trusting and weak republics; Hamilton used Mably to set forth the advantages of confederations in that they prevent neighboring nations, which otherwise would be jealous of each other, from doing each other harm.[121] Hamilton harked back three times to the worthy Abbé. As for Madison, he quotes extracts from Montesquieu to prove that a confederation unites the advantages of a republic with those of a monarchy. He also employs Montesquieu's commentaries to show that there should be a division of powers. Thus, on the capital points of this controversy, this great pamphlet made a pretense at turning to French authorities and following their counsels.[122] Just how much sincerity there is in all this is hard to say; but in any case, we have here a clear proof of the prestige that the French theoreticians enjoyed in the best circles in America. At the Massachusetts convention, Bowdouin recalled Montesquieu's praise of federations in defense of the new Constitution. At the Pennsylvania convention, Wilson cited Necker and Montesquieu at length to show that the proposed Constitution was indeed in accord with the true spirit of democracy. In Virginia, the plan was criticized as being apt to lead the United States into a régime as despotic as that of France. France was often brought into the discussion because the enemies of a strong federation claimed that the generosity of France made measures of defense and an army unnecessary. In South Carolina the same tone prevailed. Finally, with great difficulty, after much hesitation, further compromises and a definite promise that Congress, as soon as it met, should amend certain articles in such a way as to render them in keeping with the rights of man, the Constitution was ratified.[123]

Throughout this great political battle, the participants never ceased to think of France, to feel the influence of her philosophers and to seek to realize the ideal that

France had set for the United States. The democratic party, which seems to have been defeated, had in reality made concessions only in order to put the struggle upon more propitious grounds.

*
* *

Franklin, the unrivaled leader of the democratic party, was soon to pass from the scene; but he was to keep the halo that France had placed about his head and which the New World beheld at first with astonishment and later with admiration. Franklin's activity during the war had been heroic, able and sovereignly efficacious. His efforts during the years from 1782 to 1785, the date of his leaving France, however less conspicuous they may have been, were not less fruitful. An object of universal veneration, he afforded France the example of the perfect sage, whose head victory could not turn and who, in fact, took advantage of it only to do more good and to return to his intellectual works. He continued to attend the Lodge of the Nine Sisters, to be present regularly at the sessions of the Academy of Sciences and to carry on researches whenever he had time for such work.[124] He concerned himself with his harmonica, stoves and means of avoiding seasickness; people wrote him letters on these and other practical subjects, which, far from appearing as laughable as they would perhaps seem today, afforded the public a high idea of his altruism and increased his renown as a saint and a benefactor of humanity.[125] A new edition of *Poor Richard's Almanack* was brought out, and the poet Feutry wrote an appendix for it, entitled *Commandements de l'Honnête Homme*, the purpose of which was to show that these maxims should be taken as a moral code. With his support, the Lodge of the Nine Sisters undertook a campaign for the moderation of legal punishments.[126] The president Dupaty was the leader of this campaign, and Franklin contributed to it by publishing a letter at the end of the pamphlet entitled *Observations d'un Voyageur anglais sur la Maison de Force de Bicêtre*. He showed how unjust it was to punish theft with death, while in time of war privateering was encouraged. He also condemned military discipline as being worse than slavery. The author of the *Observations d'un Voyageur anglais* was Mirabeau. This was not the first time that these two revolutionary leaders had collaborated. Mirabeau had already published at Franklin's request *Considerations on the Order of Cincinnatus*. The group of Franklin's friends formed a sort of philosophical headquarters-staff. Madame Helvetius's salon continued to flourish and to reflect the ever-increasing brilliance of Franklin's glory. He inspired the masses with enthusiasm, and this impression did not displease him.[127] He tells how moved he was on seeing the poor peasant from Provence who had sent him an incredible pamphlet whose style was as bad as its spelling. This man's name was Gargaz. He had come on foot all the way from his province to see Franklin, and when he saw him, he threw himself at his feet and begged him to persuade the King to give him back his place as schoolmaster, of which an unjust condemnation had deprived him, and to submit to the King and the United States a project for a Masonic union between all the sovereigns of the world in order to assure peace and fraternity.[128] Franklin, moved to tears, interceded in his favor. And Gargaz redoubled his efforts and had his memorandum published. In the highest society, the admiration for Franklin ran quite as high, and people were astonished at the brilliant career of this man who, arriving in France as an outlaw, had become the minister of a victorious people allied to France. In 1783, the Duc de Croÿ brought his grandson to see the great man in order that he might behold "a man whose glory as creator and liberator of his country and as founder of its laws and sciences, is above any comparison that might be made." [129] When Franklin left Paris, it was in one of the King's own litters, which Louis XVI had lent him in order to lighten the weariness of the journey. Later he wrote to his friends in Paris wise and useful letters, little philosophic fables and charmingly tender messages. They saw from the newspapers that the throngs at Philadelphia had followed the example of those of Paris. Franklin's entry into Philadelphia was a triumph. His friends in Paris published a pamphlet which described in detail this ceremony with which a nation of philosophers welcomed the great man and it affords a spectacle of a philosophy apt in the things of this world, potent in the domain of the mind and imbued with a pious moral.[130]

Franklin's departure from Paris was almost coincidental with the publication in book form of the *Lettres d'un Cultivateur américain* (1784) which was published without the name of the author, but which was the work of Hector Saint-Jean de Crèvecœur. Crèvecœur who belonged to an old and honorable Norman family, had early emigrated to Canada. After having tried his hand at various trades, he had settled in the region that lay to the west of the English colonies. He had bought land and cleared a farm where he seems to have lived happily until the outbreak of the American Revolution. Then, obliged to choose between the English government and the new American government, he was in a cruel dilemma until the cruelest moment of all, when the Indians, allied with the English, drove him from his home. In his flight, he was captured by the English, who put him in prison at New York. His plight stirred the pity of an English officer, who enabled him to escape.[131] He returned to France, where Madame Houdetot, who was herself of a Norman family, took him under her protection. At her house he met Franklin and all the other leading spirits of the Americans in France. He began to show his writings—rather ingenuous but colorful and moving accounts of what he had seen and suffered in America. His friends helped him to revise and correct this work, and he set about having it published. It achieved the greatest success of the times. It consists of a series of anecdotes dealing with American life, the life that was the least known and had the greatest attraction, the life along the frontiers, at the edge of the great forests where one encountered wild beasts and Indians in red paint, savage but kindly and spontaneous. Crèvecœur depicted the rustic, wild and solitary existence, one neighbor is all of society and man loves his neighbor with a Scriptural love, the long winter days when there were no other pleasures than the crackling fire and the assembled family, silent but warm with tenderness. He pictured summer in the virgin forests, the frightful serpents, coiling and fighting among themselves. He let the reader share the happiness of a peaceful family, in whose existence the most outstanding events were the children's birthdays, when the father planted a little tree that in twenty years the daughter would contemplate with pride. He also depicted in gentle and glowing terms the devotion of the good old slaves. He described with horror the tortures that certain whites inflicted on these unfortunate creatures. But he dwelt especially on the cruelties of the English in America, and he gave the highest and most stirring appreciation of the Quakers' adoration for God. These noble and kindly Quakers, for whom death and ridicule were but petty annoyances, and who, steadfast in their morality, simple in their living and unwavering in their virtue, refused with equal determination to kill, to steal or to take oaths. Crèvecœur had not tried to make a novel out of his book. He gave it out as he had written it, at random. The reader felt that it was a confession, a perpetual effusion. Some passages had a tender and touching charm of which something remains even today. I quote as an example this one page, from among many others, which describes a rustic holiday. Crèvecœur celebrated it every year to commemorate the transplanting of a sassafras that he had found in the forest and placed in front of his house: "The anniversary of this little event has been solemnized regularly ever since by a gay though simple little celebration to which we invite our neighbors. Our celebrations, as you know, are always accompanied by dancing, or rather, we have no celebrations without joy, and our pleasure is always showed or expressed by dancing. There is no holiday in the year that I enter into with more pleasure. Our good negro, December, who for years has been too old to work, is still musician enough to preside at our dances. He enjoys telling the neighbors who attend the celebration all the details of this little event; he does not overlook the part that he took in helping me to pull up and transplant the sassafras, and my daughter loves him all the more for it. As soon as she is married, he says, he expects to divide his time and pass six months of the year at her house. 'Because,' he says, 'although I can no longer do anything myself, I know more than any other negro about how things should be done, and old December's advice will be as useful to my master's daughter when she is married as my care was in her early childhood when I used to carry her into the fields and leave her, wrapt in my overcoat, to sleep at the foot of a tree while I worked. I loved her as if she had been a little black girl.' " [132] Such pages went straight to the heart, and no one could help admiring them and shedding tears on reading them. This book, therefore, had a deep and serious success.

The public was deeply stirred by it. In France, as in America, the best magazines and the most popular newspapers reprinted pathetic passages from Crèvecœur. They praised his sincerity and admired his piety which did harm to none and seemed to be the highest type of true religion, that of the heart, just as his characters seemed to be the worthiest type of man gone back to Nature without having sacrificed his dignity.[133] It is in Crèvecœur that we must seek the concept that was held about 1785 of the "state of Nature" as the philosophers would have had it. The savages were never considered except as a curiosity, and people were delighted at seeing a white man, and a Frenchman, practicing true spontaneous virtue. The book inspired both prose and verse. In 1787, a comedy in prose by Gorgy, *Les Torts apparents*, sought to put on the stage this simple but pure life of the American colonists. The year before, in *Le Voyage d'Amérique*, L. Bourdon had sung the mystic aspects of the United States:

In them we still behold the sons of Nature. . . .
By contemplating Her and heeding Her commands,
They have through righteousness made simple all their laws;
Her hand it is that traced throughout their codes sublime
The reasonable bounds to all authority.
Behold a refuge where the never-changing law
Is to be just and kind, devout and tolerant. . . .
Where, piously constrained by Nature and Her laws,
Each household, in the throes of pious ecstasy,
Worships the One Supreme according to its lights;
Where, of their sacred rights by our sages made aware,
A people lifts the prayers of Truth and of Mankind
Before the holy shrine of Joy and Liberty
Unto Philosophy, the priestess of their God;
And where the humblest turns for redress of his wrong
And Righteousness is held the peer of daring deed.
Such is the sanctuary America shall be,
And Louis's high renown shall never pass away.[134]

This zeal was not confined to literature. On every hand there was talk of setting out for America. Lanthenas thought of going and tried to persuade his friends the Rolands to go with him, but they hesitated on account of their age, they said.[135] Nevertheless, they thought seriously of founding an agricultural colony in America. Bernardin de Saint-Pierre, the author of *Paul et Virginie*, was fired with the same idea and went so far as to gather information as to the feasibility of the scheme.[136] Benjamin Constant,[137] weary of Europe and Madame de Charrière, contemplated a similar means of escaping from them. As for the Marquis de Lezay Marnésia, he actually tried to put the plan into execution. A passionate follower of Rousseau, and sincere Catholic and devoted to the King, Monsieur de Lezay Marnésia was weary of the iniquity of mankind and thirsted after the "state of Nature." He longed to see the realization of a moral reform and set out for Ohio in search of it.[138] A large group of noble and courageous souls were pervaded with this particular form of idealism. They had read Rousseau and their minds turned toward the United States.

Their influence would not perhaps have been very wide had not this aristocratic and somewhat chimeric ideal been communicated to the middle and lower classes by one of the most daring of pamphleteers and one of the most consistent forerunners of the French Revolution: Jean-Pierre Brissot. Brissot was the son of an inn-keeper at Ouarville near Chartres. His eager soul and active mind had driven him to literature. In order to have an English air and to make an impression, he had taken the pen-name, Brissot de Warville. From his youth up, Brissot had had serious tastes and high aims. He suffered from having a heart that was eager to believe and a mind that could not be satisfied with the dogmas and faith that others accepted. When the American Revolution broke out, he immediately showed his enthusiasm for America by writing a pamphlet against England. He offered it to Vergennes, who thought it too violent. He found a publisher for it at Neufchâtel. The pamphlet attracted notice, and Morande, who was then editor of the *Courrier de l'Europe*, offered Brissot a place on the staff of this paper.[139] Brissot had found his work and, from then on, devoted himself to it completely. His aim was to lay the foundations for a social and moral reform by means of journalism and the spreading of enlightenment. The task, as he saw it, was a twofold one, and the most important part of it was to consist in substituting new, intelligent and life-giving beliefs for a faith that had outlived its usefulness.[140] Meeting Franklin and later Crèvecœur, whom he encountered at Madame Houdetot's home, turned him more and more in the direction of America. Brissot had harbored the design of establishing at London a "lycée" similar to that which the Lodge of the Nine Sisters had established at Paris, and of publishing in connection with it a periodical which should not only concern itself with the activities of the lodge, but should also strive to spread enlightenment.[141] He had not succeeded in this enterprise; he was drifting with neither work nor aim when one day he came upon *Le Voyage de M. le Marquis de Chastellux*, which had just been published.[142] He was indignant at the tone of mockery which the nobleman affected and at the scorn that he showed for the great truths. He hastily wrote a pamphlet[143] to show that this so-called philosopher had maligned the negroes, who in reality were worthy of liberty and in all ways the equals of the whites, and the Quakers, whose *mores* were pure and whose religion was wholesome since it was both moral and free from superstition. Brissot concluded by asserting that Chastellux had belittled the dignity of man when he claimed that this dignity was of no value in itself but was entirely proportionate to the personal worth of the individual. "All men are born free, equal and independent," he wrote. "It was aristocracy, your prejudice, that ruined Rome." In the name of Rousseau, Brissot proclaimed that all men, free or slaves, are endowed by Nature with an equal dignity. His pamphlet created a great stir. Chastellux was a member of the Academy, an old friend of Voltaire's, and a well-known philosopher. To criticize him was both audacious and dangerous. Brissot's pamphlet, very clear and eloquent though rather lacking in refinement and good taste, won him a public. He allied himself more closely with all those who were looking forward to reforms and trying to bring about the realization of these hopes. In his periodical, *La Bibliothèque de Jurisprudence*, Brissot had given evidence of his philosophic enthusiasm by publishing a sort of prose ode on American freedom and by printing the text of the Constitution of Pennsylvania. In 1786, he and his friend Clavière did more than this: they wrote an essay in refutation of the calumnies against the United States that were being circulated in France and England. In order to give their pamphlet a practical appeal and to reach the middle-classes, they treated the question from the commercial point of view especially and drew attention to all the advantage that France could derive from commerce with the United States. They could not, however, refrain from taking a philosophic glance at the past and future of the Americans.

They praised their tolerance and the liberty of the press that existed in America, and they declared that the new constitutions had regenerated the country and that all of its citizens were working together for the common good. With such an aim, with such enlightenment and such liberty, one might expect miracles from them. Such was the tenor of the essay entitled *De la France et des Etats-Unis . . . par Etienne Clavière et Brissot de Warville*, published in London in 1787. After such a work and the favorable sensation which it roused, Brissot was considered as one having authority.

He frequented La Fayette's house. He collaborated with Bergasse (both of them were seeking a means of banding men together under the pretext of social or scientific experiments, "but in reality to crush despotism").[144] With this purpose, Brissot founded one after another two societies: the Gallo-American Society, which was to promote friendly relations between the two peoples and to seek out everything in America's experience and institutions that might be of use to reform in France; and the Society of the Friends of the Negroes. The Gallo-American Society was made up only of a small group of prominent persons, but all of its members were valuable ones, because of either their ardor or their position. This organization bore a strong resemblance to the Masonic lodges. Like them, it endeavored to bring to accord on great general principles and a wide plan of common action men whom personal interests and petty questions separated. The first members of this society, which was founded in January, 1787, were Brissot, Bergasse, Crèvecœur and the Geneva banker, Clavière, with whom Brissot had become intimate and who shared his aspirations.[145] They set about obtaining and circulating accurate information concerning the Americans and also doing whatever they could to promote abstract morality "without any religious acceptation." They succeeded in attracting a few new members and in publishing a certain number of letters and documents in the *Journal encyclopédique*. Finally, when Brissot went to America the following year, he founded an American chapter of the society and inserted advertisements in the newspapers in Massachusetts and throughout New England inviting good citizens to join it.[146] He met with a certain response; but this semi-secret society whose avowed purpose was the spreading of enlightenment but whose immediate objectives were not precisely defined, was somewhat compromising. In January 1789 it was still going on with its work secretly and with but few members and limited resources. Brissot had more success with the Society of the Friends of the Negroes. He established this society in the early part of the year 1788, it seems, and from the first succeeded in enrolling illustrious and able men in its ranks. The first members were, beside Brissot himself, Carra, Mirabeau, Cerisier, Duchesnay, Ysaru, Valady, Bréban, the Marquis de Bourges, Volney and Condorcet. Péthion and La Fayette joined it in the course of the year, and Condorcet was chosen president. As an argument in favor of freeing the slaves and by way of proving that this step was feasible, the Friends of the Negroes cited the example of the Quakers. They placed themselves to some extent under the patronage of this sect, for they had affiliations with the English Quaker societies whose aim it was to abolish slavery and they used in their own propaganda the pamphlets that English and American Quakers had written on this subject.[147] Brissot's correspondence leaves little doubt that the true object of this society, as well as of the Gallo-American Society, was to spread enlightenment and thus to prepare the way for revolution or reforms in France; but its avowed purpose was so pertinent and the evil it combated so flagrant, that the society itself immediately met with great favor in advanced circles.[148] It grew rapidly and was known in both hemispheres. We still have an interesting letter from Jefferson thanking Brissot for having invited him to join it and refusing. "Those whom I serve have never been in a position to lift up their voices against slavery," he says. "I am an American and a Virginian and, although I esteem your aims, I cannot affiliate myself with your association."[149]

To merit his renown as a Quaker and an American,[150] it still remained for Brissot to visit the United States. Clavière, who was interested in a vast financial enterprise having to do with the redemption of the American debt, gave him the opportunity to go to America and paid the expenses of his trip. Clavière's proposition would enable him to visit the American Friends of the Negroes, to extend the Gallo-American Society, to spread his fame and to earn some money.[151] Brissot sailed with a recommendation from the Minister of Foreign Affairs which La Fayette's protection had procured for him. When the French minister at Philadelphia, Monsieur de Moustier, saw him, he was dumbfounded at the messenger that his superior had sent him, and he told him so. Brissot spoke out brazenly against the Government of France and did not hide his enthusiasm for that of the United States.[152] Boston fascinated him. He was delighted at seeing Washington and finding that their ideas were in accord. Both of them, in fact, thought that a great future lay before the young nation, and they were right. Brissot extended the Society of the Friends of the Negroes, he founded a chapter of the Gallo-American Society, he bought lands, he made arrangements for his brother-in-law to settle in America, he became acquainted with Quakers and gave a more definite form to his own faith—but he failed in his negotiations for redeeming the American debt. And when he saw in an American gazette that the States-General were about to be assembled in France, he hastened back to his destiny.[153]

He brought back powerful weapons for the Revolution. Not that he had made a fortune nor yet enriched himself with warm friendships. He seems not to have been extremely in favor with the calm and prudent

Americans.[154] But he had made a study in revolution. He had faith and a concise idea as to what he wished to accomplish. He attacked the root of the problem of reform in France, and not its manifestations. He could speak to the middle class in a language that it had long been waiting to hear.

Brissot had attempted to realize the dream that Pahin de Champlain de la Blancherie before him had entertained when he established his international institute of learning, that Quesnay had tried to realize through his University, and that one of his friends, Nancrède, professor at Harvard, was to endeavor to bring true by his publications and teaching. But Brissot had had the art of holding public attention and had employed symbols that had wide appeal. A great part of public opinion in France, and that the most active part, followed him. The word Quaker had never enjoyed such popularity before. André Chénier, the one really great French poet of the period, was preparing to glorify the humanity of this sect which, by its virtues, atoned for all the crimes of the Europeans in the New World.[155] Beside Benjamin Constant, Lanthenas, the Rolands and the Marquis de Lezay Marnésia, the famous Doctor Guillotin and his friend Saugrain, the bookseller, weary of French despotism, were considering emigrating to America.[156] A Norman gentleman named Jean de Marsillac, an ex-officer, had just been converted to Quakerism. He set himself up as the apostle of the sect in France, sent memoranda to the King, made pastoral rounds, visited the mother chapter at London, prepared pamphlets for propaganda and contemplated making the voyage to America.[157] People in high society, without leaving their social circles or changing their manner of life, adopted the manners of these "primitives." Old Monsieur de Lescure gave a card-party, and when the playing was at its height, a halt was called while prayers were said and the Bible read. Then the party went on.[158] A little book that was published in 1778 and enjoyed great popularity, *Le Calendrier de Philadelphie*, gives a just idea of this enthusiasm. It is more Quaker than the Quakers. It defines them thus: "Dogmas are for the human mind and morals for the heart. Not believing it possible to bring all minds together under the same dogmas, William Penn tried to unite all hearts in a morality which is everywhere, and always will be, the same among all peoples." This opuscule, after a short preamble devoted to an enconium of the Quakers, whom it represents as a deist and American sect in contrast to the backward and despotic Catholic Church, ends with a long calendar which gives for each day of the year moral precepts of the same nature as those of Poor Richard. This curious warping of Quakerism is intended to make it a better weapon against the Roman Church, which is directly envisaged. Thus, at the dawn of the French Revolution, the religion of the Quakers, which is and was essentially Christian, became in France a sort of deism and a common ground on which all the minds that were weary of dogmas and ecclesiastic hierarchies could meet, pray and range themselves. Condorcet, whose hostility to the French clergy and Catholicism is well known, had not hesitated to rally to this group and make use of the weapon that it afforded. We have seen that he was associated with Brissot in the Society of the Friends of the Negroes. He had also drawn up a model constitution for Mazzéi's book on the United States, in which he set forth once more Turgot's thesis; the absolute sovereignty of the people, the futility of a system of checks and balances and the necessity for tolerance. In his *Lettres d'un Citoyen des Etats-Unis à des Français sur les Affaires présentes*, he upheld the same theories and insisted on the essential equality of all men and France's duty to follow glorious examples of liberty and tolerance that the United States had afforded her.

The most amusing and widely esteemed Parisian newspaper of the time, *Le Journal de Paris*, was a willing means of spreading these ideas and popularizing this attitude; its columns were full of discussions on the Quakers, virtue, the American constitutions and social perfection. Lyons, with its Academy, was also a center of American liberalism. From 1785 to 1788, the *Journal de Lyon* published long and interesting letters from Savary, who had emigrated to America and was cultivating lands in western Pennsylvania. Without having Crèvecœur's ardent sensibility, Savary's letters had a similar tone and present an idealized picture of the New World. A traveler tells of having seen at Lyons in 1788 a poster couched in these terms: "Louis the severe, the present King of France, who has given liberty to the Americans and made slaves of his own subjects." [159]

The center of this movement was La Fayette's hotel at Paris and the house occupied by Jefferson, who did not disdain to dabble in French politics and to give advice. Arriving in France with a fairly vague ideal derived from Montesquieu, Jefferson, under the influence of his philosopher friends, had come to think as they did. He was inclined to believe that free Indians were happier than the subjects of a tyrant. From the first, he had been charmed by the refinement and elegance of the young French nobles, and this impression made him continue to the end to believe that the Revolution would be effected through them and by their efforts. The middle-class he was not acquainted with and he could not therefore estimate its strength. As for the lower classes, he admired them from a distance. He gave them credit for being the least alcoholic people in the world. He pitied certain regions of France for their poverty and filth; but in general, he had the impression that the country was rich and that there were lands in France as well, or perhaps better, cultivated than those in England. Jefferson was an honest man and a generous soul, but his discretion and reserve prevented him from playing the part of a leader in France. He might rather have been a conspirator. And this he was to a certain extent, for he incited to harmony and action the group of very influential young nobles and scholars who admired him and listened to his advice. To the masses he was an imposing and distant figure.[160] Since he was simple in both dress and bearing, his reserve was not held against him. He won wide admiration, and he did more perhaps by his prestige and his discreet counsels than a more striking personage might have accomplished.

As a matter of fact, he was obliged to observe a certain degree of prudence.[161] A powerful and alert group was forming to combat this American and revolutionary movement. In 1788 the *Année Littéraire* and the *Journal de Bruxelles* took a decidedly hostile attitude toward the United States. Jefferson was attacked by the first of these publications for his criticisms of Mably and indecent statements on the subject of religion. This periodical also characterized the current praises of America as "defectuous declamations." [162] The most able and persistent enemy of the Americans during the years 1787, 1788 and 1789 was Mallet du Pan, editor of the *Mercure de France*. Mallet was a shrewd and tireless worker. He was almost the only one of all the pamphleteers who paid any attention to documentation: we find that he had subscribed to the best American magazine of the time. He felt the Revolution coming on and he believed that the only cure for France's ills was a constitution like that of England. The increasing popularity of American ideas dismayed him.[163] He wanted to be prepared to point out the weaknesses of these ideas, and in his letters to the *Mercure* he did this often. In 1788 the revolutionary struggle had already begun in France. The young nobles, stimulated by La Fayette's example, had rallied about him; the Parliaments, resentful of the King's conduct, and the middle-class, grown restless and distrustful, made no secret of their desire to see radical changes brought about in the administration of the kingdom. Almost everybody shared this feeling. The masses felt the need of believing and feeling an enthusiasm and of having a living, applicable faith to replace the ancient beliefs which the philosophic campaigns had destroyed. They wanted the reform in France to be a moral reform. One heard the watchwords, Liberty, Fraternity, Justice and Equality. In the center of these powerful and unformed aspirations, had formed a nucleus which was firing the indifferent and aiding the fervent. It put its faith in a revolution that should follow the example of the United States in its general lines and take as its model the pious, tolerant and social deism that was believed to be one of the attributes of the Americans. It might be said that a sort of Church had been formed between 1783 and 1788 with this ideal as its tenet. Through La Fayette it attained the highest classes, through Brissot the lowest; but all those who had a definite idea of revolution belonged to it. The generation of Raynal and Mably and their ilk, with their groping about and their theoretical concerns had gone by. The fever that was smoldering in the veins of France was a fever of action and mysticism. In the France of 1788 there was already a powerful group of men who believed in the sovereignty of the people and considered man as endowed with certain inalienable rights such as happiness, property, the liberty of thought, of conscience and of commerce. La Fayette, Brissot, Condorcet, Target and their friends had agreed on these principles. Without being consciously republicans, they had rejected the very essence of monarchy, its doctrines and its claims. They tolerated it as an existing condition and did not dream of attacking it directly, for their aim was to break down aristocracy and the Catholic Church and take possession of their social prestige and spiritual power. Such, on the whole, was the attitude of the leading "patriots." It reveals the extent to which they had been influenced by the United States. In fact, although for more than a century people had turned toward England for examples of wise policies and masterly, constitutional structure, although the English Whigs were still circulating pamphlets and essays criticizing the institutions of despotism, it was America alone who had drawn the eyes of the world to the spectacle of a sovereign people, as virtuous and pious as it was free. It was America that had first wakened enthusiasm and faith and brought the world to comprehend the value of fraternity. The ideas that she typified and resumed were old ones, but she was the first synthesis of them, living and worthy of worship.

Although, in all the controversies, Great Britain and the English Whigs had furnished splendid arguments for the reformers, it was the New World that gave them a common soul and drove them into action.

Chapter IV

SPIRITUAL UNION

The importance of American ideas in France from 1789 to 1792, pp. 253-263. Their influence in the States-General and the Constituent Assembly; the *Declaration of the Rights of Man*, the Night of August 4, spiritual communion between France and the United States, pp. 263-276.

After the group of young nobles, the bourgeois who are beginning to be the leaders of the Revolution make use of the American ideal. Brissot's example, pp. 276-286. Franklin's death gives rise to an enthusiastic manifestation, pp. 286-293. With him Quakerism becomes popular and is used as a weapon against Catholicism, pp. 293-296. It is also used to prime republican propaganda, pp. 296-302.

The governments, on the other hand, have difficulty in agreeing, pp. 302-307. This is all the more true since the opposition party in America has rallied to the French revolutionary ideas and uses them as a means of attacking Washington's administration. Washington commences to feel some irritation, pp. 307-314. The Girondists, with their dream of uniting all democracies and carrying on a crusade against England, make the situation even more delicate, pp. 314-321. Genet's mission, though it kindles the masses with violent love for France and her Revolution, angers the American administration, pp. 321-332.

In France the popularity of the United States does not diminish, but Robespierre, in spite of his sympathy with them and his desire to conciliate them, does not succeed in bringing the American government to adopt a brotherly attitude, pp. 332-340. French culture spreads in the United States and has great influence, pp. 340-348. But party conflicts continued and the government was thinking of a rapprochement with England. Behind the spiritual communion of the People, was the opposition of the governments. Revolutionary mysticism prevailed, but it had not succeeded in building up a united faith, pp. 348-351.

The comte de Vergennes had died without having transmitted to his successor, it seems, the maxims and observations that had made him adopt the United States as an ally and friend of France and as an example to the European nations and a basis for a program of internal reforms. Only those who were in his intimate confidence, such as Hennin and some few of his agents, remembered his intentions. They were forgotten by the mass of the public, heedless and distracted by the roar of new events. Vergennes had tried to bring about the union of the French in opinion, government, the army and commerce, by the philosophic and profitable war of 1778, which was to have permitted the orienting of all minds toward new and positive conceptions, political, social and moral.[1] The results, vast as they were, had not had the scope that he had hoped for them; and one feels throughout the latter years of his life an anxiety that his reserve and hesitancy hide but partially. A well-informed pamphleteer has described, in a way that often seems to me to be accurate, inquietude that Vergennes felt during this period. In a pamphlet entitled *Le Comte de Vergennes, cause des Etats généraux* (1788), the author maintains that it was the war in America, its cost, and the current of opinion created by Vergennes and circumstances, that made it necessary to convoke the States-General. This view, which has often been developed since, cannot fail to seem justified when one has followed the activities of this minister from 1774 to 1784. It is probable, however, that

Vergennes never envisaged the assembling of the States-General and a series of reforms like those that were executed between 1789 and 1792. His successor, Monsieur de Montmorin, was far from such thoughts. He did not see very clearly how the United States could be of use to France, and, although he had a liberal turn of mind, he was imbued with English ideas; he scorned the rabble and failed entirely to perceive that the New World was a force.[2] From about 1785 on, and more so every year, the group that was making use of the United States and exploiting their popularity was the party of young and public-spirited nobles who desired a complete remodeling of France and were eager to play the principal part in bringing it about. Their participation in the American war had given them great prestige with the army, the middle class, the Parliaments and the women. Vergennes had made use of them, but they had learned how to turn the arms that he had put into their hands to their own advantage. The Marquis de La Fayette was the standard-bearer of this group. His reception in America had been a triumph. Washington's friendship had been both an inspiration for him to do big things and a guarantee in the eyes of the people of his own public-spiritedness. It was a sort of a school, and when people saw the master, so wise, so strong and so pious, chosen, in spite of his modesty, to be President of the greatest republic in the world, they imagined that his pupil would not fail to seek a like honor.[3] The Marquis de La Fayette, influential at the Court, in favor at the Ministry of Foreign Affairs, rich, young, elegant and skillful in keeping up his popularity, and moreover an honest man, had ostensibly taken over the leadership of the patriots' party.[4] He was in touch with the parliamentarians and in accord with the Protestants, and he kept his former companions-in-arms grouped about him. Any one who was interested in America fell automatically under his protection.[5] He was very close to Mr. Jefferson, who was kind enough to aid him and advise him discreetly. Jefferson's tact and judgment were remarkable.[6] He did not as yet know France well, but he loved her deeply, and he had social and philosophic theories which allowed him to judge and understand her.

Jefferson and La Fayette were very close friends. Jefferson was not at all jealous at seeing La Fayette intrude somewhat upon his functions as Minister of the United States at Paris, and Monsieur de La Fayette gladly consented that Jefferson should play the part of Mentor in the great tragedy of the French Revolution.[7] Jefferson, with his fine manners, his learning, his discretion and his aversion for tumult and futile discussions, was an ideal peacemaker. He helped to clear up ideas and to make them practical and to establish harmony between people. Moreover, no one could accuse him of not being democratic enough, and his moral aid was invaluable. It is difficult to determine, through the maze of all the old papers, foxed pages and immature scribblings on the subject, just what the exact rôle and the reciprocal influence of these men were. One always ends up in hypotheses.[8] However, it seems certain that, during the whole of the preparatory period of the Revolution and in the months that preceded the convoking of the States-General, Jefferson kept in steady contact with La Fayette. We have proof that when the States-General began their sessions, Jefferson's house was the headquarters of the patriotic party. They gathered there to discuss questions and, above all, to come to agreements; for Jefferson stressed the need of harmony among all the workers for the Revolution. He deemed that, in order to succeed, the Revolution should be radical in spirit and bring about a total change of ideas, but should remain moderate and progressive in practice. He had confidence in the King. He urged La Fayette and his friends to form a bloc with the people and the King against the privileged classes. La Fayette states that the most important compromises, those which eventually permitted the establishment of a constitution, were gone over and discussed at Jefferson's house. Mounier, Lally, Rabaut, Duport, the Lameths and Barnave came there, and it was there that they agreed to accept the royal veto and the system of one legislative body divided into two parts, which the good Virginian favored so strongly.[9] Thus all those among the privileged classes and the young nobles who had progressive ideas united under the guidance of the Minister of the United States; and this tendency was so general that, even in

Brittany, when the Parliament wanted to rouse the people, they distributed by night more than four hundred pamphlets recalling the American Revolution and the rights of the people.[10] All parties recognized then, and later proclaimed, that the Americans were the model that the revolutionary idealists sought to follow in 1789 and that the whole nation saw in La Fayette a new Washington.[11] This, however, does not prove that the French nation as a whole knew exactly what the nature of the American Revolution had been or what part Washington had played in it; but they felt that there was a great lesson to be learned and were moved by a mystic desire to imitate the Americans and to accept their revolution as a model, a rule and a universal truth. They had faith.

In opposition to the feudal world, which was looked upon with loathing, and the existing institutions in France, from which it was felt that no good might be expected and which the reformers distrusted and hoped to destroy, the United States and their principles and government were a banner and a symbol of hope. People felt confidence in them. They were a badge of good-citizenship for any one who had fought for them and defended them. Thus la Rouërie, in spite of his aristocratic opinions and attitude, was held in respect by the Assembly of Brittany because it was remembered that he had fought in America; and Robespierre consented to receive a noble when he was sure that he had fought for the insurgents.[12] Among the diverse classes and groups who labored together in the preliminary work of the French Revolution, America created a unity, purely idealistic without doubt, but very useful; for it provided a common language and brought about a singleness of purpose, or at least, an agreement to disagree. These somewhat vague aspirations that were accepted in principle and without having been examined closely, as a basis of accord, were responsible for the hours that seem to us to have been the most benign and noble of the Revolution. And these moments are all of them suffused with a tender, chimeric and pious Americanism.[13] In 1789, Roland, who was later to become minister, said in an address to the Academy of Lyons, "The moderation of the American government creates as zealous patriots as were ever the most famous republicans; the moderation of their principles renders them akin to the most complete cosmopolites, in their universal benevolence; and their situation ought to make them most powerful commercially. . . . The charm of their philosophy alone, which is so fit to win hearts, seems to lay the foundations for the triumph of their opinions and promises some day to gather many peoples into their consoling religion." In the *Annales patriotiques* for November 3, 1789, Carra, who was not moderate in his views, exclaimed, "O happy people, you have neither monopolists nor ministerial charlatans, neither aristocrats, archbishops nor bishops; and even Nature overwhelms you with her benefits." Even the theater, which reflects in a general and attenuated way the preoccupations of the moment, gives us an idea of what the United States meant to the Parisian in the street in 1789. In *La Vallée de Shénandoah en Virginie*, a comedy in two acts in prose interspersed with couplets, we find a virtuous colonist of Virginia welcoming European emigrants fleeing from oppression, and the regenerated Europeans love each other without forgetting that they were formerly serfs and lords.

The pious Virginian treats his slaves as friends, and the whole cast sings:

> Here there reigns equality,
> Here man to man is brother,
> And in this land reigns no false pride
> Adored in every other.

On his estate, the Virginian has a bower where every evening the family and the servants gather to chant the evening prayer, the hymn of Liberty:

> O thou whose glance puts base flattery to rout,
> O thou whose name alone doth blanch dark tyranny, etc.

Then any one kisses and marries. There is in this play, as in the speeches of Roland and Carra, no accurate knowledge of America; but nobody minded that. During these years of enthusiasm, people seldom read books that had been published earlier. Only the tender Crèvecœur and the sensitive Brissot seem to have had many readers, but Chastellux, Hilliard d'Auberteuil, Mazzéi (who did have some knowledge of the country) and Mandrillon, who had accurate commercial data, were no longer read. Raynal, himself in favor of the French Revolution, was no longer being read as generally as he had been from 1770 to 1789. Henceforth the *Lettres d'un Cultivateur Américain* set the tone. The books of travel that were published were translations from English and presented a picture of the United States deformed by spite and bitterness. Auburnet in 1790, Smith in 1791, and Long in 1793 dwelt on the ferocity and cruelty of the Americans during their war for independence and showed them in unfavorable contrast with the goodness and gentleness of the Indians. This sort of thing, however, was not calculated to be unpopular in France, then in the midst of one of the most violent crises a nation has ever come through. But these accounts, aiming as they did at the picturesque and at evoking colorful impressions, contained nothing that might give a precise and just picture of the United States in 1789. The only other source of information that lay within the reach of the French people was even more vicious. American land agents were beginning to flood Paris, London and Hamburg with prospectuses vaunting the virtues of the American people and the inexhaustible fertility of their soil.[14] Brissot had engaged in these speculations without much success and had been obliged to give them up in order to look after more important affairs. But Joel Barlow,[15] the great American poet, was in Paris and succeeding only too well in finding innocent and childlike souls to whom it seemed quite natural to buy lands along the Kentucky or the Ohio without inquiring either whether the lands really existed or whether the Indians were still in the habit of living there and making their rounds in quest of scalps. These speculators were so successful that the resulting scandal has not been forgotten even unto this day. An American company sold certain nobles and members of Parliament superb lands along the Ohio River in Kentucky. Lezay Marnésia and Duval d'Esprémesnil became the patrons of the enterprise, and the colonists set out. The party was made up mostly of liberal aristocrats who were seeking a land of "true liberty," of liberty according to Rousseau. When they arrived they found that the lands were almost inaccessible, situated in a dangerous and savage region, and that, what was more, the company that had sold the lands did not own them. The wretched emigrants would have starved to death had it not been for the charity of other colonists who took them in, and the pity of Congress who gave them other lands.[16]

The departure of these members of Parliament for the Scioto gave rise to violent discussions and much gossip. The patriots, the party then in power, thought it unbecoming of them to leave France in the midst of a period of reorganization. They were indignant at seeing aristocrats seeking refuge in a land of liberty. It was not, in fact, one of the least strange spectacles of this astonishing period.[17] This incident shows how far confidence in the United States and their ideal had penetrated into all classes and made an impression on even those who considered themselves above the giddiness of the times. Lezay Marnésia, the disciple of Rousseau, emigrated to America with the aid of Duval d'Esprémesnil,[18] one of the first proponents of resistance to absolute monarchy, and in company with officers of the royal army and nobles from the Court of Versailles. It was, in short, an example of old society seeking sanctuary in the temple of Liberty. The concept of liberty that these men entertained was not identical with that which inspired the revolutionists; in certain respects these two concepts were even opposite, but the United States formed the link between them. Chateaubriand's voyage bears further witness to this state of mind. Chevalier de Chateaubriand was at that time young, ambitious, a dreamer and favorably inclined toward the new ideas. He scorned the rabble and thirsted for the unknown. He was fond of the sciences, poetry, solitude and melancholy. Too proud to intrigue for the favor of the King or the plaudits of the mob, too ardent to brook delay, filled, like every one else, with a reverence for America, he yearned to go to this far-off land and to learn to know it, to try his fortune there and to associate with the heroes of liberty—a desire similar to that which had inspired Brissot. He needed only a reason or a pretext for the voyage. The learned Malesherbes furnished him one: the search for the Northwest Passage of which there was much talk at the time.[19]

There was something absurd in the idea: Chateaubriand was not a sailor, a geographer or a botanist; and he had no special knowledge that could possibly contribute to the success of the undertaking. However, as pretexts went, it was honorable in the eyes of his contemporaries and well calculated to impress posterity. Everything indicates that when Chateaubriand set forth he was much more eager to see Washington and the battlefield of Lexington than the Pacific Ocean. He harbored in his heart the revolutionary piety that was beginning to transform France. He combined the enthusiasms of a philosopher with those of a Christian. Later he made his choice, and from this fine frenzy whence others had derived the cult for a democratic republic, he brought forth French Romanticism. It was a loophole, a means of accepting the ideas of the times by adapting them to his own personality. Chateaubriand's voyage to America links him closely with the French revolutionary group and their ideas.[20]

Whenever it could show that it was following an American precedent or an American principle, the patriots' party was sure of having with it the weight of public opinion. It owes its most brilliant successes to principles from across the sea. There has been much discussion as to the origin and sources of the *Declaration of the Rights of Man;* but a text by Mounier, who assisted in drawing up this famous document, shows without ambiguity what the prime considerations of the authors of the Declaration were at the time.

The disciples of the Anglo-Americans in the assembly had set forth the pretended advantages of a declaration of rights, and most of the deputies did not foresee the consequences of such a step. Those who were acquainted with the American declaration of rights thought that it would be possible to bring about the adoption of one which would avoid any statement that might tend to favor license." [21] He repeats in two places that he yielded to those who were in favor of a declaration of rights only after much discussion and because they continually cited "the example of the American states." In fact, the idea was in the air. For a long while, La Fayette had thought of a declaration of rights, and he had gone so far as to draw one up, it seems, and had discussed it with Jefferson.[22] Four editions of the Constitutions of the United States had already been published since 1778.[23] Now these constitutions were usually preceded by a preamble which asserted and summed up the principal rights of citizens and of men. The most famous of these was that of Virginia, which contained formulas concerning Tolerance and Liberty that have become famous. Thomas Jefferson was believed to have written it, and it is only natural that those with whom he was associated should have read and discussed it.[24] Throughout the early months of the year 1789, pamphlets were circulated calling for a declaration of rights and holding up as an example the American documents.[25] At least three of these have come down to us. All three of them are grounded on the idea of a social contract and equality between men. We find in them the same doctrines that are set forth in the preambles of the American constitutions. This similarity of views and aims leads us to accept these words of La Fayette as typical of the opinions of the times: "The era of the American Revolution, which may be regarded as the beginning of a new social order for the entire world, is, properly speaking, the era of declarations of rights." [26] There was a feeling that every revolution should have its declaration of rights, just as every religion should have its catechism, and that the reform of society ought first of all to be internal, to correspond to a moral renascence and to be based on common aspirations and beliefs. The function of a declaration of rights was to formulate this credo and to reveal to the citizens what was already engraved in their hearts.[27] Attempts have been made to fix a distinction between the American declarations and their French equivalent and to consider the former as statements of fact and of rights that were already acquired and recognized, and the latter as a program of reforms. Such a procedure is arbitrary, for in every case, the declarations of rights were documents whose value was abstract and which, even in America, proclaimed principles that the government reserved the right to apply more or less rigorously as it saw fit. In both cases, in France as in America, one may say that the declarations of rights were acts of faith of a political religion. Their original model is much less this or that English text than it is Moses and the Twelve Tables.[28] Just as the Decalogue aims at defining the duties of men toward God, so the American and French revolutionists intended to define the duties of men toward Man. As for the details of the French declaration, most of them are inspired by the preamble of the Constitution of Virginia in 1776, as might be expected; but here and there we find articles more closely related to this or that other American constitution which was more explicit as to some particular right that had been mentioned by the writers of the time—Mably, Jefferson, Mazzéi, Brissot or the sage Franklin. The very religious and democratic Constitution of Massachusetts and the Constitution of Maryland, a state which Raynal had already praised as early as 1770 for its tolerance,[29] are the two other documents that seem to have been copied systematically by the French constitutionalists.[30] A detailed comparison of the French *Declaration of Rights* with the preambles of these three constitutions brings out a striking resemblance. Let us consider for example Article I of the French document: "Men are born and remain free and equal in their rights. Social distinctions can be founded only on common utility." Is it not similar to the American texts: "All men are by nature free and independent, and have certain inherent rights, of which, when they enter into a state of society, they cannot, by any compact, deprive or divest their posterity" (Virginia Bill of Rights, Art. I). "All men are born free and equal, and have certain natural, essential, and inalienable rights" (Constitution of Massachusetts, 1780, Article I). Mr. Jellinek's book shows that the same is true of every paragraph.

It seems therefore that the discussion may be considered closed. From the historical as well as from the ideological point of view, we have proofs that the *Declaration of the Rights of Man*, drawn up by the French Constitutional Assembly, was suggested and continually influenced by the examples of America. Undoubtedly the rigorous, logical and concise form that the French legislators gave it, the extraordinary fervor that surrounded its conception, the quarrels that it stirred up and the victories that were won throughout the world in its name, made it to some extent a universal moral code and conferred upon it a spiritual and material importance that the American declarations never had. But this changes nothing as to the question of its origins. We must add that in this domain of general phrases and great sentiments it would be futile to seek to attain rigorous precision. Since 1770 the principles embodied in the French and American declarations had been considered by many people as recognized truths. The legislators of Europe and America invented nothing; even in their phraseology there was nothing strikingly new. All of these doctrines are descended from the Reformation and the ideas that it spread through France, England and America at the end of the sixteenth and the beginning of the seventeenth centuries. To say who was the first to defend these democratic doctrines would be impossible. Even before the Renaissance, were there not philosophers during the Middle Ages to uphold them? Thus an almost unbroken chain links these theories with those of the ancient republics. Nevertheless, America was the first country whose soil gave them shelter and whose people put them into practice, while in Europe they were still being discussed vaguely, abstractly and obscurely. Roger Williams, when he proclaimed the right of liberty of conscience in Rhode Island, was the initiator of the entire mystic and democratic movement of the eighteenth century. He was the first to define in a social contract the right of liberty of conscience, and his phrases contained the germ of all the declarations that were drawn up subsequently. In 1776, the intellectual achievement of French philosophy during the entire century, the sentimental and pious attitude that Rousseau and Raynal had adopted and, finally, the discreet instigations of the French minister undoubtedly gave Jefferson the idea of drawing up the Declaration of Independence of the United States in a grandiose and dogmatic tone. These were the sources of his daring, but he was satisfying first of all a religious need and following an American tradition. In 1789 it was clearly recognized in France how very American the whole idea of a solemn declaration of rights was; and bringing about the acceptance of the project was one of La Fayette's triumphs. The monarchists always blamed him for what they considered his impertinence in taking over from a small, democratic country with no past, indefinite formulas that could have no application to a great monarchy.[31]

Still another of his initiatives seems to have been suggested to him by America and his desire to play the part of a French Washington: the National Guards. As long as he remained in command of the National Guards, La Fayette continued to hold up before his soldiers the example of the Americans. He endeavored to have the skeleton of this organization composed of veterans who had served in America.[32] He tried to inculcate into them the spirit of the militia that he had commanded in 1778 and 1779. He did not fail entirely; and when his faithful National Guards saw him in danger, they remembered his exploits in America. A scrap-book that was made by one of his friends, a member of the National Guard in 1790, has come down to us. Three-quarters of this little book is made up of citations having to do with La Fayette's conduct in America. It tells of his glory in the New World, of all that he did for Liberty and how well he understood her, and of how he came to be loved and worshiped by the sons of Penn.[33] His brother-in-law, the Vicomte de Noailles, was to have his hour of glory. In a book written at the time, Cérutti claims that, if La Fayette was responsible for the success of the American Revolution, it was the Vicomte de Noailles who, in the night of August 4th, completed and terminated the revolution in France.[34] For a long while in the secret councils that were held at his house, Jefferson had urged La Fayette and his friends to break away in a signal fashion from the nobility, to go directly to the people and the King and rule with the support of these two forces. In the eyes of an American, the existence of privileged classes was incompatible with that of Liberty.[35] We have seen how Mirabeau in 1786 used his polemic against the Order of Cincinnatus as a weapon to attack the principle of heredity. Jefferson, without being as violent (for he was a wealthy Virginian, a slave owner and a man of prudence), accepted in principle the same doctrines and asked only that they be applied with discernment.[36] The young nobles and prelates who in that famous night swayed the decision of the Assembly were led by Noailles and La Rochefoucauld Liancourt, who was also thoroughly under the influence of America.[37] Noailles had been, with La Fayette, one of the first to want to set out for the New World. La Rochefoucauld Liancourt had lived and grown up in a circle that was whole-hearted in its enthusiasm and labors for the Americans. The manner in which they accomplished their act, their willing self-sacrifice, the spontaneity of the whole Assembly and the impression that this step made everywhere—all this went hand in hand with the concept that these young men held of a peaceful, benevolent and brilliant revolution, such as the American Revolution had been for them.

In the course of the year 1789, the patriots' party, still united in appearance and already divided in reality, conducted itself in conformity to the principles that it had been proclaiming and holding up as American since 1783. To obtain action, to assure success and to win favor, it made use of the example of America. It carried this system far. For instance, it was said at the time that the names of the French departments had been chosen in imitation of the Americans, who named their states and counties for their geographical characteristics.[38] This party tried to give its entire conduct the appearance of disinterestedness, piety and morality which, along with Franklin, Washington and Penn, was considered the mark of true republicanism. On the whole, the public recognized them as faithful to their model.

The impression produced in America was similar. The American nation, which until now had been interested in France especially because of its upper classes and its culture, and had known only a limited number of the *élite* of its population, suddenly discovered France. It was no longer the learning of the French philosophers that was admired, but the nation as a whole. The Americans were delighted and proud at finding traces of their own influence and the memory of their high deeds at every point of the Revolution. It was with rapture that they recognized the unity of principles and mysticism. No matter to what group they belonged, they were carried away by this enthusiasm. Fenno, a Federalist who had founded the *Gazette of the United States* and was very close to Jay, Rufus King and all the traditional enemies of France, wrote in his number for April 18, 1789:[39] "The Revolution of America, it was very clearly predicted, would have a great influence upon the public affairs of the European world, but the most sanguine advocates for the liberties of mankind could not have anticipated those surprising events, which have already transpired to distinguish the annals of the present age. Our generous and magnanimous ally, the French nation, in their publications upon laws, government and Freedom discover a noble ardor in the best of causes, and the following communication will show that under the best of Kings they are on the eve of establishing a new and free Constitution." In all the states and in all the newspapers in 1789, one finds a considerable number of news items concerning France which, in spite of the unflagging activity and shrewdness of English propaganda, were unanimous in praising France, her efforts and her new government, and in recognizing all this as a product of American influence. Of this there could be no doubt, since "the Marquis," who was so well known over here, was leading the movement over there.[40] The newspapers of the most remote towns in the United States from Vermont to Georgia began publishing two or three times as much French news as they had in the preceding years. They sometimes printed at great length extracts from speeches by Moreau de Saint Méry and, more especially, from the speeches of Rabaut Saint-Etienne; and they inserted pages from the great French writers on liberty—Voltaire, Necker, and Mirabeau. In most of the papers there appeared articles on the Bastille and poems in which the taking of the Bastille was celebrated and compared to the former struggles in America. A profound and sincere joy was felt. There was no condemnation for any one except occasionally for the privileged classes; and blessings were heaped upon the heads of the King, La Fayette, the patriots and the army.[41] America received incoherent masses of news items that were difficult to understand because they came from London in batches. In winter there were sometimes two weeks without any newspapers whatsoever, and then they would arrive in bales at a time. Sometimes the last mails arrived first and then there would be gaps that no one knew how to bridge over in the information that was received. But public opinion never faltered, it saw immediately that the revolution was drawing the two countries together, making them more alike and uniting them in spirit, intention and faith.[42]

More anxiety was felt in governmental circles. England was bringing pressure to bear upon them, and they felt the influence of a strong nationalist party that wanted to have no relations with Europe and could not bear the thought of Europe setting herself free.[43] In their opinion it was impossible that these enslaved nations should be ripe for liberty. But Jefferson was vigilant;

his active pen presented the French Revolution in the most favorable light and dwelt on its similarity to the American struggle for independence. When he returned to America at the end of 1789, he was able to expose in person all that he had seen, and, by his speeches and his sincerity, he made a profound impression on all classes of American opinion and especially upon the opinion of those who were in power.[44] Moreover, the French minister at this time, the Comte de Moustier, was an energetic and talented man gifted with a knowledge of character. When he arrived in the United States, Moustier was not favorably inclined toward this nation of bourgeois; but prolonged contact with the American people and its politicians convinced him of the excellent qualities of the nation. It is true that Moustier had a hobby: his dream was that France should regain possession of Louisiana. His motives were purely patriotic, but the idea was ill timed. Moustier often wrote about it to Montmorin, who seems to have paid little attention to the project, for he had neither the time nor the means to do so.[45] Public opinion was not interested in the idea, and the attitude of such people as were acquainted with it was generally hostile.[46] Moustier wanted to take back Louisiana, not out of hostility to the United States, but because of the weakness and incompetence of Spain. He thought that the Mississippi Valley, under a King of France who was a good friend to the United States and would open up the navigation of the river to them, would be prosperous and could not but further French influence in the New World.[47] In spite of this project, of which he talked too much and which was highly displeasing to America, Moustier became friendly with Washington, who had just been unanimously elected President of the United States. He was able to see what Genet unfortunately did not perceive—that Washington was a great man and a wise one, that he was well disposed toward France and held an absolute dominion over the American people. With his support, France had nothing to fear from the United States. Washington was a sincere friend of France. His great soul was capable of gratitude. He had seen the French soldiers fight, suffer and conquer, and he was not one to allow it to be said that France had acted only in her own interest. He knew too well what the war for independence had been. Therefore his friendship for Moustier and confidence in him were both deep and useful.[48] He thought, and he said, that a community of principles as well as of interests would hold the two peoples together forever. There were fewer of Jay's supporters in the new Congress which was composed of elements who had not kept the spirit of the former Congress. The fact that the new régime in America was simultaneous with the Revolution in France also suggested an agreeable comparison, and the roads that the two nations were following seemed to be parallel.[49] Every one in America accepted and approved the President's policy of friendliness to France, and even

John Adams himself, who had come back to America disgusted with England, seemed to accept it.[50] The clergy and the former Tory classes also seemed to be coming around to this attitude. Moustier received a visit from the pastor Jedediah Morse, who gladly consented to insert several passages furnished him by the French minister in his geography; and his whole book, the only work of its kind that had as yet been published by an American, was very friendly toward France.[51]

*

* *

La Fayette, as commander-in-chief of the French National Guards, profiting by the support and advice of his great and old friend Washington, the President of the federal republic of the United States, seemed to loom up as a considerable moral force; and in the latter months of 1789 he might well have had the impression that the two worlds, sincerely united in spirit, asked nothing better than to work hand in hand. He was justified in hoping that his fondest wishes were about to be realized. In the eyes of the world, he had succeeded in a most daring and chimeric effort to find a common ideal for an enormous and scarcely populated federal republic and a European kingdom of twenty-six million inhabitants.

La Fayette wanted to remain at the head of the revolutionary movement. He devoted hours every day to keeping up and developing his popularity, but he was neither a great orator nor a gifted organizer.[52] His idyllic and moderate conception of a revolution that should be a succession of spontaneous effusions, reciprocal concessions and religious rejoicings was soon to appear silly and irritating. Behind the young nobles who had at first led the attack against absolute monarchy, new groups and new classes, eager for action and victory and filled with a feverish unrest, were pressing on. When one compares the enthusiastic and altruistic tone of a La Fayette at the beginning of the Revolution with the harshness of a Brissot or a Madame Roland, one quickly comprehends why La Fayette and his friends could not long be the leaders of this formidable movement.

Their aspirations were too vague and too theoretical; their religious enthusiasm was too superficial. With them, the need to believe and to feel was a vogue. In the ruder, more ardent and more sincerely religious spirits, of whom there were so many in the French middle class during the eighteenth century, the revolutionary flame was to burn more intensely and kindle everything about it. These cultured, energetic and impassioned commoners had soon felt that the Revolution could not take place without them, and they set themselves to the task of carrying it on for themselves and by themselves. They had much more to look forward to and to gain; they were less trammeled by the past, and the class spirit that united them constituted a vital force. This spirit gave every word and act a sharp, clear value, while the young nobility seemed to be strolling along through a revolution painted by Boucher. The enthusiasm for America and the hopes of the early months of 1789 had at first been a bond between these two groups of patriots; but the discussions at the Assembly and the necessity of coming to an agreement on a definite program brought about a most complete rift between them. In the course of these quarrels, the young nobles allowed the advantage of their moral prestige to slip away from them. Little by little their American laurels were withering. They had come to be looked upon as schemers bragging of past and dubious services in order to usurp a place to which their lack of zeal did not entitle them. They allowed the shining ideals of reform which they had cherished at first to become tarnished, and their American theories and zeal now seemed to be mere phraseology.[53] It is not a little surprising to see what constant and incoherent use the moderate monarchists made of the United States in 1789 and 1790.

During these two years, newspapers and pamphlets were continually holding up the example of the Americans and discussing its value. There was not a single journal but spoke of it; and some of them, such as Mirabeau's *Courrier de Provence*, Brissot's *Patriote français* and Mercier and Carra's *Annales patriotiques*—made mention of the Americans in every issue. Two translations had just revived the interest of such discussions:

John Adams' *Davila*, which was a most incoherent and vigorous defense of moderate aristocratic constitutions, and especially of the English Constitution; and the *Examination of the Government of England* by Livingston,[54] a brief and violent pamphlet which, in the name of pure democracy, took up the defense of Turgot's thesis and condemned the system of two legislative bodies as being a useless impediment to the machinery of government and one that rendered popular control too vague. This book was a source of perplexity to the monarchists and the neutrals.[55] It was published at the moment when the discussion of the division of the legislature into two bodies was at its height. Mounier, Lally and Bergasse were endeavoring to prove that the separation of the three powers and the establishment of a legislature consisting of two houses were general and universally recognized principles. Livingston's book and the stir that the most ardent patriots proceeded to make about it placed the conservative revolutionists in the annoying position of being obliged either to come into conflict with American influence or to compromise. Mounier attacked the Americans, Lally said that Livingston had failed to understand.[56] The controversy became more complex and obscure every day; the same examples were cited in support of contradictory axioms. In the end, the system of two houses came to be looked on more and more as an aristocratic English device and out of keeping with true American usages. The idea of having a single house became a moral principle and a proof of confidence in the people. It was linked with the person and the cult of Franklin, who had been the protagonist of this idea at the federal convention of 1788 and during his entire stay in France.[57] By not having been willing to yield on this point in time, the constitutional monarchists lost much of their prestige as "Americans." They came to be considered as "English." They accepted this classification and began criticizing the American Constitution, with no other result than to make themselves an object of hatred or scorn. Mounier, who was the frankest of them, suffered the most.[58] La Fayette did not commit himself and was given the benefit of the doubt. When the question of assignats came up, there was a similar battle of arguments and pens. It was true that the United States had made use of paper money and that its use had been of assistance to them during their great struggle; but they had ended up in partial bankruptcy, and their paper money did not enjoy too enviable a reputation. Those who were opposed to the use of paper money in France now had a chance to utilize the example of America to disparage paper money and thus to bring about a division among the revolutionists. It would be no exaggeration to say that more than two out of every three of the pamphlets on the question of paper money cited the example of America.[59] The supporters of the monarchy took this means of trying to turn to their advantage the American legend, of which they perceived all the benefits and weight. The *Gazette de Paris* for September 13, 1790, for instance, quotes Paine's pamphlets against American paper money during the Revolution and adds: "In spite of so many attributes, gifts and virtues, in spite of the genius of a Washington, a Franklin and an Adams, the value of American continental money fell off ninety-five per cent. Yet America was a virgin nation, closer to Nature than any other, and more favorably disposed toward the usages and daily barter of men whose needs are modest and who know no other luxuries than those born of the advantages that they have at hand." To this the patriots replied, with the greatest respect for America, that the situations were in no way parallel, since America was at war in 1776, her territory was invaded, and she offered only vague securities. Moreover, they continued, what ruined the American notes was the shameless way in which they were counterfeited at London in order to injure the credit of the insurgents, but France would be able to prevent that and, Cérutti added, Congress had just given France secrets for manufacturing them that would guarantee absolute security.[60]

Whenever the conservatives and anti-revolutionaries could find an example of anything that smacked of aristocracy or prudence in America, they immediately published it.[61] They made use of the fact that the Americans did not have universal suffrage and had laid down strict conditions for eligibility; we find this argument in several pamphlets published in 1789. Later the great powers that the federal Constitution accorded the President were used to support a demand that the King be given at least a similar power. When the critical question of the veto was raised—a question that did the constitutionalist cause so much harm by dividing its supporters, both sides adduced the American veto; and we must admit that in this case the example of the United States savored more of monarchy than their French friends allowed.[62] It became a regular procedure with the supporters of the King to quote from authentic or non-existent American sources. In 1789 the Abbé Morellet had published over Franklin's name an *Avis aux Faiseurs de Constitution*, which was intended to show that popular opposition to the government did not prove that the government was wrong or that its form was defective. About the same time, letters purported to have been written by Washington to La Fayette concerning the revolution were being printed and circulated. In these letters the American Fabius was supposed to say, "You have badly devised both your interests and the proper limits for the liberty of a great kingdom." [63] In its number 114 for 1790, the *Journal général de la Cour et de la Ville*, edited by Brune and known to be in the service of the Court, published an authentic letter from Franklin to his friend Le Roy asking for news of himself and expressing regret at the alarming news from France. "I fancy that natural philosophy is receiving but little attention at the present time," he wrote, "and that the voice of learning is with difficulty heard in the midst of all your troubles." This phrase and others of its ilk annoyed and hampered the revolutionists greatly; it was evident that the *Journal de la Cour* had played a master stroke.[64] This victory was followed up; the example of America was most often used as a means of contrasting the moderation and kindliness of the great American revolutionary leaders with the violence and party-split of their French counterparts. La Fayette was continually under attack for his ambition, which contrasted unfavorably with Washington's modesty. The moderation of Franklin, who reserved judgment on everything and wished to impose nothing by force, was often held up. Examples of American probity were also accumulated to confront the French legislators and convict them of their own unworthiness.[65] This was a maneuver in the campaign of the aristocrats, but was also pleasing to the masses; and it was decidedly dangerous to do anything that swelled the prestige of the Americans, for despite all nice distinctions, discussions of America always turned to the profit of the democrats. Some few details favorable to a strong government might indeed be found in the American Constitution, but nothing could refute the fact that the United States had created or propagated a new spirit and that this spirit was one of fraternity and fervent democracy.

Beyond the monarchists, who were trying to turn the

American moral concepts to their own advantage, and the friends of La Fayette, who were endeavoring to remain at the head of the revolutionary movement by means of this morality, the bolder patriots were taking up their position and making more and more their own the ideas, the sentiments and the enthusiasm that the American war had brought forth. There was no question but that the best weapon against Catholicism and its hierarchy was this nation where no religion, so it was believed, was recognized by the State and where priests had no other activities than preaching and doing good. All quibbles and questions of detail were effaced by the fact that the Americans had been able to build up a strong religious spirit without accepting the Catholic dogmas and almost without retaining any vestige of traditional Christianity.[66]

Before 1789 there had already been talk of the intelligent piety and social zeal that it quickened among the Americans. Voltaire had been one of the first to write about the religion of these democrats and "primitives."[67] The establishment of the liberty of the press made it easier to talk of this religion, and the conflict occasioned by placing the clergy on a civil basis rendered the discussion the more poignant. The monarchists, needless to say, did not want to be drawn into this question, and La Fayette avoided as much as possible any precise expression of his beliefs and his attitude toward the Church. This line of conduct was dictated by the respect that he still felt for the King, his desire to reconcile all tendencies, and a real lack of religious concern. His attitude was none the less displeasing to a great many of the patriots, and La Fayette lost thus much of the esteem that he had enjoyed as a free-thinking, frank and bold, American spirit.[68] Where he hesitated, others dared. Brissot's book, *Nouveau Voyage dans les Etats-Unis*, was a curious mixture of material details and religious feeling. The underlying theme of the book was faith in the ideal of the "natural man." "The prosperity of a society," says Brissot, "is always in proportion to the extent of its liberty; and liberty is always in inverse proportion to the extent of the powers of the government." He described the tolerance of the Americans, the simplicity of their clergy, who were worthy and well behaved because they led a normal life instead of being, as the French clergy was, condemned to "an artificial and immoral existence." Brissot showed the United States not only as having liberty, prosperity and a religion without dogma, but also as being very close to the "state of Nature." In sincere admiration he exclaims, "The potato! There is the food for the man who wants to be, and is capable of being, free!"[69] For, he goes on to say, it grows everywhere without being cultivated. And so it is with the man who lives in this happy state which satisfies his instincts and at the same time develops in him neither evil nor artifice; he can no longer be forced, there is neither coercion nor punishment possible for him.

In America everything is simple and rustic, and the *mores* have escaped contamination. Brissot offered his book to the French public in the hope of bringing his fellow-countrymen to an appreciation of the importance of *mores* and inciting them to acquire such ways as should naturally make for liberty. "Without private *mores*, there can be no public *mores*, no public spirit and no liberty," he says.[70] The ardent appeal and fearless initiative of this pamphleteer was the signal for a sort of crusade. There was much talk of *mores* and of the Americans as an example of *mores*. Rabaut cited their example in his orations in favor of the Protestants. The patriotic newspapers and even the anti-revolutionary organs had constant recourse to the United States for standards by which to judge the *mores* of the public men of France.[71]

This morality became a matter of mystic devotion. It took on this aspect even more markedly when the death of Franklin allowed him to be almost deified and canonized as the first "republican saint." As long as he had been alive, there had always been reason to fear that, in spite of his silence and discretion, he might express personal opinions and might not be in accord with the views of those who wanted to make use of the Franklin legend. His life could add nothing further to his glory, and his words might have been detrimental to his cult. His passing was greeted with grief not unallayed with enthusiasm. All of the French leaders endeavored to adopt him as a patron saint and to pass as his disciples. On learning, during a session of the Assembly, that Franklin had died, Mirabeau mounted to the rostrum and pronounced a few impassioned and grief-stricken words that stirred the whole assembly with emotion: "The sciences owe Franklin their tears, but it is Liberty—it is the French people who should mourn him most deeply: the liberty that we enjoy he aided us to attain, and the sparks of his genius glow in the Constitution that is our boast. . . . He went down to the grave gently with the thought that Liberty, spreading everywhere, was going to better mankind—for it was above all with the betterment of man that he was concerned. Even to the brink of the grave, he continued writing moral text-books for his compatriots." The Assembly decided to go into mourning for thirteen days.[72] It accepted the gift of the busts of Franklin and Washington which were offered by Houdon (June 18, 1790).[73] This was only the beginning of the great ceremonies in honor of the holy man. On June 13, the Duc de La Rochefoucauld Liancourt pronounced a eulogy of Franklin before the Society of 1789. With great solemnity of words and warmth of sentiment he extolled Franklin's activities as a propagator of enlightenment in the New World and forerunner of French liberty.[74] He furnished details that were both interesting and new to the French public, concerning the religious unrest that Franklin had felt in his youth and all that he had done (by means of clubs, newspapers and libraries) to create a deist center at Philadelphia. He lauded the idea of a single legislative body and attributed its adoption in France to Franklin's influence. "This great idea alarmed the legislators of Pennsylvania, but he succeeded in reassuring half of them and finally brought about the adoption of this principle which the National Assembly has made the basis of the French Constitution." The Society of 1789 approved this discourse so sincerely that they passed unanimously La Rochefoucàuld Liancourt's motion that they go into mourning in honor of Franklin. They also decided to place a bust of Franklin in their assembly hall with the inscription: "Homage rendered by unanimous vote of the Society of 1789 to Benjamin Franklin, Object of the admiration and regrets of the Friends of liberty." [75] The Commune of Paris, not to be outdone in public spirit and piety, held on July 21, 1790, in the Rotunda a great funeral ceremony in memory of the Sage of Pennsylvania; and the Abbé Fauchet, chaplain to the King and one of the most prominent leaders of the revolutionary clergy, pronounced a sonorous discourse that was intended to resemble Bossuet's funeral orations on a more republican and grandiose tone. This eulogy of Franklin is one of the most amazing bits of oratory of the period. "I praise a great man," Fauchet said, "a founder of American liberty. I praise him in the name of the mother-city of French liberty: I am a man also, I am free, I have the approval of my fellow-citizens—it is enough: my words will be immortal." Then he set forth the glory of Franklin in his triple rôle as friend of humanity, liberator of America and "one of the foremost builders of our sacred Constitution." Fauchet reviewed the life of this son of a candle-maker, who through his wisdom and goodness had become one of the greatest men in the world. He spoke of the benevolent and religious spirit that had guided him throughout his life. "That religion of righteousness through which one loves God and men, and which, according to our Holy Scriptures, is the only one pure and without blemish, was in Franklin's heart and in his works." [76] He quoted *Poor Richard*. He represented Franklin as preparing the American Revolution to be "a great example to the Universe." He compared the liberty of France with that of the United States and declared: "I have said that the first great nation to possess the fullness of liberty is the Anglo-American nation; the first nation to prepare to enjoy the perfection of liberty is France—and doubly therefore is Franklin the foremost lawgiver of the world." His grandiloquent peroration ends thus: "Venerable sage, august philosopher, founder of the felicity of thy native land, instigator of the liberty of France, prophet of the brotherhood of mankind, may gentle happiness embellish the end of thy career. . . . Thy last regards beheld about thee a happy America, beyond the sea, a free France, and in the near future the salvation of the world. The United States, thine own family, have wept for the Father of their Republic;

France, thine adopted family, honors the generator of her laws; humanity, thy great family, will revere thee as the universal patriarch who made the alliance between Nature and Society. Thy memory belongs to all centuries, thy remembrance to all peoples, thy glory to eternity." [77] This panegyric embodies the ideas that were associated with Franklin and the United States. It is typical and was accepted as such at the time. It was greatly admired, although some malicious journalists, jealous of Fauchet, tried to make it appear ridiculous.[78] On June 14, the Friends of the Revolution and of Humanity, assembled at the Café Procope, had honored the memory of Franklin by holding a funeral ceremony. The chandeliers had been covered with crêpe and the second room of the café was hung with black draperies; on the door were written the three words, "Franklin is dead." At the end of the hall a bust of Franklin had been placed on a pedestal and crowned with oak leaves; below it was the word, "Vir." Two cypresses arched their somber branches above it, on each side of it were globes and maps, and below it was the symbol of immortality, a serpent biting its tail. There was an oration and bread was distributed to the poor.[79] On November 13, 1790, the Academy of Sciences met in a public session to mourn its former collaborator. Condorcet spoke in the name of this illustrious company and, weaving together all the ideas that were dear to him, he made a crown of glory for Franklin's head.[80] He showed the young Benjamin, so eager to set men free, to reform them and to find a new moral discipline, that Pythagoras alone might be compared to him. He depicted the noble American character, so simple and so great, so near to Nature, arriving at the essential verities, not by a violent effort of the mind, but by the calm development of enlightenment in an atmosphere devoid of prejudices; and this gave him the opportunity to compare Franklin with Socrates. He exalted the progress of human intelligence, in which Franklin had been one of the foremost artisans and which is the base of all revolutions that are for the good of humanity. Although he profited by the occasion to descant incidentally in favor of a single legislative house, it is upon this principle of the amelioration of the world through education and rational forms of worship that Condorcet placed special emphasis. Such was the tribute that the Academy of Sciences laid upon the Sage's grave.

There was praise for Franklin from every quarter. Marat said bitterly: "Yes, it is time that the nations cease to bow down before the idols of fortune and learn to respect their defenders, to cherish their benefactors, to feel their loss and to make public display of their grief. But is it for the most redoubtable enemy of public liberty to propose the lament for an apostle of Liberty?" [81] He and the true patriots were pained at seeing the profane honor their hero. Brissot cried out: "Genius, simplicity, goodness, tolerance, modesty, unflagging ardor for work, love of the people—this is what Franklin represents, these are the qualities that a man must unite within him in order to aspire to such an altar as his." [82] To admire and worship Franklin became a vogue. A contractor had bought the stones from the Bastille and had them carved into little statuettes of Franklin which sold well and at a good price.[83]

The true worshipers were indignant at seeing his image displayed among puppets and billikins in shops and public squares and along the quais.[84] The famous phrase, "Poor Richard," was used for the title of newspapers and pamphlets. The name of Franklin was given to printers' shops and political clubs, for example the *section* of Bordeaux. The Jacobin Society had had his bust placed in its assembly hall.[85] On the boulevards a play entitled *L'Imprimeur ou la Fête de Franklin* by Desfontanes was produced.[86] At the back of the stage was a bust of Franklin that a pious printer had placed there to do homage to the great man. The printer, unjustly accused, succeeds in proving his innocence and the play ends with these lines in memory of Franklin:

> If you would say who among men
> Upheld the torch of honor,
> Who, like Rousseau, showed us how
> To become what we are,
> Ah! it is Franklin, ever Franklin,
> Whose name shall be our song!

But even more interesting than these rather frivolous manifestations is the reëditing of Barbeu-Dubourg's

Le petit Code de la Raison humaine, which is dedicated to Franklin and inspired by him. It is an attempt at a moral catechism based on the principles of Rousseau's *Contrat social*, the natural goodness of man, tolerance and democracy. In 1791, important fragments of Franklin's memoirs, a charming little book full of the charm of simplicity, frankness and artlessness, finally appeared. All the contemporaries looked upon it as a sequel to Rousseau's *Confessions*. This book has not the fullness of Rousseau's work, but it abounds in humanity, grace, and sound wisdom. It comes nearer to the average man without losing any of its admirable qualities. It is more moral and more practical. It corresponds very satisfactorily to the common concept of Franklin as the prophet of the gospel of Nature.[87] The worship of Franklin had become almost a sect in itself. The Lodge of the Nine Sisters continued to hold its meetings and, during the year 1790, published frequent eulogies of Franklin, among which was Milhaud's very long but fairly gracious ode wherein we find the lines:

> The ashes of Franklin are covered with tributes,
> The prayers of the poor, the shepherdess' flowers,
> The chains of the slave and the tears of the world.[88]

Two groups had set themselves up as the direct disciples of Franklin: the Quakers, grouped about Marsillac, Bonneville and the Cercle Social; and the Girondists, of whom Brissot was the leader and Roland the schoolmaster.

Jean de Marsillac, whom we have already mentioned in connection with his activities in favor of the Quakers in 1788, sought to take advantage of circumstances to develop Quakerism in opposition to Catholicism and make it the revolutionary religion. With the concurrence of the English Friends, he organized a thorough propaganda. He wrote and published under the auspices of the Cercle Social a *La Vie de Guillaume Penn* (1791) which had a wide circulation and was well received. On this subject, the *Mercure de France* of June 2, 1792, said, "The Quakers are the only people who have given the world an example of society founded entirely on morality." The *Journal général de l'Europe* praised the Quakers for "having been able to ally so much amenity with Christian mysticism." During this same period, Marsillac also published, at Amsterdam, *Le Principe ou la Règle de Vie des premiers Chrétiens*. In the beginning of 1791, judging the moment to be propitious, he came to Paris with William Rotch,[89] the representative of the Nantucket Quakers living at Dunkirk, to whom Louis XVI had been so kind. His purpose was to present to the Assembly a request that the Quakers be authorized to practice their religion according to their lights, that they be exempted from military service and from taking oaths, and that they be allowed to appear before the Assembly without removing their hats. Brissot, Grégoire and Rabaut Saint-Etienne acted as negotiators between the Assembly and the delegation of Friends. They arranged for a splendid ceremony. They chose a time when Mirabeau was presiding, for they deemed him friendly to the sect. Demeusnier, Chapelier, Lameth and, of course, La Fayette lent their support to the Quakers, who were accorded a cordial reception, a superb discourse by Mirabeau, and an invitation to be present at the session, but no very definite concessions.[90] Marsillac, however, had not wasted his time. He gave a series of lectures on the morality of the Quakers, visited a great many of the deputies and became a close personal friend of Grégoire's. These two even entertained the project of establishing a large Quaker seminary in the Château of Chambord and even took steps toward putting the project into execution. On every hand one heard it said that, as soon as the Constitution should become effective, thousands of Quakers were going to immigrate to France.[91] There was talk of organizing the Quaker sect at Paris, and in a letter dated June 1, 1792, a housewife wrote to her son: "If you meet a Quaker, kiss the hem of his garment for me. Among all the multitude of men that covers the face of the earth, there are none, to my way of thinking, who do more honor to humanity. Since I know them only through pictures, if you meet any of them anywhere, tell me about them and let me know whether the descriptions of Voltaire and the other philosophers have not flattered them." [92] The Masonic and mystic club, the Cercle Social, which was also called "The Universal Confederation of the Friends of Liberty" and whose organ was *La Bouche de Fer*, a very daring sheet edited, it seems, by Bonneville, the grandson of Racine, made use of many Quaker ideas. The Abbé Fauchet, the principal orator of this club, was inclined toward a sort of Quakerized Catholicism inspired by Penn.[93] The aims of the club, which was a federation of peacefully inclined and righteous friends, were close to the ideal of the Quakers. *La Bouche de Fer* for the month of October, 1790, declared: "The civil laws of these veritable human beings have more merit than all those which are at present in force on this earth, and I hope that both worlds will conform to them." This propaganda was not without result: people came to consider the words "Quaker," "American" and "free" as synonymous; and, especially in Girondist circles, which were daring and inclined to favor novel undertakings, there was thought of importing the customs and ideas of Quakerism into France on a large scale. Bancal des Issarts, Lanthenas and Brissot had such a plan, and there is mention of it in Madame Roland's correspondence.[94] *La Feuille villageoise*, the great rural newssheet, which the Girondists employed to effect the gradual de-Christianization of the countryside and whose editors were at first Cérutti, and later Ginguené, printed encomiums of the Quakers on several occasions and described the workings of their religion and expressed hopes of seeing it flourish in France.[95]

In the realm of politics, the Quaker religion was the starting-point of the first and most daring republican propaganda in France. The very fact that the American constitutions, all democratic and republican as they were, were constantly being republished could not fail to have an influence, especially since this publishing was the work of men like Demeusnier, who was a member of the Assembly. He produced in 1790 a volume entitled *L'Amérique indépendante* which was a *résumé* of the various constitutions of the United States. In 1791, Delacroix accomplished a similar work by his *Constitutions des principaux Etats de l'Europe et des Etats-Unis de l'Amérique.* His book went into three editions. It was impossible to speak of the United States without mentioning the word "republic," and it was not a question of republics crowded into a limited territory laden with antiquated institutions, like Venice or the Swiss cantons. The United States were a federal republic with immense resources, modern ideas and a considerable population that was continually growing and affording striking examples of its vitality. In the highest society, certain groups openly proclaimed themselves as republican and cited the example of America: Madame de Tessé, La Fayette's aunt, was an avowed republican in 1789. The Trudaines, Madame de Guibert and their friends held like views.[96] But it was very difficult for Frenchmen and revolutionists to speak of a republic in 1789, because public opinion was not yet prepared to desert the King. The nobility, out of a spirit of chivalrous fidelity, would immediately have rallied in his favor, and it is probable that the bulk of the nation would have followed them. The cahiers of 1789 indicate no widespread republican sentiment. The most radical revolutionists were silent on the subject; but to speak constantly, as Brissot did, of the moral and social superiority of the republics of the New World over the kingdoms of the Old World was in itself a bold stroke and an excellent preparation for further temerities. Condorcet was a republican at heart, but he attacked the monarchy only through the praises that he lavished on the United States. To be able to undertake a campaign in favor of a republic with any hope of success, it was necessary first of all to show how antiquated the very principles of the French government were, and to found a new code and accustom public opinion to the idea of a new régime. The Declaration of the Rights of Man proclaimed the new social and legal code. It made no provision for the King—no more than the American declarations had made for him. The controversies about the Declaration and the Constitution, without bringing up the question of a change of government, had led to the discussion of the comparative advantages of various forms of government, and, as early as 1789, we find startled monarchists arguing the drawbacks of a republic and the advantages of monarchy. The example adduced is always that of the United States.[97] Inevitably the United States brought up the question. In the course of the great ceremonies in honor of Franklin of which we have already spoken, the republican spirit and morality of the great man were extolled without any opposing voice being raised. In 1791, the United States played a more decided part in the spreading of republican ideas. Thomas Paine, who had come to France the first time in order to see the philosophers and to meet the members of the government that paid him, had come back to Paris again. He had become acquainted with the group of Brissot's friends and the men who later were to become the Girondists. He was an avowed republican and followed Franklin in favoring a single legislative house. When Burke published his pamphlet on the Revolution, Paine refuted it in a work entitled *The Rights of Man*, wherein he set forth a complete theory of democracy. Analyzing the origins of power, he showed that every government reigns either through the domination of superstition, the threat of force or the result of a contract—the only legitimate form of government. Now in order that the contract be respected, the executive should be neither strong nor independent of the people. It is the height of absurdity, Paine showed, for the executive office to be hereditary. This pamphlet, dated 1791, was widely read in England and in France. Although it did not pronounce the word republic, it could lead to no other conclusion. When the King had fled to Varennes, Paine and some of his friends took the lead in calling for his destitution and the transformation of France into a republic. Villette and he were the only ones to dare come out frankly at a moment when every one else was still hesitant for fear of an unequal struggle. It was at this time that Paine's famous controversy with Siéyès took place, with the American upholding the principles of republicanism and the Frenchman those of monarchy.[98] Brissot was just beginning to unfold his real views and expressed himself as being in favor of keeping the King for the time being, not that a kingdom was the best form of government, but for the sake of prudence and in the expectation of something better. Even his friends cried out that Paine was mad, but his example gave courage and showed how much could be said with impunity.[99] Everywhere people talked of him. In the elections for the Convention, Paine was elected in four departments, although he was known only through his writings and his personality was not a winning one. The royalists in 1791 were highly incensed against the United States; they accused them of being the initial cause of the Revolution and of continuing even now to incite the country to a change of government. Morris met with this state of mind among all his friends. The accusation was not altogether justified, for neither the government nor the American leaders had done anything to convert France to republicanism. On the whole, they had confidence in Louis XVI and would not even have wished for his downfall. But the moral propaganda that had been going on in France since 1775 had indeed brought about a profound change of principles, beliefs and purpose in a large and influential class of society. The mystic respect for divine right had gradually been supplanted by a reverence for the rights of the people and spontaneous morality. These principles had appeared to be compatible with the old order of things provided it were modified; but, in proportion as they took shape and as their applications were extended, it became more apparent that they were replacing and conflicting with the past and called for a complete remodeling of society. This is the path that La Fayette, La Rochefoucauld Liancourt, Brissot and all those who were concerned with the liberation of the world were following more or less consciously and sincerely. Some of them, like La Fayette, contented themselves with stopping halfway and found refuge in a sort of sentimental and intellectual fallacy, which did embarrass them greatly, since their interests demanded it; but more violent, courageous, and deliberate spirits had in a short time followed the road to the end. They were aided by certain Americans, notably Thomas Paine and Joel Barlow. In 1791, Barlow published an essay, *An Address to the Privileged Orders*, in which he attacked feudalism as accentuating inequalities in an immoral way, the Church as being inevitably intolerant and obscurant, standing armies as a weapon of despotism, and the tendency on the part of governments to try to increase public revenue. He condemned all these institutions of the past for corrupting the soul of man, and he called for their suppression in the name of morality. At the same time he offered the American public a virulent and mystic poem,

The Conspiracy of Kings, in which he portrayed with great lyric power the alliance of all tyrants against the light. Paine and Barlow were translated, read and discussed. They gave definite shape to the many impressions and sentiments that the tales of America and the enthusiasm for things American had engendered, but their influence was less important than that of a Franklin or a Jefferson. It was effective only in making the French public pass from ideas to actions.

*

* *

In France the United States were judged by the two or three great personalities, Franklin, Washington and Jefferson, who were known in Europe; there was no clear concept of the people themselves or of their importance. Therefore, the moral and spiritual collaboration of the two countries had difficulty in finding any practical means of manifestation. To conciliate the opposed interests of two peoples is always a delicate task. It was all the more difficult in 1789-1792 because, in France as well as in the United States, the newly established parliaments were eager to display their zeal in defending the national patrimony. Both countries, confronted with a grave economic and financial crisis, sought to make use of all their resources and were ready to renounce none of them. It was all very well to approach the study of general problems with the most high-minded idealism: material questions were always solved according to the law of the least effort and sacrifice. Such relations as existed between merchant and merchant, and government and government, from 1789 to 1792, were far from being happy ones. True, private citizens exchanged friendly letters on Franklin and the French Constitution; but the United States put a tax on French ships entering American ports, and the French Assembly, after bitter discussions that were none too friendly to the United States, refused to facilitate the importation of whale-oil and American tobacco as had been requested. The Assembly was governed by questions of local interests and failed to take into consideration the danger of weakening the commercial bonds between the United States and France. They had spoken so much of the virtues of the Americans that they had forgotten that they were also tradesmen.[100] This young government should have been handled with skill and tact, for English intrigue was rampant in America at the time; but the Assembly was not aware of this. The Minister of Foreign Affairs was too closely occupied with internal politics to keep himself informed on what was happening so far away from Paris. Monsieur de Moustier, who was a good minister and had been able to win the friendship of Washington, was not sent back to America. Various circumstances and the vile little intrigues of Gouverneur Morris, an American businessman and politician who was then residing in Paris and who, while selling land, found time to meddle with everything else, made Montmorin decide not to reappoint Moustier to the American post.[101] The pretext was that Moustier was too much of an aristocrat. The real reason was that the English faction in America, with whom Morris was closely allied, had instructed him to prevent Moustier's return to America because they were afraid of his intimacy with Washington.[102] He was replaced by Otto, who was intelligent but had neither authority nor material means at his disposition. In 1792, La Fayette, at the prompting of Morris,[103] had secured the appointment as minister to America for Monsieur de Ternant, who had shown great courage in the American war but was of an uncongenial nature and, despite intellectual qualities of a high order, lacked ability, dignity and forcefulness.[104] Moreover, what could he possibly have done, since he was entirely out of touch with his superior, who never wrote to him, and the American newspapers kept announcing the most frightful commotions in France?

France treated American trade with severity. She talked vaguely of a new commercial treaty that she was willing to negotiate with the United States on a most generous basis; but the disorganization of the Ministry of Foreign Affairs prevented the realization of these projects. The intelligence and propaganda services in America had been allowed to run down at the very moment when France had the greatest need of systematic support from her friends.[105] Without doubt she had in

Jefferson a faithful and intelligent friend, but his temperament, which was tactful rather than combative, and the disadvantageous position in which his long absence from the United States had placed him, together with the fact that he was on good terms with neither Hamilton nor Morris, both of whom were very influential, rendered his task difficult.[106] Washington, although he was well-disposed toward France and glad to see her adopting free institutions, was unfortunately in close relations with Gouverneur Morris and had complete confidence in him. Now Morris held a most equivocal position in Europe. Agent for his friend, Robert Morris, who had a grudge to settle against the French farmers-general and visited his wrath on France as a whole, and a friend of John Jay's also, Gouverneur Morris had gone to London to negotiate commercial conventions with England; but it seems that his real intent was to seek an alliance or at least to lay the foundation for one. Disappointed at having failed in his mission, he returned to France filled with an ambition to play an important part in affairs. He studied the situation, visited La Fayette, whom he already knew, Madame de Staël and Montmorin, and decided that he had a chance to distinguish himself in becoming the secret agent of the King and Queen.[107] Morris scorned the populace and did not believe in monarchy. Perhaps he felt some sympathy for Louis XVI. Even this is open to doubt. It is certain, in any case, that he made friends in both camps. The turn of his mind and his ambition led him to draw a sharp, clear and amusing picture of what he observed, but one that was cynical and tinged with pessimism. He represented the revolutionists as scoundrels and their opponents as fools. And it was from him that Washington received all the information on which his judgment was based.[108] Since at the same time the Southern and Central states were being invaded by a throng of poor people, French Creoles fleeing from Santo Domingo, then in the grip of civil war and flames, the Americans could not help being impressed by the somber news from Europe which coincided so well with what they themselves saw in America. Franklin in 1789 was already dismayed at the rumors of massacres that came from France and implored his friends to assure him that they were untrue.[109] The English propaganda, on the contrary, exaggerated them wantonly. A little newspaper in Massachusetts,[110] for example, reprints from an English paper under the date of December 15, 1789: "France seems at present to be in a state of complete anarchy. The authority is tossed about among the three orders. . . . But in view of the important part that women are taking in the revolution in France, a correspondent opines that the poor Frenchmen are in danger of being reduced to a government of petticoats. He asks the public which is to be the most feared of the three forms of government: monarchy, aristocracy or petticoats?" In 1790 many American papers said more simply: "Great troubles are coming about and continue to disturb many parts of France. A great many good citizens are falling sacrificed to this momentary rage, massacred by unprincipled brigands and ungoverned hordes." [111] At New York the *Weekly Register* for September 3, 1790, called the government of France "a mad and despotic democracy." Washington had received as a present from La Fayette a key to the Bastille which he had been disposed to accept as a harmless little souvenir.[112] But with the news and rumors of massacres, the struggle against the Catholic Church and the freeing of the slaves, America began to be more alarmed. The French Revolution ceased to be a remote and interesting adventure in which one might feel a certain pleasure at having a spiritual part and a certain glory at having served as a model. It became a domestic problem. It loomed up as an immediate danger. Morris' letters, Jay's intrigues, the wave of refugees, the English dispatches—everything combined to give an alarming aspect to this France whence there now came only grandiloquent messages and starving refugees. The rich and the clergy were commencing to be frightened, and the press was beginning to mutter.

A new situation was developing. Until now the political parties in America had been on the whole a continuation of the English parties. The American Revolution had been begun originally by the English and American Whigs to fight against the Tories in both countries. During the whole duration of their war for independence, the American patriots considered themselves as members of a single party and spoke of themselves as Whigs. In the years that followed the treaty of 1783, with the necessity of clearing up the situation and the problems that resulted from the treaty, this feeling underwent only a gradual change. In general, the American leaders remained faithful to the doctrines of English liberalism, but they came into contact with the radicalism of the French philosophers, and some of them came to have a more concise concept of democracy. Franklin was one of these. Nevertheless the looseness of the federal organization and the confusion which still reigned in national life prevented the setting-up of solidly unified parties with general platforms. In 1787 and 1788 when the Federal Constitution was discussed, it seemed as though two parties were about to take shape—the Federalists, who were in favor of the national ideal; and the anti-Federalists who battled for the protection of state-rights. It was very soon evident that the nationalist sentiment would sweep aside any opposition to the application of the Constitution, not because this document was believed to be perfect, but because the United States really existed as a nation. The Constitution was therefore adopted by all as an experiment and the first step toward a national life. Immediately two problems presented themselves to the American statesmen; that of foreign policy and that of internal organization. The United States as a nation had to choose between a rapprochement with their former mother country, England, who was still their principal customer and source of imports, and France, their ally, to whom they owed their victory and who had, more than any one else, aided them in attaining a high place among the nations.[113] The French army and fleet had been the two strongest arguments in favor of the recognition of the United States by the European sovereigns. Gratitude and economy counseled the maintaining of the French alliance: race instinct and commercial interests pointed toward England. The problem of internal politics was closely related to that of external politics. Should there be a strong government which should take an active concern in developing the commerce and credit of the nation, or a government as weak as possible which should leave individuals to act and should count on France to guarantee it the respect of other nations? The wealthy merchants in the seaports, the New England tradesfolk, who, satisfied with having beaten Great Britain and conscious of the bond of religion, language and civilization, asked nothing better than to have cordial relations with her now; the business men of New York, where George II's birthday was still a public holiday; the rich planters of South Carolina, who had many links with high English society—all these groups remembered that the Revolution had been started to force England to respect traditional liberties and rights of British citizens.[114]

All these classes were in favor of establishing friendly relations with England as soon as she should consent to treat the United States with consideration. They sought to copy the English institutions as much as possible. By the provisions of the Constitution it was these people who elected the senators. Hence we find in the American Senate from 1789 to 1792 a strong aristocratic strain. The senators even discussed the creation of titles for American high dignitaries, and they aspired to a government by the rich and the wise.[115] John Adams, who represented the attitude of the New England Federalists accurately, looked forward to seeing a nobility formed in America and to belonging to it himself.[116] Alexander Hamilton, whom Washington had chosen as his Secretary of the Treasury and intimate advisor, was a monarchist.[117] He deemed it impossible to speak of royalty in America for the time being, but he wanted to build up as strong a central power as possible, develop the executive office, whose prerogatives had not been very clearly defined in the Constitution, and work gradually toward a monarchy.

To carry out this plan it would have been necessary to crush out the influence of France in America. The French philosophers had early urged the United States toward a popular government. With the development of the French Revolution, this current became infinitely stronger and made itself felt in all spheres. It was no longer simply philosophic elucubrations after the manner of Raynal that the American newspapers translated from French, but accounts of combats in which the people had taken part and triumphed. The imagination was stirred. When they saw American leaders like Paine involved in it, people could not fail to be interested in the struggle. The European crisis, placed thus within the reach of the American populace, woke the masses to a consciousness of their strength and their rights. All those who were dismayed at the aristocratic character of the Senate, all who were discontent or jealous of the upper classes, rallied to the true democrats who held by the French doctrines and shared the French revolutionary enthusiasm. Jefferson, who had just returned from France and who combined his prestige as a pilgrim of Liberty with his ability as a leader, immediately became the standard-bearer of the resistance to the aristocratic English spirit. He and his friends did not want to put the question on the grounds of federalism.[118] They did not desire the dissolution of the federation. But they did wish to place the government in the hands of the people and to efface every vestige of aristocracy and aristocratic government. To accomplish this, the masses had to be roused, wakened from their apathy and organized. A simple slogan and a principle had to be found. From 1790 on, there were really two parties: the Federalists, supported by the merchants and most of the population of New England, and the Democratic Republicans, supported by the farmers throughout the country and especially those of the South and West. One of these parties professed complete confidence in the people; the other claimed that the people needed guidance and a strong government. Neither of the two parties was willing to admit that it aimed at the destruction of the union or the republic, but each of them accused the other of intending the dissolution of the federal bond and the establishing of a despotism. In reality, it was a combat of tendencies and beliefs. The American Constitution was brief and rather ambiguous on many points; its entire sense could be changed according to the way in which it was applied. It was much less a text than a theme—hence the importance of this conflict. In this struggle the Americans no longer took as models the English parties, but the French parties. The Republicans were called "Jacobins" and the Federalists were nicknamed either "monarchists" or "monocrats." The standard about which the battle raged was France. The Federalists wanted to be quit of the alliance. Their members in the Senate passed a law applying the same treatment to French ships as to the ships of all other nations, an act that was certainly not in accord with the spirit of the treaty of 1778. The Senate also managed to drag out the discussion of the consular convention with France. It received the cordial communications of the Constituent Assembly without enthusiasm. Washington had not yet ratified this policy.[119] He held the balance.[120] While the Federalists, supported by the newspapers that they had subsidized (the chief among these was *The United States Gazette*, published by Fenno at Philadelphia), and the Republicans, led by Jefferson, who had persuaded Freneau to found a democratic sheet, *The National Gazette*, were exchanging harsh words, the President kept silent.[121] The Republican newspapers extolled French enthusiasm and published Paine's *Rights of Man*, which held that every nation has the right to dispose of itself as it sees fit. The indignant Federalists replied with horrible details concerning what was taking place in France.[122] They printed *Publicola*, a pamphlet by the young John Quincy Adams, the son of John Adams, who denied absolutely the right of nations to revolt, and maintained that there were imperishable laws that unite nations and set limits to the rights of the citizen. He praised the Constitution of England and criticized that of France severely. It was believed that John Adams himself was the author of the pamphlet, and there was a general movement of hostility against him. He quarreled with Jefferson, who had had *Publicola* attacked in *The National Gazette*, and the discord touched even Washington's advisors.[123] The supercilious attitude of England did not render the Anglophiles' task easy, but the alarming news from France made the work of the Francophiles quite as difficult. Both sides endeavored to kindle the masses in the name of the immortal rights of the people, which France was defending, or in the name of the immortal laws of God and morality, which England was upholding against anarchy. The question was laid before the people. The two great parties that were to do battle for the power were already clearly defined, although not entirely formed, in 1790. The combat was to be violent, but the issues were clear; for both parties had consented to wage it on the question of France and French democratic principles.

The fact was, that France had identified herself with democracy and become its champion in the eyes of the world. She had just overthrown the royal government. The movement started in 1791 by Paine and his club of five republicans, Paine, Condorcet, Bonneville, Duchatel and Lanthenas, had been crowned by success. From this group, the republican idea had spread to all the revolutionary groups. In his second addition to *The Rights of Man*, Paine had set forth clearly the question of Monarchy or Republic. He had depicted the immorality of the monarchical régime, which, founded on force, does not respect the primary rights of man or consider itself bound by the terms of the social contract. Popular opinion had been so profoundly stirred by his writings that Paine, without being a candidate, was elected to the Convention in four departments. This was the most brilliant period of his life. He seems at that time to have been both disinterested and enthusiastic. He was bold and stood out as the center of the republican doctrinaries. French opinion, exalted and violent, was ripe for such propaganda. The King, by his flight and his weakness, had lost his prestige; the nobles were either disarmed or in flight; the constitutionalists felt that their position was untenable. Everywhere a tense moral restlessness reigned. When his Girondist friends had prepared the way for the 10th of August,* Paine set to work with renewed energy. He published in the *Feuilles villageoises* and the *Patriote français* anti-monarchical essays with the purpose of dissuading the French from ever returning to this régime of persecution, absurd heredity and absolutism.[124] At the same time, Barlow, in *A Letter to the Convention*, was demanding in the name of Man, whose nature was essentially good, that he be allowed to govern Himself and that governments of oppression and royalty be abolished.[125] Thus the two Americans continued their campaign, which now was victorious and without danger for them. They put zeal and sentiment into their work and implored the nation to show herself generous, abolish the death penalty and treat all citizens humanely. The Convention was touched by the letter; Barlow was voted French citizenship and entrusted with the work of organizing Savoy into a French department.

In the midst of her dangers and trials, republican France, wild with joy, proclaimed herself the sister of America. The example of the American Revolution had already been used frequently to whip up the enthusiasm of the populace; now it was only natural that Washington and his heroic barefoot soldiers should be called to mind. Regnault de Saint-Jean d'Angély in *L'Ami des Patriotes* for January 14, 1792, had said, "We shall conquer just as the Americans did, for we have had even

* Tenth of August, 1792. The date of the popular uprising which destroyed French monarchy, and put the King in prison.

more to endure than they." Perlet in his journal for September 15, tries to encourage his countrymen as to the future by reminding them of Franklin's phrase, "*Ca ira.*" [126] By way of urging the citizens to bear up under their privations, Louvet, at the Jacobin Club on January 30, 1792, told how the Bostonians had gone without tea, a beverage that was so dear to them, in order to combat England. Lemaire's *Père Duchêne* compared the National Guards to the American militia and asserted that they would conduct themselves as well. The *Journal universel* for September, 1792, pointed out that the American Revolution had suffered calumny such as was now being circulated about the French Revolution, but had triumphed nevertheless. America stood in every one's eyes as an example of patriotism and heroism. It was no longer used to stimulate republican sentiment, which had now reached a high degree of intensity, but to maintain combative instinct, which could not be too great at a moment when France, divided internally, was being attacked on all sides. Just as it served as a stimulant for the victors, the thought of America was also a consolation for the vanquished. Necker devoted his leisure as a fallen minister to criticizing the Jacobin revolution and pointing out its defects. His book, *Du Pouvoir exécutif*, extolled the Americans from every point of view for having been able to carry on a humane revolution and organize a strong republic. It was alternately an elegy and a dithyrambic. And the most illustrious victims of the Revolution turned their eyes, just as Necker did, to this land of liberty and peace. Most of the monarchists who had coöperated with the patriots and favored the Revolution in its beginnings, would have liked to seek a refuge in America. Talleyrand was only too happy to be able to flee there to escape French and English proscriptions. The Vicomte de Noailles, Omer Talon and Beaumets had taken refuge in America. A group of bankers and tradesmen had tried to provide a shelter for themselves and had bought a great tract of land in the northern part of the State of New York called Castorland. La Ray de Chaumont, his brother-in-law Chassanis, Alexander Lerebours, Bailly, Moreau de Saint-Méry and Volney were connected with this speculation, which was in the nature of an insurance against possible catastrophes in France.[127] Prospectuses of a company organized by Thomas Cooper in Pennsylvania were circulated in France to attract the *émigrés*. Everywhere victims of the persecutions were thinking of setting out for America. We find La Fayette asking to be allowed to leave for the United States and sending his son there, and Benjamin Constant, dismayed at the turn of events, wrote to Madame de Charrière: "America! America! America! If some day I leave Colombiers forever, if I see all liberty die out of Europe, there will still remain one refuge. . . . You will stay behind perhaps, but sad and embittered. I shall go to Kentucky." It was at this time that Madame de La Tour du Pin fled to America, and Madame de Genlis was contemplating doing the same. The Sulpicians of Paris sent a colony of their brethren to Baltimore. Above the fray in which monarchists and republicans, Girondists and Montagnards were slaughtering each other, there remained one sacred and absolute ideal of liberty and social justice—the United States. They were done with as a catchword of conspiracies and revolutions; henceforth they had a higher rôle; they maintained the ideal which otherwise in the turmoil of conflict and passion would have been forgotten. For some it was a moral and political ideal; for others it was religious and literary.[128]

France and America were united in the same faith and exchanged their prophets. Paine's *Rights of Man* and Barlow's *Advice to the Privileged Classes* and *Letter to the Convention* had just been published in Paris. The French public kept up its courage by reading Paine's *Common Sense* and his *American Crisis*, which he had written to sustain the morale of the American insurgents in the trying moments of their revolution. A new edition of *Poor Richard* was published. Despite the turmoil of events, people read and discussed a translation of *The Federalist* by Jay, Madison and Hamilton, as well as the American constitutions and John Adams' defense of them.[129] As seen from France, the spiritual union of the two countries seemed to be a very close one. It seemed like a federation of free nations. Already at the end of 1791 and the beginning of 1792, there had been talk of a universal confederation of nations. The Prussian Cloots, who styled himself the "Orator of the Human Race," had not been the only one to uphold this ideal. Rabaut Saint-Etienne, in his *Adresse aux Anglais*, had held up the example of the United States and had called for a constitution of the United States of Europe.[130] The Jacobins had hung English, French and American flags in their assembly hall, and discourses in praise of Franklin and the Americans had been pronounced before them. Clubs in the provinces had imitated their example: at Bergerac, Bordeaux, etc., in 1792, the flags of the nations "confederated for liberty"—Poland, England, America and France—had been installed.[131] In March, 1792, in the parade of the soldiers of Châteauvieux a symbolic group represented the free nations—France, America and England.[132] The *Annales patriotiques* for February 1792 said: "It is from the fraternal alliance of the various peoples of the earth that should finally be born the great system of peace, happiness and prosperity destined to mankind by Providence and human perfectability."[133] National celebrations were planned in honor of the free nations. Instead of the past, which they cast aside, the revolutionists revered the present, and in place of ancestors they honored brother nations.[134] The Girondists adopted this idea and practiced it, but it did not belong to them exclusively. It was only that it was easier for them to stand as sponsors of it because of their connection with the American leaders such as Paine, Barlow and Jefferson. There again America was to be the pivot. No very energetic action could be expected from Poland, who had not been able to save herself. England, for all her enthusiastic democratic elements, had a strong and hostile government. Only in America were both opinion and government free. All the elements of her society, it was believed, were friendly to France, since all of revolutionary France was friendly to America. The union of the two great republics of the world would have afforded a brilliant example of fraternity and constituted an all-powerful moral force. Paine, Brissot, Roland and the whole Girondist party dreamed of realizing this union. A curious little pamphlet, *Nouvelle Alliance à proposer entre les Républiques française et américaine* by Ducher, published in the early part of the year 1793, shows what hopes were being entertained at the time. Ducher was a fiery patriot who had been consul in the United States during Montmorin's ministry and had been dismissed as a result of his misconduct and incendiary words. His desire was that the two truly free nations of the earth should not content themselves with guaranteeing their possessions but should also guarantee their democratic institutions and endeavor to trade with each other as much as possible. Brissot and Paine conceived a brilliant plan for bringing this about. They knew that in America Louis XVI was admired and respected as a benefactor of the United States. The execution of the King would meet with disapproval in the New World. On the other hand, it would have been imprudent to keep him in Europe within reach of his partisans. They planned therefore to send him to America under a strong guard and turn him over to the Americans as a proof of France's humaneness and friendship for her sister nation. Brissot arranged to have appointed as minister at Philadelphia, which was then the federal capital, Genet, the son of Vergennes's clerk, and the nephew of Madame Campan, an intelligent and energetic young man and an ardent patriot, who had received a remarkable education from his father. Genet spoke several languages, and especially English, well. His connections, patriotism and intelligence made him the ideal agent to accomplish this generous and delicate mission. Bonne Carrière, to whom the post of minister to the United States had already been promised, was ousted.[135] Paine was to propose that Louis be exiled, and Brissot and all his Girondist friends were to force the motion through.[136] Pamphlets signed by "A Quaker" were circulated to ease the way to this solution.[137]

Paine's plan was not destined to success. On the appointed day when Louis XVI was to have been saved, Paine alone, among all the Girondists, had courage enough to play the part that had been assigned to him and plead for the King's life in the name of America. The Girondists contradicted themselves and were powerless. Genet, who had been kept waiting in order that he might take the King with him, sailed alone. But he was still under instructions to rouse the American people and their government to a pitch of generous enthusiasm that should range them side by side with France against despots. In the orders that he received, he was told to strengthen the bonds between the two countries and to negotiate a new commercial treaty to draw them closer together. These orders also denounced the duplicity of Vergennes and Montmorin toward the United States, claiming that all the while they were flattering America, they were trying to stunt her growth and to keep her from conquering Canada, Florida and Nova Scotia, in the hope of stifling liberty. Genet was to make amends for these wrongs by following a generous and disinterested policy toward the United States in order to establish "a close concord that should favor in every way the extension of the empire of Liberty." [138] He was authorized to draw up a national pact with the United States to be a mutual guarantee of the territories and forms of government of the two nations. He was to seek to free Spanish America and, if possible, unite Canada to the United States. It was recommended that he place his dependence especially on the Americans in the West, the Kentuckians and Ohioans. He was given blank letters-of-mark and advised to make use of the friends of France in Congress. He set out entrusted with both propaganda and diplomacy, with both war and provisioning. Even if he had been prudent and strong, the task would have been too great; but he was both rash and weak. His false ideas of the United States, which he imagined, after the manner of the philosophers, as being idyllic and pure, were a stumbling-block to him; and the triumphal reception that was tendered him at Charleston completed the turning of his head. He thought of himself as a Roman Proconsul. He began to distribute letters-of-mark and organized Charleston as a base for French privateers in the Caribbean and the Gulf of Mexico. The consul, Mangourit,[139] was to supervise the arming of the ships, regulate their sailings, and attend to the sale of prizes and exert all possible pressure on American opinion in order to bring about an intervention in favor of France and an expedition against New Orleans. Charleston became for some time a sort of revolutionary capital in the southern United States. Men were proud to wear the tricolor cockade and call each other citizen and even don the red liberty cap at banquets. The agitation was kept at a high pitch by the descendants of French Huguenots, who, remembering what their ancestors had suffered, celebrated with joy the fall of the monarchy. In January, they had already organized a great procession in honor of the National Assembly.[140] Thirteen salutes had been fired to begin the ceremony. Then the parade, led by Manourit, Pastor Coste of the French Reformed Church, and all the public dignitaries and officials, had begun its march through the town. It stopped before the French Church and the flag was dipped as an atonement for the persecutions of Louis XIV. At Saint Philip's Church, the procession came to a halt. Salvos were fired, and Coste made a speech. Then a Te Deum and the Marseillaise were sung.[141] It was a great day of fraternization. Such was the atmosphere that Genet found on his arrival. He had heard Brissot say that the Americans were kindled with the flame of liberty and would certainly be eager to cast their lot with France. The wild joy with which he was welcomed and Manourit's enthusiasm completely persuaded him that nothing could halt the American people on the path of war and Democracy.[142] However grave may have been Genet's faults, we should not forget the impression that this frenzied and seemingly unanimous reception must have made on an impassioned Girondist who had just come from the Russian court where he had been treated with the utmost coldness and had lived isolated amid the indifference of the people. After having conferred with Mangourit, he set out for Philadelphia and crossed the States of South Carolina, North Carolina and Virginia on the way. Everywhere the same rapturous enthusiasm greeted him. The farmers of the South were anti-clerical on the whole. They had suffered a great deal at the hands of the English from 1779 to 1783 and hated them. They distrusted the federal government and were glad to envince their attachment for France, who had just beheaded her King and declared war on England, their enemy of yesterday, and Spain, their enemy of tomorrow.[143] They especially hated the latter power for continuing to bar the Mississippi to the free Americans. The news of the death of the King and the war against England had just come, and it had not immediately stirred up an unfavorable reaction. The people excused France in the midst of her tragic struggle, and withheld judgment. It is surprising to see the calm with which the upper classes took the news: the atrocious jest, *Capet sine capite*, was heard on all sides. This man, who formerly had been so highly lauded, now seemed to be scorned by all.[144] A tavern-keeper near Philadelphia dared to hang in front of his inn a sign depicting the execution of Marie Antoinette with the inscription beneath it, "*A la Reine de France guillotinée.*" The Jacobin who had had this idea was very proud of it.[145] No more than the fate of the King and Queen, did that of La Fayette at first evoke any such warm compassion as might have been expected. When it was learned that "the Marquis" had left the republican army and gone over to the enemy and that the Austrians had put him in prison and were keeping him there with cold cruelty, people felt sorry for him no doubt; some few newspapers published notes of grief and condolence, but there was no energetic manifestation in his favor.[146] Months, years, passed, and La Fayette was still in his dungeon. A young American from Charleston, Huger, risked his life to save him. Congress discussed whether or not there was anything else that they might do. The country as a whole did not quite understand these quarrels between the revolutionists nor why La Fayette had stopped halfway on the road to revolution. Therefore, in spite of a vague pity that was felt for him, in spite of good intentions, nothing definite was done. No particular group had any immediate interest in looking after him; the Federalists considered him as a democrat and a false prophet, and the Republicans saw in him a traitor to the cause of the people. Thus during 1792 and 1793, neither the misfortunes of Louis XVI and Marie Antoinette nor those of La Fayette roused American opinion against France.

In truth, this apparent indifference was rather a stupor. The American revolutionary party, which was beginning to organize, was very obstreperous. The news from France had thrown it into a redoubtable but, thus far, purely mystic and inoffensive state of excitement. They planted liberty-trees and talked of forming legions to go to France, but they did nothing untoward; and the Federalist groups, alarmed, surprised and undecided, waited. There was a moment when it almost seemed as if the weight of public opinion in America would turn in favor of France and a benevolent neutrality toward her. Washington had proclaimed the neutrality of the United States in the war that was being waged, but he had no intention of repudiating the treaty of 1778 and was still eager to follow a policy friendly to France. At this point he learned of Genet's arrival. The French minister came on to Philadelphia, harvesting the homage of the throngs along the way. People offered him wheat for France; they asked to enlist in the French army, they formed democratic and Jacobin societies at his instigation. His entry into Philadelphia was a popular triumph. But the men of position and those in the government circles held aloof. Washington was already offended. Even before presenting himself to the President, Genet had begun his functions as Minister Plenipotentiary of France, dared to arm French privateers in an American port, and made Charleston a French naval base.[147] The President did not approve of this lack of respect and these warlike acts, which the treaty of 1778 did not clearly cover. (Only the right of arming privateers in American ports was specifically accorded France, and not that of bringing in prizes and selling or arming them.) Lastly, Washington did not like these waves of brusque and ardent sentiment that were working such sudden havoc throughout the entire country. His deliberate and profound nature considered them as both a danger and a folly. Genet's next misfortune was to fall into the hands of the Republican party, who made use of him without being of any service to him in return. The Republicans needed some one to organize an active campaign against the Federalists and the government. They lacked courageous leaders. Neither Jefferson, Madison, nor Monroe was willing to compromise himself. Genet launched a splendid movement for them. Everywhere he organized, or had organized, democratic societies, veritable political and electoral leagues against the Federalists.[148] He radiated an intense enthusiasm. He did everything in his power to separate the American people from their government. Seeing that

Washington treated him coldly, he decided that "old Washington" had seen his day, that he lacked energy, and that a courageous stand would soon force him to follow the will of the people. Genet felt an intense moral and mystic force behind him. He considered Washington an old man, worn-out and spiritless.[149] He consulted Jefferson, who answered him vaguely and promised him his support. Genet wanted to bring about the invasion of Louisiana to strike a blow at Spain and England. He delegated the naturalist Michaux to go to Kentucky under scientific pretexts and come to an agreement with General Clark, who would be provided with the necessary means for organizing an expedition in Kentucky against New Orleans.[150] Jefferson approved the project and put Genet in touch with Brown, the Governor of Kentucky. Governor Moultrie of South Carolina was also informed of the plan and approved of it. This was the means that Genet had found of taking advantage of American neutrality, which he did not hope to be able to violate or bring to an end immediately because of Washington and the American aristocracy. He continued to arm ships at Charleston and other ports. Washington, in accord with his cabinet in not desiring war, forbid him to sell or arm French prizes in the waters of the United States.[151] Genet received communications every day from all parts of the Union congratulating him warmly. He felt that he had the support of Jefferson, the Secretary of State. He believed that it would be safe to take bold steps. He made a pretense of obeying Washington's order, but he continued arming prizes secretly. Washington learned of it and openly attacked Genet, who was placed in an embarrassing position. His situation was all the more difficult because he had talked too widely. Led on by his desire to rouse the masses and feeling that they were with him, he had organized the French Consulates into bureaus of propaganda and publicity. He had recommended that they pay particular attention to the newspapers and spread in the North news hostile to the English and the Indians, and in the South attacks against Spain. He himself made tours in the course of which he spoke with violence and eloquence on the subjects of liberty, intolerance, the federation of nations, etc. At his instigation, Jefferson and other Republicans wrote fine anonymous pamphlets against England and tyrants.[152] During 1793, in the *Philadelphia General Advertiser* alone, "Junion," "Juba" and "An Old Soldier" spoke in favor of "the people's war" and criticized Washington. Genet gave dinners and presided at banquets, and good cheer inspired him. In the course of a visit of this kind to New York, he shocked Noah Webster so deeply by criticizing Washington and preaching against Christianity, that Webster, who until then had been favorable to France, became her most violent enemy. During this same visit, it seems, Genet declared that, if the American government would not listen to reason, he would make a direct appeal to the people.[153] It was just this that he had been doing ever since his arrival in America. He was only adopting Paine's formula: *the government versus the people.* But these words came to Jay's ears. Jay was shrewd. At last he saw a way of breaking down Genet's position and striking a serious blow at French influence. He repeated the French minister's words. He had Genet attacked in all the Federalist papers for this anarchistic attempt to disrupt the nation and the American Constitution. National pride was engaged. Within a few days, Genet found himself abandoned by his best friends. Jefferson disavowed him officially as he had already disowned him in deeds. Washington's cabinet was unanimous in asking the Convention to recall Genet, and the request was transmitted through Gouverneur Morris,[154] who was then American minister in Paris and who, on his own initiative and through the good offices of the discreet friends that he had among the Jacobins, had it decided that Genet should be guillotined as soon as possible after his return.[155] He would only have been following his Girondist friends who had just suffered the same fate. Thus Genet's fraternal mission came to a tragic end. It had been disastrous for France, but very useful to the Republican party in the United States, which was left strong and well organized. By means of Genet's democratic clubs, it had gathered to it and organized all the violent elements of the population. These were chiefly immigrants from Europe—Germans, Irishmen and Frenchmen of the lowest classes. Through Genet's efforts, these men had acquired a class-consciousness and learned their strength.[156] Genet had begun the battle well: his attacks against governmental aristocracy, the clergy and the executive pointed out the road that must be followed to achieve victory. He was beaten, but he left the administration and the Federalist party in a critical situation. England still seemed hostile, and even those who hoped for a reconciliation with her could not see clearly how to bring it about. France was becoming unreasonable, and the United States could foresee the time when they would have to pay dearly for her alliance. Within the country itself, a party of unprecedented violence was forming and drawing into its ranks men who had never held a place nor been of any importance in American life. A fever of democracy had laid hold on the land. The people as a whole wanted no war, either foreign or civil; but even the majority of the New England preachers were lauding France in lyric terms for combating tyrants, destroying the Papacy and the Catholic Church, and laying the foundations of a new era.[157] In the face of this outburst, which in the ports and along the frontiers was becoming dangerously active, the government was badly armed. In July, even more feverish and enthusiastic demonstrations had taken place.[158] The tone employed by the Republican newspapers and the clergy was becoming worthy of the Apocalypse. Although few people were in favor of it, a war with England was possible, and a material and moral cataclysm seemed inevitable. The supporters of the government, who thus far had been wealthy and orderly citizens, felt that in self-defense they would have to exert themselves more than formerly. Their newspapers began to employ a more energetic tone. They counted on the minister whom the English had at last sent to America. They procured pamphleteers, among whom Noah Webster,[159] the lexicographer, and William Willcox were the most prominent.[160] Webster was quite sincere. Willcox's activities seem to have been more open to suspicion.[161] In order to fight on equal terms, while working toward a reconciliation with England, the Federalists turned their attention to the clergy, especially in New England, and tried to raise up the old religion in opposition to the new one. This was difficult, for the clergy was bound by liberal traditions of long standing and imbued with democratic tendencies. Nevertheless, the impiety of the French was a good theme to exploit. In 1793 the American clergy did not seem decided as to the direction it should follow, and Federalism stood wavering before a Republican party, heterogeneous it is true, but very numerous and filled with a mystic fervor. The ardor of French Jacobinism was in its veins.

*

* *

The Republican party followed all the transitions of the moral and political conflict in France. It accepted the French Revolution in all its phases and pronouncements. When Brissot, the great apostle of Americanism, fell, no one in America regretted him or took his part. Sympathy was felt for La Fayette, who still enjoyed some of his prestige and was looked upon as being mistaken but not guilty.[162] Brissot, who was not widely known and who had done nothing for America, went down unmourned. Yet, the party in France that had made the most use of the United States and placed the greatest store on her friendship sank with him. Robespierre, as we have seen, had been a worshiper at the shrine of Franklin from his youth up. He remained faithful to this worship in his maturity; and even when he was attacking Brissot's partisans in the name of patriotism and morality, he spoke with profound veneration of Franklin.[163] His devotion had nothing of the sentimental effusiveness that characterized that of the Girondists; but the deist religion, rational and mystic, was still the point on which he and his adversaries had most in common. Both sides aimed at setting up a republican religion, but each of them wanted to be its founder. In their attitude on this point, the followers of Brissot were more hostile to Catholicism and more given to pure negation than Robespierre, for they had begun their attacks earlier than he and believed that there was more to be demolished before beginning to build anew. Moreover, their constructive spirit was limited and vague.[164] Robespierre seemed more moderate, since he personally had come into power at a time when Catholicism was helpless. He therefore sought rather to make use of its ruins; but nothing proves that he had any sympathy for the Church. The Jacobins were directing a heavy attack against the federalism of Brissot's followers and their imputed desire to imitate the United States. There is no conclusive evidence that they entertained this desire. There was indeed a discussion at the Jacobin Club in September 1792, during the course of which some citizens defended federal government as it was practiced in the United States; but these men seem to have been obscure and to have had no connection with the Girondist chiefs.[165] The only ground on which they might be accused of federalism is the insistence with which they always proclaimed, in accord with Franklin, that democracy demanded a government as weak and as lax as possible in order to leave the people the real master of its own destinies.[166] In the danger that menaced France in 1792-1793, this theory was impracticable. Robespierre triumphed easily. But, after all, his efforts to moralize the Revolution are only, all things considered, the systematic prolongation of the sentimental concept that Brissot voiced when he said, "Without private *mores* there can be no public *mores* and no liberty."

With the fall of Brissot, the most prominent American figures among the French Revolutionists dropped out of sight—particularly the great apostle of the republic, Paine, whom the Jacobins, friends of Robespierre, put in prison where other Jacobins, friends of Morris, saw to it that he remained.[167] Once master of the situation, Robespierre set about realizing his projects for a religion. One after the other, France saw launched Hébert's Religion of Reason, Robespierre's Cult of the Supreme Being and the decadary cult. It will be remembered that the spectacle of the American Revolution had long inspired the French pamphleteers and philosophers with the idea that a deist and social religion with its holidays was necessary to a well-ordered state. A lay calendar entitled the *Calendrier de Philadelphie* had already been printed in 1778. In 1792, Manuel proposed following up this idea.[168] In the various forms of worship that functioned in France during these years, whatever the label may have been, the contents were always largely American. Children were baptized in republican fashion with the name of Franklin.[169] The life of Franklin was published in the newspapers under the heading "Morale." [170] In the *Alphabet des Sans-culottes, pour former la Jeunesse républicaine*, to the question, "Who are the great men who by their writings laid the foundation for the Revolution?" [171] the answer was, "Helvetius, Mably, J. J. Rousseau, Voltaire and Franklin." In the decadary ceremonies, homilies were read on the subject of the Americans, their virtues and the union of the republicans of the world to bring about the world's salvation. The Americans were represented as making an appeal to the French, as for example in the discourses pronounced by Citizen Maurin at the Temple of Reason of the Bonne-Nouvelle Section from the tenth of Pluviôse to the twentieth of Ventôse, of the year II.[172] The *Chansonnier de la Montagne* and the *Lyre républicaine* show that Franklin and the United States were still used as perfect examples of republican virtue.[173] In short, if through the turn of party politics, things American enjoyed less vogue than formerly, the moral influence of the United States continued to be felt along the same directions as it had been for the past twenty years. This influence was still strong and popular. Its diffusion makes it difficult to follow it in all its varied manifestations, but it is to be felt wherever spiritual ardor reigns and wherever minds are concerned with other aspects of the revolution than the mere armed conflict.

The policy that Robespierre followed was not hostile to the United States. He wanted to win back the Americans and continue the policy of the monarchy, which had been interrupted by Brissot's blundering, and reconcile statecraft with a frankness befitting republics. He blamed neither America nor her leaders for anything, but considered Genet at fault. He decided therefore to send to America a young, intelligent and able man, Fauchet.

The new minister was to be supervised and aided by a committee composed of the French Consuls in America: La Forest, Pétry and Le Blanc. This commission was instructed to disavow Genet and all his works, arrest him, tender friendly words to the American government and, by way of a guarantee, order French privateers in American waters to disarm, and condemn those who had armed them originally. They were also to put an immediate stop to the expedition against New Orleans, which violated American neutrality, to see that the treaty of 1778 was respected and to negotiate a new commercial treaty. Lastly, Robespierre recommended that the commission win the confidence of Washington. These instructions, wise on the whole, were, however, very vague; and, whether because the mails had been intercepted by the English or because his superiors at Paris had no time to give to such remote questions, Fauchet was never to receive any others.[174] Since, beside this, he quarreled with two of the members of his council, his task was not an easy one. The aim of his instructions was to restore order, clarity, and moral rectitude in the international relations, which had been muddled by intrigue and ill-advised enthusiasm. But Fauchet again was one who knew the United States only through their legend, and his instructions and Robespierre's counsels to him were inspired only by this legend. His effort toward political honesty was as futile as Genet's impassioned virtue.

In fact, before Fauchet's arrival, Genet had struck a most serious blow at France's reputation by publishing his instructions. These instructions claimed that, in going through the archives of Foreign Affairs, it had been established that the old régime had always been dishonest, mercenary, jealous and selfish in its relations with the United States. This declaration, which seemed to be a confession, did not cause any great scandal at first; but it was noted down carefully. Gradually it was circulated throughout the United States, and it greatly complicated the task of Fauchet, who had come to speak in the name of France eternal.[175] He was well received, however. Throngs acclaimed him, democratic societies wrote to him, Randolph, who had become Secretary of State in place of Jefferson, treated him as a friend, and Washington showed him flattering attentions. Along his way, "*Ca ira*" was played.[176]

Fauchet wanted to avoid entanglements. He tried to keep on friendly terms with the Federalists, but it was impossible to be in favor with both parties; he was obliged to make a choice. He soon became the agent of the Republicans, not conspicuously as Genet had, but discreetly and by back-stair intrigue. Out of contact with the country that he represented, attacked by his own colleagues, suspected by the principal American dignitaries, harassed by the Republicans, who wanted guarantees of his good faith,[177] Fauchet was also obliged to combat the disastrous influence of the French refugees who were arriving by the thousand from Santo Domingo, starving, disgruntled and miserable. In the larger cities there were former Conventionalist *émigrés*, filled with hatred for Robespierre; and in the country districts there were monarchists and Constitutionalists.[178] Everywhere Fauchet found the prestige of La Fayette still flourishing and increased by his afflictions. Thus every move he made was dangerous. He found himself prisoner of the enthusiasm that Genet had stirred up and which, swelled to the proportions of a social force, carried him along just as a regiment carries a flag that it appears to follow. In addition to his official duties Fauchet tried to carry on secret negotiations. In this he was going against the instructions that had been given him officially. Necessity forced him to it perhaps, for his enemies were unscrupulous; but he was punished for his secret audacity as severely as Genet was for his unbridled tongue.[179] His great error during these first months of 1794 lay in believing that the American people loved France for herself and were ready to serve her. He did not see that the Republican politicians loved France above all as a weapon in national politics, as an all-mighty lever for moving minds and raising enthusiasms to a high plane. He failed to distinguish the differences between a common ideal and a community of interests.

As a matter of fact, the situation of the American government, and of Washington, who at that time *was* the American government, was as perilous as that of the French minister. Washington was caught between the intrigues of Fauchet, who wanted a treaty but had nothing precise to offer, and the Federalists, who undertook, by coming to an agreement with England, to avoid war and realize all the benefits that had been expected of the peace of 1783 and calm the rising tide of turbulence, license and the French doctrines, which threatened to wipe out the old Anglo-American civilization.

It was no longer, as it had been in the preceding years, a matter of slow infiltration through the upper classes. French influence was seeping into the masses. From 1780 to 1788, through the efforts of the group of intellectuals and philosophers in France who concerned themselves with the United States, interesting attempts had been made to introduce European education into America. French professors had settled in all the cities, and all the larger colleges either offered French or allowed it to be taught. This tendency continued and became even more pronounced from 1789 to 1794.[180] Montesquieu was studied at Yale. At Brown and Harvard commencement orators discussed the French Revolution and praised it. At Cambridge a learned professor, Monsieur de Nancrède, exerted a real influence.[181] Students entering William and Mary College were obliged to know the elements of French. At Williams College, students who so desired could study French and be examined in this subject. At Columbia University a Frenchman, Villette de Marcellin, was engaged to teach his mother tongue. It is even more significant to find the preparatory schools that were then being founded, providing their students with facilities for learning French.[182] On the other hand, no institution had adopted Quesnay's plan; there was no longer any question of offering a more purely cultural education like that of the old régime in France.[183] Quesnay himself, interrupted in the midst of his work of organization by the Revolution, had remained in France.

There he had at first concerned himself with moderate revolutionary politics and had even published a newspaper. Later he dropped out of sight in the turmoil and nothing further was heard of him.[184] The building that had been constructed at Richmond to house his university was finally used as a theater. Jefferson and John Adams, to make up for his defection and do something of a like nature, had thought of transporting the entire University of Geneva to America; but public opinion was not favorable to the plan.[185] It was felt that foreigners, speaking a language unintelligible to the masses, would be lost and useless in America. Popular sentiment, elated at the triumph of American ideas throughout the entire world and proud of its new country, demanded a practical and democratic education suited to the needs of the country. Noah Webster expressed this thought in *The American Museum*, the most prominent magazine of the time, in 1792. It was admitted, however, that the education of girls should be more complete and cultural. In this same magazine we find articles whose intent it is to show how necessary French is in the education of women. The men had no time to lose. They wanted knowledge that would be of use to them; hence we find many professors of French keeping schools of dancing and fencing for young men at the same time.[186]

In the libraries French books were becoming increasingly numerous. They were also of a less intellectual and more popular character. There was still, it is true, a goodly proportion of the works of Voltaire, Rousseau and Raynal; but the writings of Sully and Fénelon, which formerly were to be found everywhere, were becoming rarer.[187] Most of the French books that were coming into America were books of travel, historical works and novels. The works of Marmontel and the sentimental tales of Madame de Genlis were in the greatest demand. Throughout the magazines and newspapers, one finds numerous translations and adaptations from French novels concerning the poor black slaves, the virtues of the Swiss and the life of the French peasants.[188] One of the most famous American novels of the time, *Charlotte*, is a sentimental and heart-rending tale, bedecked with ornaments from Sterne, in which a French villainess plays a dramatic part. In 1789 Mrs. Morton of Boston had published a novel entitled *The Power of Sympathy*, whose virtuous, emotional and worldly tone was inspired by Sterne and Marmontel. This influx of French sentimental novels into the cultivated circles of the United States was favored by the ever-increasing number of *émigrés*. Girondists, Constitutionalists and even Monarchist refugees were coming to the New World in search of a simple life and an ideal inspired by the reading of Rousseau. They were so deeply penetrated with this sensibility that it left its stamp on everything they touched. Nancrède, professor at Harvard and faithful disciple of Brissot, published a moral and literary manual, *L'Abeille française*, in which he printed long extracts from Bernardin de Saint Pierre.[189] To their American acquaintances, Madame de La Tour de Pin, the Marquis de Lezay Marnésia, the Vicomte de Noailles, Omer Talon, etc., appeared as apostles of a refined "state of Nature"; and a new sentimentality invaded American literature, which until then had been somewhat rude and unpolished.[190] The innumerable poems of the period have the soft romantic breath and lyric flame of the revolutionary spirit. In cultured and religious minds, the French influence led to a mystic concept of life and took on a literary form. With politicians and men of action, it became a practical, and at the same time, impassioned, cult. To the former, the turmoil of revolution revealed the infinite value of tender, delicate and profound sentiments, and inspired the desire for a world in which the dictates of the heart should be the supreme law for actions and works of art. For the others, revolution was the means of laying hold on happiness and establishing it on earth.[191] The magazines were continually publishing practical recipes of agriculture, natural sciences and applied physics, translated from French. The philosophic Society of Philadelphia also was guided by the spirit of practical philanthropy. It elected to its membership statesmen, such as Brissot and Moreau de Saint-Méry, and benefactors of humanity, such as Crèvecœur and Artaud, the president of the Cercles des Philadelphes de Cap Français, journalists such as Luzac, and refugees from the Cape, the Antilles and France. The period of great names had passed; that of practical work had come.[192]

It was through the masses that French influence was filtering in. A French theater was opened at New York and *Le Devin de Village* was played there in 1791. At Boston, in spite of protests, plays were produced.[193] All the large cities had French benevolent societies, which were founded with the purpose of helping the poor, but soon became clubs where good food and gay living were the rule. The Philadelphia club is typical of its kind and is still in existence.[194] The French Masonic lodges of Santo Domingo had been transplanted and were functioning in Philadelphia as well as in the other ports, it seems. They had a tendency to introduce a new and radical spirit into American Masonry, which until then had been very conservative.[195] Everywhere French influence tended toward deism. At Boston, where French Catholics had been allowed to build a chapel and, it is said, Protestants attended Catholic services, this was taken as a sign not of intense faith, but of tolerance and indifference.[196] The same was true in Baltimore and in the West, where French Sulpicians had settled. At Baltimore they had established a university and, in the West, missions; but, although they were tolerated, they made almost no conversions and had no American followers.[197] Genet preached deism unchecked; and in Massachusetts, Citizen Godineau pointed out the impossibility of believing in the divinity of Christ (1794). The same year the Boston papers published letters discussing and praising Robespierre's speech of April 21, 1794, on science and religion. The American clergy preached the destruction of the Papacy and Catholicism, and seems not to have perceived that its blows rebounded against itself. Until 1794, on the whole, no fear of French deism was manifested. Much to the contrary, writers and orators turned it to their own uses and exploited it.[198] Thus everywhere in the realm of words, the French Revolution accomplished its work. Seven French newspapers, at least, were published in the United States and kept up a close contact between the French *émigrés* and the American nation. Among these publications were: *Le Courrier politique de l'Univers* of Boston, moderately republican; *Le Courrier français* of Philadelphia, Jacobin; *Le Courrier politique de la France et de ses Colonies* of Philadelphia, the organ of the French Creole refugees; *Le Journal des Révolutions* (1793); *L'Etoile américaine* (1794); *Le Patriote français* at Charleston. There was also *Le Niveau de l'Europe et de l'Amérique septentrionale*, the first journal of political economy to be published in America. It was edited at Philadelphia by a French *émigré*, Tanguy de la Boissière.[199] Everywhere, under French influence and as a product of increasing excitement, newspapers sprang up. They were divided clearly into opposition and governmental organs; some of them were unreservedly Francophile; others were tacitly hostile but pretended to be fired by an enthusiasm for Liberty.

All the works of the intellect in America, and particularly those that emanated from the masses or appealed to them, reflected the struggle that was going on. Poetry, which was the most spontaneous, democratic and widespread form of literature, seemed entirely consecrated to France and dominated by a Jacobin lyricism come from Europe. Freneau, the greatest and most original of the American poets of the period, celebrated the taking of the Bastille in vigorous and eloquent verses.[200] In spite of a vocabulary that is sometimes colorless or bombastic, he succeeded in producing works that are great because of his sincerity and passion. His prose-works, which were published in his curious and admirable *National Gazette*, are of equal merit. His work abounds in pleas in favor of the republic, written in a brief, violent, sardonic and compact style. As a polemic writer, Freneau is harsh and forceful without being coarse. His sincerity glitters like steel. In comparison with him, Fenno, the editor of *The Gazette of the United States*, is heavy and dull. These two papers, together with the Federalist *Columbian Centinel* and the Republican *Argus* and *American Apollo* of Boston, were the most interesting and best presented of their kind. Every number of them contained a variety of verses, letters from the readers on the burning subjects of the day, official proclamations, prices, European and American news, local advertisements, etc. Hamilton, Rufus King and John Quincy Adams were the greatest purveyors of pamphlets in favor of peace and neutrality. They maintained that the treaty signed with the King of France could not be valid under the French Republic and that, moreover, there was no means by which the United States could be of real assistance to France in the war. These essays, lucid and without emphasis, are colorless and have lost whatever interest they had in their time. As a rule, they are well constructed and plausible. The replies that were written by Madison under the name of Helvidius, and the other Republican leaders under various antique pseudonyms, defended Genet, who was then under fire, and represented him as a martyr to the cause of the people. They strove to show that the execution of Louis XVI was justified by the dangers that beset France and the crimes of the monarchy. They made appeal to the sentiment of the brotherhood of the nations and the passion for Liberty. Their vehement tone and prophetic pronouncements were intended to impress the imagination. The modern reader finds their dogmatic tone and superficial mysticism wearying, but it is easy to understand how new and striking they must have seemed to the readers of the period.[201] The most eloquent clergymen followed the same lines. In their sermons they praised France as the scourge of God, the exterminating angel, and even as a sort of Messiah, guilty but justified. Many pastors sought to wake the slumbering zeal of their congregations by preaching a new variety of millenarianism.[202]

It was into this atmosphere of religious excitement and political intrigue that Fauchet came in April 1794. The pro-English Federalists, feeling how insecure was their hold on public opinion, sought to avenge themselves by diplomatic means. Jay was to save the day for them if Washington would allow it and if the tide of popular indignation could be stemmed.

Washington, despite his popularity, ability and glorious past, had not been able to restore spiritual harmony and soothe over party quarrels; on the contrary, the Republicans, who were becoming aware of their strength and numerical superiority, were beginning to go so far as to call for war against England. They controlled the greatest number of newspapers and the most truculent ones. In spite of the opposition of powerful interests, in spite of the merchants and the former Tories, who naturally joined forces with the enemies of France, their influence was everywhere felt. People like Samuel Adams, who formerly had been so suspicious of France, rallied to her ideals and allowed themselves to be carried away by her enthusiasm.[203] In such a moment Washington was obliged to do one of two things: yield to the rising tide, or employ stratagems and place his confidence in the conservative Federalist party. He doubtless did not share all their hatreds nor yet the blind hostility that kept them from recognizing past services, but he dreaded war and had no sympathy for the new and turbulent party that treated him so slightingly. Therefore, before Fauchet could begin his intrigues, he sent Jay to England to try to obtain a treaty that would regularize relations between England and America and allow the renewal of their former friendship and intimacy. Thus French culture, the pro-French party and the French tribunes could be combated. Provided with extensive powers, Jay set sail. His primary purpose was to bring England to respect the terms of the treaty of 1783 and surrender the post in the West that she was still occupying. He was authorized to make concessions. He was to make haste; for the Republicans were beginning a campaign to bring America into war, and in Congress, Madison was urging the adoption of a measure placing an embargo on English commerce if Great Britain did not respect the American ships engaged in transporting goods to France. This vociferous discussion was a further embarrassment to the government. It was then that the administration had a happy inspiration. In order to obtain favorable terms from England, have a free rein in America and calm excited public opinion, there was an advantage in pretending to be negotiating with France.[204] Although every one expected to see him choose a Federalist or a veteran politician like Chancelor Livingston for this task, Washington selected a young politician from Virginia who was known for his republican opinions, James Monroe. Monroe's sincere friendship for France and revolutionary enthusiasm were beyond suspicion. He accepted the mission in the hope that his devotion to the cause of Liberty would enable the two republics to find a common ground on which to unite. Morris, he was told, had been recalled in order to please the French. He was instructed to come to an agreement with Robespierre without sacrificing the dignity of the United States. He was asked to draw up a detailed report on France and her moral, religious and political conditions, and instructed to represent Jay's negotiations as a purely formal step whose purpose was to prove the good faith of the United States in case war should become necessary. He was to say that Jay would take up only the question of reparations to be obtained and to add that the friendship of the United States and her President was assured to France.[205] These instructions, which were in contradiction to those given to Jay, delighted Monroe, who, in his zeal and enthusiasm, did not suspect the adventure in which he was engaged. He set out for France and arrived just after the Ninth of Thermidor, in the midst of the joy and relief that followed the fall of Robespierre. The Convention, still hesitant and bewildered, was delighted to receive this representative of the United States who arrived at such a fortunate moment. A house belonging to the government was placed at his disposition. His reception was an elaborate ceremony, and French and American flags were hung in the hall where the Convention held its sessions.[206] Before this body, Monroe proclaimed the brotherhood of republics and exalted the cause of Liberty. A speech in the same tone was pronounced in reply to him. He was deeply touched, for he had expected no such reception as this. He admired everything he saw. Even the riots and successive executions of the revolutionary leaders he justified by the necessity of keeping a watch over the probity of men in power. France, he said, had cast off her leaders as soon as they had given the first sign of a spirit of tyranny or corruption.[207] Thus once more the spiritual union of the two peoples was proclaimed, once more the masses might believe in the moral unity of all free peoples, and the doctrine of the universal and inevitable Revolution that was to save the world was proclaimed to the nations. The effort had been sustained since 1788, and in 1794 Monroe must have thought in his zealous and upright soul that the hour had come to realize all the great hopes, "a consolation that those who desire good and have served the cause of Liberty may feel."

Chapter V

THE GREAT SCHISM

John Jay involves Washington and the Federalists in a policy of rapprochement with Great Britain in spite of the resistance of public opinion, pp. 353-362. At the same time the American clergy begins attacking France as anti-religious, pp. 362-368. The French ministers try in vain to combat this movement; they are prisoners of the Republican party in the United States and cannot appease the government, although they have a great moral influence on the people, pp. 368-376.

A mystic love for France and her revolutionary ideal guides Monroe, the American minister, in his mission, but he fails, pp. 377-382. French public opinion is roused against the American government, although the political ideals and liberty of the United States are still admired, pp. 382-394. The Directory tries to intimidate the American government without losing the favor of the American people. Talleyrand's influence in this direction, pp. 395-403. The Directory refuses to receive the minister sent by the United States. Talleyrand tries to extort money from the three commissioners that the United States send subsequently, pp. 403-406.

This immoral act stirs the American people to great indignation: the Republicans are dismayed, the Federalists endeavor to profit by the crisis to carry out their program, a strong government, war with France, destruction of irreligion, pp. 406-420. The Republicans feel that public opinion is turning once more in their favor because of the progress that "French" ideas have made in America. They resume their democratic and mystic campaign, emphasizing French ideas, pp. 420-424. President Adams makes advances to France, pp. 424-425.

At this moment Talleyrand is alarmed and seeks a reconciliation. Negotiations are undertaken and Bonaparte signs a convention. He tries to utilize the memory of Washington as a standard around which to rally both democrats and monarchists, pp. 425-441.

But the establishment of a Bonapartist government in France marks the true separation between the United States and France, the moral separation. Nevertheless an American ideal of deist morality, a vision of liberty that wins over even the monarchists and exerts an influence on the writers of Romantic tendencies remains in France, pp. 442-451. America renounces pagan France and her political corruption, pp. 451-458. But France is still a powerful stimulant in American drama and literature, as well as in political, social and religious life, pp. 458-471. Thus thirty years of spiritual commerce between France and the United States brought about the creation and diffusion of a new democratic ideal. This friendship was as fruitful as it was impassioned, pp. 471-478.

JOHN JAY IS AN EXAMPLE OF WHAT PATIENCE CAN achieve. His mission in 1794 marks the triumph of his fixed idea. Jay mistrusted France already in 1782: he was the first to wish to see the alliance broken off. In 1783 he had succeeded in making a peace with England without France, at the end of a war that America had won by the aid of France.[1] From 1784 to 1788, as Secretary of the Department of Foreign Affairs, he was able to prevent the signing of consular conventions between France and America; and in 1787 he declared that the treaty of 1778 had already lapsed since it was signed only for the duration of the war.[2] In 1793 he was again one of the first to say that an alliance concluded with Louis XVI could not rightfully remain in force with the republic that had decapitated the King.[3] As he had hated and despised Louis XVI and Vergennes, so did he visit his hatred and spite on Brissot and Robespierre. The sentiment that animated Jay was a violent, all-embracing and vague fury against French culture and the French spirit. Religious zeal and rancor made him hate this Catholic and revolutionary country.[4] He set out for England in 1794 to link once more the destinies of the United States with those of England; and in the early part of the year 1795, he submitted to the approval of the American government the text of a treaty that was at last to break down all accord between France and America. Jay had been sent to England to obtain reparation of all the wrongs done the United States—the retention of the forts in the West in spite of the formal stipulations of the treaty of 1783, the illegal seizure of American ships on the high seas and the forcible enrolling of American seamen in the British navy, and the systematic destruction of all the commerce that the Americans might have with France and her colonies. Jay accepted a treaty that promised once more the evacuation of the West, which had already been promised in 1783, but refused any redress of the other wrongs that America suffered, bound the United States to some degree to the English policy by establishing the principle that England should always be accorded the treatment of the most favored nation, that no other nation at war with England should have the right to arm ships or sell prizes in American ports, and that England herself should have this right. No American citizen was to be allowed to accept a commission as a privateer from any government at war with England under pain of being considered as a pirate and treated as such. These articles were aimed directly at France, who, by virtue of the treaty of 1778, believed herself entitled to arm ships in American ports and who, in 1776, had not disavowed her citizens who went to serve in the American forces.[5] Thus, without formally breaking the treaty of alliance with France, Jay's treaty rendered it impossible of execution and substituted a defensive alliance with England for the one with France. To imagine that America might aid England in blockading France and laying waste her commerce and still remain her ally would have been absurd. In reality what Jay proposed was a complete reversal of policy, although there was some attempt to hide by hypocritical phraseology the advantages that were to be given England. An illusory reciprocity in all points concerning warships and armaments was laid down as a principle; but the only condition under which this reciprocity could be brought into play was in case of war between the United States and France. Moreover, even from a commercial point of view, the treaty was all in the favor of England, for while England was allowed to send ships of any size to trade between America and the British West Indies, the only American ships that were allowed to engage in this trade were those displacing less than seventy tons; and also the Americans were not to have the right to trade between the British West Indies and other countries.

This treaty, with everything offensive to American dignity that it contained, the position that it accorded to England and its dissimulation and pitfalls, could not be satisfactory to any sincere American patriot. Washington looked upon it with disfavor; but, impatient with France and determined not to enter the war on her side, he was inclined to accept the text of Jay's treaty, as Hamilton urged him. However, perceiving how dangerous might be the indignation of the people, Washington wanted the treaty to be kept secret as long as possible.

The Senate discussed it and, faithful to its principles, ratified it without the nation at large having learned its contents (June 24, 1795). But a Senator from Virginia, Thomas Mason, a friend and supporter of Jefferson, took it upon himself, despite the wishes of the administration, to give the text to a great democratic newspaper, *The Aurora* of Philadelphia, which immediately published it.

Then began one of the most violent conflicts that American politics have ever known. The nation as a whole was hostile to Jay's treaty and considered it as an insult. It offended both American dignity and the religion of revolution. It was unfair to France and a blow to the French party in America. It joined in hypocrisy the bonds that had been burst asunder in ecstasy in 1776 and 1783; and for an honorable alliance on a footing of equality with a great European nation, it substituted a one-sided pact with the former sovereign. In his letters to his friends, Jay declared that it was impossible to act with "more delicacy, friendliness and seemliness" than England had displayed during these negotiations.[6] His friends defended this point of view stubbornly, and a conflict that at first seemed unequal was waged between the nation on the one side and the group of Federalists who were in power on the other. Citizens of towns addressed petitions to the government. On all sides there were demonstrations. At Charleston Jay, Adams and the Devil were hanged in effigy. The newspapers published articles and letters from all parts of the country attacking Jay and his treaty. The House of Representatives was opposed to it, and the merchants, who were ordinarily so pro-English, condemned it.[7] Washington said on July 29, 1795: "At present the cry against the treaty is like that against a mad dog and every one in a manner seems engaged in running it down." The battle lasted from the beginning of 1795 to the end of 1796, and the Federalists triumphed.[8]

Even before the publication of the treaty, the conflict had begun. The President, anxious to make a clean sweep of the remains of the Jacobin influence that Genet had spread throughout the country, had published a proclamation against the Jacobin clubs and democratic societies, thereby attacking the instrument to which the pro-French party and the Republicans owed their strength. In fact, these clubs were the place where the immigrants, the poor and uneducated, mingled with certain intellectuals, became conscious of the force that their organization represented and began to put it into action. The President of the United States and the Federalist leaders were alarmed at the new force that was coming into being. It was all the more violent for the fact that its dogma was easily summed up and communicated in the three words, "Liberty, Equality, Fraternity," or in the briefer American formula that it took for its credo: "Equal Liberty." In order to discredit them and stamp out their influence, the President made use of the religious prerogatives that belonged to his office: in his Thanksgiving Proclamation calling on the nation to render thanks to God for the protection that He accorded the United States, he inserted a denunciation of the Jacobin clubs and their spirit. The Republican newspapers immediately began a campaign to defend these societies against the accusations of illegality and being an evil influence. They showed that, on the contrary, they constituted a salutary check on the too great powers of the executive. They proved that these groups gave the people a means of exercising a continual control over their representatives. They were very outspoken in their criticisms of Washington for refusing to obey the wishes of the people and turning deliberately toward England. They evoked the memory of Franklin in order to condemn these machinations. *The Aurora* of Philadelphia and *The Argus*, published by Greenleaf at New York, were continually assailing the government and taking the part of France.[9] These two great papers were copied in every city in America. It was *The Aurora* that procured the text of Jay's treaty and dared to publish it. While the surprise and indignation that followed this exposure were at their height, Greenleaf published long series of articles written by B. and R. R. Livingston under the pseudonyms of Decius and Cato. *The Independent Gazetteer* of Philadelphia published a series of articles signed Atticus, and *The Aurora* contributed to the campaign by printing articles signed variously Hancock, Valerius, Pittachus, Belisarius, etc. The theme of these attacks was, with a varying degree of violence, always the same: the President was reproached especially with having tried to impose this treaty on the people without taking their wishes into consideration, and with having sought a reconciliation with a country that stood out as the champion of tyranny. As much as possible, the Republicans confined the argument to the grounds of democracy. They also spoke of the violations of the alliance with France that were contained in the new treaty, but by preference they drew attention to the question of the principle involved. The dangers resulting from the highhandedness of a despotic executive and an alliance with an enslaved people were the main points of their argument. On every hand were heard protests of this kind. Samuel Adams and John Dickinson, the author of the famous pamphlet, *The Letters of a Pennsylvania Farmer*, openly came to the support of the Republican cause.[10] French cockades were worn on the streets, and militia companies could not give a dinner without drinking cordial toasts to the triumph of France. The Americans celebrated the victories of France and the liberation of Holland.[11] Freneau wrote:

> Genius of France, pursue thy chase
> Till Reason's law restore
> Man to man in every clime.

He also wrote an ode of vengeance against Jay.[12]

The publication of the text of the treaty with England had surprised the Federalists, but it had not caught them altogether off their guard; for the campaign that they had begun against the democratic societies tended to refute in advance every argument that their adversaries might bring up in the name of the principles of democracy. *The Gazette of the United States*, the most typical of all the Federalist papers, since it was under the direct control of Hamilton, the real leader of the Federalists, had filled its columns in every issue from January to July 1795 with attacks against the democratic societies and with letters advocating an alliance with England. When the wave of indignation broke, it had only to refute point by point everything that the Republicans said about the treaty itself. Hamilton, with his marvelous lucidity, did this in a long series of articles which he signed Camillus. It is indeed the poorest of his works. He tries in vain to prove by a long discussion of details that the treaty is advantageous to the United States, consistent with international law and judicious. He takes the trouble to cite French jurists in order to show his impartiality; but the work is long, heavy and unconvincing.[13]

All this while, Hamilton and his friends were receiving powerful assistance from the English minister and the many agents that England had stationed throughout the Union. This minister, Hammond, who seems to have been a clever man, had a large budget at his disposition and knew how to be generous with it in rewarding such members of Congress as were willing to heed his counsels.[14] He also employed publicists, the most remarkable of whom was a certain Cobbett, an Englishman by birth and nationality, who had but recently settled in America. He wrote at first for the *Massachusetts Sentinel*. Cobbett's specialty was attacking the Jacobins with their own weapons. His vehemence and coarseness, his gift for calumny, his talent for introducing anything into the realm of political discussion, made him a redoubtable adversary but also a compromising friend. In the first phase of the campaign, he was very useful to the Federalists, who were rather lacking in popular leaders; and it is curious to note that the only truly democratic voice that the Federalists found to plead their cause was that of an Englishman.[15] In addition to bribery and polemics, the English minister made use of pamphlets and indirect means. Mallet du Pan's pamphlets attacking the French

Revolution were published in translation by the old Rivington (who seems not to have ceased acting as an English spy), and were given a wide circulation. Boissy d'Anglas's speeches against the Jacobins were reprinted from the French newspapers.[16] The old but still serviceable trick of having the papers announce that France was about to seize Louisiana was brought into play again.[17] In such a game, England had everything in her favor; for ignorance of things French was still rife in America, where certain newspapers even went so far as to say "the Abbé Volney" in speaking of the famous Jacobin philosopher. English propaganda in America was once more in full swing. The government of Great Britain, without having changed its sentiments toward the former colonies, considered them as a useful weapon in the conflict with France. To spur them on, it kindled their hatred against the Jacobins and their suspicions against France, who was denounced as the seat of Jacobin intrigues. Little novels, such as *The Democrat or the Intrigues and Adventures of Jean le Noir*, brought these accusations within the comprehension of all the people.[18]

The New England papers were the most forward in disseminating and favoring this news and these pamphlets and novels. A movement that almost amounted to a crusade had begun in the Northern States and was of great service to both England and the Federalists.[19] New England had always been inclined to consider itself as being under the special protection of God and chosen by Providence for the mission of purifying the world. Many clergymen had been pleased to compare the Puritans and the Pilgrims, in their colonization of Massachusetts, to the Jews fleeing from the persecutions of the Egyptians. In 1793 Dwight wrote to Wolcott: "Not only young gentlemen from our sisters States, but from every quarter of this globe would do well to pass a few years of their life amongst us, and acquire our habits of thinking and living. Half a dozen legislators or even scholars bred in New England and dispersed through the different countries of Europe every year would in half an age change the political face of affairs of the old world." This comparison between Israel and the United States, and particularly New England, recurred continually in the sermons of the Puritans.[20] Such an attitude naturally led the preachers to consider the French Revolution as an appeal from God to the United States, either to magnify their virtues or to exhort them to penitence. As long as they could make use of the French mysticism to reënforce the old faith of the Puritans, they did not evince any hostility against the revolutionary tendencies, remembering doubtless how much France had helped America toward her independence. They protested but little at first against the execution of Louis XVI. They greeted the battle between France and Catholicism with joy. For years they had predicted the downfall of papistry and despotism; for years they had sought to unite the dogmas of Christianity with the zeal for Liberty and enliven one with the other. The great emotional tumult that the French Revolution occasioned throughout the world had at first appeared to them to be something similar to the religious movements that came about from time to time in the world and brought the masses back to the spiritual life. At first they saw in the French Revolution only mystic transports, heroic devotion to Liberty, and Christian deism. It seemed to them that here was a new and formidable force working toward the same ends as they themselves, and one that they might utilize.[21] But when the French Revolution and the French party in America had revealed their purely deistic tendency, the New England clergy began to change its attitude. The openly anti-Christian speeches of Genet and the echo that they found in America were an unmistakable warning. It was no longer a valuable auxiliary that they saw in the French Revolution, but a powerful enemy that would have replaced the religion of Christ with the worship of man deified. Noah Webster in his work on the French Revolution (1794) pointed out that, no sooner had France escaped from the domination of papist superstitions, than she fell into new forms of bigotry, such as the Cult of Reason, which, he said, derived from the same pagan stock.[22] Webster's book had been widely read in New England. It made the more impression since, almost at the same time, America was beginning to receive copies of Paine's latest book, *The Age of Reason*, written during his imprisonment, as a supreme insult to the God of the Christians, against whom he cited everything that he judged incongruous and incredible in the Bible, as well as the old arguments of Voltaire and Rousseau, to conclude in favor of the existence of a Supreme Being, architect and astronomer, who regulated the general course of things without concerning himself with details. This book contained a rich harvest of blasphemies and profanations. It roused indignation everywhere. Now, in the eyes of the American patriots, Paine was the most concrete link between their own Revolution and that of France. Preachers and publicists hastened to confute him. Belknap refuted him with citations from the Bible, J. Dennie with insults, and Cobbett with revilings mingled with calumny and vituperation.[23] A little later there was published in London a third book which was to have great success in America, where it was translated, published and widely circulated: *Memoirs on Jacobism*, by Abbé Barruel.[24] This great work was the first systematic attempt to show that the French Revolution was a product of a satanic activity and establish a connection between the campaigns of the German Illuminati, the Masonic lodges and the Jacobins. In short, he defined the French Revolution as the Antichrist. This view was certain to please the preachers of Massachusetts and the other Northern states, for it suited their own mystic tendency and allowed them to appeal to a fervor that was no longer grafted upon the revolutionary mysticism, but was, on the contrary, opposed to it. This France, papist, monarchist and corrupted, now suddenly overwhelmed by an inexplicable wave of new and diabolic mysticism—was not this one of the tokens of the end of the world, the Beast against whom America alone, pure and Christian, her feet set on the true path, stood as the representative of the Church, decimated but still resisting?

David Osgood, a clergyman of Medford, Massachusetts, was the first to perceive it. In a sermon preached on September 20, 1794, he belled the cat. He was the first to condemn France and her revolution formally from the pulpit, when most of his colleagues were still saying with Morse: "While we felicitate ourselves on a freedom from the various calamities which afflict this magnanimous nation, we cannot but feel deeply interested in their happiness and wish for their success in all virtuous measures to advance a cause dear to mankind and in defense of which we formerly experienced their generous aid." [25] Osgood opened up a new road. He had followers; he created a sensation. Sullivan, under the pseudonym of Nouvion,[26] refuted him with vehemence; but the blow had been a telling one; and from that day forth, we find this same theme in dozens of sermons. The orthodox Congregational clergy was the most zealous producer of such homilies. Also it is in the newspapers of the North that we find the most attacks against France. They criticized her republican bigotry, the which, after having been considered for six years as a sound doctrine, was now branded as a false teaching. They condemned her for her low morality and her bloody violences wherein there was nothing pure. They condemned her Constitution which, while finally recognizing the value of the balance of powers, did not understand how to go about putting it into practice. Lastly, they repeated that France was a mere beginner in the school of liberty and that she had tried to imitate the United States but had failed because of her lack of *mores* and virtues.[27] They supported their argument with the documents that Genet had foolishly published after his disgrace; by way of justifying himself, the former minister had made public the instructions given him on his departure from France, which, as the reader will remember, contained a thorough and false arraignment of Louis XVI, whom they accused of duplicity toward the United States because he had not considered it natural that they should increase their territory indefinitely at the expense of his Spanish allies. These documents had had a tremendous effect. Everywhere they had been accepted as proof of French immorality, and at this moment no argument could have shaken the French influence, reposing as it did on a sentimental and religious enthusiasm, more profoundly. There was hardly a pamphlet attacking France during the years 1795-1796 but cited Genet's instructions and drew from them the most bitter conclusions. Thus clergy, pamphleteers and politicians struck at the very heart of the Franco-American alliance.[28]

The response was furious and worthy of the attack. Aside from the customary vilification, its special aim was to save the republican cult. The French minister led the chorus, but the popular sentiment of the poor and farming classes joined in enthusiastically.

The situation of the French minister was not an easy one. To combat the calumnies and inaccuracies that the English newspapers circulated throughout the American public and press, he had only two weapons at his command, intrigue and faith. French newspapers were not reaching America or were arriving too late and irregularly.[29] Since 1785, the French press service had been disorganized and seemed in a fair way to remain so. Certain consuls, among them Mangourit at Charleston, undertook to carry on controversies, but it only brought them into discredit. Robespierre's instructions to Fauchet when he set out for America had been very friendly to the United States and very moderate: he was simply to try to draw the two countries together by making the Americans forget Genet and by offering them very considerable advantages, namely, Louisiana and Canada. Fauchet had behaved with reserve and had made a favorable impression on Washington. Unfortunately, the moral crisis through which the United States were passing and the influences that were working on Washington, had brought about a coolness between the President and the

French minister. Despite anything he might do, Fauchet had found himself, like Genet, prisoner of the Republican party and enemy of the Federalist party, with which Washington was now patently allied. Monroe and R. R. Livingston had become Fauchet's secret counselors and exercised an absolute control over his decisions. They urged him on to a war to the knife against the Federalists. Fauchet had the wisdom to conduct himself with prudence. However, when Jay's treaty was submitted to the Senate, he could not refuse to take action.[30] He had come into close relations with Randolph, Washington's Secretary of State, and it might be said that they collaborated. It is perhaps through Fauchet's influence on Randolph that Monroe was chosen as envoy to France. It was certainly Randolph who advised Fauchet to use indirect and dubious means to procure a majority in the Senate against Jay's treaty. Tazewel, a senator from Virginia, was his agent. Fauchet at that time was worried and discouraged, for he had just learned of Robespierre's fall and his own replacement by Adet, who arrived shortly after. He therefore turned over his powers and his intrigues to his successor, who was so lacking in vigilance and shamelessness that the senators eluded French influence, took dinner with Hammond, passed part of the night at his house and voted the treaty by a large majority.[31] The worst of it was that Hammond, who knew of Fauchet's machinations, was clever enough to secure a dispatch proving that Randolph had been concerned in them. He had this paper turned over to Washington; and by this one stroke the political career of Randolph and the reputation of Fauchet and France were compromised.[32]

It seems to be true that Randolph received no money from Fauchet, but it is certain that he did help him in distributing it. Fauchet's efforts to exonerate him were futile; everybody persisted in believing him guilty. Fauchet's failure can be laid at the door of the French government; he had been left without instructions and without support in the midst of the most difficult conditions and in a most critical situation.[33] He returned to Europe embittered. As with Genet, his enthusiasm had given place to indignation. In this nation whom he had seen at first as the apostles of a common faith, he now saw hypocritical bigots. He recommended an energetic policy to the French government and urged that France retake the Mississippi valley in order to bring the Americans to appreciate her force and the value of an alliance with her. He advocated neither violence nor interference with American internal politics, but a close accord with the Republican party.[34]

Adet, who succeeded him, tried to follow this program. Like Fauchet, he was still young and a scholar (chemist) whom the Revolution had drawn into politics. He regretted leaving Geneva where he had been the French minister, and he did not hide his dejection at being sent to America. He wrote an imprudent letter in which he compared the Republic of Geneva with that of the United States, much to the detriment of the latter. This letter was discovered and published in the United States. He also lacked adaptability. His scruples frustrated Fauchet's immoral machinations. He did not however refrain from sending three agents into the West to spy out and stir up the inhabitants of the region. His antipathy for America was so marked that he could not possibly make a favorable impression.[35] He employed an *émigré* from Santo Domingo, Tanguy La Boissière, to draw up a report on commerce between the United States and France. This work, which was very remarkable for its documentation, was published in an edition of one hundred copies, and Adet did not allow any of these copies to be sold or shown to the Americans, lest it should be used as a weapon against France. By temperament he was a dogmatic Jacobin and a reformer. For him the love of France was an article of faith, not only for Frenchmen, but for all men. He said scornfully of Jefferson: "Although an admirer of the efforts that we have made to break our chains and dissipate the clouds of ignorance that hang over mankind, Mr. Jefferson is an American and, as such, he cannot sincerely be our friend." [36] The Committee of Public Safety had directed him to present a French flag to President Washington. For fear of seeing the flag neglected and slighted, Adet waited until Congress was in session to execute this commission. The presentation occasioned a very impressive session in the House of Representatives, who accepted this token of friendship with the deepest and most sincere emotion. The flag was accompanied by a note from the Committee of Public Safety exalting Liberty, the Republic, the republican brotherhood of nations, and the French victories that were preparing the way for a republican universe. The House replied in the same spirit; but Washington, in his speech of thanks, said that the flag would be deposited in the archives of the United States. The American flag was hung in the assembly-hall of the Convention. The difference of treatment roused Adet's indignation. "This flag," he said, "will be hidden away in an attic and destined to become the provender of the rodents and insects that live there." [87] Filled with resentment against the Federalists and the government, he began carrying on a furious propaganda in favor of the Republicans. Despairing of obtaining any satisfaction from the President and the existing Congress, he went through the country stirring up support for Jefferson. When the critical moment of election approached, he published in *The Aurora* of Philadelphia four open letters to the American government couched in pompous and sentimental terms and threatening reprisals if the American government did not change its attitude and cease violating the treaty of 1778. He announced that France, by way of showing her disapproval, was about to recall him. His intention was to evince a melodramatic change of heart and show himself once more as a generous friend as soon as the triumph of the Republicans should be assured.[38] It is painful and sad to recall all these intrigues when one remembers the sincere enthusiasm that the masses in America felt for France.

In many churches, the victories of France were still celebrated as triumphs for Liberty. The majority of the newspapers still represented France as defending the cause of humanity. This was particularly true in the South and West where almost all of the papers spoke in these terms. There was rejoicing at the "liberation" of Holland. The 14th of July was celebrated. South Carolina distinguished itself by its ardor, but Baltimore was not far behind. The Irish members of Tammany were almost all of them Francophiles, as were the Germans. News of French victories was eagerly published throughout the country. Nevertheless, public opinion and French propaganda suffered two defeats: Jay's treaty was ratified by both Houses; and Adams was elected president over Jefferson, who lost by two votes. The fear of war had given the Federalists the support of the House of Representatives. Through the efforts of the clergy, their party had gained strength in the North and had not been defeated in the South.[39] Moreover, they had at their disposition all the resources that their position as the party already in power afforded. They had scored a victory, but not without great difficulty, and the fight was not over. Between *their* ideal of a strong government that should dominate the people and mark out their path for them according to the dictates of traditional morality, and the *other* ideal of a weak government that should accept the orders of the people as its political and moral code, there could be no truce. The Republican party, which had been so weak in 1792, was now of equal strength with the Federalists, and thirsted for vengeance. It had consolidated itself; and slowly its great man, Jefferson, drawing from French examples whatever he judged assimilable in America, had formulated a doctrine. He still took refuge behind the French doctrines, which helped him to elaborate his own; but his party was becoming a national party with a world-wide platform and mission.

Thus in 1796 and 1797 all those in whose hearts the democratic ideal burned, all those who were to become the leaders of the Republican party, came under French influence and derived their doctrines from those from across the sea. Nothing is more curious than to see John Dickinson, the enlightened patriot of 1770, the methodic and moderate revolutionist, so firmly attached to the French Republic in 1797. In the letters that he published under the name of Fabius, he took a generous and philosophic attitude that was in keeping with his idealistic soul. He saw the French Republic as the heir of Louis X, who in 1315 declared all citizens of France equal, and Louis XVI, who freed the United States. It is the daughter of Rome, fighting in the name of immortal principles, against the venality and despotism of England, resembling Carthage in these respects. Thus in the cultured and religious mind of Dickinson, France had become the incarnation of an eternal liberating force, the guide of groping Humanity.[40] At the other extremity of the United States, in western Pennsylvania, the democratic leader H. H. Brackenridge, a fiery orator whose eloquence swayed throngs, offers a striking example of the worship of France. His novel, *Modern Chivalry*, undoubtedly the most amusing and original American novel of the time, shows the extent to which France dominated all imaginations in the West. The hero of the book is a certain Teague O'Regan, a shrewd and pusillanimous Irishman who has hired out as a servant to a land-owner, Captain Farrago.[41] The master, who resembles somewhat Don Quixote, lacks originality and is used merely as a double for the author of the book, but Teague is a living character, and although Brackenridge imitated rather puerilely Scarron's *Roman comique* and Lesage's *Gil Blas*, Teague is truly an Irish-American colonist of 1797. His adventures at Washington's court where he goes to ask for an appointment, his efforts to acquire elegant manners, the lessons that he takes from a French dancing-master, his joy at being appointed tax-collector in Pennsylvania, the trials and tribulations that he encounters in the exercise of his office, which lead to his being tarred and feathered by people of his district in wrath at his greed—all this is told in a lifelike, true and clean-cut way. With rapid and sure strokes, Brackenridge depicts life in the taverns, along the roads, in the ministries and in the camps of the new-born country.

Nothing gives a more accurate notion of the social conditions and the ideas that prevailed in those days. But the purpose of the book is to show that, even in a republic, care must be taken to maintain the spirit of democracy and keep magistrates from arrogating personal power and forgetting that they are merely public servants.[42] One of the most characteristic episodes of this book is the meeting between Farrago and the old Marquis de Lezay Marnésia in the mountains where the illustrious old man has retired in his flight from demagogy. An elegant and rather moderate discourse condemning the French Revolution is put into the mouth of Marnésia. Farrago answers him skillfully and earnestly and proves that in its essential principles the French Revolution is right, because it upholds the inalienable right of all men and all generations to direct their own destinies. Without this there would be no progress, says Farrago, and through him, Brackenridge.

In Brackenridge's novel, as in Dickinson's pamphlet and many poems and articles of the period, reverence for France is intimately connected with faith in the rights of man. These two elements form a sort of cult: it is no longer, as it was in 1776, a mixture of Biblical spirit and national consciousness; it has become in itself a religion that dominates and threatens to exclude all others.

*

* *

No one, with the possible exception of Paine, was more imbued with this faith than Monroe; and again, the difference between the faith of these two men was one of tendency rather than intensity. Each of them is a prototype of the revolutionary intellects that Jacobinism created. Monroe had gone to France, not for the realization of personal ambitions or national aims, but to bring about a unity of action between the two great republics of the world and establish their collaboration on a base of profound spiritual intimity. He considered himself as the envoy of the American people to the French people, and he sought to see all problems not from the American or French points of view, but from the standpoint of the rights of man.[43] He had believed in the good faith of the American government that sent him to France at the same time that it sent Jay to England. In France he did not hesitate to take the Convention into his confidence and open his heart to them. At a time when every one distrusted his neighbor, he made it a principle to have confidence: he had confidence in the future of the French Republic. He believed that France was not trying to draw the United States into war and that she wished the Americans only good, as she asserted. He believed that France would defend the interests of the United States sincerely against Spain and England (1794). He believed that at the same time the United States would endeavor to help France in the full measure of her means. He suggested in America and in

France that the Americans might advance money to France in 1795, as France had done for America from 1776 to 1783.[44] He felt sure that the American government wanted to make Jay's negotiations with England as acceptable as possible to France, and he candidly wrote to Jay to obtain a text of the treaty (1795). He saw in the discussions between France and the United States concerning commerce and privateers, a question of principle which the two republics would settle in a friendly way according to the dictates of the right and their hearts. He had but scant sympathy for the American merchants who, under the protection of a friendly flag, carried on a commerce hostile to France; and he concentrated his efforts on bringing the American government to comprehend that the French Revolution had been the renovation of the world and that it was an accomplished fact, and endeavored to show the French that they had everything to gain from the friendship of the United States, but that violence would spoil everything. His diplomatic correspondence is curious and admirable; his notes, which expose all of his relations with the members of the Conventions and later with the Directors and their ministers, bear witness to his good faith and his intelligence.[45] He was the dupe of no one except his faith, and he was the dupe of every one. The American government hid the true nature of Jay's treaty from him and let him lie involuntarily to France. The Directory made subtle attempts to persuade him to be its political agent in America and, since he was too honest for this, tried at least to use him as a means of obtaining money from the United States.[46] In spite of the resentment that he justly felt against his government for sending him on a mission with misleading instructions, in spite of the difficulty of his position in France after the signing of Jay's treaty, Monroe did not give up hope; he remained in Paris in expectation of better times to come, a Republican election in America or a return to prudence and idealism in France.[47] He importuned the Directory with efforts to prevent them from sending Vincent, the Governor of Santo Domingo, to the United States with an ultimatum and appointing Mangourit, Genet's famous collaborator, who had caused so much disturbance and carried on so much propaganda as French consul at Charleston, to the post of Minister to the United States.[48] He succeeded (1796); and he would thus have gained enough time for a change of attitude to take place in the United States, if the counsels of Fauchet, Adet and Paine had not at last persuaded the Directory to try to impress the Americans by recalling the French minister at Philadelphia shortly before the electoral campaign in favor of Jefferson.[49] Even then this decision was only provisional and was to have been revoked in the event of Jefferson's victory. Thus Monroe, by his conviction and devotion, not unmixed with a certain naïveté withal, had been able to maintain a degree of harmony between two governments inclined to hate each other. Paine shattered his work. Imprisoned through the efforts of Robespierre and Gouverneur Morris, so it seems, Paine had come to harbor a boundless hatred against his persecutors, and he considered Washington, the friend and protector of Morris, as one of them. Instead of seeking to establish accord through confidence, as Monroe did, he attempted to accomplish it by suspicion. He began making denunciations. Also, he was in need of money, he drank too much, he led an irregular life, he had lost his seat in the Convention, and a sort of belated ambition made him seek to play a part in diplomacy. Monroe had been instrumental in securing his release from prison and in keeping him alive. Both men held to the same principles; but Monroe was a mystic and trusting believer, while Paine had become a suspicious fanatic and inquisitor.[50] He attacked Washington publicly as a scoundrel and the author of his own sorrows, in an open letter which caused the greatest scandal both in America and in France (July, 1796). In various pamphlets he urged the Convention to adopt a highly radical constitution, and at the same time he wrote articles against England to be circulated in America for the French government.[51] He furnished information concerning America to Delacroix, the Minister of Foreign Affairs. He tried to influence this minister and public opinion by the information that he gave and by inspiring the communications of the fiery patriot, Jacques Ducher, the former consul at Wilmington, who continued to concern himself with American affairs. There is still preserved in the Archives of Foreign Affairs the memorandum from Paine and Ducher recommending that the Directory refuse to receive as minister Pinkney, whom the American government had just appointed to this post, in order, as Paine said, to ridicule Washington, who had chosen Pinkney, and to safeguard the principles of Democracy.[52]

Paine's advice received more consideration than Monroe's. Monroe, accused in America of supporting Paine, and in France of being disloyal, was recalled (1797). However, before leaving, he attended a ceremonial reception that the Directory gave as a farewell to him, in order to show the high esteem that they would ever feel for a patriot, even when they considered his government as a traitor. Monroe did not try to evade it, whether because he himself was exasperated at last, or because he counted on this fraternal ceremony to open the eyes of the American people. He ended his diplomatic career as he had begun it, with a confession of faith in the Rights of Man, without fearing or caring what his government might think of it.

While Jefferson, Monroe and their friends were trying to rouse the American people in the name of the new morality, a like problem confronted the French people. The action of the United States in ratifying Jay's treaty with England had placed France in the necessity of deciding the question as to whether it was better to keep up an alliance whose very spirit had been violated, or to sever relations with a nation to whom they were united by sympathy, common principles and similarity of government. From 1795 to 1797 public opinion in France was greatly preoccupied with this question, and it may be said that it was one of the moral worries of the Directory. This government, which succeeded the Convention without adhering to its principles, had to solve in this question one of the gravest and most delicate problems of doctrine that ever confronted it. From September, 1796, to January, 1798, the reports of the Paris police mentioned at least every month great agitation concerning the United States in the cafés where politics were discussed. It is one of the subjects that recurs most often; and behind the euphemisms of the agents of the Directory, we divine the restlessness and dissatisfaction occasioned in the mind of the public by the policy that the French government was following in the New World. The public, moreover, was very badly informed, and these discussions and rumors prove how ignorant it was of the most essential facts: John Adams was considered as a friend of France, through a confusion, no doubt, with his cousin Samuel Adams, and a thousand absurd rumors were current. Paine and the Paris group of United Irishmen seem to have contributed to stirring up French opinion against the American Federalists, Jay's treaty and, in a general way, the United States.[53]

In fact, the two most general sentiments among the public were disapproval of the Directory for persisting in an arrogant and unjust policy, and wrath against the American government for having abandoned France in favor of England. All the French newspapers, except those that were in the pay of England, gave echo to these opinions during the year 1795. They still employed a friendly, affectionate or admiring tone, according to their tendencies, in speaking of the American people, whose hostility to Jay's treaty was everywhere mentioned and praised. They laid much emphasis on the opposition between Washington and the American nation—the one grown old and beguiled by England, the other generous and loyal. They brought out the facts that the French West Indies lay at the mercy of the wrath of America, that French commerce needed American ships and ports, and that a break between the two great republics would be a shameful calamity. More than all this, it was felt and said in all circles that the United States represented a moral force that France needed and an ideal that she could not deny without renouncing the principles of 1789 and 1793.[54]

Even among the Royalists, a current of opinion very favorable to the United States had set in. In proportion as the French Republic deviated from the American type of government, it became easier and more tempting for them to laud America.[55] They recalled that she owed her pure liberty to Louis XVI. But above all, there was the fact that the *émigrés* who had been able to flee to the United States and who, for the most part, hoping to see the end of the Revolution, had not remained there, had come back to France filled with a profound and indelible sentiment of affection and gratitude for the country that had welcomed them so generously. Received by the aristocracy of New England, New York and Philadelphia, they had seen all the pleasantest and most winning aspects of America. After the turmoil of France, they had enjoyed these homely and wholesome ways. Steeped in the spirit of Rousseau, they had seen the Indians, the negroes and the farmers in a poetic light. They had appreciated the beauty of the soil, the plants and the race. A poetic rapture pervaded them.[56] They had wept on eating their first slice of white bread on this free and virgin soil. They had shed even happier tears on freeing their slaves, wild with gratitude, before returning to Europe.[57] The best and most fascinating descriptions of the United States about 1795 have been left us by Royalist *émigrés;* but the finest of these is unquestionably the one written by Henriette-Lucie Dillon, Marquise de La Tour du Pin de Gouvernet, daughter-in-law of Louis XVI's Minister of War. Saved by Madame Tallien, she passed what were doubtless the two happiest years of her life in America. There she lived the life of a farmer-philosopher, milking her cows, making her butter, superintending her slaves and servants, giving bits of ribbon to the Indian women, who adored her, and winning over the braves by the charm of her smile and the splendor of her manners. She frequented Talleyrand, who was kindly and sincere with her. Her best friends were the Schuylers, the Van Rensselaers, Alexander Hamilton, all the finest and most intelligent society of the New York aristocracy. But above all she loved her farm, her country dog and the starry sky. When she came back to France, her heart seemed rent in two. "I felt no pleasure at returning to France," she says.[58] Many an *émigré* knew this sentiment. Europe was a disappointment to them. We might mention first of all Chateaubriand, who owed to this sense of disappointment his America, the America of which he dreamed during the long nights in bivouac along the Rhine and in the garrets of London, the America that he created and revealed to the world. His first book, *Essai historique, politique et moral sur les Révolutions anciennes et modernes considérées dans leur Rapport avec la Révolution française* (1797), shows his enthusiasm and disappointment; he admires the French Revolution and he condemns it. He exclaims: "I have seen the fields of Lexington. I stood there in silence, like the traveler at Thermopylae, contemplating the graves of these warriors of two worlds who were the first to die in obedience to the laws of Country. On treading this philosophic ground which told me with mute eloquence of how empires disappear and rise, I confessed my nothingness before the paths of Providence and bowed my forehead to the dust." [59] Then he added: "The American Revolution is the immediate cause of the French Revolution." [60] In the pages that he devotes to America, Chateaubriand shows himself as a faithful disciple of Raynal, and some of his phrases are directly inspired by those of Raynal. Like the Abbé, he condemns on moral grounds the action of France in intervening to defend rebellious subjects; like him, he admires the patriotism of the Americans and their doctrines; like him, he praises their principles and fears lest they prove unable to remain faithful to them. There is a gibe at the Quakers and a eulogy of Major André.[61] All this might have been written in 1786 and links Chateaubriand with the past, with the group of pre-revolutionary philosophers. But his lengthy and moving description of an evening along the Hudson and the songs of the American women bemoaning the fate of André, and the new tone that he uses in speaking of the land of America bear witness to his personal impression. The essay ends with the magnificent description of "a night among the savages of America." To him, as to Madame de La Tour du Pin, the United States had revealed new conformities between man free and spontaneous, and living things.[62] He was filled with a longing, an obsession, not political but lyric and emotional. In order to forestall any confusion with the Jacobin and patriotic mysticism, he is inclined to describe the United States as the land of the Indians, but this is essentially only a literary artifice; he knew nothing, or almost nothing, of the Indians; what he did see and what moved him were the fields of Lexington. His attitude is typical of that of the most intelligent and sincere of the *émigrés:*

Lezay Marnésia, wandering throughout Europe after his return from America, retains the delightful image of a world where earth, principles and man move together in a natural and tranquil liberty, illumined by the fear of God.[63] Madame de La Tour du Pin, Chateaubriand and Lezay were converted in the New World to the worship of natural liberty as it is born from the contact of man, living in isolation and free from the restraint of an imperious government, with Nature. And with *them* this worship was emotional, artistic and personal.[64]

Many other *émigrés* had lived in America at Marietta in Ohio and Gallipolis, the colony founded by the Scioto Company, which struggled along until the end of the century. Others, with the Vicomte de Noailles, Omer Talon and Dupetit-Thouars, had tried to found the Asylum in Pennsylvania and had lived there for some time; but all of these undertakings had finally failed for lack of capital, practical intelligence and physical strength. Nevertheless, all of these colonists who had returned to Europe had brought back sentiments similar to those of Madame de La Tour du Pin: they denounced the speculators as the cause of their sorrows, but they loved the soil, Nature and the life of the "American wilderness." [65]

Thus it is not surprising to find the Royalist papers at Paris and outside of France taking the part of the United States in their quarrel with France, satirizing Thomas Paine (who, in truth, was legitimate prey) and exalting Washington, who henceforth was held up as the noblest example of a man of order guided by a prudent love of liberty. This was the attitude of Mallet du Pan, Peltier, etc.[66]

Such also was the attitude of the conservatives, the great mass of citizens, yesterday monarchists, who had joined the Revolution only to save their lives and were seeking to gain control of the Directory and, if possible, to bring it around to a policy of liberalism. Some of these conservatives were only Royalist conspirators in disguise, but most of them were former Feuillants, patriots of 1789, Constitutionalists and sincere reformers who, impressed by the magnitude of the French Revolution, adopted the democratic idealism spontaneously. They were sincere in dreaming of a general conciliation and a gradual adapting of France to the Republic. Many of them had no projects for the future but sought only to live: after the sufferings of the Terror, they accepted the inevitable and tried only to make the government bearable. Everything led them to admire the United States and use them as an argument. The happiness, simple life, tolerance, order and religious spirit that reigned in the New World made it a democratic Eden for these conscientious and apprehensive minds. As a general thing, they saw it from the Federalist point of view and felt a strong sympathy for that party. A voluminous book, *Le Tableau de la Situation actuelle des Etats-Unis d'Amérique* by C. Pictet of Geneva

(Paris, Year III), which was printed in 1795 and enjoyed popularity during the following years, bears witness to this state of mind. Pictet was an honest citizen of Geneva, a philanthropist who had devoted many years to the service of his country and the improvement of agriculture. He believed in the progress and goodness of humanity. He was also a man of letters like his brother Marc Antoine Pictet, in collaboration with whom he published the *Bibliothèque britannique*, one of the best literary, economic and philosophic reviews of the period. Pictet's picture of the United States is taken from the works of Pastor Morse, Tench Coxe and Jefferson; his compilation is not highly original, and its only merit is to bring American books within the reach of the French public and to show the United States as a rare example for the world at large, and one so admirable that Pictet exclaims: "Other nations will pay dearly perhaps for imitating the dangerous example of so noble a revolution." He shows the American uprising as having its origin in a concern for the noblest of principles and as remaining always peaceable and moderate; he shows the colonists as capable of maintaining "an orderliness, son of Liberty," and he cries out to Heaven, "O Liberty! Liberty! Daughter of Heaven! Precious gift, meet only for righteous nations! Source of virtues, glory and prosperity!" [67] He proves that the Americans owe their good fortune to their *mores*, their morality and their religion, which makes them understand the rights of man.[68] This is the same lesson that is contained in the letters of the Duc de La Rochefoucauld Liancourt, then a refugee in America, whence he sends his friends, the former Constitutionalists, patriotic and philosophic exhortations. He even published in 1796 a little work on the prisons of Philadelphia, in which he praises the justice and humaneness of the Pennsylvanians for seeking, not to punish, but to improve their convicts. Although he does not make it himself, a comparison between this humane and generous republic and the Convention naturally suggests itself to the reader's mind. It is in the name of the United States and the ideal that they represent that the conservatives carried on their battle against the absolutism of the Convention, and later, of the Directory.[69]

In 1795 a complete series of pamphlets criticizing the Constitution in the name of Liberty had already appeared. The most spirited of these is undoubtedly the one written by Adrien Lezay, the son of the Marquis de Marnésia.[70] It was entitled *Qu'est-ce que la Constitution de 1793?* but the police having forbidden criticism of the Constitution, Lezay renamed his pamphlet *Considérations sur les Etats de Massachusetts et de Pennsylvanie, ou Parallèle de deux Constitutions, dont l'une est fondée sur la Division, l'autre sur l'Unité de la Législature.* Lezay proclaims that there are no more great men, and no more pure men, in this world unless it be beyond the seas in America and that it is therefore to that country that France should turn for examples if she would have a good Constitution. He preaches in favor of two legislative houses, the balance of powers, liberalism and tolerance, as practiced by the Americans. He imagines Samuel Adams looking out over the superb Boston Bay with the rich, peaceful and virtuous city spread out before him, explaining to the author the workings of the constitution to which the land owes its prosperity. It is a sort of Socratic dialogue—in intention at least (for as a pamphleteer, Lezay is straightforward and daring, but prosaic). He brings out clearly enough the dangers of a single house, even in Pennsylvania where men are almost perfect. This pamphlet made a great impression, and the arguments that it contained were used by other writers. Lenoir Laroche utilized them and also cited the example of America in his tract, *L'Esprit de la Constitution qui convient à la France.* Mounier did the same in *Adolphe.* In all these works the example of Massachusetts was taken as being the perfect type of liberty within the law, and the American *mores* as being the highest degree of virtue. In 1796 Roederer [71] wrote that the United States were the happiest nation on earth because they had an agricultural civilization, and La Harpe [72] stated that common sense had taken refuge in America.[73] All parties took the United States as a standard by which to judge the corruption of the times. Delacroix, making a study of the means of regenerating France, demanded that she should first come to a reconciliation with the United States "who preceded us in liberty and almost inoculated us with it." [74] In his *Considérations sur la France*, Joseph de Maistre was halted in his criticisms of all the various governments, by the United States in which he found nothing to condemn.[75] He declined to pass judgment on them by saying, "Let them grow up," and he respected them. We see what a privileged situation that North America enjoyed in the opinion of all the philosophers, even the monarchists and conservatives. This esteem and influence are also apparent in the newspapers and political controversies. Many papers excused Washington's government for accepting Jay's treaty by asserting that French inferiority on the seas put the United States at the mercy of England. They exposed the sins of the Convention and the ruin of American commerce by French privateers. Finally, when it was learned that the Directory had refused to receive Pinckney, although he had arrived in Paris with a regular appointment as American Minister to France,[76] Louis Philippe de Ségur dared to take up the defense of the United States in two stirring articles in which he stated that the French Republic was to be blamed for its treatment of its allies (April-May, 1797).[77] A few weeks later in the Council of the Five Hundred Pastoret [78] took up the same theme and asked that the government be condemned for having insulted the United States (2 Messidor, Year V) and be obliged to return to a juster policy. He wanted first of all an investigation. This motion, urged with great insistence and supported by a vigorous newspaper campaign, caused a great stir and would undoubtedly have produced results if the Directory had not put an end to all this opposition by the *coup d'état* of the eighteenth of Fructidor. At this date Dupont de Nemours' paper, *L'Historien*, which had been the most ardent defender of the United States and their ideal, also disappeared.[79] One feels to what extent the Jacobins and the supporters of the Directory had been worried by this attack and how great a danger they had considered it. The *Conservateur* for the first of Complémentaire, Year V (September 17, 1797) contains a significant paragraph: it says that the Directory was wise to put an end to royalist plots by the *coup d'état* of the eighteenth of Fructidor, because the monarchists were trying only to prevent the functioning of the government and "such was the purpose that inspired Pastoret's motion of order." In this year 1797, the United States were to some extent the standard around which the parties fought. The conservatives used them as a means of criticizing the executive and discrediting the integrity of the Directory. The Directory sought to prove that it was following the true tradition of the heroes of 1776 and 1793; it wanted to break with the American government without ceasing to benefit by the moral prestige of the United States. Its position was an awkward one. Its material triumph over the conservatives afforded it only a breathing-spell.[80] It could not live without a doctrine;

and it needed the American principles, although they embarrassed it more and more every day.

Great changes had taken place among the Jacobins and the revolutionary patriots since 1792. The enthusiasm, mixed with confidence and hope, that had reigned among them then had given way to a somber determination in which distrust and resentment had a part. And the government established by the Constitution of 1794 had not reassured them; it gave the political power to the wealthy peasants and bourgeois. It sought its support in the most conservative classes, among whom monarchist tendencies still survived. In spite of foreign victories, it was no longer the spirit of Valmy that was dominant among the Jacobins of 1795. The Convention attacked them and closed their clubs; the Directory kept them out of power and used them as a weapon against the reactionaries. Thus they collaborated with a government that they despised or, at least, distrusted. This government still used the revolutionary vocabulary frequently and tried to take advantage of the patriotic ardor, but above all it sought to safeguard material interests and satisfy personal ambitions. Any too definite moral code was a hindrance to them. Thus the Jacobins, through resentment, and the Directory, as a ruse, were to have the same attitude toward the United States and a common policy. They sought to rouse the nation against its government, they praised the people and attacked the administration in word and deed.

The opinion that the Jacobins and the Directory formed of the United States was derived from the accounts and descriptions of the latest French ministers to America, Fauchet and Adet, and the impressions of the revolutionary *émigrés* who had been restored to favor, such as Moreau de Saint-Méry, Demeusnier, Talleyrand, Hauterive, Volney, etc. We have also seen how much influence Paine exercised on all the French revolutionary groups in matters that concerned the concept of America and the policy to be followed with regard to her. Fauchet and Adet both came home very much dissatisfied with their mission. But Fauchet seems to have studied the United States more thoroughly and understood them better than his successor. He perceived their importance.[81] In the reports that he submitted to the French government on his return from America, he said: "The United States have shown to great advantage in these latter times of revolution and disputes concerning the nature of governments.[82] The American institutions have been held up as a model to which governments pride themselves on having more or less conformed; and, since the most complete happiness that may be desired in the social order has resulted from them, they are everywhere adduced as a conclusive authority in matters of political controversy. Cabinets like to acquire a standing in the eyes of the people by claiming to be in good intelligence with a nation that is regarded as being the most wisely governed." Fauchet recognized the close moral bonds between France and the United States, as well as the blunders of the French revolutionary governments in the New World; but, filled with resentment against the government at Philadelphia, he urged a policy of "firmness" toward the United States. He wanted France to give effective aid to the pro-French party and intimidate the pro-English party. Adet went further than this. Of a less judicious character than Fauchet and resentful at having been sent to America, he was prejudiced against this country, of whose value and importance he was nevertheless aware. He had confidence in the American people. "The party in the government of the United States which is devoted to England seems to me to have filled the measure of outrage toward the French nation," he wrote in Nivose of the Year IV (1796), "but the people remain constant in their attachment for us. It would doubtless suffice for the Directory to adopt firm and judicious measures to recall our allies to their true interests and make them declare themselves against England, their natural enemy." Adet's plans were adopted and put into application—and miscarried. This defeat made Adet only the more bitter and finished making him a dangerous advisor.[83]

It is strange that the whole group of intelligent, patriotic men and sincere revolutionists who had gathered around Talleyrand and his friend the Constitutionalist bookseller, Moreau de Saint-Méry, should have been so bitter and so harmful to a good understanding between

France and the United States. Coming to America filled with a longing for liberty and a desire to see a land where it was being given an honest trial at last, these illustrious personages were also filled with an extraordinary vanity that caused them great suffering. Equality, as it was practiced in America, at first annoyed and later enraged them. Moreau de Saint-Méry has left us an interminable account of his stay in the New World, which is a masterpiece of wounded conceit and short-sightedness. Obliged to earn his living at Philadelphia by engaging in trade, and later, selling and printing books, he could not forgive the American authorities and upper classes for neglecting him.[84] With only the rabble as associates, he preferred to associate with nobody; his undertakings failed and he became embittered. The judgments that he pronounces on American life and morality are a gross and blind injustice. He could not forgive the young republic for ignoring, or rather, for being averse to, the use of enemas, and he drew from this prejudice on their part the gravest conclusions against the good sense and sincerity of the Americans. In spite of himself, he still admired their tolerance, liberty, popular government and simplicity, but he did not understand them; and he circulated, together with the cruelest calumnies, the silliest inaccuracies. Those who came to his shop every day to talk with him and discuss the destinies of the world around his counter while they sipped Madeira wine—Talleyrand, Demeusnier, Théophile de Cazenove,

Beaumetz, Nancrède, Volney and Boislandry—could not fail to be influenced by the ideas of the eloquent Moreau. It is curious to see Talleyrand's views correspond so faithfully with his. Talleyrand had, however, been received in the best society of Philadelphia. Hamilton had entertained him royally. He had grown wealthy. But this was not enough. Of a caustic wit and unlimited ambition, Talleyrand was unhappy and restless in the United States. He was humiliated when Washington refused him an audience. He suffered at feeling himself despised by the middle class as one of the causes of the French Revolution. He waxed indignant at the artlessness of the Americans and the "religious prejudice" that prevailed among them. The immoral life that he led, by making him an object of opprobrium, led him to despise American society. He accused it of hypocrisy. Liberty without license was beyond his understanding. In short, this man, one of the most intelligent of his time, returned to Europe without having in the least understood the New World. He could not withhold his admiration, for his mind retained its perspicacity, but even this sentiment was mixed with hatred. He had found himself dwarfed, out of his element, even somewhat ridiculous, in this country that he had hoped to dazzle, instruct and direct. This impression and their inability to recognize the religious character of the entire American population, including even the revolutionaries, explain the attitude of Moreau de Saint-Méry, Talleyrand and their friends, without excepting Volney, of whom we shall speak later.[85]

Talleyrand's influence had great weight; and in order to comprehend the conduct of the Directory with regard to the United States, we must examine closely the activities of the former Bishop of Autun. After his return to France, thanks to the protection of Madame de Staël, he immediately succeeded in being admitted to the Institute to which he addressed two communications. That of the fifteenth of Germinal, Year V, was entitled *Memoranda on the Commercial Relations of the United States with England*. This work, clear, brief, intelligent and composed well and in a delightful style, could not fail to impress the Institute and, at the same time, political circles. Into this paper Talleyrand had put all his dissatisfaction with the United States, whose moral greatness he still endeavored, however, to exploit. He showed the United States as being entirely devoted to England, with whom they had language, genius and commercial interests in common. With the greatest inaccuracy, though not unskillfully, he accused Louis XVI and his government of having tried to discourage merchants from trading with the United States, and he stated that it was now too late to begin such commerce. He concluded therefore that France could scarcely hope to have close relations with the Americans. He depicted them as being governed on all occasions by their interests and as being still incapable of forming a nation, because their character was unformed. His judgment was most harsh and arbitrary. He cited very few facts in support of his views. He contented himself with saying "How *could* America have a character of her own when her population is composed of fishermen and woodcutters?" Fishermen, living continually at sea, form attachments for no land and have no country. As for the woodcutters, he goes on, "The American woodcutter takes no interest in anything; any emotional idea is far from him: the branches that Nature limns with such elegance, beautiful foliage, a bright hue that enlivens one part of the forest, a strong wind that spreads gloom over another—all this is nothing to him; he has no memories to attach to anything. His only concern is the number of strokes that it will take to fell his tree. . . . The product of his toil does not go through all the stages of growth so endearing to the farmer; he does not follow up the destiny of his products: he does not know the pleasure of new experiments, and if, on leaving the spot where he has lived for years, he does not forget his ax, he leaves no regrets behind him." [86] After such poetic reasoning and this scarcely scientific exposition of American shortcomings, Talleyrand praised the perfection of the social life of the United States, where every one was free, where absolute tolerance reigned, and where one of the most violent revolutions that the world had ever seen was followed by an era of peace, prosperity and liberty. From this he drew the following moral, which was addressed rather to the

Directory than to the Institute: "After a revolution that has changed everything, we must be able to lay aside our hatreds, unless we are prepared to renounce our happiness for ever." [87] The work closed with this reflection.

Talleyrand could not but be satisfied with his work. He had given vent to his spite, flattered rather basely the powers that were, proffered the fashionable counsels and proved his talent as a diplomat as well as a philosophic writer. His phrases suited the taste of the times, and they were abundantly reprinted and praised. Even the friends of the United States did not seem to perceive how much wrong the *Memoranda* would do. They were too delighted with this adroit appeal to tolerance to care to quibble with Talleyrand. The Jacobins made use of it, but they took but few extracts from it, because of the moderate counsels that it contained.[88]

From the end of 1794 to the middle of 1797, the Jacobin newspapers and the periodicals subsidized by the Directory received much information in the spirit of Talleyrand's contribution. We find Mazzéi giving out to the French papers a letter in which Jefferson describes with indignation the autocratic spirit of the Federalists. A certain M. de Bulow's attacks on the character and customs of the Americans were given wide circulation. Paine was writing his articles against Washington. There were also here and there virulent letters from American Republicans denouncing the Federalists and Adams. *La Décade philosophique* published a letter from Marsillac, the

Quaker, who, under the influence of, and perhaps in collaboration with, Volney, furnished information on life in the United States and painted a sad picture of the condition of the arts in America.[89] With less severity, a friend of Brissot's, F. M. Bayard, brought out a book on the United States in 1791 in which, mingled with delightful picturesque and romantic scenes and warm praises of the people, we find violent criticisms of the American character.[90] If we add that the French newspapers drew their information concerning the United States from the English press, we shall understand the tone of the Jacobin papers. They noted with joy and accuracy, however, all the celebrations held in America in honor of France, all friction between England and the United States, and all the symptoms of a revolt of the American people against their government. They did not fail to praise the two sister revolutions of France and America. They came out in favor of following the example of the United States, who had banished the Tories for ever and never allowed them to return, who tolerated all religions but scorned them all. The papers continued to cite Franklin as a republican saint. In short, they mixed bitterness and enthusiasm according to the needs of the polemic. They would have liked to continue utilizing America as the example of a perfect and complete revolution, while despising its government and, if possible, its people. But this was difficult. Thus, from the criticisms of Jay's treaty, which began in the middle of 1795, to articles hostile to Pinckney, and virulent denunciations of Ségur and later Pastoret (May and June, 1797), their tone grew more vociferous. In June, 1797, it was a curious mixture of insult and affection, of material and moral concerns, of violence and flattery.[91]

The action of the French government unfolded along the same lines. On May 9, 1793, and July 27, 1793, the Convention had already passed decrees subjecting American ships to the enterprises, supervision and depredations of French privateers. A series of other measures to the detriment of American commerce had been adopted. In November, 1794, Monroe had succeeded in obtaining satisfaction for some of the American wrongs and even a decree proclaiming anew the principle that any neutral flag protected merchandise; but in 1796 the Directory, seeing that this more conciliating attitude had not produced favorable results, returned to harsher measures. It decided that France would treat neutral ships as they allowed themselves to be treated by England. The Minister of External Relations, prompted by Adet and feeling personally aggrieved, urged the Directory to take steps to intimidate the United States. Barras, weary, it seems, at hearing the American virtues too much praised, was hostile to America. Carnot had seen with indignation the United States making common cause with England through Jay's treaty. He desired a frank and energetic move on the part of France. He wanted her to act in all honesty. La Réveillère-Lépaux hedged; Monroe, a mystic like himself, had persuaded him to have patience, and La Réveillère may also have preferred more indirect means. Rewbell and Letourneur seem to have followed the lead of the others.[92] Barthélémy was the most peacefully inclined, as much by taste as in consequence of the tendencies of the conservative party to which he belonged, but he alone could do nothing and he was looked on with suspicion. Thus, as soon as Monroe had left, violence had a clear field. The Directory refused to receive C. C. Pinckney, who presented himself at Paris with papers drawn up in due form proving that he was the minister chosen by the United States. He was sent back under vain pretexts suggested by Paine.

The appointing of Talleyrand as Minister of External Relations in July, 1797, was the final blow to friendship between France and the United States. It is here that the saddest incident in the period, and the most shameful one for the good name of France, occurs. John Adams, the President of the United States, in spite of the conduct of France with regard to America, sought a reconciliation; for he was not inclined to give over to the tutelage of England, and he was on unfriendly terms with the fervent Anglophiles.[93] He therefore designated three envoys-extraordinary to France; two moderate Federalists, John Marshall and C. C. Pinckney, and one moderate Republican, Elbridge Gerry. They reached Paris in 1797 and immediately tried to get in touch with Talleyrand. The French minister sent them three unofficial agents, Hottinguer, Bellamy and Hauteval, to tell them that the Directory was highly incensed and would not treat with them until it received a "douceur." The United States must also furnish money to France in the form of a loan. The Americans, justly indignant, refused. Talleyrand's emissaries renewed their propositions, while the amiable Marquis de Villette tried to cajole Pinckney and poor Beaumarchais was sent to wait on Marshall. Beaumarchais, down to his last penny, ruined by the refusal of the United States to pay him, went to call on Marshall and asked him to help him to win his suit, in which event he promised to reconcile him with the Directory at his own expense. This imprudent step achieved Beaumarchais's disgrace in the eyes of the Americans and was of no avail. These intrigues lasted three months. Finally the American envoys decided to send Talleyrand a letter explaining and discussing the points in question (January, 1798). Talleyrand replied in March by an insolent letter in which he mingled the just protests of France with exorbitant claims and criticisms. He asserted that the United States had done everything to bring about the rupture and accused Marshall and Pinckney of being hostile to France.[94] He offered to negotiate with Gerry alone. In January the Directory had taken new measures against American ships to prevent them from trading with England. Pinckney and Marshall decided therefore to leave France immediately, while Gerry, prompted by the hope of bringing around Talleyrand, with whom he had had personal relations, to more favorable sentiments, remained a few weeks longer.

Talleyrand had played an infamous part in this affair. He knew the United States, he knew the spirit of morality that reigned in this country, he knew it only too well for having come into conflict with it so often during his stay in Philadelphia.[95] The pleasure of humiliating the Americans in his turn, shocking them with impunity and winning money at the expense of people who claimed to be incorruptible, led him to this base and stupid act. His tastes and his skill at subterfuge led him to think that he would easily be the winner at this game that the innocent Americans could hardly know how to play. He was mistaken, for the Americans had in their favor their indignation, and behind them an impulsive and idealistic people. And he himself was the agent of a corrupt government. On this occasion Talleyrand was lacking in both honesty and judgment.

*
* *

He provoked in America one of the most violent and unanimous reactions that has ever been seen—and this at a time when the triumph of the Republican party seemed certain and would have brought about a good understanding with France. The fact was that, in the elections of 1796, Adams had won by a very slight majority. Jefferson, who was Vice-President, had such great prestige and had been so near to victory that his increasing influence could be counted on, the more so since the new President, although a Federalist, had been exasperated by the intrigues of Alexander Hamilton, the former cabinet-member in 1789 and the power behind the throne in Washington's administration. Hamilton, anxious to keep control over everything that went on at Philadelphia, had secretly sought to have Pinckney elected in place of Adams. Adams was therefore prone to bear a grudge against him and to distrust him. Moreover, Adams, with his natural spirit of contradiction, was inclined, at the time when his party was playing into the hands of England, to remember what he had seen at London after the war for independence; his culture, which was really a wide one for the times, and the knowledge of French writers that he had acquired during the last ten years made him tend to greater moderation than was usual with the Federalists or than his own character suggested. Lastly, he knew that he was looked upon with disfavor in a goodly number of Federalist circles; and this feeling, together with his pride, his honesty and his lack of political subtlety, made him a man independent of parties, as much as this was possible in 1797. He kept the same cabinet that Washington had had, out of deference to his illustrious predecessor; but he drew nearer to Jefferson and drifted away from Hamilton. He spoke of France in severe terms, but he would have done the same with regard to England; and he thought, and wrote, that France was less evil than his Federalist friends claimed.[96] Since there was also a solid Republican majority in the House of Representatives, led by a few such able men as Madison, Gallatin and Nicolas, France, during the spring and summer of 1797, was once more well defended before American opinion. It is true that she no longer had an accredited minister in the United States, but the chargé-d'affaires, Letombe, was a man ripe in years and judgment and respected.[97] She had also a secret agent, Monsieur Hauterive (*ci-devant* Comte d'Hauterive), who acted as an intermediary between the French government and its supporters. Volney, Collot and the sons of the Duke of Orléans were traveling about the United States; and at Philadelphia the bookseller, Moreau de Saint-Méry, was carrying on a discreet propaganda and printing pamphlets favorable to France; here and there French agents distributed Paine's writings.[98] At Philadelphia the *Courrier français* was voicing the Jacobin doctrines of Paris, while at New York the *Gazette française* was evincing greater prudence. Everywhere French politics were being discussed.[99] At New York an impresario, M. Maison, presented "the Democratic Citizen, Monsieur Aristocrat and Mademoiselle Moderate in their surprising performance." These puppets seem to have achieved great success, whether it be because of their personal charm or because of the pleasure of the allusions to which their performance gave rise. Discussion was rife, and France was always the center of the debate—when the House tried to oblige the President to help La Fayette, when it wanted to reduce the American armament, and when it replied in moderate terms to John Adams' message announcing the return of Pinckney, rejected by the Directory. Ames pronounced impassioned discourses setting forth the good fortune of the United States, the people chosen of God. Harper attacked violently the blind friends of France. Gallatin, summing up the "French" ideas, said solemnly: "If we complain of the prodigality of the administration or want to control it by refusing to appropriate all the money which is asked, we are stigmatized as disorganizers; if we oppose the growth of taxation we are charged with the design of subverting the constitution and of making a revolution; if we attempt to check the extension of our political connections with the European nations we are branded with the epithet of Jacobins." [100]

In the newspapers the conflict took on a harsher form: there were headings, "French Friendship," under which were listed all the acts of piracy committed by French privateers; and columns headed "English Friendship," in which were published all the acts of pillage committed by English privateers and the agents of that nation; there were essays on equality, details concerning French victories [101] and this young leader called Bonaparte, whom certain well-informed people asserted was an American born in Connecticut. [102] But the battle raged particularly around the question of religion. Volney was the standard-bearer of the deists; he was attacked on all sides by the pastors and the faithful. Even Priestley, the English liberal scholar, who had taken refuge in America, wrote an open letter condemning his impiety. The controversy caused so much stir that every one wanted to take a hand in it. Dwight took the trouble to give a course before his students at Yale on the dangers of unbelieving philosophy, and at commencement the students held Volney up to ridicule.[103] But above all this, rang out the voice of the great poet Freneau, exalting Bonaparte, the destruction of the Papacy, the capture of Rome, and Monroe's generous mission. The vehement pamphlet which the latter had circulated widely to justify himself and show the grandeur, the beauty and the nobility of France, had been well received.[104] Thus, in the midst of discordant rumors and brutal polemics, the thing that stood out most brilliantly was the passion of the American people for Liberty and their sentimental attachment for France, despite quarrels, misunderstandings and politics. In spite of the rebuffs of the Directory, the American government, while continuing to arm, sent to France a new commission composed of the three ambassadors whose difficulties with Talleyrand we have already followed. But the year 1798 began with sinister rumors threatening war.[105]

Yet no one was prepared for what did happen. Adams was the first to receive the announcement of the strange negotiations. He kept it to himself and only asked Congress to take measures for the defense of the United States, for he had no hope of bringing France around to peaceful views. A violent discussion took place in the House, and the Republicans were indignant that the executive should thus alarm the country without furnishing evidence to support his words; they demanded that the correspondence between the President and the envoys to France be communicated to them. In reply Adams transmitted to Congress a copy of the reports that Marshall and Pinckney had sent him (April 2, 1798); then he had these documents published in the newspapers. Thereupon the opposition melted away, the country was unanimously back of the President. From Congress, from which many of the best Republicans retired, judging that the struggle was in vain, even into the streets, where French cockades, hitherto so popular, vanished entirely, the whole nation was swept by a wave of stupefaction, indignation and wrath.[106]

With a single impulse, all New England rose in support of Adams and the Federalists. The newspapers were unanimous in declaring that Talleyrand's negotiations were shameful, and even in the coffee-houses, that until now had been Jacobin, the crusade against France was preached. A like movement ran over the Central States, where English propaganda was strong and well organized;[107] even the Quakers, it is said, took a warlike attitude. At Philadelphia, Cobbett,[108] the great English pamphleteer, poured forth on the United States his furious and powerful prose; he had at this time more than 3,200 subscribers, which was enormous for those days, and he had just inaugurated a rural edition of his paper.[109] Even in the South, there was a profound change of sentiment, especially in Virginia; the Federalist party suddenly found itself in control of public opinion. The West, which received the news more slowly and was more intensely democratic, was touched only much later and less deeply. From all parts of the Union, messages, addresses and petitions came to the President, telling him of the country's grim resolution not to give in to French corruption and tyranny.[110] "Millions for defense and not one cent for tribute," was the slogan adopted by all; and, in accord this time with his party, his country and his own conscience, Adams responded to this enthusiasm with an enthusiasm quite as vehement and with energetic measures. He felt himself to be great and strong, the head of a powerful and united nation resolved to die for its liberty.[111] Jefferson, discouraged, looked on and dared do nothing.[112] Meanwhile, the Federalists, popular for the first time since 1788 and strongly organized, were in a position to realize the program that they had been meditating for so long; failing a monarchy, the establishment of which was impossible in America, they could set up a solid government by and for "the best people." After the X Y Z scandal (these were the initials under which Adams, not wishing to reveal the names of Talleyrand's agents, had designated them), this was easy; it sufficed to take France as the example of what should not be done and to show the nation clearly that this was their intention. Thus in a few months Congress decided to declare the treaties with France null and void and to arm a fleet and an army, at the head of which Adams placed Washington, the patriarch of American liberty. Adams, supported by the United States, solemnly declared that he would "never send another minister to France without assurances that he would be received, respected and honored as the representative of a great, free, powerful and independent nation." The government did not yet declare war, for it judged that France, furious at the publication of the X Y Z Correspondence, would immediately sever relations and that the war would be a defensive one and therefore very much easier to bring the Republicans to accept. On his arrival in the United States, John Marshall was welcomed by a throng wild with joy and enthusiasm. His journey to Philadelphia was comparable only to that of Genet in 1792. To the Federalists this crisis was the unique opportunity to found a healthy government at last. They bent their efforts to this end. First of all, it was necessary to reënforce the powers of the executive. Profiting therefore by a rumor that was everywhere in circulation to the effect that the country was overrun by French spies, Adams had a law voted giving the President the power to expel all foreigners from American territory. Another law, the Sedition Act, which provided for heavy fines and as much as two years of prison for any one who should plot against an American government official or hinder the execution of a law or libel an official or defame the government, etc., was also passed. This amounted to gagging the press and crushing out opposition.

In vain had the Republicans protested against measures so contrary to the Declaration of Independence; in vain had Gallatin fought to the last ditch in the House; in vain had the great Republican paper of Philadelphia, Franklin Bache's *Aurora*, tried to defend France. Public opinion was not with them. Bache had adroitly tried to prove that X Y Z were not agents of the Directory, but men employed by the enemies of the French government to ruin its reputation. This interpretation had convinced but few people. Bache had laid stress on Talleyrand's conversations with Gerry and the conciliating spirit that the French minister had shown; but it was no longer possible to make people listen to praises of Talleyrand, and his labor was lost.[113] Souvaroff and Nelson were the two men the most popular in America.[114] There were no more toasts drunk in France at banquets, but invocations of American liberty and praises of Adams were voiced. A colored engraving was everywhere circulated showing a turbaned monster with five heads dressed like a Turk, who menaced the three American envoys standing in a group at the left, dignified, calm and well dressed. The Devil-Directory was demanding a great deal of money from them and treading under foot a book labeled "Equity." At the right a white man, a negro and a monkey seemed to be busy eating frogs, while an ignoble woman was beheading a man. The verse beneath the caricature ran:

> Americans never
> From Freedom will sever.[115]

Letombe at Philadelphia and Rozier, the consul at Boston, did indeed succeed in circulating clandestinely a few documents and pamphlets proving the pacific spirit of France; and the Chevalier de Yrujo and Moreau de Saint-Méry worked shrewdly along with them at the same task, in which *The Aurora* assisted them.[116] But this was merely a proof of the courage and ingenuity of these men, for their efforts were of no avail and exposed them to severe punishments. The propaganda in favor of peace that a few of the faithful carried on found no echo except in the West.[117] The rest of the country listened only to voices praising Adams, recounting the American naval victories and exalting national dignity.

The Federalists were too clear-sighted not to endeavor to maintain and organize their dominion over popular opinion. Federalist literature from 1788 to 1800 is considerable. In prose and in verse it concentrated its attacks on France. From insidious propaganda to emphatic diatribes, it neglected nothing. At the instigation of the principal Federalist leaders, works on the conquest and occupation of Switzerland by France were translated.

The newspapers published extracts from them and also printed pages from Miss Williams' account of her travels in France, those pages on which the cruelties of the revolutionists were best described. They brought out in this way the character of France as a conqueror and the danger of America's being invaded as Geneva and Holland had been. The speeches in which Harper, the most prominent Federalist orator, criticized the policy of France and showed its crafty ways and ulterior motives were published. The veterans of Federalism, Joseph Dennie and J. Hopkinson, published brochures denouncing France and her disorders. The Federalist poets of Connecticut joined their voices to those of the politicians. Richard Alsop wrote *The Political Greenhouse for the year* 1798, in which he described American Jacobinism in darkest colors, denounced its supporters and declared that Barlow was

> Trained in Illumination's School
> And hired by rogues to play the fool.[118]

This sarcastic and coarse tone prevailed in all these productions, which resembled literature only by the fact that they were printed. *The Stand*, the great pamphlet that Hamilton produced at this time, was vastly superior to the others in form, although quite as violent. It is skillfully composed in order to answer all the arguments in favor of France and to impress the imagination. Hamilton depicts France as cruel, thirsting to conquer Europe, acquire a universal dominion such as Rome formerly had, and in the name of Liberty, Equality and Fraternity, impose an impious gospel everywhere. He pictures America, innocent, faithful to her treaties, suddenly assailed by this monster that hopes to filch her wealth and corrupt her. This violent attack is well written, but its tone is sometimes burdened with a wearying insistence scarcely in character with Hamilton, due to the passion that impelled him and his desire to show clearly that morality and religion were involved.[119] In fact, from now on, the whole Franco-American quarrel took on this character, and the fight against France was preached in almost all the churches of America as a crusade.[120] This was the result of an initiative on the part of the New England clergy, so pious, enthusiastic and zealous, so eager to do good, and so accustomed to exercising a political influence which they were anxious to retain.[121] Looking on the United States as a land blessed by God, they were led to consider France as the Antichrist, and two works had just confirmed these views; these were the books of Robison and the Abbé Barruel on the Bavarian Illuminati, the Freemasons and the Jacobins. The latter were represented as the agents and successors of the Illuminati and Freemasonry. A great conspiracy united them: they aimed at the destruction of Christianity. The books of Robison and Barruel, documented at length and somewhat obscure, were not easy for American readers to digest. Synopses of them were made and quoted by all the newspapers. They were commented and abridged;

and there was not a zealous pastor, were he Congregationalist, Reformed Church or Huguenot, Dutch Church, Presbyterian, or Episcopal, but preached from the pulpit the gospel that should save his flock from "The Beast." As early as 1794, Osgood had outlined this theory, but it was spread and vulgarized by Jedediah Morse, the famous writer who was so prolific and erudite and had already produced so many bulky and fairly interesting books on the geography of America and the world.[122] Morse had been a defender of France, and now he set about attacking her with all the zeal of a convert. It was hardly before the years 1796-1797 that he changed his opinion of her. Until then, the mysticism propagated by the French Revolution had seemed to him to be good and useful.[123] By a process of logic, this new faith that he had loved, if it did not come from God Himself could only be a very dangerous work of the Devil. The change in Morse and his colleagues was so complete that they forgot the praises that they had lavished on France as the destroyer of papism, and preached the condemnation of France in accord with the Catholic priest Barruel. It is almost comic to behold their violence when one thinks of all the great men from Washington to Franklin who had belonged to Freemasonry or were still among its initiates. Most of the lodges had been very patriotic from 1770 to 1783, and it might well be said that they had been one of the cradles of the spirit of independence. Morse's argument presented itself therefore under a well-chosen religious and mystic aspect, but it was not without entailing some few difficulties in practice.[124] Although Washington had condemned the Jacobin societies and all spontaneous and extra-constitutional organizations, the fact remained that Freemasonry in America in 1798 had by no means a revolutionary aspect. Nevertheless, the Federalist leaders and the New England clergy felt that the evil was a deep-grounded one and not merely a political crisis. They wished therefore to cauterize the wound. Morse denounced France, the Illuminati, the Masons and the Jacobins in a great sermon on May 9, 1798, just at the moment when the X Y Z scandal was causing the greatest stir. Like a flame in a forest, the idea ran over all New England and then gained the other states where, however, it was more disputed. It was particularly in Connecticut and Massachusetts, at Harvard and Yale, that these ideas were set forth, defended and maintained. Elsewhere they were accepted, but people asked for evidence. As proofs, Morse furnished in two new sermons, of which the second was pronounced in 1799, various French diplomatic documents tending to prove that France had not dealt frankly with the United States in 1778-1783, quotations from Robison, informations against Monroe and Paine, letters attacking French propaganda in America and extracts from Miss Williams concerning the Worship of Reason in France.[125] These, in general, are the documents that were used everywhere, with here and there criticisms of the French Revolutionary calendar (which was taken as testimony of the Convention's rage for dechristianization), a discourse by a priest from the Rhône in defense of religion, and declarations by Cloots proclaiming religion to be useless. All this made an impressive collection. Thus did victorious Federalism attempt both to fetter the press and win over souls.[126]

The Republicans, who seemed decisively beaten in the field of politics and government, found courage to defend their doctrine. This they did forcibly and with ability. Although it had been difficult for them to justify the conduct of France, on the other hand, it seemed easy to them to defend the French *ideas* when the attack was turned against them. Had not the revolutionary spirit that animated France come from America? It was important to save it at any price. The Republican party could do nothing else, for all the power was in the hands of the Federalists. Their rebuttal was solely on the grounds of ideas and principles, but it was none the less effective for that. This time, as often since, it was made evident that a cause is never lost with American people if it can make an appeal to their spirit of idealism and their optimistic sentiments. In opposition to the Federalists, who wanted to curb the individual in order to preserve his virtues, the Republicans recalled the Rights of Man and proclaimed that the best way to develop good instincts in the individual is to let them grow freely. To the ideas of restraint and religious discipline, they opposed those of spontaneity, liberty and religious enthusiasm. James Sullivan, for instance, in his pamphlet, *An Impartial Review of the Causes and Principles of the French Revolution by an American* (Boston, 1798), explains that the "state of Nature," being one of ideal and perfect liberty, is therefore not accessible to any nation, but every nation enjoys a greater liberty in proportion as its *mores* and its morality are better. The government of the old régime in France having brought up its subjects badly, the French could not be ready for a strong dose of liberty, and if there were excesses during the French Revolution, it was due to the priests and the King. It was therefore just that these latter should have suffered, and the destruction of the papacy should be considered as one of the greatest triumphs of the Revolution; for it was the spirit of the English revolution and one of the principles that guided the American revolutionists. Sullivan concludes with an encomium of republics and an appeal to defend them, since they are the hope of the world.[127] Philip Freneau in a prettier and more delicate brochure, *Letters on Various Interesting and Important Subjects*, shows a farmer arguing with his pastor, not from party spirit, but from a concern for truth.[128] This pamphlet was in the tone of Franklin's *Poor Richard*, but it was more supple and literary. These political letters presented scenes in taverns and rural life; they were moderate but biting and very hard on the clergy behind a veil of respect. He blamed the Directory for having immoral agents, but cleared France of the charge of atheism; she has a religion of her own, that is all, he said. In splendid verses written in 1798 he explains this religion:

> O Liberty, seraphic name
> With whom from heaven fair virtue came,
> From whom through years of misery toss'd
> One hundred thousand lives were lost,
> Still shall all grateful hearts to thee
> Incline the head and bend the knee.[129]

And the great poet mingled the bitter accents of satire with hymns of piety in order to make clear the grandeur of Liberty and the ignominy of her enemies. Barlow, the other great pamphleteer of the Republicans, published in Paris in 1798 a little booklet full of bitterness against Adams and the monarchical tendencies of certain Americans. Its harsh, popular and lawless, though inspired, tone was certain to create a sensation. To make amends for this outburst, he produced in 1800 a serene and pure work entitled *Letters from Paris*. In this book he proclaimed the necessity of the United States and the entire world achieving Liberty; but the United States, favored by circumstances, ought to set the example. He called on his fellow countrymen to cease deifying the executive, and to remember the great principles, and especially this one: "The art of government is in reality the art of substituting a moral force for a physical force." He lauded the federal system as furnishing the easiest means of applying these principles, as the good King Henry IV of France had been the first to see and proclaim.[130]

The newspapers circulated these verses and copied or summed up these pamphlets in their columns. The first to reopen the fight against Federalism had been certain democratic newspapers of New England, such as *The Independent Chronicle* of Boston and *The Bee* of New London, certain western sheets, and of course *The Aurora* of Philadelphia. These papers also published the text of speeches pronounced by the Republicans.[131] They attacked Cobbett with his own weapons, insult and calumny; they criticized the clergy for concerning itself with politics instead of attending to its own business; finally, they silenced Morse. Morse had received a letter from a German named Ebeling, who was very learned and well-informed on American affairs, warning him to take care, because he was mistaken in attributing any revolutionary activity to the Illuminati of Bavaria. Morse had kept this letter without showing it. But the papers learned of it and published it, thus rendering Morse ridiculous at the same time that they refuted his arguments. A letter in the same tenor from Weishaupt arrived shortly afterward.[132] In short, protests and criticisms flowed in from all sides. Morse had the humiliation of seeing his own weapon turned against him. *A Description of the Illuminati of New England* was a pamphlet by J. C. Ogden, who claimed to have learned of the organization of a secret sect in New England composed of Federalist pastors and resembling that of the Illuminati. He said that Jay and his friends belonged to an association of this kind.[133] The denunciation of the Illuminati ended therefore in ridicule, and the effect of mysticism that had been sought was not attained. The same was true in other fields, but the most striking event was the success of Jefferson and Madison in having resolutions voted in Kentucky and Virginia recalling the fact that the Union was a contract and that the States, as members of the Union, had the right to break it in case of usurpation of power or violation of the rights of individuals. Never before had the doctrine of the Rights of Man been so formally taken as the rule of American national life. Thus American opinion, which had been scandalized by the unseemly conduct of the French government, was still attached to the principles which France represented and which had become those of the Republican party. In trying to break them down, the Federalist party had only paved the way to its own final fall.

Adams himself felt this. He was an honest, strong and intelligent man, when he was not in bad humor, which, it is true, happened almost never. He saw Washington and Hamilton eager to arm, fight, conquer Florida and kill Frenchmen. He saw the campaign of the ardent Federalists and joined in it, but he perceived that the people with all their enthusiasm were not flocking to their standards, that they were weary of the war before it had begun, and that to fight beside England against

France would be to go backward fifty years. All this he saw, and also the fact that he himself could by no means acquire military glory. He thought that Hamilton was plotting too much to become the leader. He was irritated. He was quite ready to admit that true Americanism would consist rather in abstaining from European quarrels than in mixing into them. Together with a few other clear-sighted Federalists, he was worried at the part that English agents were playing in America. Finally, as he often did, he preferred his enemies to his friends and had foresight in spite of his advisers.[134] Since Talleyrand had made known to him that the French government would gladly receive an American ambassador, he asked the advice of his cabinet and, in spite of their most explicit opposition, sent a new delegation of three members to Paris.

In France the situation had changed greatly. Talleyrand was too intelligent not to see his error and appreciate its gravity as well as its possible consequences. The pleasure of vengeance and the illusion of vice had led him too far. As soon as he learned of the departure of Marshall and Pinckney, his attitude changed. He tried to negotiate with Gerry and adopted a conciliating tone. Gerry, recalled by Adams, was unable to accomplish anything, but he brought back to America certain evidences of good intentions. Shortly after, the account of the X Y Z negotiations, published at Philadelphia in April, reached Paris with remarkable rapidity. It was in Talleyrand's hands as early as the month of Prairial, Year VI (May 1798). He felt that Adams was angry and would go to great lengths. He was frightened; immediately he sent a report to the Directory (the twelfth of Prairial, VI) in which he denied formally having been in any way concerned "in these shocking propositions." In his conduct, he said, "all was simple, all was pure, all was worthy of the loyalty of a Frenchman." He gave an exact analysis of the documents published by the American government, then he proceeded to draw a very dark picture of the situation of the United States, directed by a government allied with that of England, and monarchial. He recommended calmness, prudence and moderation. He begged the Directory to issue a manifesto along this line. In short, he sought to clear himself and wriggle out of unpleasant straits. All that was needed for him to make advances to the United States was the opportunity.[135] In fact, public opinion was astonished and indignant at seeing this new difficulty that the Directory had created by its arrogant policy. The cafés were hostile, as the reports of the police allow us to see; the royalist newspapers gloated; the English were circulating throughout Europe the American version of the X Y Z affair. Finally, the Jacobins were casting doubt on Talleyrand's probity and recalling his antecedents.[136] No one was willing to take the responsibility for a break with the United States, and Talleyrand was in a fair way of being chosen as the scapegoat.[137] Advice and counsels of moderation were raining in from all sides. Volney, arriving from America, stressed the danger of a war and urged that the government treat with Adams politely. Kosciusko, who had just returned from a triumphal journey in America, where the Republicans had received him with open arms, gave the same advice. Logan, a prominent and influential Republican who had just arrived in Paris with letters from Jefferson, presented a memorandum to the Directory in the same tone. This cost him dearly moreover, for the Federalists never forgave him this act which they considered an intrusion on the functions of the executive.[138] These travelers and all the Frenchmen returning from America agreed in saying that the X Y Z negotiations had united the Americans against France and that, unless something were done in haste, there would be war. Finally, Dupont, the French Consul-General to Philadelphia, whom Adams had sent back without allowing him to exercise his functions, presented Talleyrand with a report which the minister received with joy and which got him out of his difficulties. Dupont very skillfully threw the blame on the governments that had succeeded each other in France during the past ten years, the tendencies of the American government, the acts of violence of certain French officials in the West Indies and the exactions of French privateers. Talleyrand's "awkwardness" was buried under this pile of reproaches, the which were, moreover, justified.[139] Talleyrand submitted the report to the Directory and asked it to take action in the direction indicated by Dupont. The Directory approved. Circular instructions were sent to the West Indies to put a stop to the capture of American ships. The Directory entered into indirect relations with Vans Murray, the American minister at The Hague, and let Adams know that his representative, or representatives, would be received with pleasure and due honor.

This change of front, which was in part the result of the pressure of public opinion, the circumstances of the moment, and Talleyrand's personal fears, was due above all else to moral factors. The Directory had very little to fear from the United States either on land or on the sea; and it had nothing to expect from them, as it knew. But America was still a great moral force; and for a government that was feared but held in little esteem in Europe, and violently combated within the country, and that wanted to claim the sanction of principles from which, however, it often departed, to quarrel with America would have been a further and disastrous loss of prestige and a cruel handicap.[140] America was the only nation in the world that could appear to be guided by the same ideal as France; to break this spiritual unity, even though it was fictitious, would have been dangerous. At least, this is what all the memoranda presented to the Directory at this time say or insinuate. In the newspapers under its control, such as the *Rédacteur*, the Directory had articles published setting forth its moral purity and proclaiming its desire to extend a fraternal hand to the American republic. Talleyrand circulated a pamphlet containing the proofs of his innocence and moderation.[141] The French government sought no advantage except friendship. She had no political end in view. She desired only to help the Americans to preserve their federal union and their fine democratic spirit.[142] Such is the conclusion of the complete final report that Talleyrand submitted to the Directory the twentieth of Pluviôse, Year VII (January 1799).[143]

This policy of conciliation inaugurated by Talleyrand was to succeed, thanks to Adams' decision to send negotiators in spite of his cabinet and his party, in spite of even Washington. He had in his support the opinion of the majority, which was opposed to a war and grieved at seeing the two great republics of the world fighting among themselves at the risk of discrediting their common ideal. When the three envoys, Vans Murray, Oliver Ellsworth and Governor Davie of South Carolina, arrived in France, a new government had been set up. The Consulate had succeeded the Directory, and no one knew what attitude it would take on the American problem.

On November 11, 1799, Napoleon Bonaparte had come into power and had established, under the name of Consulate, a government that aspired to be stable and constructive, to derive its support from property-owners, to bring about peace and continue the Revolution while making it more humane, tolerant and generous. The conservatives, the discouraged royalists, the wealthy classes and the great mass of the people who had had enough of war and turmoil, had rallied to Bonaparte, whose personal prestige was so great. Nevertheless Bonaparte, still a novice in the art of carrying on revolutions, had hesitated in the course of his enterprise: all his past was Jacobin and revolutionary. He, more than any other, held the cult of Country and the great ideals of 1789. It was these ideals that had made him. Sincerity and the need of defending himself against the royalist movement that was taking shape made them necessary to him in 1799. The death of Washington and the revival of popularity that it brought to this great man came along at the right moment to furnish Bonaparte an outburst of revolutionary mysticism that was both tinged with a conservative spirit and dominated by a pleasing concept of the dictatorship of virtue. In the first days following his accession to power, Bonaparte informed himself on the American questions, which had remained at the point where Talleyrand had left them: that is to say, inclined toward moderation and accord, but with nothing precise about them.[144] The weight of public opinion was in this direction, and one pamphlet after another called for an understanding with the United States.[145] On the thirteenth of Pluviôse of the Year VIII (January, 1800), the news of Washington's death spread through Paris. It attracted public attention immediately. For some years there had been less talk of Washington in France.[146] The liberator of the New World had been very popular from 1780 to 1792, the period during which his former French companions-in-arms and lieutenants had carefully maintained his renown, from which they were not without deriving some benefit. La Fayette, who from 1789 to 1792 had been known under the name of "the French Washington," had been most assiduous in furthering and utilizing the glory of his illustrious friend. Thus Washington, admired between 1775 and 1783 as a great general, a powerful personality and an able dictator, had become, for the needs of the cause and as a result of events, the model of the great Citizen, modest and devoted, for whom political offices are only a means to service, who has no other will than that of the people and whose majesty is made up of abnegation, poise, and —I should almost say—mediocrity.[147] From 1793 to 1798 his glory underwent an eclipse; the French could hardly pardon him for his policy of rapprochement with England and his distrust of the Revolution. They were inclined to portray him as the leader of the anti-French party in America and to hate him accordingly. Never had the popularity of Washington been so imperiled as in 1797, in France as in America.[148] But his death repaired all this. For the Americans, whatever might be their opinions, he became once more the great man who had brought about the military victories of the war for independence. They no longer feared him, and he became a subject of pride. In France, Bonaparte hastened to lay hold on his glory and make it an emblem about which to rally all Frenchmen who were revolutionary in spirit but men of order in deed. It was to be a symbol, in the eyes of the public, of the reaction against Jacobism and the Directory, without denying the principles of 1789. It was the emblem of morality and wholesome republicanism. It would once more give the new régime in France the means of profiting by the American revolutionary mysticism, so important ever since 1778.[149] On the 13th of Pluviôse, as soon as the news of the death of Washington was known at Paris, a member of the House of Representatives, F. Faulcon, asked that body to vote a funeral oration in honor of Washington such as Franklin had received formerly, and forthwith he began a eulogy of the great man. Faulcon was a conservative, a Catholic with monarchial tendencies; he belonged to the group which even during the Directorate had supported the American government and called for a policy of peace abroad and tolerance at home. After various discourses in which many favorable things were spoken of Washington, the House passed to the order of the day. It was no longer 1790, and the legislative body still contained too many Jacobins who had not forgotten Jay's treaty.[150] But the First Consul went over their heads. His Minister of External Relations, in a report on the

United States, had advised him to have a statue of the Great Man erected in a public place at Paris. The Minister said: "A people who will some day be a great people and is today the most orderly and happiest people on earth, mourn the death of Washington, who had aided them more than any other man to win their liberty. . . . The name of Washington is attached to a period forever memorable: he will honor this age by his talents, the elevation of his character and his virtues, which even envie dared not disparage. . . ." He therefore desired that "France, who had foreseen all the glory that humanity might attain and all the benefits that the policy of enlightenment might derive from the new kind of social institutions and the new sort of heroism of which Washington and America were to furnish the common examples," should offer a striking testimony to her emotion.[151] Bonaparte decided that Washington's statue should be placed in the Tuileries, where twenty-seven statues were to be set up. It was to be made by Houdon and would be enthroned in this palace amid a host of heroes, among whom Franklin, intentionally excluded, would not figure. Bonaparte decided that the mourning for Washington should be celebrated on the very day when the flags captured in Egypt were to be installed in the Invalides. A funeral oration was to be pronounced. He himself ordered that all the flags should be draped with crêpe; and he addressed an order of the day to the consular guard, in which he exclaimed: "Washington is dead. This great man fought against tyranny. He consolidated the liberty of his Country. His memory will always be dear to the French people as well as to all the free men of both worlds, and especially to the French soldiers, who, like him and like the American soldiers, fight for liberty and equality."[152] The orator who composed and delivered the eulogy of Washington in this ceremony was M. de Fontanes, a moderate monarchist who had recently returned to France. He was on friendly terms with Elisa Bonaparte, and it was she who had recommended him to Lucien.[153] His discourse on this occasion was undoubtedly the greatest literary and political triumph of Fontanes's career. It won him the favor of the First Consul and the public. Fontanes knew what he ought to think, and he expressed it with emphasis. He depicted Washington as good, kindly, firm and, above all, humane, devoted to Liberty, but capable of imposing order on political parties. The whole eulogy was a series of allusions and lauded the First Consul, not *equally* with Washington, but much *more* than Washington.[154] This superiority, due to the fact that Bonaparte was a living hero instead of a dead one, also resulted from the incomparable luster of the First Consul's victories and all that the people expected of him. In his peroration Fontanes said, "It seems to me that, from the heights of this magnificent dome, Washington cries out to all France, 'Magnanimous nation, you who know so well how to honor glory, I conquered in the name of independence, but the happiness of my country was the prize of my victory. Do not content yourself with imitating the first part of my life: it is the second part that recommends me to the eulogies of posterity!' Yes, thy counsels shall be heard, O Washington! O Warrior! O Legislator! O Citizen without reproach! He who, though yet young, has surpassed thee on the fields of battle, will, as thou didst, close with his triumphant hands the wounds of his Country. . . . The acclamations of all the centuries will at last accompany the hero who bestows this blessing on France and on the world that she has too long unsettled." Fontanes adroitly showed the continuity of French sympathy toward the United States. He also evoked in one way or another all the governments that had succeeded each other in France since 1775, in order that their spiritual union, at last refound, should penetrate the hearts of all his hearers. This timely theme had already been utilized by the newspapers that supported the Consuls: *Les Débats* had said: "If Alexander shed tears on the grave of Achilles, if Caesar in Spain meditated at the foot of a statue of Alexander, Washington's grave will be the retreat to which the man who now holds the reins of the government in France will sometimes withdraw in spirit to reflect again on what he already knows—that there is a glory more noble, more moving, more worthy of the applause of all men, than that of arms and conquests." [155] The *Gazette de France* and the *Journal de Paris* took the same attitude. The latter published an ode on the death of Washington, whose lyric platitudes were not at all out of place in 1800.[156] What these papers, the most conservative as well as the most influential and best directed organs of the time, said all the others repeated. At the *Portique républicain*, the fashionable literary assembly of the day, Billardon de Sauvigny read a scene from his play on Washington, which was produced in 1791. In certain cities of the provinces, Angers for example, ceremonies were held in imitation of the one at Paris. The Masons, who had had an illustrious brother-member in Washington, and the Theophilanthropists, who were in search of lay saints, made their meetings resound with the name of the Hero. The eulogy pronounced by Dubroca at the assembly of the Theophilanthropists is the most noteworthy testimony to this worship.[157] These enthusiastic words were not addressed to Washington alone, they were uttered for the benefit of all the Americans and manifested the desire for reconciliation that prevailed in France. The First Consul worked deliberately toward this end. He had formed a commission of three members, Jerome Bonaparte, Roederer and Fleurieu, to treat with the American plenipotentiaries, and he attached great importance to the success of the negotiations. At the Ministry of External Relations, every one was in favor of this step, especially Hauterive and Otto. Since France was unwilling to renounce the treaties of 1778 or pay an indemnity to the United States for the American ships captured, while the American government, stirred up by the X Y Z scandal, had strictly ordered its delegates to obtain these two concessions, nothing more than a convention could be signed.[158] Postponing until later the solution of these problems, the convention settled that the two countries should mutually restore all prizes and confiscated property and that they should pay their debts. It thus permitted the renewing of relations without, however, reëstablishing them on a secure basis. To compensate for the partial failure and to take all possible advantage of the partial success, the First Consul had a celebration held at the Château de Mortefontaine to bid the American delegates farewell and thank them. The entertainment was as sumptuous and brilliant as possible, and was given great publicity. A rather ill-assorted banquet in which statesmen, Jacobins, actresses, and a few unexpected guests thronged about the First Consul and the delegates, was followed by an allegorical exhibition of fireworks representing France and the United States, their revolutions and their renewed friendship. Then a play was acted. Mlle. Contat played *Les Jeux de l'Amour et du Hasard*. It is even related that the First Consul, having received from the prefect a present of some Roman coins that peasants had just discovered in the surrounding country, wanted to distribute them among the American delegates as a token of friendship. They answered that the laws of their country prevented them from accepting anything; but Bonaparte replied, "There is nothing better to be done with these relics of a great republic than to make a present of them to the citizens of the American republic." He insisted that "these relics of a free people be given to the freest of all men who live in society on earth." And this was the last grandiose scene of a well-arranged spectacle.[159]

Doubts have been cast on Bonaparte's sincerity during this period. But everything tends to prove that as a young man he had sincerely admired the United States and Washington.[160] Since then, he had been but little concerned with them, but he had never ceased to subscribe to his revolutionary credo; and it must have been a real pleasure for him to use his power to forward so republican an act as the reconciliation of the two great democracies. It has further been alleged, especially in America, that he was on the point of signing the treaty of Saint-Ildefonse which gave back to France her empire of Louisiana and the Mississippi and made her an American continental power. American historians ordinarily deduce that he was dealing underhandedly with the Americans when he evinced friendship for them while he was preparing to reoccupy Louisiana. But it seems as if these two things may have been compatible in his mind and in the minds of the French citizens of the time. The United States had neither rights nor claims to Louisiana. They had often had causes for complaint against Spain. France had colonized these regions and had always felt a lively interest in them and a strong attachment for them. Only the wisdom and philosophic spirit of Vergennes had kept her from doing anything to reconquer them or even desiring to do so. But times had changed. With the French Revolution, national sentiment had taken a new form and fresh strength. To hope for the extension of one's country was to hope for the triumph of the moral ideal in which one believed: it was therefore a mystic action and sentiment, and not a mere material calculation. Neither Bonaparte nor the public opinion that supported him had any reason to blush for coveting Louisiana in 1800.

In America, however, they were condemned for it. It was no longer, as in 1778, a mere survival of the old Anglo-Saxon hatreds against France: it was national sentiment and the consciousness of the great destiny to which they were called that made the American people take this attitude. It was also an attachment to democratic principles and the desire to create for themselves a new world in which liberty should reign.[161] Jefferson had just been elected President of the United States. America had once more proclaimed—and that brilliantly—her will to remain a democratic state. In spite of the bitter campaign carried on against Jefferson, who had been represented as an atheist, an agent of France and a man of no constructive ability, he had received a majority throughout the country. By its mistakes and its internal weakness, the Federalist party had paved the way to its own defeat.[162] It had enacted energetic laws, but it had not enforced them. It had denounced France violently, but except for fairly brilliant naval operations, it had done nothing against her. The Federalist leaders, with their aristocratic tendencies, desirous of a strong government under the guidance of the best and wealthiest people, had neither dared nor known how to realize their program in the brief moment when popular enthusiasm would perhaps have permitted it. The rivalry between Hamilton, with his monarchist tendencies, and Adams, with his aristocratic republican spirit, had been fatal and had brought about defeat.

But this would not have happened if the country and Adams himself had not been imbued with the ideas that were then known as French and that called for the sovereignty of the People and a religious respect for them. These principles—most of them had already been involved in the American Revolution—had changed character under the influence of the French Revolution. Instead of being taken as axioms resulting from the religious and political traditions of England, they were henceforth truths in themselves, a religion apart, and they had taken on a universal and absolute character that they were far from having in 1770. They had gradually begun to acquire this character after 1770 under the influence of the French philosophers and impassioned discussion. Thus they formed a much more general theory and a much more definite discipline. They had a much more profound authority over human thought and occupied a much greater place in the life of man. This transformation is all the more curious since, from 1788 to 1799, the American Constitution was composed, interpreted and applied by a party which, for the most part, had no confidence in the dogmas of democracy and sought, with the support of a considerable portion of the clergy, to turn the people away from them. By his tact, his external moderation and internal violence, Jefferson, with the support of the masses and the immigrants with French tendencies, had just come into power; it was both the continuation of the revolution of 1776 and a new revolution. Coming three years earlier, it would without doubt have drawn France and America together; in 1800 it was, on the contrary, to put an increasing distance between them, for Bonaparte's military dictatorship, his despotic empire of conquest, could not fail to look with hostility upon sincere democrats.[163] Moreover, the policy of unlimited expansion which he seems to have adopted for France alarmed every one, even in America. Lastly, the continental blockade and the English blockade, by making intercourse between Europe and America almost impossible, completed the widening of the breach between the two peoples. The world of ideas is not autonomous to such a degree as to permit the exchange of ideas and sentiments when nations have neither commerce, navigation nor interests in common.

*

* *

Nevertheless, thirty years of intellectual and sentimental collaboration cannot be wiped out without leaving a trace. After 1800 the American argument still retained great value in France; and it had so strong a hold on minds that no party neglected it. We have already pointed out how much it had discommoded the Jacobins since 1796, especially those who felt a violent antipathy toward the Christian dogmas and all religious sentiments. Volney expressed this point of view and this annoyance in the book that he produced after his return from America, *Tableau du Climat et du Sol des Etats-Unis d'Amérique.* As a matter of fact, Volney had personal grievances: he had not been very well received in America. The newspapers and the clergy had scarcely left him any peace, and a law had been passed especially to permit him to be deported. A more patient man than he was would have been irritated. Now Volney had neither modesty nor patience in excess. He therefore wrote a book asserting that the United States were bigoted, avaricious and tiresome, that their women never washed themselves and that only patriotism made them think that their climate was a good one. For all its bitter and violent tone, the book has savor and contains curious information, but it is lacking in accuracy and justice.[164] Monsieur de La Rochefoucauld Liancourt, although he showed better breeding and wrote less colorful French, was scarcely more amiable. His feelings also had been rumpled. His first enthusiasm had faded in the course of his long stay in America. He had not been widely enough received and listened to. He took his revenge in eight very heavy, very monotonous and very pedantic octavo volumes. They are in reality the notes of his travels and those of Moreau de Saint-Méry, almost without revision or completion. Here and there we find in it documents that are of use in the history of this period, but the heaviness of the style and the mediocrity of thought render the book futile and intolerable despite its material importance. Liancourt cannot help admiring the liberty and tolerance that prevailed in the United States, but he understood neither the genius nor the character of the country. He takes every occasion to rail at priests, pastors and believers; he does it without grace and usually without reason. Nothing of his book was to live.[165]

Beside these books, and quite as futile as they were in promoting good relations between the two countries, there was during several years a complete Bonapartist literature whose purpose was to bring the example of America to the support of the moderate revolutionary policy of the First Consul. These books, of which the two most typical are doubtless *L'histoire politique et philosophique de la Révolution de l'Amérique septentrionale* by the Citizens J. Chas and Lebrun (Paris, Year IX) and *Coup d'Oeil politique sur le Continent* by Charles Saladin (Paris, 1800), aim at proving by the example of America that all revolutions can, and ought to, end in an era of assuagement and reconciliation. They compare

Bonaparte to Washington. But the obscurity of the writers and their lack of talent made their labors vain. Very soon they became impossible: it was no longer Washington whom Bonaparte imitated, but Caesar and Augustus.

The American tradition, which still persisted and refused to be uprooted, had its center and stronghold in the ideal of Liberty and a religious love of Democracy. It is surprising to see how much influence America continued to have over those of the revolutionaries who still felt the need of mysticism and worship. Thomas Paine was one of the founders of Theophilanthropy in France and he organized a chapter in America. And as long as the revolutionary cults were followed, Franklin was glorified. In the month of Vendémiaire, Year III, when Rousseau's remains were transferred to the Pantheon, a statue of Franklin was carried in the procession. During the whole Directorate, a life-size fresco painting of Franklin beside Rousseau, Voltaire, Helvetius and Marat was to be seen in a café at the corner of the Boulevards and the Rue du Faubourg-Montmartre. In the Year VIII a celebration was held in honor of Benjamin Franklin in the Temple of Victory (Saint-Sulpice), and a conjurer called up his ghost together with that of Mohammed in the Cours des Capucines (Place Vendôme). The newspapers frequently printed letters and paragraphs taken from his works, and his biography published in the Year VI was very well received.[166] He did not cease to be regarded by the republican worshipers as one of the sublime men whom they were pleased to oppose to the Catholic saints, whose cult was beginning to revive. In the Year III, people were singing:

> Give us back the names of all the saints
> At the corner of each street.
> Rousseau, Buffon and Franklin—
> Let us throw their statues down.[167]

La Décade and the other great revolutionary papers faithfully cherished the memory of Franklin. The second part of his autobiography was published for the first time in *La Décade* for February, 1798. It is about his form that popular imagination in France grouped everything that it remembered of America. Once more Franklin was a more popular personage in France than in the United States. Bonaparte did not like Franklin and tried to stifle his influence. Gradually he pulled away from the United States and ceased to employ them as a proof of his republican spirit. It was with the followers of La Fayette, the democratic idealists and dreamers, that the American tradition, with all its pious, noble and generous qualities, then took refuge. We can follow its trace through the first forty years of the nineteenth century as far as de Tocqueville. When we remember that La Fayette rode into triumph on the crest of the Revolution of 1830, we perceive that this survival, which still enjoyed a great moral prestige at least, is not to be belittled. It alone is worthy of a complete study, and this is not the place to broach it. It will suffice to have mentioned its importance.

On the other hand, it is curious to see the American legend develop among the monarchists. Almost all of the royalist *émigrés* came back to France filled with enthusiasm, and they conserved the memory of this simple, happy and truly free life in the New World. We have seen how much regret Madame de La Tour du Pin and the Marquis de Lezay Marnésia felt at leaving this land of liberty. The same was true of the sons of the Duke of Orléans, who were so well received during their stay in the United States. Their memoirs bear witness to this; and already the books of the period revealed the favor that the United States enjoyed in certain royalist circles.[168] The good Abbé Bonnet de Fréjus,[169] who saw in Bonaparte a new Monk, wrote a thick book, *Les Etats-Unis de l'Amérique à la Fin du XVIIIe Siècle*, with the sole purpose of exalting the natural liberty, humane, tolerant and benign, that reign in this country and of contrasting it with the false liberty that was obtained by violence in France. Saint Jean de Crèvecœur, whose book had had so much success before the Revolution, published another of the same nature in 1801, *Voyages dans la haute Pennsylvanie*, whose dominant ideas are similar to those of Abbé Bonnet. But is it not most curious to find them again in *Le Voyage en Amérique*, which Chateaubriand published in 1827? This writer, who was considered the great upholder of monarchy by divine right during the first third of the century, expresses in this book a boundless admiration for Washington, whom he compares with Bonaparte at the expense of the latter, depicting the great emperor as a destroyer and the great democrat as a creator. Who can forget these marvelous phrases? "A quietude envelops the activities of Washington, he moves slowly; it seems as if he felt himself the representative of the liberty of the future.[170] This man, who does not stand out greatly, because he is natural and in true proportion, blended his existence with that of his country; his glory is the common patrimony of increasing civilization; his renown looms up like a sanctuary whence flows an inexhaustible spring for the people." This admiration is not mere resentment against Bonaparte; it has a positive quality. Chateaubriand cannot help seeing, in the United States, the future; and in the form of government that they have adopted, a model of perfection. "The discovery of the representative Republic in the United States is one of the greatest political events of the world. It has proved, as I have said elsewhere, that there are two kinds of practical liberty: one belongs to the infancy of peoples. It is the daughter of simple living and virtues; it was that of the first Greeks and the first Romans; it was that of the savages of America. The other is born of the old age of peoples. It is the daughter of enlightenment and reason; it is the liberty of the United States replacing that of the Indians.

Happy land that in the space of less than three centuries has passed from one liberty to the other almost without effort and by dint of a struggle that lasted less than eight years! . . . Whatever the future may be, liberty will never disappear entirely from America; and it is this that we must account as one of the advantages of Liberty, the daughter of enlightenment, over Liberty, the daughter of *mores* . . . it increases as time goes on instead of deteriorating as the other form does." Lastly, the United States, having a sparse population for an immense territory, will be protected: "For a long while its wildernesses will be its *mores*, and its enlightenment, its liberty." In the light of these texts, does it not seem as if Chateaubriand, at the time when out of fidelity and ostentation he was playing the part of an unflaggingly faithful servitor of monarchy, thought and believed that the future of the world lay in "Liberty, the daughter of *mores*" such as he had seen in America? Can we help seeing in him a worshiper of Liberty who learned from America, and not from France or her Revolution, that it is possible for men to be free? Throughout his life he did not forget this lesson, even when he was serving a cause that seemed opposed to this faith.[171]

In 1801 he wrote *Atala*, in 1802 *René*—always the wildernesses, the purity, the rapture of this new world. The brightest dreams of his youth Chateaubriand gave to America, or, perhaps, derived them from this land. Whether or not he heard "the voice of the flamingo that, hidden in the reeds of the Meschacébé, foretold a storm for the middle of the day," whether or not he saw "at the ends of the forest avenues, bears drunk with grapes swaying on the branches of the elms, caribous bathing in the lake, black squirrels playing in the thickets, mocking-birds, Virginia doves the size of sparrows alighting on lawns red with strawberries, green parrots with yellow heads climbing in spirals to the tops of cypresses, humming-birds sparkling against the jasmine of Florida, and bird-catching serpents hissing as they hang, swaying like grape-vines, from the domes of the forest"—whether he saw, heard and touched all these things, or dreamed it, is of little import. He had felt it intensely; it was *his* America. The germ of all this was in the first impression that the United States had made on him. The good Crèvecœur says in his book, at a time when, filled with enthusiasm, he tries to depict the falls of Niagara, and fails in it: "How shall I describe the effect that is produced on the mind by a long contemplation of this movement, this eternal struggle; and on the senses by the uninterrupted flow of so violent an uproar, such an image of chaos? How shall I analyze the impressions that result from the view of these gigantic and menacing objects whose immensity is so disproportionate to the weakness of our organs? It is only in the calm of the study, and not on the spot, that it is possible to draw a picture of it." [172] Crèvecœur saw all that Chateaubriand saw and tried to express all that Chateaubriand expressed. But he lacked genius; his book is bad. Their descriptions are identical except for the single difference of genius. Crèvecœur was no more true to life than Chateaubriand. Artistic impression cannot be measured like scientific or experimental knowledge; intensity is of greater worth than precision, accuracy or breadth of knowledge. Thus the testimony of Chateaubriand is one of the most important documents that might be found. On this impression, many another is modeled, and it summed up many of the faltering and ill-defined yearnings that others felt. For Chateaubriand, as for Madame de La Tour du Pin, Lezay, Crèvecœur and Desjardins, America and the United States represent a certain physical joy, an intense and ecstatic perception of Nature that no other place affords. All these travelers have spoken the delight of the first piece of bread eaten on American soil.[173] But only Chateaubriand found the image of the flamingoes of the Meschacébé to express it. All of them came under the influence of American religiousness, which made lay preachers of Crèvecœur and Lezay and a convert of Madame de La Tour du Pin; but Chateaubriand wrote *Le Génie du Christianisme*. It is in America that Nature made felt most keenly her substantiality and divinity during these last years of the eighteenth century. The American influence afforded a transition between the influence of Rousseau, which it prolonged and transformed, and Romanticism, for which it prepared the way. After the concept of an abstract and chimeric "state of Nature," which was finally becoming empty and visionary, it created and developed the idea of a modern civilization that would be perfected by the intimate contact of man with Nature and by liberty and piety. It furnished the example of this civilization; it turned the imagination away from the past and directed it toward the future. Thus it provided a marvelous stimulant, and the impulse that it communicated to the minds of men, for all its being coördinated, mingled and later blended with other currents, remains none the less one of the great intellectual forces of the eighteenth and nineteenth centuries.

If France in drawing apart from America was still to retain the profound imprint that this nation had made on her sensibility, it is not less true that the United States, scandalized by the X Y Z Correspondence and irritated by the policies of Napoleon, was to remain for a long while under the influence of French thought. It is true that the newspapers rarely printed any news except from English sources—the French papers arrived with too much delay; but in these English articles and intelligences, they sought out faithfully everything that might evoke the French spirit and ideas. The conflict of the years 1795 to 1800 had been reëchoed in all fields of activity. The position of privilege that France had enjoyed in education in the United States underwent a sharp attack from 1797 to 1800. All the ground gained between 1774 and 1795 was lost for twenty years. In

1795 and 1796 the newspapers still carried advertisements of French courses and lessons (three at Philadelphia, four at New York, two dancing-masters at Baltimore, one at Pittsburgh, one at Princeton, eight at Charleston, one at New Haven, etc.). After 1797 there were no more. Except in the West, we find almost no more of these advertisements, innocuous and pacific as they were; either through coercion or timidity they had been given up.[174] The French professors took to cover; many of them returned to France. In the colleges where French was taught, it happened, as at Harvard, that the students rebelled against their professors under the pretext that all Frenchmen were Jacobins. There were no more French cockades; only the black cockade, the badge of the Federalists, was to be seen. A two-fold movement came about in the large universities; an increasing unruliness and a surprising irreverence for religious exercises manifested itself, and this wave of immorality was attributed to the influence of French ideas; on the other hand, the majority of the students and professors were Federalists and hated France. The discourses pronounced by the young men in their clubs or at commencement ceremonies bear witness to this. Volney and his impiety bore the brunt of these attacks in 1797, while in 1798 the principal concern was the defense of American dignity. Volney has left us several pages full of indignation at this persecution, which he endured with rage, although to us they seem mild enough. Yale, Harvard,

Princeton and Brown were the ringleaders.[175] A young Princeton student in 1798 characterized the French Revolution in these terms: "France has been governed by a succession of tyrants with whom the Neros and Caligulas of antiquity do not merit to be compared."

The same moderation prevailed at Harvard; in 1798 a young man there said in speaking of the French Revolution: "It has in a manner annihilated society in one country of Europe." And in 1799 he used this comparison in a poem describing the students corrupted by the French spirit:

> Like pigs they eat, they drink an ocean dry.
> They steal like France, like Jacobins they lie.[176]

In these conditions the French professors and the professors who had the French spirit were obliged to go. Harvard in 1798 omitted the French oration from its commencement exercises in order not to raise a storm of protest. Gradually the teaching of French was abandoned. Harvard, Columbia and Brown seem to have given it up at the beginning of the nineteenth century. In the South, which was less touched by the wave of hostility to France, we still find the University of South Carolina beginning to teach French in 1804, as the University of North Carolina had done in 1802; but it was only for a few years—it was eventually done away with because of the immorality of French authors.[177] Institutions of the West still persevered in teaching French, but this region was not the center of learning.[178] In the teaching of medicine and law France continued to hold an important place, for these subjects had a less direct relation to politics. Nevertheless, Montesquieu, Burlamaqui, Grotius and Valtel, although they expressed French culture in a certain measure, hardly represented the French judiciary concept of the beginning of the nineteenth century. When France adopted the Civil Code with its precision, its Roman logic and its rigidity, this was a fresh obstacle to the French judiciary influence in America; for the United States held to customs and laws that resembled those of England, and their law was based on usage, the decisions of the courts and tradition. Only Louisiana, which had received the French system of laws in 1801, kept the new system and still adheres to it. The friction between the two countries even modified the relations between the learned societies of France and the United States.[179] The Philosophical Society of Philadelphia, which, having been founded by Franklin, was liberal and daring by tradition, no longer dared to take into its membership a considerable number of Frenchmen, as it had done heretofore. Before 1798 Liancourt, Talleyrand, Adet, Volney, Alexandre Lerebours, etc., had been accorded this honor; from 1798 to 1802 Dupont de Nemours was the only Frenchman elected, and communications from Frenchmen, hitherto very frequent, became rare.[180] In all these domains there was somewhat of a lull to hostilities after 1800, but it was only a temporary calm and not a return to the glowing popularity of 1788.

America had been too deeply shocked by French immorality. Even leaving out of consideration the X Y Z affair and the blasphemies of Volney, there were other scandals that, for all their being neither literary nor political, had made no less impression on public opinion. Could the Americans forget Talleyrand, the former bishop, refined grandee and illustrious revolutionary, walking the streets of Philadelphia with his mulatto mistresses on his arm? [181] Two scandals in particular stirred the upper classes deeply from 1798 to 1800. The reader will remember Monsieur de Marsillac, the former officer and student of medicine at Montpellier who was converted to Quakerism and had been its exponent in France and later had gone to America to follow this religion in a place where his piety was more secure from the guillotine. The Quakers of Philadelphia received him as a brother and honored him. This lasted several years. He piously attended the meetings of the Friends, and the spirit often descended upon him. One day he was almost killed by a runaway horse, and all the Quakers of Philadelphia went to bear him their consolations. When the *émigrés* returned to France, Marsillac thought of going back home to see his native Alençon once again. In 1798 he paid farewell visits to all the brethren. Then he embarked, and the rumor later reached Philadelphia that, as soon as he set foot aboard the ship, John de Marsillac had changed his clothes, put on a velvet suit and shoes with silver buckles, drunk, sung and even rolled under the table. It was said that he had taken delight in denying his brethren and in playing a flute in public. Every one talked of it, and he was solemnly excommunicated from the congregation. He had been the leader of the French Quakers and the link between the Friends in France and those in America.[182]

This incident which made a painful and profound impression among pious people in America, did not have the disastrous publicity of the Tilly-Bingham scandal. This affair upset society throughout the United States. Mr. Bingham was a successful and very opulent merchant who had represented Congress in the French West Indies during the Revolutionary War. Later he had traveled in France. He had married a charming and refined woman, Miss Willing, had been elected senator and, as a rich man, an outstanding Federalist senator, the husband of a fascinating woman and the father of two charming daughters, he led an ostentatious life at the court of Philadelphia, where he had built a superb residence in the English style. There he gave many dances and entertained royally, for Mr. Bingham was much attached to his wife and wanted to divert her. It was the best house in Philadelphia. Only the most aristocratic Frenchmen were received: Talleyrand appeared there, as did Liancourt; the Vicomte de Noailles was an habitué of the house. Louis Philippe of Orléans would have been only too glad to have married into the family.

There were others who went there, and among them a certain Count Alexandre de Tilly, a man already ripening in years but not in wisdom. He had led an adventurous and obscure life, in the course of which his fortune had disappeared. He was amusing, without doubt, and clever. He won favor. He paid his court to the younger of the Misses Bingham, and between the third and the fourth of April the young lady disappeared about one o'clock in the morning. The next day it was learned that she had married Count Alexandre de Tilly. Every one was astounded and indignant. "Oh, those Frenchmen!" people said on every hand. There was as much ado as there had been over Messrs. X, Y, and Z; and Mrs. Bingham would have died of chagrin if her friends had not been able to find the girl and persuade Tilly to allow her to pay a visit to her mother. So Miss Bingham left her new husband for a few hours and never returned to him. Thereat Tilly, whose grief had not taken away his sense of realities, put advertisements in the papers announcing the abduction of his wife as if it had been a question of a runaway slave or an adulteress. At the same time he commissioned a lawyer by the name of Samson Levy to summon her parents to restore his young wife to him. Mr. Levy, a Jew, it is said, carried on the negotiations so well that he obtained, not the young lady, whom the offended husband perhaps no longer desired ardently, but the payment of Tilly's debts and an annual income of £5,000 sterling. Tilly, who had had his face slapped, also received satisfaction on this point: Mr. Baring, the offender, declared that he had forgotten himself "in a moment of agitation." Then Tilly returned his wife's letters and engaged himself to leave Philadelphia and to facilitate a divorce, a step which he had moreover rendered easy in advance by his admirable foresight in furnishing a slightly inaccurate name on the marriage license. He kept his promises, and in 1800 everything was settled. But the scandal became a legend.[183-184]

It is true that Marsillac and Tilly were isolated cases. There were at that time hundreds of honest, worthy and upright Frenchmen in America, and their neighbors and friends respected them; but these shocking incidents and a few others, adroitly circulated and compared with the libertine novels of France and Volney's irreligious declarations, sufficed to develop the legend of an atheist and guilty France. The Federalists made the most of it, and throughout this vast but provincial America the effect produced was tremendous. This happened at the moment when Washington's virtues and greatness of soul were everywhere being celebrated. They were seen as a symbol of the American people. Thus, in contrast to a corrupt France, there stood a pure America.

In spite of this opposition, in spite of the almost complete breakdown of French education in America, something remained, and France had given the United States a treasure of great price. One feels it during the years when, throughout the New World, calumny and outrage against France are being circulated. At the same time French books do not cease to be current; thought from across the sea holds its own and French civilization continues to have a fascination. There is a tendency to evict the philosophers. Voltaire and Rousseau, although we still find advertisements of their works, seem to be read less. Rollin and Fénelon have retained their popularity. The Abbé Barthélemy with his young Anacharsis * scored a considerable success; American writers went so far as to compose imitations of it. History and books of travel are still in vogue. As for French novels, they seem to be more and more appreciated, especially those of Mme. de Genlis. The magazines also are full of extracts and translations of works with philosophic and religious tendencies: Bernardin de Saint-Pierre, Mme. Roland, etc., are the principal authors whose works are thus exploited. *Les Etudes de la Nature*, translated and published at Boston by Nancrède, seem to have had a wide success. On the whole, readers were seeking therefore a certain mysticism more vague and more artistic than they found in the churches and in American works of art. It goes without saying that many revolutionary articles, especially those by Mercier, are translated and quoted; but

* *The Travels of the Young Anacharsis in Greece* by the Abbé Barthélemy affords an interesting picture of public and private life in Greece in the fourth century.—*Translator's note.*

this is rather by way of documentation than in answer to any literary concern or any taste for them.[185]

It is in the theater that French influence is most direct. The very introduction of drama into the larger American cities had been due in a great measure to the arrival of French officers, writers, hairdressers, dancers and actors in the United States. During the Revolutionary War, the theater was forbidden in America. The first man to produce a play was Quesnay de Beaurepaire, who played Beaumarchais's *Eugénie* and thereby raised a mooted question. It was only in 1784 that a company began playing regularly in New York and Philadelphia.[186]

With the progress of the French Revolution and the wars in Europe, a troupe of French actors, and later a troupe of dancers, emigrated to America. An English company came also, but it was filled with the French spirit and was at first patronized by the revolutionaries. To tell the truth, the American theater on the whole was very audacious. In 1793, when the French fleet was at New York, the Marseillaise was sung in the theater and a great democratic manifestation took place. Baltimore also was visited by the French troupe, and it was one of the factors in the strong French influence that prevailed in that city.[187] At New York in 1795, a play was produced representing the capture of the Bastille; the crimes of the Court were discussed, a son discovered his father who had been a prisoner for years, and the Iron

Mask and skeletons brought out of secret dungeons appeared before the eyes of the spectators. At Charleston an Italian impresario named Colomba exhibited puppets representing the execution of Louis XVI and the Queen. The audience saw the guillotine fall and the heads drop into the basket. "All is done by an invisible machine without any visible aid," the artist announced. The authors were not less subject to French influence.[188] Dunlap, the leading playwright of the period, translated a great many of his plays from French. He imitated farces like *Jérôme Pointu* and melodramas like *Bella, ou la Femme aux Deux Maris* by Alexandre Duval.[189] After 1797 he imitated and exploited Kotzebue, Schiller and the whole German theater, without, however, neglecting the French. His melodramas have all the paraphernalia of Romanticism, knights, abbeys, mysterious monks, hermits, ghosts, etc. He was rather a producer than an original playwright on the whole; he always exalted liberty in his plays. John Daly Burk, a fiery Irishman and democrat, is more original and interesting. In 1798, the year that was so critical for Franco-American friendship, he dared to produce a play entitled *Female Patriotism or the death of Jean d'Arc, an historic Play in five Acts* in which Jeanne d'Arc exclaims:

> It is not to crown the Dauphin Prince alone
> That hath impelled my spirit to the wars,
> For that were petty circumstance indeed;
> But on the head of every man in France

To place a crown, and thus at once create
A new and mighty order of nobility,
To make all free and equal, all men kings,
Subjects to justice and the laws alone:
For this great purpose have I come amongst you.
[Shout: Liberty and Equality.] [190]

These lines give an idea of the nature of original drama in the United States and of the vogue for things French.

The novel, written especially for and by the upper classes, was less easily bent to the French mode than the theater. It was the refuge of pious and religious souls. There were here and there imitations of the good Madame de Genlis, the virtuous Marmontel and Anacharsis, but most of the inspiration for novels came from England. A single writer of great talent, Charles Brockden Brown, seems to have sought originality. He attained it by complicating infinitely his plots, whose general plan often reminds me of that of *Coelina, ou l'Enfant du Mystère*. There are many things in these novels, and although time has rendered them somewhat difficult to read, we find certain beauties in them. They also are full of a strong, pungent and original sap. Pirates, robbers, incendiaries, heroines, somber monsters athirst for blood, and mysterious specters—all these appear, and many scenes have a German tinge. The flame of liberty that burns in them is French, however. In *Arthur Merwyn* (1799) we have Martinette who, born at Ragusa, enlists as a volunteer in the French army and kills thirteen officers, among whom are two *émigrés*, at Jemmapes. If

Brunswick had not beat a retreat that day, Martinette would have gone to assassinate him with his own hands "out of a generous attachment for Liberty." In *Ormond* (1799-1800) there are French privateers, French deputies beheaded by Robespierre, etc. While remaining under the influence of England and undergoing that of Germany, the American novel acts as a vehicle for French ideas. This is even more true of poetry, which was then the popular form of literature.[191] There were almost no newspapers that did not publish verses every day during this period when there were no serial novels. The most gifted American writer of the time seems to have been Philip Freneau, the descendant of French Huguenots whom we have already seen writing and fighting for liberty. Animation, eloquence, power of vision, ease of expression, a naturalness that was rare at the time, and a remarkable sense of reality, such are Freneau's principal qualities. His articles are as good as his verse. He was a champion of France to the end. In the years 1798-1800 he gave himself freer rein than ever before, he satirized Cobbett superbly in verse, he glorified Liberty and fought against the idea of a war with France who was defending the cause of humanity. He worshiped the People and did not want great men to usurp its dignity. In speaking of Washington he said:

> He was no god, ye flattering knaves,
> He owned no world, he ruled no slaves,
> But—exalt it if you can—
> He was the upright honest man.

He had read Rousseau and was sometimes inspired by him.[192] His knowledge of French was good but not complete, and we find few literary procedures copied from French authors in his work.[193] He had taken a religion and not a literature from France, but in this religion he was an impassioned and heroic believer. The same was true of the young men who wrote revolutionary verse without having his gifts; France had transformed them all, but she had not made French poets of them, nor had she persuaded them to imitate Joseph Chénier, Roucher, Delille, or Baour-Lormian, the greatest French poets of the day, nor even Racine. As for Voltaire, he was already too tiresome to be read carefully or copied in America. Songs, quatrains and stray verses—this is what we do sometimes find coming over from the French. But after all these scraps of poetry belong to all countries. The very extensive reading of French books in America at the end of the eighteenth century did not bring about a movement toward imitating them. The forms remained Anglo-Saxon even when the spirit was thrilled with an ecstasy that came from France. A book by Samuel Miller, *A Brief Retrospect of the Eighteenth Century*, shows that France was esteemed as the nation the most advanced in chemistry, natural history, geography, philosophy, and history. Her art was admired, although it was considered to be in decadence; and as for her language, it was said, "It has indeed become what Latin was, a universal tongue." It is therefore not that

French authors lacked the intellectual and literary esteem necessary to give them a more concrete influence over the United States; it was a general and curious phenomenon: French writers roused American minds and created original reactions in them at a time when English writers were less interesting and stimulating, but afforded examples that could easily be utilized and imitated. French culture in America was a means of liberation, not a model to be copied. Indeed its great rôle seems to have been to aid hardy and simple minds, who might have lacked enterprise or imagination, to find themselves and adopt a new spirit that should lead them to create a new form for themselves. Barlow, Freneau and Brackenridge are three cases of this. Out of enthusiasm for France they celebrated the revolutionary spirit; and without wasting any vain concerns on form, they composed, in forms that were already known, crude but original and sincere works that are the first expressions of the genius of the United States, straightforward, frank, strongly idealistic, tenderly attached to material life, noble with a tinge of stiffness, humble with glory.

Was it not the same with politics? The victory of Jefferson in 1800 was considered as the triumph of French ideas. It is true that Jefferson owed much to France. The man who, as early as 1776, had written the Declaration of Independence as a moral and religious code, the man who had always fought for the rights of the individual and who in 1788 had extolled revolts as being wholesome and of value to democracies—for this man the French Revolution had been a formidable revelation. It is not sufficient to define a doctrine, to practice it, or even to bring about its acceptation in order for it to attain fullness of life; it is necessary that it become incarnate in a social form and that it become a dominant passion. Thus a concept which seems immutable is modified by its internal growth, its radiations and incarnations.[194] Jefferson was fully conscious of all the spiritual value that the success of the French Revolution had for him and for the United States. It cannot be denied that in 1800 he was the champion of French philosophy. But this term designates rather a tendency than a coherent body of doctrine. Since 1775 France had sent to America moderate revolutionists, Jacobins, royalists and skeptics; each of them, in a circle more or less wide, had had influence and contributed in forming the concept that America held of France. Jefferson had had an intimate friend in La Fayette; he had also kept up continuous relations with Genet, Fauchet, Mazzéi and other revolutionists. In France he had especially frequented and loved the upper class that had been overthrown by the Revolution.[195] When he wrote to France, it was to order his wine, objects of art or books on architecture, rather than to procure political works or revolutionary documents.

Jefferson, considered by the patriots of 1789 as timorous, had made a common cause with the Jacobins of

1793 and had been considered in America as a theoretician of atheism, anarchy and violence. In 1788 he condemned the Constitution of the United States as being too monarchical and centralized; when he had been in office eight years, he left the central power stronger than in 1800. He, the friend of France, was the artisan of the definitive rupture between France and the United States. Never were there so few relations between the two countries as during this period; and Jefferson acceded to this state of things. What then had he retained from his association with France?

Before him, the ruling group had had visions of building up a strong government, creating a stable power based on the support of the upper classes and the clergy and capable of imposing on the nation whatever it considered to be for its good and of turning it away forcibly from what it judged detrimental. Jefferson transformed this internal policy; his own policy was based on the respect of the people and confidence in their judgment as well as their strength. Now this is an idea that he had already voiced in Paris in 1788 and that the group of patriots of 1789 had cherished. Before him the government had worked toward a policy of reconciliation with England and a sort of commercial and naval cooperation with her. Jefferson turned the interest back to America. He refused the friendship of England. He was the first to set in movement the peaceful conquest of the interior of the immense continent on which the United

States had founded a free nation. He spread the empire of liberty beyond all boundaries, and his conquests were peaceable, as all the conquests resulting from this policy were to be. This again was the great idea that he and his Girondist friends of 1793 had harbored.

America, the purified continent, America, the liberated continent, America turning away from Europe—these precepts would have brought tears of joy to the eyes of the French philosophers, the Mablys, Raynals, and Condorcets who had counseled the new-born United States to fill in their harbors in order to remain agriculturalists and upright men.

How much they would have admired this deist religion whose sway was marked by a most extraordinary impetus on the part of the Christian churches in America. From 1800 to 1815 was the great period during which the Baptists, the Presbyterians and the Methodists conquered the South and the West.[196] The Federalists declared that French atheism would be rife under Jefferson's administration; they cited the dissenting newspapers that supported Jefferson, *The Aurora* at Philadelphia, *The Argus* at New York, *The Independent Chronicle* at Boston, *The Temple of Reason* at New York, which represented Christ as the greatest deist that ever lived,[197] *The Argus* of Virginia, etc. As a matter of fact what did flourish under his administration was French Catholicism which, introduced in 1792 by the Sulpicians, traveling companions of Chateaubriand, had at first been slow to grow but had taken new life after 1802. The Sulpicians had had only one American student in their seminary at Baltimore before 1800; from 1800 to 1810 more than twenty were ordained in the Order.[198] They had founded a college at Georgetown. Their brethren were evangelizing all of the West, the Mississippi valley where the French had already done so much. All of the first Catholic bishops of this region were French; what is even more, the first Catholic bishop of Boston was a Frenchman, Mgr. de Cheverus, and it is said that if he had remained there, his personal prestige would have brought to Catholicism a part of the high aristocracy of the city.[199] And all this took place under a Republican administration! The reign of tolerance and democratic enthusiasm foretold by Franklin, Raynal, Mably, Condorcet, and others had brought about, not a disappearance of the Protestant churches, but an adaptation of them. The Presbyterian, Baptist and Methodist preachers who converted the West were not ordinarily scholars, but rather they were popular leaders who, mixing with the crowd and speaking its language, appealed to its good sense, and even to its senses, while angling for souls. They stirred the masses as they had been stirred in the Jacobin clubs.[200] In the North, the emancipation took on more subtle forms; minds eager for liberty and optimism turned toward the Unitarian doctrine, which refused to believe in one God in three persons. For more than thirty years the Congregational church in Massachusetts had seen faith in precise dogmas, and most especially in that of the Trinity, decreasing; but these tendencies remained vague and no scission occurred between the reformers and the orthodox believers. It was only in 1785 that the first church that officially renounced the trinitarian dogma was opened at Boston. Salem became the center of the Unitarian movement. A group of laymen and three clergymen led the fight. One of the first laymen to adopt the new ideas had been Thomas Pickering. According to his own story, doubt had first come into his mind during the Revolutionary War one day when he heard General von Steuben express the deist ideas that he had received in France and say that he would believe more easily in an absurdity than in the Trinity. Of the three pastors who preached Unitarianism at Salem, William Bentley seems to have been the firmest and the most ardent. He was a great democrat, a friend of Jefferson and a supporter of the French, whose philosophy he had studied. Thus almost everywhere in New England the Unitarian doctrine spread along with zeal for France. In 1800 it could be said that "there was not a single clergyman in Boston who believed strictly in the Trinity." Harvard tended to become the center of the new sect. In fact, although the students, carried away by their youth and patriotism, were ardent Federalists during the last years of the eighteenth century, the faculty was continually being reënforced by liberals and democrats. President Willard (1781-1804) was on intimate terms with friends of Voltaire, corresponded with Price and Priestley, and favored the philosophic spirit. Thus in these years of formation, Unitarianism grew up in the shadow of the "French doctrines." Catholicism, which was developing at the same time, had a much more popular character than in Europe. It was to be a long while before there were American monks and a rich and artistic ritual. It was a humble and combatant church. The Frenchmen in this church represented, on the whole, culture, broad-mindedness and a tendency toward mysticism.

*
* *

At the conclusion of this study we find ourselves therefore in the presence of two phenomena, which characterize the relations between France and the United States from 1770 to 1800, and which we have often had the occasion to point out in these pages: the collaboration of France and the United States in elaborating and spreading a democratic doctrine which won over hearts as well as nations; the reciprocal action of the two peoples in stimulating each other's desires and revealing and exalting each other's most characteristic forces.

From 1770 to 1800 a body of ideas that seems to be the product of their relations and represents in the eyes of the world the true spirit of democracy has formed in these two countries. England had played a considerable part in the preceding century in defining and propagating liberal ideas. After 1770 she seems to undergo an eclipse. It is true that the English Whigs still have great philosophers and vehement spokesmen; Wilkes, Price, Priestley, maintain the traditions of the party and expose the most daring political views. But they turn toward America and toward France to find the land of their hearts' desire. As a people, England exerts an influence hostile to new ideas, reforms and democracy during this period. On the contrary, the world at large begins to consider with admiration the United States, who on a virgin soil are building an ideal and Arcadian republic; then, with a mixture of alarm and fervor, it sees France establish a democratic form of government in the place of the oldest monarchy in Europe. Therefore it is truly in America and France that we find the stronghold of revolutionary ideas at the end of the eighteenth century.

It is impossible to define these principles with exactitude and to determine what their first origins were. In fact they are not definitely fixed, and they have varied continually according to the governments in power in America and in France from 1774 to 1800. The sovereignty of the people, the liberty of the individual, social and political equality, the necessity of good *mores* in order to establish a republic, the infallibility of the nation—such were in short the principal doctrines that constituted the Franco-American revolutionary spirit from 1770 to 1800. No one of them was original. They came from Rousseau, Montesquieu, Locke, the Reformation, the Renaissance, the Middle Ages, Rome and Greece. They were given their first complete expression in the Declaration of Independence and in the Constitution of Virginia in 1776; then we find them embodied without great change in the Declaration of the Rights of Man in 1789, in the writings and proclamations of Bonaparte and in the messages of Jefferson in 1801. The purely intellectual work has not therefore been intense during these thirty years.

The original element, as early as 1770, was the religious fervor with which people set themselves to the task of solving political problems and seeking out a code of principles that might serve as a rule for life as a whole and food for the soul. In 1770 the Declaration of Independence was the first response to this appeal. It proclaimed briefly, but in a grandiose tone, a moral and political catechism. Its novelty consisted in treating as universal and necessary truths principles theretofore discussed and upheld only by isolated individuals. It brought the ideas of the Encyclopedia, Rousseau and the English philosophers into the realm of collective thought, sentiments and faith. It was not merely a daring stroke risked at hazard by the spirit of reform in America. French philosophy had prepared souls for it, and the French ministry urged it.

As the years went by, this new moral code of these nations seemed so noble that all peoples dreamt of imitating and developing it. The French Declaration of the

Rights of Man is an example of this zeal. It contributed precisions and deductions that had been lacking in the American texts. It transformed these admirable and remote principles into a formidable moral reality for Europe and for the world. For Europe, democracy in America was a benign, chimeric and innocuous dream; democracy in France, the democracy spread by the French armies, was the most violent emotion of modern times. Thus the ideas of the Franco-American revolutionary system are original, not for themselves, but for the fact of their being grouped into a body of doctrine and for the sentiment that proclaims them axioms and eternal truths. These ideas, through the work accomplished by the American people and the French people, have laid hold on the entire human being—intelligence, sentiment, and will, although in 1770 they enjoyed only the theoretical adherence of the mind.

Their domination was to be durable. La Fayette had been the most famous symbol of this transformation. Apostle of pure democracy, hero of America, one of the first leaders of the French Revolution, he remained, even though he had deserted the revolutionary camp in 1792, the symbol of democratic idealism and Franco-American friendship. His popularity, tarnished by his ill-advised move in favor of monarchy in 1792, recovered its luster under the Empire, when once again he roused admiration by his resistance to arbitrary government. He maintained this courageous attitude all his life and he was rewarded for it. The Revolution of 1830 brought him back in triumph. Later still the theory that he represented and defended was to find in Alexis de Tocqueville a masterful historian and philosopher. It is curious to find in Tocqueville after more than half a century the concepts, with but little change, of the young nobles who had visited America and had derived from her a democratic philosophy scarcely adapted to their condition, their tastes and their instincts, but one from which they could not escape. Thus there was formed again in the middle of the nineteenth century a school which the violence of events had been able to bend but not to break, and which maintained faithfully the cult of the principles of 1776.

From these principles America had derived less a body of doctrine than a method for finding itself and creating her true personality. France and her revolutionary spirit aided her in forming herself but did not impose a form upon her. We have seen that many of the errors and successes of the French policy in America were the outcome rather of the use that the Republican party in the United States made of France, than of the action of France herself. Jefferson and his French ideas were marvelous stimulants for all the natural originality of this country and the blending of its fertile races. Jefferson was not under the domination of any French prejudice; he was able to admire the revolutionary ideas without accepting them as a tyrant. They afforded him the means of rejecting England whom it would have been so dangerous for this young nation, closely related to Great Britain, to imitate. They provided America with a new religiousness and new forces of enthusiasm even when, as a nation, she had no common faith.

And all this has dissolved, blended and disappeared in the gigantic personality that is taking shape—the American nation. Ideas have become irrecognizable, sentiments have developed so much that sometimes they have turned on themselves; deist tolerance, for example, brought about in certain ways an expansion of Catholicism. But without the first impulse of faith and desire, everything would undoubtedly have taken another course. I am not prepared to pronounce here on the value of this faith or to say whether or not another would have been preferable, as the Federalists claimed; but on contemplating the sway that is still exercised over the American masses by the two or three great principles that guided Jefferson and his party—confidence in the people as a spontaneous force, impassioned attachment to religiosity and morality without dogma being in the least involved, jealous love of the American soil which they consider sanctified—on finding these ideas still so dominant, one feels how much the shock of the French Revolution stirred these souls and how much they were transformed by it.

Yet to see in their intimity only an effort toward democracy would be to limit the part that France played in the life of the United States and that of the United States in the life of France. As we have mentioned,

America wakened in the French mind the taste for Romanticism. By its physical beauty, the diffusion of its religions, and its spontaneous liberty, it prompted eager and sensitive spirits like Chateaubriand to conceive a modern, religious and sentimental literature, wherein liberty should be the daughter of enlightenment, the ecstasy of Nature should be pious and illuminated, and strangeness and appeal should lie in the present instead of in a remote past. In return, France, while she was stirring up a wave of republicanism, introduced Catholicism, the arts, the theater and French culture into America. She woke a thousand contradictory yearnings and enriched American civilization beyond measure.

It seems therefore that from 1775 to 1800 there reigned an impassioned intellectual union between the two countries which was to be severed only by the disappointment of the French Empire and the almost total suppression of commercial relations, due to the continental and British blockades. France and the United States were dazzled by each other. The best minds of both countries threw themselves recklessly into this friendship. All the admirable qualities that they did not comprehend enticed them. A thousand tendencies, theretofore obscure, took shape and became images and desires; the revolutionary spirit, eager to transform the world and to act immediately, took the place of the spirit of reform. French intellectualism and American religiosity formed a torrent that swept over the world. The two countries loved each other for their differences. These they often misunderstood even while admiring them greatly. They did not succeed in exchanging their characteristics, as for a moment they had hoped they might. They did what was better than this: thanks to these very differences, they discovered in themselves resources of which they were unaware. Among nations, as among individuals, there seem to be those whose personalities are so much alike that in loving each other, even in a mediocre way, they imitate each other, and again, there are those whose beings are so distinct that in admiring and cherishing each other and trying in all ways to act one on the other and one for the other, they can only create. Men who have this gift are veritable "revealers" for their friends. These are the loftiest, the most difficult loves, and the most fruitful. When such friends part, it seems as if they had lost all, as if they had conserved nothing of each other. Nobody discerns anything in common between those who have just separated; for what they have retained is the great mystery, it is life and personality itself, the form that they needed. These generous intimacies, so rare even among men, are even rarer among nations. But the friendship of France and the United States between 1774 and 1800 affords such a spectacle. It is a mistake, I believe, to try to find intricate contrivances in it. If we consider it from an intellectual point of view, it is above all a mirage, a story of love.

Appendix 1

Abbé De Pauw's theory concerning the origin and age of America, taken from RECHERCHES PHILOSOPHIQUES SUR LES AMERICAINS, Vol. I, pp. 105-107 (edition of 1770).

If we admit that the American continent had been upset by secondary causes, floods and earthquakes, later than our continent, we shall comprehend why there existed such a marked difference between all the possible objects of comparison of these two parts of the globe.

Our horizon had an air of antiquity, because human industry had had time to repair the ravages occasioned by the convulsions of Nature. In the opposite hemisphere men had just climbed down from the rocks and elevations where, like new Deucalions, they had taken refuge; coming down into vast prairies still covered with sloughs and slime, their constitutions had been vitiated by the vapors of the earth and the humidity of the air. The lack of warmth in their temperament, their unbelievably sparse population, their feeble and enervated bodies, the endemic sickness to which they were subject, all this indicates that they had undergone an essential and recent alteration.

The character of newly cleared and drained lands is widely enough known: the heavy and fetid vapors that rise from them are everywhere equally unhealthy and engender chronic maladies among the inhabitants. By what happens in one canton, in one province, we can judge what should happen in an entire country and pass from the little to the great: if it takes a long succession of years to purify the least beach from which the water has receded, what lapse of centuries will it not take to clear up a considerable portion of the globe invaded by the ocean and dried by evaporation or other causes of one kind or another?

The consequence involved by a deluge seems to have escaped the notice of the most enlightened Authors; it is not enough that the overflow should have subsided and that the waters should have receded; in order to become inhabitable and healthy the soil still needs a thorough drying out which only time can accomplish: the most favorable spots become covered with vegetation and trees, and it is only then that men can go in and finish the work of clearing their abode by labor and industry.

The peoples of America are therefore, in this sense, more modern than the nations of the Old World: they are weaker because their native soil is more unwholesome, and we now perceive the reason why they were all found in a state of savagery or half savagery. The time to police themselves thoroughly had not yet sounded for them; their climate had first of all to ameliorate itself, the valleys and meadows had to dry out more, their constitutions had to grow stronger, and their blood to purify itself.

Appendix 2

Controversy between Favier and M. de Vergennes concerning the legitimacy of French intervention in America and the propaganda that should be carried on against England. (*Archives of the Ministry of Foreign Affairs. Memoirs and documents. France. Vol. V, Folio* 6 *to* 30).

(The phrases and words in italics are those underlined in the original text.)

PARIS, March 18, 1778.

MY LORD,

When I had the honor of waiting on you on Thusday last, you deigned to ask me for a work concerning the right that the King had or might have to *make a treaty of commerce or to contract an alliance with the United States of America, in short, to recognize authentically the independence and the sovereignty of this new Republic.* Since that day I should have written a volume on any other subject that lies within the field of my competence. I shut myself up in my study, I meditated a great deal, made researches, worked—*and I have done nothing.* I did not foresee that, neither by me nor by any one else, is there anything to be done on this subject.

I ought however to report to you the obstacles that I encountered in this work as I set about it. You know my devotion and you deign to render me justice; this is the reason for the respectful confidence with which I permit myself to expose to you freely what I think of the project of the work in question.

My desire to please you and to make myself useful made me seize upon the ideas that M. Gérard presented to me the more eagerly, since you appeared to approve of them at first glance. I therefore engaged myself to undertake this work, and I promised you to *execute it, although very imperfectly*.

But on returning alone to Paris, I began to meditate on an outline. Accustomed to establishing principles first and then deducting the corollaries from them (according to the *Wolfian method*), I immediately perceived that, in a work which might become the material for a manifesto, the usage to make of these principles becomes a very delicate question.

In fact, nothing would be easier for an American, for an Englishman even, than to prove according to the general principles adopted by the two nations that *the united colonies, being almost independent* DE FACTO, *are independent* DE JURE *on the grounds of their separation from England; that from their respective independence and the pact of their union, follow necessarily their sovereignty and the legality of the powers delegated by them to the general Congress; that this body has become the representative of their collective sovereignty; that it is therefore a* DE FACTO *and* DE JURE *power, and that any* *other power* may without violating international law * make not only treaties of commerce and navigation with it, but also offensive and defensive alliances, as the States of Europe are accustomed to do among themselves.

But: 1st, these Anglo-American principles are not generally recognized and adopted in all the rest of political society of the States of Europe. They are equally outlawed in the most prudent republics and in true Monarchies. In England itself, those of the Tories who are called strict have never adopted these opinions of the *Whigs*, the twelve *judges*, *organs* and interpreters of the laws, *the King's Council* † (or *les Gens du Roi*), the majority in the administration, especially the Scottish party formed by My Lord Bute, maintain constantly, though to palpably little avail, approximately the same dogmas in favor of the reigning House, for which the dethroned family were so much reproached; 2nd, Would it be proper to put into the mouth of a King of France or his minister paradoxical assertions concerning *natural liberty, inalienable and inadmissible rights of the people and its inherent sovereignty*, which have not ceased to be repeated, commented, ransacked and compiled for two centuries, from François Hottoman's *Vindiciæ contra tyrannos* to J. J. Rousseau's *Contrat social?* Would it be prudent even? (Pardon, my lord, a liberty that cannot concern you.) If the King, if the government, appeared

* *Jus gentium.* In the original French, *le droit des gens.—Translator's note.*

† This phrase is in English in the original.—*Translator's note.*

to profess such maxims, would we ourselves be exactly safe from their application and from their being turned against us? Has France no province which might appeal to the *original Contract*, or at last to a subsequent pact, definite, written and preserved, by which she gave herself to the crown of her own free will? Are not Languedoc, Brittany and Provence in this position? And even some of the conquered provinces, having yielded and having been ceded only on condition that they *retain all rights, customs, laws and privileges*—could not they also oppose the title of possession itself to manifest abuses of domination?

Yet, we must admit that, for a long while and especially during the last thirty years of the preceding reign, these abuses were carried so far by that of authority, even under a mild prince, that they became flagrant and unbearable.

Undoubtedly we may expect of the new reign the reform of a part of these abuses, and France already blesses her young King for having at least put a stop to their progress. Produced by necessity and existing for the same reason, the state of finances does not allow the moment of their suppression, even in the most happy future, to be envisaged.

If, therefore, the rights of a people were imprescriptible and consequently irrevocable, if after having ceded them to a State or a sovereign by a formal but conditional pact, by a *synallagmatic* contract; the sovereign having failed in the condition *sine qua non*, the people would resume its rights and might legitimately take back what it had ceded, that is to say, the *Sovereignty*, which would belong to it and be *inherent!* What other right would the State, this abjured sovereign, have save that of force? And could this right always, in all combinations of eventual, or at least, possible, circumstances, retain its energy and efficacity?

What usage against France then could not England herself make of the application and retortion of these principles which France would have freely sponsored against England? But, supposing that this latter country should never be strong enough to stir up and support a rebellion in France, what would not this Monarchy have to fear for its internal tranquillity from the *sanction* that the government itself would have accorded to these maxims from across the sea? The propagation of these ideas is already only too apparent. It had begun a long while ago with the writings of sects and the proclamations of parties. But the effervescence of American liberty is completing the work of turning many heads at Paris, and the contagion is spreading throughout the kingdom. Your prudence, my lord, and your sagacity had without doubt foreseen the observations that I have taken the liberty to make on this subject in a few notes of my *Hypothetic Speculations*. M. Gérard, whose abilities and competence are far above mine, has moreover the advantage of knowing and understanding the circumstances, of which

I am still ignorant. He seemed to have forestalled the objections and settled the difficulties by very ingenious solutions: 1st, that England, having accepted the *principles of Revolution*, could no longer deny the colonies the right to abjure the mother country, just as she herself had abjured the Stuart family; that this latter right, being derived from the former, is only a natural consequence of it, and that the [English] nation could not deny it without disavowing the principle itself, that is to say, the principle of its present constitution. In accepting this parity, which after all is very just, I shall merely take the liberty to remark that England might dispute it entirely, at least as to form. In the first case, it was the Nation assembled in Parliament which declared the throne vacant and chose for itself Kings from another house. In the second, it is colonies, members of the British Empire, which separate themselves from the main body without any other sanction than their own will. They do not abjure an individual or a family, but a whole nation of which they are a part. This nation, assembled in parliament, has not abjured explicitly (nor even implicitly, as did James II) its rights and authority. These rights still hold in all their force. No foreign power has the right to be the judge or arbiter of them, nor consequently to decide the question by a formal recognition of the Independence and Sovereignty of the separated colonies.

Such might be the answer of the Minister of St.

James's if he cared to discuss *constitutional questions;* but, too much occupied with these matters of contention, he would at least have no account to render on this score to foreign powers, and would probably not condescend to enter into the discussion.

Europe herself might feel some surprise at seeing France, the perpetual sponsor for the Peace of Westphalia and the born arbiter of all differences that may arise between the head of the Germanic body and its members, looking with a tranquil and indifferent eye upon the usurpation of Bavaria and, at the same time, without right, title, competence or the consent of those involved, setting herself up as a tribunal between England and her colonies. For, after all, to treat with these latter from Crown to Republic, to be the first to recognize them in this character, would be to judge the case and to pass sentence;

2nd, That the danger or at least the embarrassment that might be foreseen in treating so delicate a subject in a Monarchy and, perhaps, in the name of Monarchy, would easily be avoided by means of a distinction that suggests itself; namely, that each State has its own constitution, that that of France is not that of England, that the difference between them is known and does not need to be proved; that, in consequence, there are no applications or retortions to be feared and no annoyance could result from it.

I shall admit, if you wish, the principle established

by M. Gérard, *that each State has its own Constitution*, although in truth this seems to be more of a conventional axiom than an actual truth. In England, *fundamental law is the latest act of Parliament.* In France, the thing that might make one suspect that there is no constitution is the fact that, among all the bodies and all the individuals who have written so much, harangued so much and disputed so much on this subject—as if a constitution did exist, none of them have been able to agree, either with others or among themselves, as to the nature of this constitution. In view of the conflict of their systems, the contradiction of laws, facts and examples for and against, in the confusion that results, any reader a bit difficult to convince is obliged at least to suspend his judgment; and the more he observes, the more he puts things together, the more he is tempted to believe that this constitution is yet to be born. But, in admitting the existence of these two constitutions, I shall permit myself to feel some doubts as to the consequence. I have already exposed some of the at least very probable dangers for the internal tranquillity of his kingdom, which might sooner or later result from a French Monarch's adopting, in a manifesto, these Anglo-American maxims. I shall only add that the development of these same principles in favor of the English colonies would be a very bad example for our own.

Ordinarily I write without books, the matter of which I treat having for a long while been constantly in my mind. I felt obliged to make some researches as to the abstract principles of this matter. I dug up an old Grotius from the bottom of a closet. I thumbed it over and I found in Book II, Chapter IX, Paragraph 10, M. Gérard's opinion on the subject of the ancient colonies: *that their submission to the mother country was not in obedience to natural law.* And in fact (as M. Gérard has so justly remarked), it is certain that the Greek colonies did not remain in the dependence of the mother country long after their establishment. It was not the same with the Roman colonies. They followed the fortunes of the provinces in which they were incorporated and were detached from the Empire only by force at the time of its fatal downfall.

Grotius would without doubt have spoken further and more discreetly of colonies if those of the Europeans had been more important in his time. But they were still in their infancy. He therefore does not mention them and says only a word in passing about the colonies of antiquity. Also he cites on this subject only Thucydides and Denis of Halicarnassus.

But even if this doctrine were intended to apply to modern colonies, it would not be a reason for the government to encourage its propagation by its own example. We have already only too many fanatics who believe in it and charlatans who preach it. However that may be, supposing the existence of *our constitution*, let us admit at least that its nature is as yet not well enough known and clearly enough determined for us not to fear compromising it by the comparisons and analyses that this controversy might occasion. Silence on this subject is to be recommended; perhaps in the end we shall be obliged to command it and to have it rigorously observed. Is it then the place of the Monarch to break this silence?

3rd, M. Gérard has cited the famous example of Elizabeth's conduct toward the United Provinces as soon as they had shaken off the yoke of Spain. I myself cited this in *Questions importantes* and *Spéculations hypothétiques.* I had also recommended that we imitate it. But, whenever I have proposed treating with the United States, I have always distinguished between *a secret convention between unofficial intermediaries and informal agents* and *a formal treaty of alliance or commerce. I have not ceased to emphasize the necessity of having such a treaty preceded or accompanied by a strong diversion against England elsewhere even than in America.* I presupposed the existence of certain *conventions of assistance*, and I should have desired that this aid had been more prompt and efficacious. Indeed I have thought and said that such aid would hasten the moment for an inevitable rupture. I have added that this constituted another reason for making our aid so forceful, so consistent and of such weight that it would make an impression on these new allies and keep them from making peace with England. But also I have always supposed that this alliance would remain hidden and indirect, like a germ ready to hatch out, and that its development by a formal and direct treaty would be postponed until the moment of the first open hostilities on one side or the other.

I know that here the example of Elizabeth might be raised against me. I myself have mentioned the fact that, a long while before entering into open warfare against Spain, she had concluded a formal alliance with the United Provinces, that she had furnished them money, troops and generals and had taken over strongholds. What is the consequence of this? It is that Elizabeth was in a position with regard to Philip II which differed from that of Louis XVI toward George III. The Spanish monarch was not yet waging open war against her, but he was employing all the resources of intrigue and fanaticism to hatch conspiracies and to stir up rebellions in England and Ireland.

He was flooding the two kingdoms with emissaries and agitators. He disputed this Queen's title to her possessions. Even her life was not in security. Several conspirators convicted of having made attempts against it had admitted their relations with Spanish agents, ministers and governors and confessed to having received money and encouragement of all kinds. Finally, Elizabeth rightly felt herself justified in going beyond the limits of international law in order to thwart the attempts of a prince who respected them so little. If Philip's dark and slow-moving policy made him prefer the continuation of this underhanded war to open warfare, it was because he hoped to succeed better by it; and it was only after having tried vainly all other operations, that he finally decided to declare war. It was really a mere further formality, for hostilities on both sides had begun long before and were being carried on vigorously in both the Old and the New World. The King (of France) would not have the same griefs to allege to-day against the King of England.

But what need would we have had to justify a treaty of alliance with the United States if we had contented ourselves with a secret convention such as I had defined and imagined? There would still have been time to change it into a formal treaty dated, if we wished, the day after the declaration of war or after the first open hostilities.

Then the King might without difficulty have openly avowed the treaty of alliance. *The law of war*, being in itself only the suppression of all other laws, there follows naturally that to harm a declared enemy by all sorts of means, even to furnish aid and encouragement to rebellious subjects (or those whom this enemy may consider so), as Louis XIII and Louis XIV did for the Portuguese and then later for the Neapolitans, the Messinese and the Hungarian malcontents. From this right also proceeds that of making offensive and defensive alliances with revolted subjects and even, when they are joined in a body to give themselves a king or to form a republic, that of recognizing their sovereignty and their independence.

Things have come to such a pass that there is no longer any way to retreat; and if a formal treaty with the United States exists, if we have been obliged to admit it, if we have felt obliged to notify the King of England of it officially, if, in consequence, his Ambassador has received orders to quit Paris without taking leave, if in fact he is to leave next Monday; it is no longer the time to discuss the legality or illegality of the treaty in question, and much less, the motives that the government doubtless had for concluding it. The ability and prudence of our ministry ought to make one suppose that these motives were so preponderant that there was apparently no other course to choose. It now remains only for us to draw up a manifesto to precede or accompany a declaration of war.

In my humble opinion (to use the English expression) there is no necessity of speaking of the treaty in question in this manifesto. It will be only too thoroughly discussed in the English manifesto, and the Minister of St. James's will not fail to lay stress on this *secret hostility for a long while inavowed* to refute our just complaints concerning the *open hostilities* of 1775, committed by England against France in time of peace. France is not under any obligation to justify the treaty by principles, dissertations and citations. She has only too many excuses for declaring war without this. The reports of the Admiralty, those of the governors and other officers of our colonies should furnish a writer abundant enough material.

It must be admitted that the aggressions, violations of territory and depredations committed of late by the English in our seas, along our coasts and even in our ports might be justified in certain respects *in themselves*, but they are none the less irregular and none the less vicious *in form*. And of what is it a question save form, in a manifesto as in a legal process! Right and wrong on both sides, it is the form that counts. The form is the only thing to be considered—and with reason; for however we set about it, we shall prove nothing by considering the *matter* itself. If it is the *matter* that decides, it is by the cannon's mouth; and this will perhaps be the only reply that will remain for us to make on the subject of this treaty. May it be unanswerable!

I am with profound respect, my lord, your very humble and very obedient servant.

(Signed): FAVIER

[The remainder is in Favier's handwriting.]

P.S. I have explained the motives of my excuses, deign now to accept my very humble thanks.

When you asked me for the work in question, you were so kind as to tell me that *it was to be placed before the eyes of the King*.

This step on your part would imply that I have your favor, which would undoubtedly have assured me the approbation of his Majesty. What greater good fortune could have befallen me? Concerned only with the glory of the King and of your ministry, I feared lest I should compromise both of them in following the outline that M. Gérard had traced for the *plan of the manifesto.* I thought it my duty to sacrifice personal interest to such great motives.

It seemed to me impossible to *justify* a formal treaty with the colonies before *a declaration of war*, by any other principles than those of the *preambles of their constitutions.* And these principles cannot be ours. We might at most *palliate* in a manifesto the irregularity of this step by reasons of *fact* and not of *right.* We should hasten to bury *the English grievance* under the multitude of our own grievances. Any one of our own griefs is in itself of less weight, but their number and the accumulation, with the aid of a little hyperbole, would not have failed to give them, as a whole, a weight that would put the balance in our favor.

After having enumerated all these grievances then and placed the picture in the light the most unfavorable to England, one might slip in a word concerning the treaty (since it is no longer possible to deny it). It could be stated that the King was in the right in negotiating and concluding it; because the excesses, violences, and the *hostile procedures* of the English against the flag of His Majesty and French Commerce, had put him in a *de facto* state of war with that nation; that from this state of war would result the same dangers and the same need of taking precautions as from an open and declared war; that consequently and in order to protect and assure the navigation and commerce of his subjects, the King had found himself obliged to conclude a treaty with the nation the most interested in maintaining the liberty and security of commerce, etc., etc.

Pardon, my lord, this crude scrawl. These are a few ideas that presented themselves to my imagination after my letter was written; they are not exactly marvelous. They will merely prove that I am keeping the subject in mind and that, at least, like Diogenes, *I am rolling my barrel.*

I have finally consented to dine with M. Fullarton tomorrow. I shall have the honor of waiting on you on Saturday, my lord, and of telling you why I accepted this latter invitation. Perhaps something interesting will come out of our conversation.

PARIS, April 17, 1778

MY LORD,

You have undoubtedly been surprised at my silence during the last two or three weeks, after the orders that you did me the honor to give me when we last met in the presence of M. Gérard.

I admit that I still feel the same hesitation as to how to go about a task, easy in appearance, but, to my way of thinking, most difficult. I despaired of doing it, and I went to Versailles last Saturday to have the honor of telling you so. I did not have that of waiting on you, your door was closed. Not having found M. Moreau, I left a note for him.

Since then I have reflected as to how I might write something reasonable and, at the same time, fitting, without doing violence to my principles. If I had not always had these unfortunate scruples, I should have achieved success long ago, as so many others have done.

You yourself, my lord, approved the observation that I made to M. Gérard, that these principles being those of Monarchy, we must above all avoid compromising them, even under the cover of anonymity. And I shrunk from doing so all the more after you were so kind as to inform me of its particular destination.*

I needed a frame-work; and only two days ago one presented itself to my imagination. I submit this idea in all humility to your superior judgment. I should consider myself very fortunate if you deigned, my lord, to indicate to me means of handling the subject better.

I know the extent and the multiplicity of your occupations. Perhaps you will hardly have time to glance at this mere outline during the next few days. On my return from the country, where I am going to pass the holidays, I expect to pay you a visit Friday to renew my homage.

I am, with profound respect, my lord, your very humble and very obedient servant.

(Signed): FAVIER

* The pamphlet was to be read by the King, as Favier mentions in his preceding letter.—*Translator's note.*

[All this is in Favier's handwriting, and the enclosures include the manuscript of *La Lettre du Comte d'Albany au Lord Bute.* Vergennes replied to these letters in the following communication.]

VERSAILLES, April 22, 1778

I received, sir, the letter that you were so kind as to address to me. This work is a new proof of your zeal and talents, and I am all the more grateful to you since you were working in contradiction to your own principles. I understand how much hesitation and constraint you must have felt; and this, as well as my duty to respect your scruples, would prevent me from having further recourse to your talents to expose more fully the principles which ought to be the essential bases of the work that I had proposed to you. Be persuaded however, sir, that I shall always seize with pleasure the opportunity to make use of your abilities and learning and to give you proof of the sincerity of the sentiments with which I remain very sincerely, sir. . . .

P.S. [In Vergennes's handwriting.] I do not want to impose too much on your complaisance. To convince others, one must first be convinced one's self, and I see that you are not. I hope that other subjects will afford me the occasion to ask you for new proofs of your zeal and new fruits of your learning.

Notes

CHAPTER I

[1] The American newspapers are the principal source from which I have drawn for the study of public opinion. As early as 1760, under the impulsion of Franklin, the Press had attained a high degree of organization in the English colonies in America, and the liberty that it enjoyed permitted it to give expression to all points of view. Every town of any importance had its gazette, which printed, it is true, only a small number of copies (from a few hundred, it seems, up to a thousand, rarely more than this). The newspapers of the large ports were of course the most important and the most valued. In fact, it was through them that all European news was disseminated. European news items were taken from English papers and the accounts of travelers, merchants and sailors. After 1775, French papers from the West Indies, Dutch papers and, finally, newspapers from France were circulated and translated; but it was still from England that most of the news came. The American papers were in the habit of copying each other; an editor would make up his paper (usually a weekly appearing on market-day) from clippings taken from ten or a dozen other papers to which he subscribed. In addition to such news items, these papers also printed official announcements (acts of the State Legislatures or Continental Congress), local news, letters from readers, and usually poems and sometimes literary selections in prose. Advertisements often filled half the space and were even accompanied by illustrations. Among these advertisements we find announcements of stolen horses, runaway slaves and unfaithful wives.

Franklin had made Philadelphia the veritable center of information for the New World. The situation of this city allowed him to circulate his papers in all the other colonies. Philadelphia enjoyed great liberty. Boston and New York, as ports and rich and cultivated cities, had a well-directed and influential press. The New York newspapers were inclined to be English in tendency and those of Boston to be American. The South, which had very good newspapers before the Revolutionary War, does not seem to have been able to rebuild them. Baltimore and Charleston possessed flourishing gazettes, but they never had the prestige of the Northern papers. In each chapter we have mentioned the most important organs of the period under consideration. There is no modern book on the American press during the eighteenth century. The book on this subject by I. Thomas, which is already very old (it dates from the beginning of the last century), is a curious and useful, though very incomplete, document. As for the alphabetical catalogue of all the American newspapers from 1620 to 1820, which M. C. Brigham is publishing in the collections of the American Antiquarian Society, it is of great value.

[2] For the pacific inclinations of Louis XV, see the news from English sources printed in the *Boston Post Boy* (Dec. 31, 1772); *Boston Evening Post* (Aug. 10, 1772); *Massachusetts Spy* (July 2, 1772); *Pennsylvania Gazette* (March 21, 1771); *New York Gazette* (March 25, 1771), etc.

[3] For the riots in France, see the *New York Gazette*, *New York Journal*, *Pennsylvania Gazette*, *Pennsylvania Chronicle*, *Massachusetts Spy*, *Boston Post Boy*, *Boston Evening Post*, *passim*, etc. (1770).

[4] Concerning internal quarrels in England, see *Nouvelles extraordinaires de Leyde* (Jan. 13, 1770); *Journal Encyclopédique de Bouillon* (Sept. 2, 1771); *Mercure de France* (October, 1771). *Gazette de France*, *passim*, during the winters of 1770 and 1771.

[5] Saurin (Bernard Joseph), 1706 to 1781, was a dramatic poet and a philosopher. He is especially known for his *Spartacus*, a tragedy in five acts (1760), and his *Anglomane*, a one-act comedy (1772).

[6] Concerning Voltaire, see *Histoire de France*, published under the direction of M. Lavisse, Book VIII, Part II, p. 304.

[7] Concerning Helvetius and the revival of Freemasonry in

France see Louis Amable, *Une Loge maçonnique d'avant* 1789; *La R. L., les Neuf Sœurs* (Paris, 1897), pp. 1-8 and 9-10.

[8] For the odes on navigation and crises of fever, see *Mercure de France*, No. 2 (January, 1770), p. 12, and No. 1 (October, 1773), pp. 5-13.

[9] Concerning the use of the terms "patriot" and "citizen," see *Mercure de France*, May, 1770, pp. 125-128, and July, pp. 87-88.

[10] John Wilkes (1727-1797), Whig politician of an extraordinary violence, who was very popular in England between 1770 and 1779.

[11] Madame Roland, *Lettres de Madame Roland*, published by Claude Perroud, new series, Vol. I, pp. 229-244 *et seq.*

[12] Concerning Chateaubriand and Raynal, see *Mémoires d'Outre-tombe* (edited by Biré), Vol. I, p. 192.

[13] Abbé Roubaud (Pierre-Joseph-André, 1730-1792), economist and author.

[14] Quérard mentions fifteen editions and modifications of Raynal between 1770 and 1798 and adds that there were others. The American version is entitled *Sentiments of a Foreigner on the Disputes of Great Britain with America. Translated from the French* (Philadelphia, 1775). See also *Bibliographie critique de l'Abbé Raynal*, by A. Feugère (1922), pp. 15-18.

[15] For the collaborators of Raynal, see *Un Précurseur de la Révolution, l'Abbé Raynal*, by A Feugère (Angoulême, 1922), pp. 175-201.

[16] For Raynal's errors as to the boundaries of Pennsylvania, see *Histoire des Etablissements des Européens dans les Deux-Indes* (Amsterdam, edition of 1770), Vol. VI, p. 195.

[17] Polly Baker's speech is found in the same edition, Vol. VI, pp. 157-262.

[18] The anecdote concerning Franklin and Raynal is related by Jefferson, *Writings of Thomas Jefferson*, Vol. X, p. 121, and A. H. Smyth, *Writings of Benjamin Franklin*, Vol. II, p. 470. For these and other errors committed by Raynal, see *Un Précurseur de la Révolution, l'Abbé Raynal*, by A. Feugère (Angoulême, 1922), pp. 200-231.

[19] The pages of Raynal concerning the English colonies in America are found in Vol. VI, pp. 176-426, of the work cited above.

[20] Henry Fabry (Comte d'Autrey), Catholic theologian and apologist, especially known for his refutation of *Christianisme dévoilé* (1776).

[21] Raynal, *Histoire des Etablissements des Européens dans les Deux-Indes* (edition of 1770), Vol. VI, pp. 309-311.

[22] Abbé Corneille De Pauw (1739-1800), philosopher and author, uncle of Anarcharsis Cloots.

[23] Dom Pernetty, Benedictine of Saint-Maur (1716-1801), known for his researches in alchemy and his disputes with his superiors.

[24] De Pauw's book had at least one edition at Berlin in 1768, one at London (Berlin) in 1770, one at Berlin in 1771, one at Clèves in 1772. Dom Pernetty's book was brought out at Berlin in 1770, had one edition in two volumes in 1771, and was re-edited with De Pauw's book at Berlin in the same year.

[25] See *Œuvres complètes de Buffon* (Paris, 1845), Vol. III, pp. 353-357.

[26] See *Writings of Thomas Jefferson*, Vol. II, pp. 60-61.

[27] See articles expressing the typical attitude of public opinion concerning the New World and the Americans, *Journal d'Agriculture*, January, 1773, pp. 15-30; *Mercure de France*, August, 1786, pp. 36-42.

[28] For Guillard de Beaurieu, see the article by M. Legouis in *La Suisse universitaire* (April, 1901), sixth year, No. 7.

[29] See *Ephémérides du Citoyen* (1771), Vol. XI, pp. 74-80; *Journal d'Agriculture* (February, 1773), pp. 156-165.

[30] See *Le Journal des Savants* (February, 1773), p. 87; *Observations sur la Physique* (1773), Vol. I, p. 38, etc.

[31] L'Abbé Chappe d'Auteroche (1722-1769), astronomer, member of the Académie des Sciences; Father J. E. Berthier, of the Oratory (1710-1783), philosopher and naturalist, famous for his kindness; Dalibard (Thomas-François), botanist and Franklin's disciple in electricity.

[32] Pierre Dupont de Nemours (1739-1817), economist, editor-

in-chief of the *Journal d'Agriculture* and of the *Ephémérides du Citoyen.*

[33] Concerning Franklin in France in 1767, see *Writings of B. Franklin* (ed. by A. H. Smyth), Vol. I, pp. 418-419; Vol. V, pp. 49-52, 92-93, 153-154, 192-193, etc.

[34] Julien David Le Roy (1728-1803), architect and scholar, member of the Académie des Inscriptions et Belles Lettres.

[35] We find an example of this philosophical attitude in favor of America in the very important *Gazette de Leyde* (1773), *passim.*

[36] Concerning the hatred of the Indians in the United States, see the news items from America in the *Mercure de France* (January, 1773), pp. 206-208; August, p. 209; April, 1774, etc.

[37] This opinion is expressed notably in *The History of the American Indians . . .* by James Adair, Esq. (London, 1775).

[38] On the accounts of French travelers and missionaries among the Indians of North America, see Gilbert Chinard, *L'Amérique et le Rêve exotique dans la Littérature française au XVIIe et au XVIIIe Siècles.*

[39] See *Writings of B. Franklin* (ed. Smyth), Vol. III, p. 203, and *Old Family Letters*, Series IV, pp. 2-7.

[40] Concerning irreligion in Virginia: *Old Churches, Ministers, and Families in Virginia,* by Bishop Meade, especially pp. 174 and 175.

[41] On the spread of the Baptist Church in America, see *The American Church History Series. A History of the Baptist Churches in the United States*, by A. N. Newmann, Chapter I.

[42] Concerning the schism in the Congregational Church, see, in the same series, Williston Walker's book.

[43] Concerning the formation of the Unitarian and Universalist churches, see *The Religious Forces of the United States*, by H. K. Carroll.

[44] Concerning the development of Methodism, see *Massachusetts Historical Society Proceedings* (1914-1915), Vol. XLVIII, pp. 254-268, M. J. S. Bassett's article, "Popular Churches after the Revolution," and in *The American Church History Series*, the volume on Methodism by J. Buckley.

[45] Concerning the political philosophy of Samuel Adams, see *Writings of Samuel Adams*, by H. A. Cushing, Vol. II, pp. 287-289, and 233-234.

[46] In 1773 the Society Library of New York was already publishing a catalogue. We have the catalogue for 1770 of the Library Company of Charleston. The Philadelphia Library regularly published advertisements in the newspapers, and Francis Daymon was the librarian in 1774 (*Pennsylvania Journal*, June 15, 1775).

Boston had had, as early as 1640, the first and largest public library in the Anglo-American colonies. That of Harvard University, which did not cease to grow, was already excellent in 1773, as the catalogue published that year proves. It had been imitated. Boston was the city of books on the American continent. See particularly *Voyages dans les Colonies du Milieu de l'Amérique septentrionale* by M. André Burnaby, pp. 152-164.

[47] Dartmouth College was founded in 1769. Rhode Island dates from 1764, but it did not begin its full development until later (see *Historical Catalogue of Brown University*).

[48] *The Records of the College Faculty* at Harvard, for the years 1763 to 1775, afford a very striking document concerning the development of education in America.

[49] Concerning Charles Carroll's voyage to Europe, see *The Life and Times of John Carroll, by Peter Guilday* (New York), pp. 6, 14, etc. For the voyage of H. Laurens, who was President of the Congress, and later prisoner in England, see *Lives of American Merchants*, by John Frost, *passim.* For Franklin's voyage, see *Writings of Franklin* (ed. by A. H. Smyth), Vol. V, pp. 49-52.

[50] See *The Loyal Verses of Joseph Stansbury and Dr. Jonathan Odell* (ed. by Winthrop Sargent), p. 4.

[51] John Adams, schoolmaster, member of the Congress, and later ambassador to England and President of the United States. See *Warren-Adams Letters*, p. 31.

[52] Concerning Louis XIV and his reputation in the United States, see *Works and Writings of John Adams*, Vol. IV, p. 38.

[53] Concerning the Pope and the United States, see *Papist Idolatry*, by J. Mayhew (Boston, 1765); *A Discourse on the Man of Sin*, by Gad Hitchcock (Boston, 1770), and the whole series of the *Dudleian Lectures*.

[54] See *Literary Diary of Ezra Stiles*, Vol. I, p. 179.

[55] See especially the years 1772 and 1773 of the *Boston Gazette*, the *Massachusetts Spy*, the *Pennsylvania Gazette*, the *Pennsylvania Packet*, the *New York Post Boy*. See particularly in *Rivington's Gazette* of Oct. 28, 1773, the comparison of France with a sparrow.

[56] *New London* (Connecticut) *Gazette* (July 22, 1770).

[57] See *New York Gazette* (Aug. 21, 1771).

[58] See *United States Bureau of Education Bulletin* (1913), No. III, *The Teaching of Modern Languages in the United States*, by Charles Hart Handschin, pp. 16, 17, and 22.

[59] *Writings of B. Franklin*, Vol. III, pp. 24-28; Vol. IV, pp. 419-423.

[60] *Diary of Ezra Stiles*, Vol. I, p. 409.

[61] Concerning Giraut, *New York Gazette* (Feb. 5, 1770); for Tétard, *id.* (Oct. 5, 1772); for Haumaid, *id.* (May 14, 1774); for Saint-Pry, *New York Gazetteer* (March 23, 1775); concerning the three Italians, *id.* (May 19, 1774); for Delille, *Diary of Stiles*, Vol. I, pp. 388, 408, 409, etc., and *Boston Gazette* (June 8, 1772, and May 17, 1772). For Régnier, *Boston Post Boy* (June 20, 1774). Concerning M. de Viart, see *Essex Gazette* (Dec. 1, 1772).

[62] Concerning Daymon, see *Pennsylvania Gazette* (Jan. 3, 1771; April 23, 1771; Sept. 19, 1771); *Pennsylvania Journal* (June 15, 1774) and Doniol, *Participation de la France à l'Etablissement des Etats-Unis*, Vol. I, pp. 267-287.

[63] *Writings of Jefferson*, Vol. I, p. 3.

[64] I have deliberately refrained from giving the numbers of the catalogues in which the various French books that I have spoken of here are mentioned. The value of these catalogues varies greatly according to the man who composed them and the person or persons who owned the library. Each of them has its

own particular intention, and they cannot logically be considered as a whole.

In fact there are three distinct categories to be distinguished:

1. The catalogues of public libraries whose books were read and circulated in the larger cities.

2. Those of the booksellers, who sometimes kept on their shelves books that were unsalable and continued offering them for sale year after year. (The American booksellers did not always choose the books that they sold; they received them from England by the ships that brought over tea, hardware, furniture and cloth. Their furnishers often sent them books whose vogue had passed in order to get rid of them, and these books were badly received by the American public. Sometimes they sent very modern books which the American public rejected as being too worldly and scandalous.)

3. The catalogues of private libraries, which were scarce and of little interest. In fact, in almost all the libraries of celebrated men the majority of the books were gifts from the authors or their friends and the owners did not read them. We know that this was true in the case of Washington, whose splendid library was merely a proof of his popularity in Europe and by no means indicates that either he or his family took any interest in literature. We are justified in feeling the same suspicions with regard to Franklin, Jefferson, John Adams, Madison, etc.

Thus we may say that in America at the end of the eighteenth century a book that is often mentioned in the catalogues of the public libraries may well be a popular book, a book often mentioned in the advertisements of the booksellers may be one that has been coldly received by the American public, and one often mentioned in the catalogues of private libraries may be altogether unknown in America.

The only indication that would show that the book had been read would be marginal notes in the handwriting of the owner and having to do with the contents of the book. In every case in which such evidence was to be found, I have taken it into account.

Such are the reasons that have made me refrain from giving

statistics on this point in which the reader would have found only a deceptive accuracy.

[65] *Writings of B. Franklin*, Vol. IV, pp. 267-268.

[66] *Warren-Adams Letters*, p. 18.

[67] See the catalogues of the *New York Society Library*, *Charleston Library Company* and *Philadelphia Library Company* already mentioned.

[68] See *Pennsylvania Gazette* (Sept. 20, 1770), for example.

[69] *South Carolina Gazette* (Nov. 24, 1772).

[70] See *New York Journal* (May 26, 1774), *Maryland Journal* (Nov. 3, 1774).

[71] *Boston Post Boy* (Aug. 13, 1770).

[72] See *The Harmony Between the Old and New Testament*, by T. Coombe (Philadelphia, 1774), p. 17.

[73] See *Transactions of the American Philosophical Society* (1879), Vol. I, pp. 1-25.

[74] See *South Carolina Gazette* (Aug. 6, 1772).

[75] *Massachusetts Historical Society Proceedings* (1915-1916), Vol. XLIX, p. 440 *et seq.*

[76] *Early Proceedings of the American Philosophical Society* (Philadelphia, 1884), pp. 168, 169, 170.

[77] See *New York Gazetteer* (Nov. 9, 1775), for example.

[78] See *Gazette of Boston* (Oct. 20, 1768).

[79] *Writings of B. Franklin*, Vol. V, p. 47.

[80] *Works and Writings of John Adams*, Vol. II, p. 110.

[81] Simon-Nicolas-Henri Linguet (1736-1794), lawyer and famous pamphleteer, editor of the *Annales politiques du XVIII me Siècle*, exiled under Louis XVI, beheaded under Robespierre. Vergennes and Louis XVI took an interest in him and protected him. See *Correspondance publiée par M. de Lescure*, p. 254.

[82] See *Mémoire de Vergennes, pour le Roi*, dated Dec. 8, 1774, *Archives des Affaires étrangères, France, Mémoires et Documents*, Vol. 446, pp. 32-33.

[83] Concerning Vergennes's ideas, see the very curious book of Doniol, *Le Comte de Vergennes et P. M. Hennin*, p. 98 *et seq.*

[84] See Doniol, *Participation de la France à l'Etablissement des Etats-Unis*, Vol. I, pp. 280-283.

[85] *Le Comte de Vergennes and P. M. Hennin*, pp. 90-92.

[86] *France in the American Revolution*, by James Breck Perkins, pp. 25-26.

[87] Patrick Henry, whose famous words of revolt were pronounced in 1765, later became one of the Anti-Federalist leaders in Virginia. Charles Galloway, a patriot in 1765, became more and more interested in a reconciliation with England, and his opinions brought him into disfavor with the insurgents.

[88] This discovery was made by M. Abel Doysié, who published this journal in *The American Historical Review*, Vol. XXVI, No. 4, and Vol. XXVII, No. 1 (1921).

[89] Friedrich Kapp, *Life of Johann Kalb*, pp. 1-46.

[90] See Doniol, *Participation de la France à l'Etablissement des Etats-Unis*, Vol. I, pp. 280-283.

There were undoubtedly several other secret missions. At the Ministry of Foreign Affairs, we find indications that the Chevalier d'Annemours, who was later consul at Baltimore, traveled in America to obtain information, about 1773 (see *Archives des Affaires étrangères, Etats-Unis, Mémoires et Documents*, Vol. I, pp. 18-40). I am even inclined to think that the Chevalier d'Annemours may have been the mysterious agent of 1765.

[91] Concerning the opinions of the Prince de Montbarrey, see *Mémoires du Prince de Montbarrey*, Vol. II, pp. 259, 267-8, 294, 297, 308, etc. The Prince de Montbarrey attracted attention by the various memorandums that he drew up in 1775; immediately afterward he entered the King's council and was appointed Minister of War in 1777.

[92] *Correspondance complète de Madame du Deffant*, Vol. II, p. 499.

[93] See *Journal historique et politique de Genève* (January, 1775), article on the political situation.

[94] *Mémoires historiques sur la Vie de M. Suard*, by Dominique Joseph Garat (Paris, 1820), Vol. XXVIII, pp. 122-123.

[95] *Gazette de France* (May 12, 1775).

[96] See Doniol, *Participation de la France à l'Etablissement des Etats-Unis*, Vol. I, pp. 275-285, 359-365, etc. See the references in the index under the name of Louis XVI. This is the only con-

clusive and irrefutable body of documentation concerning the attitude of the King at this period.

[97] Concerning Caron de Beaumarchais, see Doniol, *Participation de la France à l'Etablissement des Etats-Unis, passim;* Loménie, *Beaumarchais et son Temps*, Vol. I, p. 19; Perkins, *France in the American Revolution*, pp. 58, 64, 68-85, 104, and 105. For the Chevalier d'Eon, see the same work, pp. 74-77.

CHAPTER II

[1] Anti-French polemic in America. See *Massachusettensis* (Boston, 1776), by D. Leonard, p. 57 *et seq. Plain Truth. Written by Candidus* (Philadelphia, 1776). *A Discourse on the Times* (Norwich, 1776). *A candid Examination of the Mutual Claims of Great Britain and the Colonies* (New York, 1775), by Galloway. *The Church's Flight into the Wilderness. An Address* by Samuel Sherwood (New York, 1776) and *Loyal Verses of Stansbury and Doctor Johnathan Odell*, p. 4.

[2] Concerning the adventurers of the Antilles in America, see *Writings of Washington*, Vol. VI, p. 37. *Mémoires, Correspondances et Manuscripts du Géneral La Fayette*, Vol. I, pp. 16-20, and *Journal of the Continental Congress*, Vol. VI, pp. 595, 768, 857, 904, etc.

[3] Concerning Pinto, see *Bibliographie des Ouvrages français sur les Etats-Unis.*

[4] For the attitude of Turgot, see Doniol, *Participation de la France à l'Etablissement des Etats-Unis*, Vol. I, pp. 280-283. Concerning the attitude of the Physiocrats, see articles by the Abbé Roubaud in the *Nouvelles Ephémèrides économiques* (1776), Vol. III, pp. 48-76.

[5] *Correspondance inédite de l'Abbé Galiani*, Vol. II, p. 203, and *Mercure de France* (January, 1777), pp. 127-137.

[6] *Journal de politique et de Littérature de Bruxelles*, edited by Linguet, article concerning the letter of Kerguelen (Jan. 5, 1776).

[7] *Journal inédit du Duc de Croÿ*, Vol. I, p. 302.

[8] *Mémoires autographes de Monsieur le Prince de Montbarrey*, Vol. II, pp. 268-293.

[9] Doniol, *Participation de la France*, Vol. II, pp. 70-73, and the Historical Society of Pennsylvania's Franklin Papers, Vol. II, the *Projet de J. de Sparre* and the *Mémoire* of July 2, 1779, which follows.

[10-11] Concerning Favier, see *Archives des Affaires étrangères, Mémoires and Documents, France*, Vol. V, pp. 6-11. Concerning Madame du Deffant, see *Correspondance complète de Madame du Deffant*, Vol. III, pp. 306-307. Concerning Moreau, see *Mes Souvenirs*, by Jacob-Nicolas Moreau (Paris, 1808), Vol. II, pp. 25, 315-318. Concerning Malouet, see *Mémoires de Malouet*, Vol. II, pp. 414-417. Concerning d'Alembert: *Œuvres de d'Alembert*, Vol. V, pp. 372, 374 and 386.

[12] See, for example, *Gazette de Leyde* (Jan. 1, 1776; Jan. 30, 1777, etc.), *Courrier d'Avignon* (Jan. 3, 1777; Jan. 17, 1777), etc.; *Journal historique de Genève*, No. 1 (January, 1777).

[13] Doniol, *Participation de la France*, Vol. I, p. 281.

[14] *Id.*, Vol. I, pp. 282 and 283.

[15-16] Mirabeau, *Considérations sur l'Ordre de Cincinnatus*, pp. 199-201.

[17] *Id.*, p. 190.

[18] Doniol, *Participation de la France*, Vol. I, pp. 2 and 267-270.

[19] *Life and Works of John Adams*, Vol. II, pp. 454-459 and 474, and *Journal of the Continental Congress*, Vol. III, p. 392.

[20] *Literary Diary of Ezra Stiles*, Vol. II, p. 10.

[21] See *Life and Works of John Adams*, Vol. II, pp. 502-510, Vol. IX, pp. 387, 396, 409; *Writings of Thomas Jefferson*, Vol. I, pp. 18-23.

[22] See the very typical letter from William Livingston to Henry Laurens, Feb. 5, 1778, in *A Memoir of the Life of W. Livingston*, by Theodore Sedgwick, p. 185, and the not less curious answer of Laurens, *id.*, pp. 167-258. See the letter of John Randolph to Thomas Jefferson, and the letters of the latter in 1775-1779 in *American Antiquarian Society Proceedings* (April, 1920). See, further, *Warren-Adams Letters*, pp. 184 and 259; *Correspondence of Ralph Izard*, Vol. I, p. 120; *Virginia Gazette* of Dixon (April 20, 1776; Aug. 10, 1776, etc.), and *Massachusetts Spy* (June 21, 1776).

[23] Concerning this edition of Rousseau, see *Journal of the Continental Congress*, Vol. III, p. 507. It was published by John Roberts, and P. L. Ford is the first to have pointed it out.

[24] See "Jefferson and the Social Compact Theory" by G. P. Fisher, in *Yale Review* (1894).

[25] See *Gazette de France* (Aug. 22, 1777).

[26] See *Courrier de l'Europe* (March 11, 1777).

[27] *Lettres de Gustave III à la Comtesse de Boufflers*, p. 102.

[28] See *Correspondance secrète de Métra*, Vol. III, p. 307.

[29] See *Deane Papers*, Vol. I, pp. 179-183, 194, etc. See Doniol, *Participation de la France*, Vol. I, pp. 494-520.

[30] Concerning the attitude of Gérard, see particularly the memorandum that Doniol cites (*Participation de la France*, Vol. I, p. 243).

[31] See *Journal of the Continental Congress*, Vol. V, pp. 575-588, 768, 813, 817, and 827.

[32] See *Journal of the Continental Congress*, Vol. VII, dated March 14, 1777.

[33] Concerning the arrival of Franklin and his immediate triumph, see *Calendar of the Papers of Benjamin Franklin*, Vol. I, pp. 200-300. There is not a page without an enthusiastic letter and an offer of service. The poems are found p. 200 *et seq*. See, further, *Journal du Duc de Croÿ*, Vol. III, pp. 294-295, etc.

[34] Concerning the departure of La Fayette, see *Mémoires de Lafayette*, Vol. I, pp. 9-16.

[35] See *France in the American Revolution*, by J. B. Perkins, p. 115.

[36] *Lettres de la Marquise du Deffant à Horace Walpole*, Vol. III, pp. 374-375.

[37] See *Recueil Clairembaut Maurepas*, by E. Raunie, Vol. IX, p. 118.

[38] Same *Recueil*, pp. 134-135.

[39] Concerning Hennin, see Doniol, *Le Comte de Vergennes et P. L. Hennin*, *passim*. Concerning Gérard, see Doniol, *Participation de la France, passim;* concerning Garnier, see *Journal inédit du Duc de Croÿ*, Vol. IV, p. 141. Concerning Genet, see *Souvenirs d'Alexandrine Pannetier d'Arsonval*, pp. 1-10, and

Calendar of the Papers of Benjamin Franklin, Vol. I, pp. 450, 464, 536, etc.

[40] Concerning Vergennes's procedure with regards to the censorship, see the typical example of a book that he authorizes on condition that it be refused by the censor: *Archives des Affaires étrangères, France, Mémoires et Documents*, Vol. DLXXXII, p. 115. Concerning the secret organizations of Genet, *The Calendar of the Papers of Benjamin Franklin* gives suggestive details; see the pages cited above.

[41] See *Mémoires de Brissot*, Vol. I, pp. 157-165.

[42] Thévenot de Morande, pamphleteer and journalist, lived principally at London and published a collection of scandalous anecdotes under the title of the *Gazetier cuirassé*. He was chief editor of the *Courrier de l'Europe*, into which he took Brissot. Then they quarreled, and at the beginning of the revolution, Morande was the principal enemy of Brissot. He was then in the pay of the Court.

[43] See *Calendar of the Papers of Benjamin Franklin*, Vol. I, pp. 450, 465, and 536, and Vol. III, p. 56, etc.

[44] It is in Vol. I of the *Affaires de l'Angleterre et de l'Amérique*, pp. 33-103, that the extracts from Paine are cited.

[45] It is in Vol. III of the *Affaires de l'Angleterre et de l'Amérique* that Price's *Observations on Civil Liberty* were published, pp. 45-231.

[46] See the *Archives du Ministère des Affaires étrangères, France, Mémoires et Documents*, Vol. DLXXXII, pp. 85-87.

[47] See *Calendar of the Papers of Benjamin Franklin*, Vol. I, p. 229.

[48] Concerning the attitude of Louis XVI, *Mémoires historiques et politiques du règne de Louis XVI*, by Jean-Louis Soulavie, Vol. III, pp. 347, 393, 395, and especially 397-480, and *Mémoires, Souvenirs et Anecdotes* by the Comte de Ségur, Vol. I, pp. 154-156.

[49] Anecdote related by Madame Campan, Vol. I, pp. 232-234.

[50] See, for example, *New York Gazette* (1777: June 9, Sept. 29, Oct. 6 and 27, etc.; and further, July 12, 1779).

[51] *Correspondance secrète de Marie-Antoinette et de Mercy*,

letter of Marie-Thérèse to Mercy (dated Nov. 3, 1777), Vol. III, p. 127. See also *Mémoires de Madame Campan*, Vol. I, pp. 233-234, and Vol. II, p. 30.

[52] See *La Cassette Verte de M. de Sartines* (1779), pp. 22-23.

[53] *Reply to the Declaration of the Congress* (London, 1777).

[54] Concerning this opposition in conservative circles, see the typical pages of *Mes Souvenirs*, by Jacob-Nicolas Moreau, Vol. II, pp. 318-319.

[55] Doniol, *Participation de la France*, Vol. II, pp. 572 and 628.

[56] *Gazette ou Journal politique des Deux-Ponts* (additional number, Jan. 15, 1778).

[57] Concerning the Club of Marseilles, see *Gazette ou Journal politique des Deux-Ponts* (same date, same number).

[58] See *Journal du Duc de Croÿ*, pp. 300-302.

[59] Hale in *Franklin in France* has treated at length this question of Franklin's friends, but it is sufficient to read *Calendar of the Papers of Benjamin Franklin*, Vol. I, from p. 200 to the end, to have a clear idea of them. One even derives from these papers an impression of reality which is more interesting than any compilation.

[60] *Lettres de la Marquise du Deffant to Horace Walpole*, Vol. III, pp. 349-350.

[61] *Correspondance littéraire, philosophique et critique* by Grimm, Vol. XII, p. 85.

[62] See *Journal de Perlet* (Sept. 15, 1792).

[63] *Correspondance complète de Madame du Deffant*, Vol. III, pp. 313-314.

[64] See *Mémoires de Lafayette*, Vol. I, pp. 18, 45, 103, 109, 126, 133, etc. The text cited is p. 108.

[65] *Correspondance secrète de Métra*, Vol. V, pp. 388-392.

[66] This farce was entitled *Matroco*. See *Bibliography of Franklin* by P. L. Ford, p. 318, and *Affaires de l'Angleterre et de l'Amérique*, Vol. VII, p. 28.

[67] Concerning the situation in Germany, see *Gazette des Deux-Ponts* (1777), No. 89. Concerning the state of mind in Italy, see in *Calendar of the Papers of Franklin* the various letters coming

from Italy; for example, Vol. II, pp. 42-43, No. 13; pp. 283, 293, 507, etc.

[68] See Doniol, *Participation de la France*, Vol. III, p. 153.

[69] Concerning the *Mémoire sur la Louisiane* imputed to Vergennes, see the excellent article by Edward S. Corwin in *The American Historical Review* (1915), Vol. XXI, pp. 33-61, on the subject of "French Objectives in the American Revolution."

[70] See especially the memorandum of Turgot to Louis XVI, in which these ideas are expressed: Doniol, *Participation de la France*, Vol. I, pp. 280-283. All the newspapers seem to share this opinion, but the economists are the most explicit. See the article of the Abbé Roubaud in the *Nouvelles Ephémérides économiques* (1776), Vol. III, pp. 48-76.

[71] Concerning the question of Canada, see Perkins, *France in the American Revolution*, pp. 45, 46, 227 and 471, and *Journal of the Continental Congress*, Vol. XII (Oct. 24, 1778; Dec. 5, etc.).

[72] See *Archives des Affaires étrangères, Etats-Unis*, Vol. VI, p. 150; Vol. X, p. 140.

[73] See *Archives des Affaires étrangères, Etats-Unis*, Vol. IV, pp. 120-125.

[74] *Memoirs of the Life of Richard Henry Lee, by His Grandson, R. H. Lee*, p. 195.

[75] *Writings of Samuel Adams*, Vol. IV, p. 10 *et seq.*

[76] *Writings of Washington*, Vol. VII, p. 2.

[77] *Boston Continental Journal* (April 13, 1778).

[78] See *Boston Continental Journal* (May 21, 1778).

[79] See *Journal of the Continental Congress*, Vol. XI (July 11-Aug. 1, 1778).

[80] *Journal of the Continental Congress*, Vol. XI (dated Aug. 6, 1778).

[81] *Archives des Affaires étrangères, Etats-Unis*, Vol. IV, pp. 120-135.

[82] Concerning this surprise, see *Journal du Duc de Croÿ*, Vol. IV, pp. 72-74.

[83] For evidence of this enthusiasm see *Journal historique de Genève* (1779). Preliminary speech in January.

[84] *Œuvres de Voltaire*, Vol. I, p. 276.

[85] For Vergennes's attitude toward England, see Doniol, *Le Comte de Vergennes et P. L. Hennin*, p. 103.

[86] See, for example, the pamphlet by Charles Inglis, *The Letters of Papinian* (New York, 1779).

[87] See *Songs and Ballads of the American Revolution* by Frank Moore, pp. 236, 269, 274 and 289.

[88] *New York Weekly Museum* (Dec. 17, 1781).

[89] See *Rivington's Royal Gazette* (March 28, May 27, and Oct. 21, 1778).

[90] See *Rivington's Royal Gazette* (March 28, May 27, Oct. 21, Oct. 24, Dec. 5, 1778, etc.).

[91] *Rivington's Royal Gazette* (May 17, 1780).

[92] See *Rivington's Royal Gazette* (March 1, 1780).

[93] *Writings of Madison*, Vol. I, pp. 299-300.

[94] See this authentic evidence in *Deane Papers*, Vol. II, p. 368, and the history of the question, Vol. III, pp. 374, 392, 419, 434, 467, 477, 497, etc.

[95] The whole question is well summed up in *France in the American Revolution*, by J. B. Perkins, pp. 86-117.

[96] *Deane Papers*, Vol. IV, p. 494 *et seq.*

[97] The book of M. Phillips, *The West in the Diplomacy of the American Revolution*, in its first fifty pages contains a detailed and exact analysis of the situation of Gérard at Philadelphia in 1778-1779, p. 37. See in this book the analysis of the two parties.

[98] *Writings of Samuel Adams*, Vol. IV, p. 244.

[99] See *Literary Diary of Ezra Stiles*, Vol. II, pp. 370-373.

[100] Concerning the gifts and loans made by France, see Department of Interior, Census Office, *Report on Valuation, Taxation, and Public Indebtedness in the United States* (June, 1880), p. 299; *History of National Loans* by R. N. Baylay.

[101] See *France in the American Revolution* by J. B. Perkins, pp. 503-513, and *Correspondence of John Jay*, Vol. I, p. 377.

[102] See *Works and Writings of John Adams*, Vol. III, pp. 270-280, and Doniol, *Participation de la France*, Vol. V, pp. 55-59.

[103] J. B. Perkins, *France in the American Revolution*, pp. 222-225.

[104] See, for example, the discussions and decisions of the Congress (dated Nov. 28 and Dec. 12, 1780), Vol. XVIII of the *Journal of the Continental Congress.*

[105] Concerning the discussion relative to the terms of the treaty of peace, see Phillips' book, *The West in the Diplomacy of the American Revolution*, which is a detailed *résumé* of these interminable discussions.

[106] Concerning the opinion of Vergennes, see *Archives des Affaires étrangères, Etats-Unis*, Vol. XIV, p. 379; Vol. XIX, p. 43; Vol. XXII, pp. 372, 414-417, 578, etc.

[107] All this is the *résumé* of Phillips' book, already cited, and of the *Journal of the Continental Congress*, Vols. XIX, XX, XXI.

[108] Concerning La Rouërie, see *Journal of the Continental Congress*, Vols. XI and XII (Jan. 1, Jan. 13, Feb. 3, June 25, 1778), Vols. XIII and XV (Jan. 13, Feb. 4, 5, 12, 13, and 17, and June 26, 1779).

[109] For example, on Feb. 23, 1776, the Continental Congress gave $13.50 to Francis Daymon for translating from the French the regulations of the Continental Army. All the military books published by the Congress were French; see *The Art of War* by M. de Lamont (Philadelphia, 1778). The book also contained an article by the Chevalier de la Vallière, "*Le Réglement militaire*," translated from the English by Francis Daymon (Philadelphia, 1776). *L'Ingénieur de Campagne, written in French by the Chevalier de Clairac, and translated by Major Lewis Nicola* (Philadelphia, 1776).

[110] The Comte de Damas, born in 1758, later an *émigré*, and Brigadier-General during the Restoration. Charles-Louis-Victor de Broglie (1758-1792), member of the Constitutional Government, guillotined. The Vicomte Louis-Marie de Noailles (1756-1804), member of the Etats-Généraux, famous for the part he played in the night of August 4, later emigrated to America and was killed in a naval battle while he was serving in the French navy in 1804.

[111] Concerning the impression that the French troops made, see *Maryland Journal* (Aug. 27, 1782) and *The Magazine of Amer-*

ican History, Vol. IV, *Diary of a French Officer* (Cromot Dubourg), pp. 229, 383, etc.

[112] Concerning the attitude and the success of La Fayette, there are innumerable sources to be cited. See in the *Carnet de la Sabretache* (1896), p. 436, "Souvenirs de Villebresme"; *Boston Gazette* (June 8, 1778; Apr. 19, 1779; July 30, 1781; Dec. 17, 1781, etc.).

[113] See, for example, Quesnay de Beaurepaire. His very typical story is told in his *Mémoire concernant l'Académie des Sciences et des Beaux-Arts des Etats-Unis de l'Amérique*, pp. 19, 24, 25, 28, 35, 95, 101, and 106. See also *The Life of Albert Gallatin*, by Henry Adams, pp. 26-44.

[114] See, for example, *Massachusetts Spy* (Feb. 1, 1781; Sept. 13, 1781) and *Voyage du Marquis de Chastellux*, Vol. I, p. 267.

[115] *Writings of Washington*, Vol. VI, pp. 160-161.

[116] *Mémoires de La Fayette*, Vol. I, p. 384.

[117] Concerning Robin, see *Freeman's Journal* (Aug. 15, 1781); concerning Quesnay, see *id.* (Oct. 31, 1781, and Sept. 29, 1782). Concerning Brival, see *Pennsylvania Ledger*, Jan. 21, 1778, etc.

[118] See *Literary Diary of Ezra Stiles*, Vol. II, pp. 296, 297, 299, 301, 304, etc. (I owe these supplementary details to the kindness and erudition of Professor Newhall of Yale.)

[119] Concerning Vandal, see *Harvard Record of the College Faculty* (March 3, 1779); concerning Poullin, *id.* (Seut. 15, 1780); for Gallatin, *id.* (Aug. 20, 1882); concerning Gébelin, *Voyage of M. Carver*, p. 183.

[120] See C. H. Handshin, *The Teaching of Modern Languages in the United States*, p. 21.

[121] *Harvard Records of the College Faculty* (Nov. 27, 1780).

[122] *Id.* (July 18, 1781) and *Salisbury Family Memorial*, pp. 319-320.

[123] See in *William and Mary Quarterly*, Vol. XIV, No. 2, "Early Courses and Professorships at William and Mary College" by L. G. Tyler, p. 77.

[124] *Calendar of the Papers of Benjamin Franklin*, Vol. IV, p. 347.

[125] *Id.*, p. 460.

[126] *Works and Writings of John Adams*, Vol. IV, pp. 260-269.

[127] *Rivington's Royal Gazette* (April 12, 1780; Jan. 24, 1781, and Nov. 22, 1777).

[128] *Massachusetts Spy* (Sept. 5, 1782); *Freeman's Journal* (Oct. 17, 1781; Apr. 4, 1783), etc.

[129] See Bassett, *Popular Churches after the Revolution* (Massachusetts Historical Society Proceedings, 1914-1915), Vol. XLVIII, pp. 254-268.

[130] *Writings of Thomas Jefferson*, Vol. I, p. 91.

[131] *Life and Works of John Adams*, Vol. II, pp. 490-500.

[132] See *Catalogue of the Library of John Adams* and notice all the French books on diplomatic history that it contains, all of them earlier than 1780.

[133] *Freeman's Journal* (Oct. 31, 1781).

[134] See *Archives des Affaires étrangères, Etats-Unis*, Vol. X, pp. 215-220; Vol. VI, pp. 75-76 and 258.

[135] See *Freeman's Journal* (Jan. 16, 1782).

[136] Concerning Gérard and the propaganda, *Archives des Affaires étrangères, Etats-Unis*, Vol. IV, pp. 183 and 321; Vol. VI, p. 70.

[137] *Archives des Affaires étrangères, Etats-Unis*, Vol. VI, pp. 178-179.

[138] *Id.*, Vol. VI, pp. 167-168.

[139] *Id.*, Vol. XIII, pp. 413-414, and especially Vol. XXI, p. 30.

[140] See, concerning Samuel Cooper, *id.*, Vol. VI, pp. 168-169; Vol. XIV, p. 176, etc.

[141] See especially *id.*, Vol. VI, p. 140.

[142] See *id.*, Vol. VI, pp. 178-179; Vol. XIII, pp. 413-414; Vol. XVI, pp. 265-276; Vol. XVII, pp. 309-405 and 481.

[143] See particularly *The Massachusetts Spy* (Boston) and the *Freeman's Journal* (Philadelphia), the two most typical, most Gallicized, and best edited "patriotic" newspapers of the time. See years 1779-1783.

[144] See *The Motley Assembly, a Farce* (Boston, 1779). See *Essays on the Free Trade by a Cityzen of Philadelphia* (Philadelphia, 1779), of Pelatiah Webster.

[145] *Massachusetts Spy* (Oct. 7, 1779). See also *id.* (June 26, 1778).

[146] Concerning the Lees' situation, see *Writings of Madison*, Vol. I, pp. 65 and 301 *et seq*. See also *Archives des Affaires étrangères, Etats-Unis*, Vol. VI, p. 296, and Doniol, *Participation de la France*, Vol. IV, pp. 153 and 200.

[147] *Life and Letters of Simeon Baldwin*, p. 60.

[148] See especially *Writings of Madison*, Vol. I, pp. 299-304 and 403-415, and *Journal of Eliza Drinker* (Jan. 25, 1781).

[149] See *Service hydrographique de la Marine*. Maps and diagrams. Library, Manuscript 7228B, Vol. II, pp. 216-223, and Vol. I, *passim*. This very curious diary was discovered by M. Abel Doysié. It is to be regretted that he has not yet been able to publish it. See also *Souvenirs d'un Officier Royaliste* by the Comte de Romain, pp. 49-51.

[150] *Works and Writings of John Adams*, Vol. III, p. 195.

[151] See *Journal du Duc de Croÿ*, Vol. IV, p. 229; *Lettres de M. de Kageneck*, p. 128, etc.

[152] *Mémoires secrets de Bachaumont*, Vol. XIV, pp. 269-278.

[153] See *La Cassette verte de M. de Sartines*, pp. 37-39 and 56-60, and *Journal du Duc de Croÿ*, Vol. IV, p. 159.

[154] *Mémoires adressés aux Souverains de l'Europe* by M. Pownall, translated from the English by M. . . . (London, 1781), and *Cui Bono* by J. Tucker (London, 1782).

[155] See *Mémoires secrets de Bachaumont*, Vol. XIV, p. 269.

[156] *Gazette des Deux Ponts*, number of January 21.

[157] Concerning Genet's activities in those years, see *Works and Writings of John Adams*, Vol. VII, pp. 59-63, 160-180.

[158] See *Archives des Affaires étrangères, Etats-Unis, Mémoires et Documents*, Vol. V, pp. 27-30. Concerning Vergennes's attitude toward the press, see the pamphlet of 1780, *Rêveries d'un Suisse*.

[159] See Doniol, *Participation de la France*, Vol. IV, p. 587 *et seq.; Archives des Affaires étrangères, Etats-Unis, Correspondance politique*, Vol. XXIII, p. 363 *et seq.*

[160] See *Journal du Duc de Croÿ*, Vol. IV, pp. 167-168; *Correspondance publiée par M. de Lescure*, p. 167, etc.

[161] *Lettres de M. de Kageneck*, p. 17.

[162] See *Journal of the Continental Congress*, Vols. XIX, XX, and XXI (Jan. 2, Feb. 23, 1781), etc.

[163] See *Writings of Franklin*, Vol. VII, pp. 289 and 400-402, Vol. VIII, pp. 24-30 and 39, etc.

[164] Concerning Franklin's ideas, see *Writings of Franklin*, Vol. VII, pp. 427-431.

[165] Concerning Franklin's attitude and that of his grandsons, among the great mass of documents, see J. P. Brissot, *Mémoires publiés par Claude Perroud*, Vol. I, p. 138 *et seq.; Correspondance publiée par M. de Lescure*, p. 180 *et seq.; Mémoires secrets de Bachaumont*, Vol. X, p. 121, etc.

[166] See in *American Historical Review* (1915-1916), Vol. XXI, pp. 708-719, "A Missing Chapter of Franco-American History" by D. J. Hill.

[167] See *Works and Writings of John Adams*, Vol. III, pp. 160-161.

[168] See *Calendar of the Papers of Benjamin Franklin*, Vol. I, p. 229.

[169] *Writings of Benjamin Franklin*, Vol. IX, p. 27 *et seq.*, and "A Missing Chapter of Franco-American History" by D. J. Hill.

[170] *Writings of Benjamin Franklin*, Vol. VIII, pp. 440-448; Vol. IX, p. 27; *Calendar of the Papers of Benjamin Franklin*, Vol. I, pp. 225, 450, 452, and 466; *Mémoires secrets de Bachaumont*, Vol. XXII, p. 5.

[171] See Louis Amable, *Une Loge maçonnique d'avant* 1789, Introduction and pp. 45-93.

[172] See *Mémoires secrets par M. le Comte d'Allonville*, Vol. II, p. 48.

[173] Concerning the Epée de Bois, see Doniol, *Participation de la France*, Vol. I, p. 663.

[174] See Louis Amable, *op. cit.*, pp. 1-18. Everything that follows is but a synopsis.

[175] All this is taken from Amable's book, pp. 18-180.

[176] Concerning the *Lycée de Paris* and the Museum, see Amable, same book, pp. 187-204.

[177] See *Journal intime de l'Abbé Mulot*, pp. 71, 79, and 82.

[178] The best evidence of this fact is given by the *Mémoires secrets de Bachaumont*, Vol. XIV, p. 65; Vol. XXII, p. 154.

[179] See *Nouvelles de la République des Lettres* (1777).

[180] *Calendar of the Papers of Benjamin Franklin*, Vol. I, p. 563; Vol. II, pp. 128, 272, and 371; Vol. III, pp. 32, 150, etc.

[181] *Correspondance de Grimm*, Vol. XII, p. 29.

[182] *Affiches de province* (Jan. 7, 1777).

[183] *Journal du Duc de Croÿ*, Vol. III, p. 302; *Souvenirs and Portraits par M. de Lévis*, pp. 51-52; *Mémoires de l'Abbé Morellet*, pp. 295-322; *Works and Writings of John Adams*, Vol. IX, p. 623, and p. 69, 1, 13. Concerning Franklin, Voltaire's successor in the eyes of public opinion, see *Correspondance publiée par M. de Lescure*, p. 180 *et seq.*

[184] All this is taken from the *Calendar of the Papers of Benjamin Franklin*, save Condorcet's letter, which is to be found in the archives of the *American Philosophical Society*. See Rozengarten, *Early Proceedings of the American Philosophical Society* (Dec. 30, 1774). The Benedictine is Dom Bernard, Vol. I, p. 196. The schoolmaster is Gargaz, *id.*, Vol. II, pp. 25 and 39; see the very interesting little book by G. S. Eddy; *A Project of Universal and Perpetual Peace Written by Pierre-Andre Gargaz. Introduction and Typographical Note by G. S. Eddy* (New York, 1922). See also M. Aulard's article in the *Revue de Paris* (Sept. 1, 1922). For the other, see *id.*, Vol. I, pp. 234-240; Vol. II, p. 39; Vol. III, p. 29, etc.

[185] See *La Comtesse d'Houdetot* by Hippolyte Buffenoir, p. 44.

[186] *Discours sur la Naissance de Mgr. le Dauphin*, by M. Poissonnier (1782), p. 25 *et seq.*

[187] *Calendar of the Papers of B. Franklin*, Vol. IV, p. 468.

[188] See *Paul Jones ou prophéties sur l'Amérique, l'Angleterre, la France, l'Espagne, la Hollande, etc.*, by Paul Jones. *Corsaire, Prophète et Sorcier* and *L'Apocalypse britannique ou les Révélations d'un bon Breton* (London, 1782), etc.

[189] See *Correspondance publiée* by M. de Lescure, p. 294; *Correspondance secrète de Métra*, Vol. XIII, pp. 387-390, 403, etc.

CHAPTER III

[1] Concerning the rôle of John Jay, see *John Jay*, by G. Pellew, pp. 1-96. On his anti-French sentiments, *Correspondence and Public Papers of John Jay*, edited by H. P. Johnson, Vol. I, pp. 181 and 275; Vol. II, pp. 69, 353, 371, etc.; and *Archives des Affaires étrangères, Etats-Unis*, Vol. V, pp. 353-354.

[2] The exact account of the negotiations is found in *France in the American Revolution*, by J. B. Perkins, Chap. XXV, pp. 470 *et seq.* This author's conclusions seem correct and are justified by all the documents I have seen in the Archives of Foreign Affairs.

[3] See *Writings of Madison*, Vol. I, pp. 199-305 and 403-406.

[4] See *Archives des Affaires étrangères, Etats-Unis*, Vol. XXV, pp. 64-70. We find here and there the indication that a part of the American opinion held these "moderate views" and did not desire the acquisition of the West. In 1787, a Southern newspaper expressed satisfaction at the idea that France was going to occupy Louisiana. See *Virginia Independent Chronicle*, March 7, 1787.

[5] *Archives des Affaires étrangères, Etats-Unis*, Vol. XXVIII, pp. 320 and 437-439.

[6] See *Writings of Madison*, Vol. I, pp. 406-407.

[7] See *Archives des Affaires étrangères, Etats-Unis*, Vol. XXXIII, pp. 33 *et seq.*, and 208-212.

[8] See *Archives des Affaires étrangères, Etats-Unis*, Vol. XXVIII, pp. 137, 173, and 178, and *Le Courrier de l'Amérique* (*imprimé chez Cist, distribué par Boinod et Gaillard*) (Philadelphia), July-October, 1784. Nine numbers out of fourteen are known, thanks to M. A. Shearer, librarian of the Grosvenor Library at Buffalo, where the collection is found. See also the various advertisements inserted in the American newspapers by Boinod and Gaillard, *Gazette of the State of South Carolina*, Aug. 2, 1784, and *Philadelphia Freeman's Journal*, Jan. 12, 1785.

[9] See *Archives des Affaires étrangères, Etats-Unis*, Vol. XXVIII, p. 369.

[10] *Id.*, Vol. XXIX, p. 51.

[11] On this question see, for example, the *Pennsylvania Packet*, Jan. 27, 1781.

[12] See particularly *The Dying Legacy of an Aged Minister* (Boston, 1783), by S. Mather.

[13] *Correspondence of John Jay*, Vol. III, p. 69 *et seq.*

[14] See *Journal de Madame Campan*, Vol. II, p. 30.

[15] See, for example, *Considérations sur la Paix de* 1783, *envoyées par l'Abbé Raynal au Prince Frédéric Henri de Prusse* (Berlin, 1783).

[16] See, for example, the *Année littéraire* (1784), Vol. VIII, pp. 289-304.

[17] See *Mémoires secrets de Bachaumont*, Vol. VIII, pp. 20-24.

[18] Concerning Vergennes's attitude, see *Archives des Affaires étrangères, Etats-Unis*, Vol. XXIV, pp. 340-343; Vol. XXV, pp. 64-70; Vol. XXVIII, p. 320; and *Mémoires et Documents, France*, Vol. CDVI, pp. 351-357.

[19] Concerning La Luzerne, see, for example, *Archives des Affaires étrangères, Etats-Unis*, Vol. XXVII, p. 213.

[20] See *id.*, Vol. XXIX, pp. 148-150; Vol. XXX, pp. 42-43 and 140.

[21] L. G. Otto, Comte de Mosloy (1754-1817), native of the Duchy of Baden, private secretary to the Chevalier de la Luzerne, later *chargé d'affaires* at Philadelphia. He returned to France in 1792 and joined the Girondist party, which appointed him chief of the first division at the Ministry of Foreign Affairs. Cashiered and imprisoned in 1793, he was saved by the Ninth of Thermidor. He returned to his post at the Ministry of Foreign Affairs through Sieyès's favor and became very influential. In 1800, he was appointed ambassador in London. Later he was sent to Munich and Vienna. He was appointed Counselor of State and finally Minister of State under Napoleon (1813). He lived in retirement under the Bourbons. From 1798 to 1800 his influence on American affairs was important.

[22] See, for example, *id.*, Vol. XXVIII, pp. 57, 412, etc.

[23] *Id.*, Vol. XXVI, pp. 199, 252 *et seq.*

[24] Concerning the Nantucket fishermen, see *Memorandum Written by William Rotch* (Boston, 1916), pp. 1-15.

[25] For the average opinion on the treaty, see, for example, in the *Journal historique de Genève* (1784, the first number of that year), the *Tableau de l'Europe.*

[26] Concerning the Abbé Colin de Sepvigny, see *Literary Diary of Ezra Stiles*, Vol. II, pp. 517-519.

[27] See, on the Abbé Robin, *Mémoires secrets de Bachaumont*, Vol. XXI, p. 191, and Louis Amable, *Une Loge maçonnique d'avant* 1789, pp. 21-25.

[28] *Discours sur la Paix*, delivered Jan. 11, 1784, by M. l'Abbé Racine (Toulouse, 1794).

[29] *Archives des Affaires étrangères, Etats-Unis*, Vol. IV, pp. 425, 426, 427, etc.

[30] See, for example, *Mémoires du Comte de Moré de Pongibaud*, pp. 109-118, 122-123, 141-148, and especially 171-174; and also in *Collections of the New York Historical Society*, for the year 1878, pp. 384-396, La Rouërie's letters, p. 13, Letters 1-16. See, among many others, the charming memoirs of the Prince de Broglie and of the Comte de Ségur in *Mélanges publiés par la Société des Bibliophiles* (Paris, 1903), *Deux Français aux Etats-Unis.*

[31] *Archives des Affaires étrangères, Etats-Unis*, Supplement No. 3, Letter from La Fayette, Sept. 10, 1780.

[32] See, for example, in *Le Comte de Fersen et la Cour de France*, published by the Baron R. M. de Klinckowstrom, Vol. I, pp. 42-45, 46-72, and *My Campaigns in America, a Journal Kept by Count William de Deux Ponts.*

[33] See Perkins, *France in the American Revolution*, pp. 322-324.

[34] See *Voyages de M. le Marquis de Chastellux*, Vol. I, pp. 119-121.

[35] See *id.*, Vol. II, pp. 32-46.

[36] Eugène Berger, *Le Vicomte de Mirabeau*, pp. 46-67.

[37] See, for example, *Mémoires de Rochambeau*, pp. 322-328.

[38] See, for example, *Souvenirs du Lieutenant-Général, Comte Mathieu Dumas*, Vol. I, pp. 112-130.

[39] *The American Traveller* (Amsterdam, 1782), p. 64.

[40] *Travels in the Interior of North America*, by Jonathan Carver (1783).

[41] *Voyage dans les Colonies du Milieu de l'Amérique septentrionale faits en* 1759 *et* 1760, by M. André Burnaby (Lausanne, 1778).

[42] *The Beginnings of Kentucky*, by John Filson (1775).

[43] See *Le Spectateur américain*, p. xi.

[44] *Œuvres de M. Arnauld* (Paris, 1803), Vol. I, *Amélie*, English anecdote. See especially pp. 316-330.

[45] This poem was of *Chavanne de la Giraudière*, as we learn from Brissot's *Mémoires* (Perroud edition, Vol. I, pp. 332-334).

[46] *Les Amours du Chevalier de Faublas*, by Louvet du Coudray (new edition, Paris, 1789), Vol. I, pp. 219-224.

[47] See *Ami des Lois* of the nineteenth of Germinal, Year VI, Durand-Maillane's article concerning La Fayette's ambitions before 1789. See in the *Mémoires de La Fayette* the nature of his relations with Washington; for example, Vol. I, pp. 140-142; Vol. II, pp. 121-125, 109-113, etc.

[48] *Mémoires de La Fayette*, Vol. II, pp. 157-161, 163-168, 226-233, etc. See also *Correspondence of John Jay*, Vol. II, p. 313.

[49] See *The Correspondence of John Jay*, Vol. III, pp. 135 *et seq*., 200-220, 326 *et seq.;* Vol. II, pp. 42-43.

[50] See *Salisbury Family Memorial*, pp. 319-323.

[51] See *Memorandum Written by William Rotch*, pp. 1-20, and *Letters of an American Farmer* (Crèvecœur), Vol. III.

[52] See *Mémoires de La Fayette*, Vol. II, p. 60, and especially Brissot's typical note, in *Mémoires de Brissot*, Vol. I, p. 279.

[53] Doniol, *Le Comte de Vergennes et P. M. Hennin*, p. 90.

[54] See *Journal of the Friends' Historical Society*, Vol. XV, p. 49 *et seq.; Memorandum Written by William Rotch*, pp. 1-20; *Archives des Affaires étrangères, Etats-Unis*, Vol. XV, pp. 15-17.

[55] Concerning La Fayette and the negroes of Guiana, see *Mémoires de La Fayette*, Vol. II, pp. 140-143.

[56] See *Lettre d'un Correcteur des Comptes à M. le Marquis de La Fayette*. Pamphlet without locality or date, written about 1787 or 1788.

[57] Mazzéi was an Italian from the Duchy of Tuscany, who settled in Virginia and was a great democrat and a friend of Jefferson.

[58] See, for example, the *Boston Independent Chronicle*, Aug. 26, 1784.

[59] See *Writings of B. Franklin*, Vol. IX, p. 326.

[60] Concerning the prize offered by the Academy of Lyons, see *Journal de Lyon*, Sept. 29, 1784, and Jan. 9, 1788, and *Esprit des Journaux* (1791), Vol. XII, pp. 120-134.

[61] *Révolution de l'Amérique*, by M. l'Abbé Raynal (Dublin, 1781), pp. 66-67.

[62] Letter addressed to Abbé Raynal concerning American affairs, published in translation, Paris, Buisson, 1791. See also *Archives des Affaires étrangères, Etats-Unis*, Vol. XXI, p. 20, and especially Vol. XXII, pp. 160-163.

[63] See *Journal de Lyon*, Sept. 29, 1784, the same references as for note 59.

[64] *Correspondance de Grimm*, Vol. XIII, p. 264.

[65] *Writings of Thomas Jefferson*, Vol. VI, p. 3 *et seq.*

[66] The author of the American pamphlet attacking the Order of Cincinnatus was named Ædanus Burke. See Mirabeau's account of the whole affair in *Considérations sur l'Ordre de Cincinnatus*. See also *Mémoires biographiques* by Mirabeau, Vol. IV, pp. 156-162.

[67] One of the most striking examples of the penetration of French documents and ideas is that of the *Massachusetts Spy*, one of the best American newspapers of the time. During the years 1783-1788, it published extracts from Raynal, Turgot, Target, Voltaire, Rousseau, Lesage, Necker, Calonne, Crèvecœur, etc. It reprinted articles from the *Journal de Paris*, *La Gazette des Deux Ponts*, *La Gazette de Santé*, etc.

[68] See especially *Loudon's New York Packet*, Jan. 16, 1786, and Jan. 23, 1786; *Massachusetts Spy*, Feb. 1, 1787; *Maryland Journal*, Feb. 17, 1786; Feb. 26, 1786, etc.

[69] See Note 67. See also the collection of the *New York Packet*, 1783-1788, and the *Philadelphia Independent Gazetteer*, 1786-1788.

[70] Concerning La Rouërie, see *Massachusetts Spy*, Aug. 21, 1786. La Fayette is continually mentioned; see especially the year 1784 in the volumes of the *Massachusetts Spy*.

[71] For advertisements in French, see *The Maryland Journal*, Feb. 14, 1786. See the eulogy of the French press in the *Pennsylvania Journal*, July 13, 1785; comment on anti-Papist France in the *Massachusetts Spy*, June 30, 1785; praise of Louis XVI and his generous conduct in the *Massachusetts Spy*, Sept. 17, 1784; concerning Vergennes, *New York Daily Advertiser*, April 10, 1787.

[72] For the sentiment of spiritual union between the two countries, see, for example, the *Maryland Journal*, Oct. 5, 1787; Aug. 5, 1788; Aug. 9, 1788.

[73] See *The Boston Independent Chronicle*, May 25, 1785.

[74] See *The New York Daily Advertiser*, March 23, 1787.

[75] See *Works and Writings of John Adams*, Vol. IX, p. 530-540; *Old Family Letters*, Series I, p. 57; *Writings of Thomas Jefferson*, Vol. V, pp. 87, 152-154, and 186; and *A Collection of Essays*, by Noah Webster (Boston, 1790), p. 1-20.

[76] See *Calendar of the Papers of B. Franklin*, Vol. II, p. 401.

[77] See *Maryland Journal*, March 14, 1786.

[78] Concerning French instruction for girls, see *Columbian Magazine*, September, 1787, pp. 643 *et seq.*

[79] See *Freeman's Journal* (April 5, 1786); *Pennsylvania Packet* (Sept. 14, 1784; Feb. 22, 1785; Oct. 1, 1785); *New York Gazette* (Nov. 20, 1783); *New York Journal* (July 12, 1784); *Maryland Journal* (Aug. 3, 1784; Jan. 18, 1785; March 24, 1786; June 2, 1786; Dec. 1, 1786; Sept. 11, 1787); *Maryland Gazette* (June 4, 1785; Oct. 14, 1785); *Norfolk and Portsmouth Journal* (Jan. 9, 1788); *Georgia State Gazette* (Nov. 11, 1786; Oct. 28, 1786; April 3, 1787; Nov. 11, 1788); *Massachusetts Spy* (Sept. 17, 1788); *New York Daily Advertiser* (Dec. 30, 1786; June 16, 1786); *New York Packet* (Dec. 1, 1785); *Providence Gazette* (April 2, 1785).

[80] It would be very difficult to determine the exact number of French professors in America. In fact, the only means by which this could be found out would be reading the newspapers of

the time in which professors of all kinds usually published their announcements. Unfortunately, we have only a relatively small number of complete files of American newspapers published during the eighteenth century. Although for cities like Boston, New York, and Philadelphia, it is possible to find almost complete collections of the four or five principal newspapers after 1783, this is not true of the smaller cities or of the Southern cities. Any statistics therefore would favor the North unduly as compared with the South. They would also exaggerate the difference between the years of peace and the troubled years, since the latter have left us only fragmentary newspapers of small size, which were not numerous and did not represent contemporary intellectual life.

[81] See *The Diary of Ezra Stiles*, Vol. II, pp. 296-304 and 534, and Vol. V, p. 347; see also *Hartford Courant*, March 13, 1783.

[82] See *Harvard Records of the College Faculty* under the dates of Aug. 16, 1787, and Oct. 8, 1787, etc.

[83] See *Harvard Records of the College Faculty* under the dates of Sept. 18, 1783, and Harrington, *The Harvard Medical School*, Vol. I, pp. 285-295. See also *The Harvard Medical School in* 1788-1789, by D. Head, pp. 2-12.

[84] This journal was in such demand that Crèvecœur could not fill all the requests for it that were sent him. See *Boston Independent Chronicle*, July 8, 1784.

[85] See *Archives of the American Philosophical Society*, *Letters*, Vol. I, the letter from Rozier. See also *Boston Gazette*, March 8, 1784.

[86] See *Harvard Records of the College Faculty* under the dates of Jan. 9, 1784; Sept. 8, 1788, etc.

[87] See *The Works of John Witherspoon*, Vol. V, p. 237; Vol. VI, Letters 34-128; Vol. VIII, pp. 25, 29, 44, 86, 193, 198, 202, and 308; and *Archives des Affaires étrangères*, *Etats-Unis*, Vol. XXVIII, p. 125.

[88] See *The Teaching of Modern Languages in the United States*, by Charles Hart Handschin, p. 14.

[89] See the same book, pp. 13-14.

[90] See *The Harvard Law School*, p. 185.

[91] See, for example, *Writings of Thomas Jefferson*, Vol. VI, p. 167.

[92] See *Autobiography of John Trumbull*, p. 67 *et seq.*

[93] See *Revue rétrospective*, July-December, 1789, and Aug. 1, 1789.

[94] See *Mémoire, Statut et Prospectus, concernant l'Academie des Sciences et Beaux-Arts des Etats-Unis de l'Amérique établie à Richmond, Capitale de la Virginie, presentés par le Chevalier Quesnay de Beaurepaire* (Paris, 1788). See also for further information *New York Gazetteer*, Dec. 17, 1784; *Virginia Independent Chronicle*, November and December, 1787; *Virginia Gazette*, Sept. 11, 1788; *Virginia Gazette or the American Advertiser*, Sept. 13, 1786, and Dec. 13, 1786; and *Gazette de France*, Oct. 31, 1788, and *Maryland Journal*, Sept. 2, 1788.

[95] See *Transactions of the American Philosophical Society* (1789), between the dates Sept. 26, 1783, and June, 1786. See also Rozengarten, *Early Proceedings of the American Philosophical Society* (1884), after Jan. 13, 1783.

[96] See *Writings of Benjamin Franklin*, Vol. VII, pp. 400-402 and 411-413, and Vol. IX, p. 286; and *Writings of Thomas Jefferson*, Vol. V, pp. 87 and 137, and Vol. VI, pp. 23, 96, etc.

[97] See especially *The Charter, Bye-laws . . . of the New York Society Library* (1789). *A catalog of the Books Belonging to the Library Company of Philadelphia* (Philadelphia, 1789).

[98] See *American Magazine*, January, 1788.

[99] Concerning Hector Saint-John de Crèvecœur (1735-1813), see *Saint-John de Crèvecœur*, by Robert de Crèvecœur (Paris, 1883), and *Saint-John de Crèvecœur*, by Julia Post Mitchell (New York, 1916). See in particular, in this latter work, the list (pp. 346-359) of the American magazines and newspapers that mention Crèvecœur.

[100] See *Miscellaneous Works of David Humphreys* (New York, 1804), pp. 1 and 13.

[101] See *The Vision of Columbus*, by Joel Barlow (Hartford, London, 1787). See particularly the preface, p. xiii (edition of 1807).

[102] See *The Poems of Philip Freneau*, edited by Fred Lewis

Pattee (Princeton, 1902). Concerning Louis XVI, see Vol. I, pp. 167 and 247; concerning the balloons, p. 276, etc.

[103] *The Anarchiad, a New England Poem. Written in concert by D. Humphreys, Joel Barlow, John Trumbull, and Dr. Lemuel Hopkins* (New Haven, 1861). The original edition, which is very rare, was published in 1786. Barlow separated from this group a short time later.

[104] See *Popular Churches after the American Revolution*, by J. S. Bassett, already cited.

[105] In the Collections of the *Massachusetts Historical Society*, Vol. I, Series V, Belknap Papers, p. 60.

[106] See *id.*, Series V, Vol. I, p. 249; and Vol. II, pp. 116-240, and *Massachusetts Spy*, Nov. 13, 1788. See also *Writings of Benjamin Franklin*, Vol. IX, p. 303.

[107] See, for example, *A Sermon Delivered to the first Religious Society in Roxbury*, December, 1783, by Eliphalet Porter (Boston, 1784), and *A Sermon Preached at Lexington*, by Zabdiel Adams (Boston, 1783).

[108] See G. R. Minot, *History of the Insurrection in Massachusetts* (Boston, 1810), pp. 60-61.

[109] See, for example, *Writings of Thomas Jefferson*, Vol. VI, pp. 392-394.

[110] See, for example, *Correspondence of John Jay*, Vol. III, p. 217, and *Works of Washington*, Vol. XI, p. 54.

[111] See, for example, *New York Journal*, Oct. 25, 1787; Nov. 8, 1787, etc.

[112] See, for example, *The Federalist*, pp. 14-19 (*Works of Alexander Hamilton*, Vol. XII).

[113] See *A Study of the Monarchial Tendencies in the United States*, by Louise Burnham Dunbar, University of Illinois Studies in the Social Sciences, Vol. X, p. 55.

[114] See *Works of Alexander Hamilton*, Vol. I. The original draft which Hamilton prepared for his speech on June 18, 1787, in which he says, "The advantage of the monarch is this: he is above corruption, he must always intend, with respect to foreign nations, the true interest and glory of the people. Republics liable to foreign corruption and intrigue. It is said a republican gov-

ernment does not admit a vigorous execution. It is therefore bad, for the goodness of a government consists in a vigorous execution," etc.

[115] See *Works of Alexander Hamilton*, Vol. I, pp. 347-360; *Correspondence of John Jay*, Vol. III, p. 227.

[116] See *Debates in the Federal Convention of* 1787, *Reported by James Madison* (New York, 1920), under the dates June 2, 1787; May 31, 1787, and Sept. 17, 1787.

[117] See *id.*, pp. 443-446.

[118] See, for example, *Pamphlets on the Constitution of the United States*, edited by P. L. Ford (Brooklyn, 1888), p. 248. *Debates in the Several State Conventions on the Adoption of the Federal Constitution*, by Jonathan Elliot (Philadelphia, 1881), Vol. II, p. 208. It is also to be noted that the *Mémoires de Sully* was one of the most widely read books in America at this time.

[119] See, for example, Elliot, *Debates*, Vol. III, p. 421, and *Essays on the Constitution*, by P. L. Ford, pp. 257-279.

[120] See Elliot, *Debates*, Vol. III, p. 422 *et seq.*, and p. 483 *et seq.*

[121] See *Works of Alexander Hamilton*, Vol. XI, pp. 42, 140, 141, 156, 62, 67, 358, 359, and 363; Vol. XII, pp. 14-19 and 256.

[122] See same references as for Note 121.

[123] See Elliot, *Debates*, Vol. II, *Massachusetts Convention*, pp. 209, 421, and 483; Vol. III, pp. 53, 79, 105, 152, 213, and 361.

[124] The very particular rôle that Franklin played inspired a page of Sainte-Beuve whose accuracy and far-sightedness seem so remarkable that I think it should be quoted here: "If all those who conversed with Franklin at Passy had hearkened well to his precepts and propositions, they would have looked twice before undertaking a complete remodeling of the Old World. At the same time we must add (even at the risk of uttering a contradiction) that it was difficult for those who heard him not to be kindled and not to be tempted to reform society radically: for he himself, in his manners, was a great—a too great—simplifier.

"There was nothing about this positive man to discourage utopianism; rather, he invited people to it by the novelty and the perspectives that he seemed to open upon the future. While he conversed, he made his hearers long to apply his ideas; but he did not give equally to those who listened to him (the Condorcets and Chamforts, for example) his temperament, his discretion in details, and his prudence." (*Causeries du Lundi*, third edition, Vol. VII, p. 181.)

[125] See *Writings of Benjamin Franklin*, Vol. IX, pp. 79, 182, 183, 286, etc.

[126] See Louis Amable, *Une Loge franc-maçonne d'avant* 1789, pp. 150-186.

[127] *Id.*, pp. 1-20.

[128] Concerning Gargaz, see *Journal de la Littérature française et ètrangère* (Deux Ponts), May, 1786; *Calendar of the Papers of B. Franklin*, Vol. II, pp. 25, 140; Vol. III, p. 29, etc.

[129] *Mémoires inédits du Duc de Croÿ*, Vol. IV, p. 272.

[130] See, for example, *Journal de Paris*, Oct. 20, 1785; *Writings of Franklin*, Vol. IX, from p. 470 on, and especially pp. 495, 503, 575, etc.; *Mémoires secrets de Bachaumont*, Vol. XXIX, p. 181, and Vol. XXX, p. 23; and *Extraits des Gazettes américaines*, No. 1 (Paris, 1786).

[131] See the references to Crèvecœur in Note 99.

[132] See Crèvecœur, *Lettres d'un Fermier américain*, edition of 1784, Vol. I, p. 229.

[133] The circulation of Crèvecœur's works was incredibly rapid, and it would take twenty pages to furnish a complete bibliography of them. See particularly *Le Mercure de France*, Jan. 21, 1785, and Jan. 29, 1785.

[134] *Voyage d'Amérique. Dialogue en vers entre l'Auteur et l'Abbé* (London and Paris, 1786), p. 20 *et seq.*

[135] See *Lettres de Madame Roland*, published by Claude Perroud (Paris, 1813), Vol. II, p. 688.

[136] *La Jeunesse de B. Constant*, by M. Rudler, pp. 241 and 250.

[137] See *Œuvres complètes de Bernardin de Saint-Pierre*, Vol. V, p. 51; Vol. XI, pp. 147 and 173; Vol. XII, pp. 112-137 and 176-185, and *Correspondance de Brissot*, (Perroud edition), p. 174.

[138] Claude-François-Adrien, Marquis de Lezay Marnésia, 1735-1810. Poet, utopian, and philanthropist.

[139] All this is taken from the information that Brissot gives about himself in his *Mémoires* (Perroud edition).

[140] *Mémoires de Brissot*, Vol. I, p. 54.

[141] *Id.*, Vol. I, pp. 191 and 239.

[142] *Id.*, Vol. II, p. 46 and thereafter.

[143] The pamphlet was called: *Examen critique des Voyages de M. le Marquis de Chastellux*, by J. P. Brissot de Warville (London, 1786).

[144] *Mémoires de Brissot*, p. 54.

[145] See *Correspondance de Brissot* (Perroud edition), pp. 140-146. See *Massachusetts Spy*, Dec. 25, 1788, and *Saint-Jean de Crèvecœur*, by Julia P. Mitchell, *passim.*

[146] Concerning the efforts of Brissot to establish the Gallo-American Society in the United States, see the manuscripts relative to this society in the John Carter Brown Library at Providence, and the announcements in the newspapers: *Massachusetts Spy* (Dec. 25, 1788); *New York Journal* or *Weekly Register* (Dec. 26, 1788), and *Hartford American Mercury* (Dec. 15, 1788).

[147] Concerning the Society of the Friends of the Negroes, see *Mémoires de Brissot*, pp. 71-80. *Correspondance de Brissot*, p. 165-175.

[148] *Correspondance de Brissot*, pp. 167 and 171.

[149] See *Mémoires de Brissot*, pp. 74 and 64; *Correspondance de Brissot*, pp. 143-145 and 157.

[150] See *Correspondance de Brissot*, pp. 165-166.

[151] *Correspondance de Brissot*, pp. xliii-xlvi and pp. 179-183.

[152] *Correspondance de Brissot*, pp. 171-179, and *Ministère des Affaires étrangères, Etats-Unis*, Vol. XXXIV, pp. 6-9.

[153] All this is taken from *Correspondance de Brissot*, pp. 180-265.

[154] See *Old Family Letters*, Series I, pp. 82-83.

[155] See *Œuvres de A. Chénier* (Dimoff edition), Vol. II, pp. 100-101.

[156] Concerning Saugrain and Guillotin, see *Writings of B.*

Franklin, Vol. IX, p. 367 *et seq.; Nouveau Voyage de Brissot*, Vol. I, p. 376; *A Memoir of the Life and Work of Dr. Antoine-François Saugrain* (St. Louis), by W. V. Byars; and the article by N. P. Dandridge, "Antoine-François Saugrain de Vigny," in *The American Surgical Association Bulletin* (1904). This information and these references were obligingly furnished me by the Pettus family of St. Louis, who count Saugrain among their ancestors.

[157] See *The Journal of the Friends Historical Society*, Vol. XV, p. 49 *et seq.;* Vol. XVI, pp. 18-22 and 81-90.

[158] See *Mémoires de Madame de la Rochejacquelin*, Vol. I, p. 21.

[159] *Journal de Lyon*, March 15, April 12 and 27, Aug. 30, Sept. 13 and 27, 1786.

[160] See *Writings of Thomas Jefferson*, Vol. V, pp. iii, 152-153, 395-397, and 402; Vol. VI, pp. 50-58, and pp. 103-106 on the happiness of the Indians; Vol. VII, pp. 88-89 and 114; Vol. XVII, p. 153 *et seq.*, etc.

[161] *Writings of Thomas Jefferson*, Vol. I, pp. 154-157.

[162] See *Année Littéraire*, Vol. II, pp. 46-48, 256, and 172; Vol. V, pp. 242-283, etc.

[163] *Mercure de France*, October, 1788, pp. 11-24. See also *American Museum*, January, 1788, list of subscribers at the beginning of this number.

CHAPTER IV

[1] See Doniol, *Le Comte de Vergennes et P. M. Hennin*, pp. 90-100.

[2] *Archives des Affaires étrangères, Etats-Unis*, Vol. XXXII, p. 350.

[3] See, for example, *Recherches historiques et politiques sur les Etats-Unis de l'Amérique septentrionale*, by Mazzéi, Vol. IV, pp. 120-126.

[4] See *Mémoires de Brissot*, Vol. II, pp. 137 and 279, and *Mémoires de Lafayette*, Vol. II, pp. 163, 188, and 220-233.

[5] See *Salisbury Family Memorial*, Vol. I, pp. 319-325.

[6] See *Writings of Thomas Jefferson*, Vol. V, p. 331; Vol. I, pp. 150-160, and Vol. VII, p. 333.

[7] See *Mémoires de Lafayette*, Vol. II, pp. 141, 157, 219, 230, and 296.

[8] See *Writings of Thomas Jefferson*, Vol. V, p. 331; *Mémoires de Lafayette*, Vol. II, pp. 1-12.

[9] See *Mémoires de Lafayette*, Vol. III, p. 202 *et seq.*, and *Writings of Thomas Jefferson*, Vol. I, pp. 154 and 158; Vol. VII, p. 226 *et seq.*

[10] See *Premiers Mouvements de Bretagne ou Principe des Efforts du Peuple breton contre les Projets de l'Aristocratie de Robe et d'Epée* (1789).

[11] See, for example, *Réclamation du Tiers Etat et Supplique au Roi* (1788), *Le Despotisme des Parlements ou Lettre d'un Anglais à un Français*, p. 10. *Observations sur le Principe qui a produit les Révolutions de France, de Genève et d'Amérique*, by M. Isnard, October, 1789, pp. 4, 5, 38, and 46. See also *Mémoires de Brissot*, Vol. II, pp. 278-280. *Correspondance de Brissot*, p. 157. *Souvenirs sur Mirabeau*, by Etienne Dumont, pp. 211 and 297. *Mémoires d'un Voyageur qui se repose . . .*, by M. Dutens (Paris, 1806), Vol. II, p. 317. *Mémoires historiques sur la Vie de M. Suard et sur ses Ecrits*, by Dominique-Joseph Garat, Vol. XXI, pp. 318-320.

[12] See *Collections of the New York Historical Society for the Year* 1878, pp. 384-387; *Hérault de la Nation sous les Auspices de la Patrie*, p. 221, and *Mémoires d'Outre-Tombe* (Biré edition), Vol. I, p. 309. Concerning Robespierre and America, see *Mémoires de B. Barère*, Vol. II, p. 201.

[13] See, in *Modern Philology*, Vol. XV, No. 8 (December, 1917), pp. 91-92, M. F. Baldensperger's very interesting article, where this page can be found.

[14] See, for example, *Observations générales et importantes sur l'Affaire de Scioto* (no date) and *Etablissements français dans les Etats-Unis d'Amérique* (press of the *Patriote français*, published in 1789 or 1790).

[15] See *Correspondance de Brissot*, pp. 458-460.

[16] See J. G. Rozengarten, *French Colonists and Exiles in the United States*, pp. 19-25, and H. Carré's article in *Revue de Paris* (fifth year, 1898), pp. 310-340. See also "The Methods

and Operations of the Scioto Group of Speculators," in *Mississippi Valley Historical Review*, Vol. I, No. 4; Vol. II, No. 1 (March and June, 1914). *Ohio Company Series*, Vol. I (published by Archer Butler Hulbert, Marietta, 1915), p. lxxv *et seq.* "Andrew Craigie and the Scioto Associates" in *The American Antiquarian Society of Proceedings* (1913), New Series, Vol. XXIII, Part II, p. 222.

[17] See *Le Parlement de Paris établi au Scioto* (1790); the articles in *Le Fouet National*, Jan. 9, 1790; *Le Journal de la Cour et de la Ville*, March 6, 1790, and *La Chronique de Paris*, May 15 and Aug. 5, 1790; *Le Songe d'un Habitant du Scioto publié par Lui-même* (Paris, 1790). See also *Lettre de M. de V. à M. le C. D. M. à l'Occasion des Observations publiées sur l'Etablissement du Scioto* (Paris, 1790); *Le nouveau Mississippi, par un Patriote Voyageur* (1790); *Considérations sur les Fonds publics des Etats-Unis* (Paris, 1793); and *Pennsylvania Journal*, June 2, 1790.

[18] Duval d'Espremesnil (1746-1794). He was interested in the Scioto project, but he died before he was able to set out for America himself. Concerning his rôle, see the article by H. Carré in the *Revue de Paris*, Vol. V, pp. 318-340.

[19] See *Mémoires d'Outre-Tombe* (Biré edition), Vol. I, pp. 276, 305-309, etc.

[20] See *id.*, pp. 311 and 356, and Giraud, *Nouvelles Etudes sur Chateaubriand*, p. 163.

[21] See *Recherches sur les Causes qui ont empêché les Français de devenir libres* (1792), by M. Mounier, Vol. II, pp. 22-23.

[22] See *Mémoires de Lafayette*, Vol. II, p. 303 *et seq.*; Vol. II, p. 309.

[23] The edition of 1778, the two editions of 1783, and that of 1790.

[24] See *Writings of Thomas Jefferson*, Vol. VI, p. 10.

[25] These pamphlets are entitled *Déclaration des Droits du Roi et de la Nation française, précédées de Celles de la Chambre des Pairs et des Communes d'Angleterre et de Celles des Provinces unies d'Amérique à l'Epoque de la Révolution, par l'Auteur du Droits des Nations; Projet de Déclaration des Droits de l'Homme*

et du Citoyen, by M. Servan, advocate in the Parliament of Grenoble (1789); *Déclaration des Droits, traduite de l'Anglais avec l'Original à Côté* (London, 1789).

[26] See *Mémoires de Lafayette*, Vol. II, p. 303.

[27] See especially *Mémoires de Brissot*, Vol. II, p. 64.

[28] See what I. Herzberg says about the influence of the Bible on the Declaration of Independence in *Thomas Jefferson as a Man of Letters*. See also *Mémoires de Lafayette*, Vol. II, p. 309, in which he calls the Declaration of Rights "the Catechism of France."

[29] See Raynal, *Histoire philosophique des Etablissements européens dans les deux Indes*, Vol. VI, pp. 311-330.

[30] See the very exact statement of the traces left by the American declaration on the French texts in *La Déclaration des Droits de l'Homme*, by G. Jellinek, pp. 39-44. Concerning the Constitution of Virginia and the Act for Religious Freedom, see *Writings of Thomas Jefferson*, Vol. VI, p. 10.

[31] See, for example, the monarchist pamphlet, *L'Intérêt de la France à une Constitution monarchique* (Berlin, July 15, 1791), in which we find the tirade: "It is not the philosophico-political dogmas placed at the head of the ephemeral Constitutions of some few American States, at a time when it was a question of spurring the people to an insurrection, that became the political principles of the Americans after the acquisition of their independence. The object of their government is set forth in the very short preamble of the present Constitution, which has replaced all this metaphysical trash. The material rejected by the Americans has been gathered up by the French, and it is with this refuse from the Americans that the French nation has consented to allow the constitution of a government to be built, which, if it would not satisfy the Americans, will certainly be even less satisfactory to the French, who are as dissimilar from the Americans, and perhaps more so, as from the Chinese."

[32] See in particular the speech that La Fayette made to the officers of the Garde Nationale in October, 1789; *Extrait d'un Discours adressé par M. Le Marquis de La Fayette, vers la Fin-d'Octobre, aux Officiers de la Garde Nationale, assemblés chez*

Lui, especially p. 5. See, further, *Mémoires de Lafayette*, Vol. III, pp. 227-229.

[33] See same pamphlet as above and *Mémoire historique de M. La Fayette* (Paris, Year II).

[34] *Lettres à M. le Vicomte de Noailles sur sa Motion du 4 Août*, 1789 (Paris, 1789), by M. Cérutti, pp. 3-11.

[35] See *Writings of Thomas Jefferson*, Vol. I, pp. 154-158.

[36] See *Writings of Thomas Jefferson*, Vol. I, pp. 154-158. Note what Montmorin thought of the rôle of Jefferson during those days (same reference). See, further, *Souvenirs d'un Nonagenaire*, by Yves Besnard, p. 353, which seems to attribute a much more active rôle to Jefferson. In reality, the two texts are in accord, for Jefferson attacked the clergy and the nobility at this time but supported the King. Concerning his moderation, see also *Writings of Thomas Jefferson*, Vol. VII, pp. 227, 256, and 371 *et seq.*

[37] François Alexandre Frédéric, duc de la Rochefoucauld Liancourt (1747-1827), peer of France, member of the Institute, famous for his philanthropy and his activities during the Revolution. He was president of the Constituent Assembly, and later emigrated to England and the United States.

[38] *Courrier français*, Feb. 27, 1790.

[39] See *Gazette of the United States*, April 18, 1789.

[40] Concerning the relations between the French and American Revolutions, see especially *Herald of Freedom*, July 20, 1790; *Pennsylvania Gazette*, Dec. 23, 1789, etc. For praises of France and translations of French revolutionary documents, see *Pennsylvania Gazette*, Oct. 14 and 21, 1789; *Gazette of the United States*, March 24, April 21, and Dec. 16 and 23, 1789; *Herald of Freedom*, Nov. 17 and Dec. 1, 7, and 15, 1789, etc.

[41] See the same articles as above and also *Massachusetts Sentinel*, July 18, Aug. 5 and 15, Sept. 2, and Oct. 7 and 14, 1789, etc. This is only an example of what may be found in the line of French citations and literary extracts in an American newspaper in 1789. At least thirty newspapers are quite as abundant in them: *Gazette of the United States* (Philadelphia), *Herald of Freedom* (Boston), *Philadelphia Gazette*, *Boston Gazette*, etc.

[42] It is in the dispatch of July 20, 1789, published by the

Herald of Freedom, that we find this attitude most clearly explained. We cannot place much confidence in some dispatches published in the American newspapers at this period which seem to have emanated from the French government or its agents, such as the letter in the *Massachusetts Centinel*, Jan. 4, 1790.

[43] Concerning the pressure brought to bear by opinion and the English government, see *Writings of Washington*, Vol. XI, pp. 177 and 493; Vol. XII, pp. 25 and 53; *Journal of William Maclay*, pp. 249, 349, 350, 386, 394, etc. See *Archives des Affaires étrangères, Etats-Unis*, Vol. XXXIV, p. 10, to the effect that France was not ripe for liberty; *Works and Writings of John Adams*, Vol. XI, p. 563 *et seq. Diary of Gouverneur Morris*, Vol. I, pp. 110, 113, 139, 143, and 251.

[44] See, for example, *Writings of Thomas Jefferson*, Vol. VII, pp. 398, 406, 448, etc. *Archives des Affaires étrangères, Etats-Unis*, Vol. XXXIV, p. 343, etc.

[45] See *Archives des Affaires étrangères, Etats-Unis*, Vol. XXXIII, p. 104, 223; Vol. XXXIV, p. 154.

[46] *Id.*, Supplement 2, Vol. VI, p. 330 *et seq.*

[47] Concerning Moustier's project, see *Archives des Affaires étrangères, Etats-Unis*, Vol. XXXIV, p. 32 *et seq.* See also *Diary of Gouverneur Morris*, Vol. I, pp. 139-143. A study of the Archives of Foreign Affairs shows that the bureaus and the minister were silent as to Moustier's suggestions.

[48] See *Archives des Affaires étrangères, Etats-Unis*, Vol. XXXIV, p. 154 *et seq.* These dispatches are remarkable.

[49] Concerning this period, see *Archives des Affaires étrangères, Etats-Unis*, Vol. XXXIV, pp. 5-8; Vol. XLIV, pp. 460-500; Vol. XLVII, p. 403.

[50] Concerning John Adams, see *Archives des Affaires étrangères, Etats-Unis*, Vol. XXXIV, p. 109; Vol. XXXV, pp. 147 and 375.

[51] See *Archives des Affaires étrangères, Etats-Unis*, Vol. XXXIV, p. 253.

[52] See the account of La Fayette's attitude and methods in the *Diary of Gouverneur Morris*, and especially Vol. I, pp. 165-172, 262-265, etc.

[53] See a whole series of pamphlets attacking La Fayette: *Vie privée, impartiale, politique, militaire et domestique du Marquis de Lafayette, Général des Bleuets*, by F. Robert, member of the Society of the Friends of the Constitution of Paris (1790). Concerning the divisions among the moderate revolutionists, see Théodore de Lameth, *Mémoires*, pp. 106-109.

[54] Robert Livingston (1746-1813), of one of the best New York families, member of the Continental Congress, Chancellor of the United States. He was a prominent Francophile and a great democrat.

[55] The pamphlet that Morellet hastened to write on this subject bears witness to this: *Lettre écrite à l'Occasion de l'Ouvrage intitulé Examen du Gouvernement de l'Angleterre.*

[56] See *Considérations sur les Gouvernements et principalement sur Celui qui convient à la France*, pp. 14, 16, 22, 34, and 37. *A Monsieur le Comte de Lally Tollendal en Réponse à sa Lettre à ses Commettants*, pp. 117-118, etc.

[57] See in particular *Extraits du Journal de la Société de* 1789. *Discours de La Rochefoucauld Liancourt*, June 13, 1790, p. 8.

[58] See the pamphlets of Mounier and Lally cited above as well as that of Morellet. See also *Lettre à M. Mounier* (Paris, 1789), by M. Blin, Deputy from Nantes, in particular pp. 22-23. On Mounier's attitude toward the Americans after 1789, see *Recherches sur les Causes qui ont empêché les Français de devenir libres* (1792), by M. Mounier, Vol. II, pp. 22-24, 93, 1, and 200. Concerning the increasing unpopularity of Mounier and his friends, see *Patriote français*, Sept. 8 and 9, 1789, etc.

[59] See, for example, *Lettre de M. Bergasse à ses Commettants; Le Financier philosophe et patriote* (Paris, 1780), by M. C. I. B., p. 10; *Au Peuple français sur les Assignats, par un Citoyen des Etats-Unis* (Paris, 1790), p. 12; *Lettre écrite au Bonhomme Richard, concernant des Assignats*, etc.

[60] See *Idées simples et précises sur le Papier-Monnaie* (Paris, 1791), by M. Cérutti. See *Réflexion sur la Dette publique exigible*, in *Courrier de Provence* (September, 1790), No. 193.

[61] See in particular *Théorie des Etats-Généraux* (Paris), pp.

33 and 50. *Considérations sur les Gouvernements*, by Mounier, p. 22.

[62] Concerning the executive, see all of the voluminous book by Necker, *Du Pouvoir exécutif dans les grands Etats*, especially Vol. I, pp. 68 and 179-180, and Vol. II, pp. 1-250. Concerning the veto see this work and *Patriote français*, Sept. 8, 9, and 14, 1789. See, further, the *Diary of Gouverneur Morris*, Vol. I, pp. 69, 108, 150, and 165, and in *La Feuille du Jour*, the article of Jan. 8, 1791, etc.

[63] See, in *Etrennes de la Nation, Extraits d'une Lettre du Général Washington à M. le Marquis de La Fayette.*

[64] See especially *Le Patriote français*, Jan. 2, 1790.

[65] Concerning the moderation of the Americans, see *Vie privée du Marquis de La Fayette* (Paris, 1790), pp. 48-52; *Journal de la Cour et de la Ville*, June 19, 1790; and *Courrier français*, supplement to its number of Nov. 19, 1789. Concerning La Fayette, Washington, and Franklin, see *Actes des Apôtres* (1789), No. 5, p. 12; (1790), Vol. VIII, p. 45 *et seq.; Avis aux Faiseurs de Constitutions* (1789), *par Benjamin Franklin; Je crains la Banqueroute*, pp. 26-27, etc.

[66] Concerning the rôle of the United States and the Americans from a religious point of view during the Revolution, see *Souvenirs d'un Nonagenaire, Mémoires de François Yves Besnard*, Vol. I, p. 353.

[67] See *Œuvres Complètes de Voltaire*, Vol. XII, pp. 419-423; Vol. XVIII, pp. 498-501; Vol. XX, pp. 311-313.

[68] See *Mémoires de Lafayette*, Vol. III, pp. 59 and 202.

[69] See Vol. I, pp. 15, xxiv, 146-150, 283-293, etc., in *Nouveau Voyage dans les Etats-Unis de l'Amérique septentrionale*, by J. P. Brissot (Warville).

[70] See *id.*, Vol. I, pp. xii and 24-31.

[71] Jean-Paul Rabaut, called Rabaut Saint-Etienne (1742-1793). See *Œuvres de Rabaut Saint-Etienne*, Vol. V, p. 368. Concerning the criticisms of public men by means of American examples, see *L'Ami du Peuple*, Oct. 2, 1790; *L'Union*, Feb. 22, 1790; *Journal universel*, Oct. 31, 1792; *L'Orateur du Peuple*, No. 48, etc.

[72] See, for example, the account in *Le Patriote français*, June 13, 1790.

[73] *Logographe*, June 19, 1790.

[74] See *Extrait du Journal de la Société de* 1789. Speech by La Rochefoucauld Liancourt, delivered June 13, 1790.

[75] *Id.*

[76] See *Courrier de Versailles à Paris*, by M. Gorsas, July 26, 1790, pp. 371-380.

[77] *Id.*

[78] See among these criticisms *Actes des Apôtres* (1790), Vol. VI, No. 157; *Folies d'un Mois*, Dec. 3, 1790, etc.

[79] See *Chronique de Paris*, June 17 and 19, 1790.

[80] See Condorcet, *Eloge de M. Franklin* (Paris, 1791).

[81] See *L'Ami du Peuple* (1790), Vol. II, No. 134.

[82] *Patriote français*, June 13, 1790.

[83] See *Souvenirs de la Terreur de* 1788 *à* 1793 (Paris, 1841), by M. Georges Duval, Vol. II, p. 185.

[84] *Vie privée, impartiale, politique de M. le Marquis de Lafayette* (Paris, 1790), pp. 48-51.

[85] See the whole series of pamphlets published by the Franklin Press; for example, *La Vie privée et politique de J. R. Hebert* (Paris) is from the Franklin Press, Year II. See also *Recueil de Documents pour l'Histoire du Club des Jacobins de Paris*, by F. A. Aulard, Vol. III, p. 291; Vol. IV, p. 489; and *Suite des mémoires du Général Dumouriez*, p. 326.

[86] This play is in the Bibliothèque Nationale, Mss. fr. N. A., Collection Solienne, No. 9284. It contains twenty-three pages, and its title is *L'Imprimerie ou la Fête de Franklin* (anonymous).

[87] See *Chronique de Paris*, Feb. 22, 1791, and introduction to Franklin's *Autobiography*.

[88] See *Tribut de la Société Nationale des Neuf Sœurs*, July 14, 1790, pp. 51-59.

[89] Concerning Marsillac and his action, see *The Journal of the Friends' Historical Society*, Vol. XV, p. 49; Vol. XVI, pp. 18 and 81; and *Memorandum written by William Rotch*.

[90] In addition to the two sources cited above, see *Chronique de Paris*, the editorial for Aug. 12, 1791; *Patriote français*, edi-

torials for Jan. 8, 1790; *Le Postillon*, Feb. 11, 1791; and *Pétition respectueuse des Amis de la Société chrétienne, appelés Quakers*, presented to the National Assembly, Thursday, Jan. 10, 1791.

[91] See at the headquarters of the Society of Friends at London the collection of Marsillac's manuscripts. I feel a deep gratitude to this Society for having put its archives at my disposal with the greatest generosity. Among these documents we find a correspondence between Marsillac and the General Assembly of the Department of Loir-et-Cher (at the end of 1792) and enthusiastic letters from Grégoire recommending the Quakers to the authorities of that department. The whole plan for the installation at Chambord is explained in them. The intention was to create a School of Moral Industry. See also *Journal of the Friends' Historical Society*, Vol. XVI, p. 21 *et seq.; Memorandum written by William Rotch*, pp. 56-60. See also in the manuscripts of Marsillac his letter of May 1, 1791, in which he speaks of the establishing of the Quaker sect at Paris.

[92] See *Journal d'une Bourgeoise pendant la Révolution* (published by Edouard Lockroy, Paris, 1881), p. 103.

[93] See *La Bouche de Fer*, patriotic and fraternal newspaper, and especially the prospectus in the heading. See also Vol. II of this publication, No. 2, p. 14, etc.

[94] See *Lettres de Madame Roland* (published by Claude Perroud), Vol. II, pp. 77, 80, 273, 688 *et seq.*, and 744.

[95] See particularly *La Feuille villageoise*, Aug. 24, 1791, and Jan. 12, 1792, etc.

[96] See *Diary of Gouverneur Morris*, Vol. I, pp. 29, 34-36, 428-429, etc.

[97] See, for example, *Observations sur le Principe qui a produit les Révolutions de France, de Genève et d'Amérique* (Evreux, October, 1789), by M. Isnard, Engineer of Bridges and Highways, and *De la République et de la Monarchie*, a pamphlet without date but published in 1789.

[98] See the preface to Vol. III of *Life and Writings of Thomas Paine*.

[99] *Id.* and *Annales patriotiques*, July 14, 1791.

[100] For the discussions of the Assembly concerning American commerce, see *Courrier de Provence*, Feb. 13, 1791; *Annales patriotiques*, Jan. 27, 1791; *Journal du Soir*, Feb. 13, 1791; *Courrier français*, Feb. 24 and March 2, 1791, etc.

[101] See *Diary of Gouverneur Morris*, Vol. I, p. 513.

[102] See *Writings of Washington*, Vol. XII, p. 5 *et seq.;* Vol. XI, p. 493, etc.

[103] See *Diary of Gouverneur Morris*, Vol. I, pp. 249, 139-143, and 262-295. At that time Montmorin and La Fayette were completely at the mercy of Morris, to whom they had confided too many secrets. See also *Mémoires de Lafayette*, Vol. II, pp. 8-12.

[104] See *Diary of Gouverneur Morris*, Vol. I, pp. 139-143 and 249, and *Archives des Affaires étrangères, Etats-Unis*, Vol. XXXV, pp. 301-305.

[105] See *Diary of Gouverneur Morris*, Vol. I, p. 275.

[106] See *Archives des Affaires étrangères, Etats-Unis*, Vol. XXXV, pp. 301-304; Vol. XXXVI, pp. 266-268, etc.

[107] Concerning Gouverneur Morris and his activities, see the excellent dispatch from Otto in the *Archives des Affaires étrangères, Etats-Unis*, Vol. XXXV, pp. 301-305; and *Diary of Gouverneur Morris*, *passim*. For his opinion of the people, see Vol. I, pp. 110 and 545 *et seq.;* concerning the Queen, Vol. I, p. 100; concerning the King, pp. 436-438, etc.

[108] See *Diary of Gouverneur Morris*, Vol. I, p. 492; Vol. II, pp. 9-11, etc., and *Writings of Washington*, Vol. XII, p. 203.

[109] See *Writings of B. Franklin* (Smyth edition), Vol. X, p. 66, letter to D. Le Roy.

[110] See *Stockbridge Western Star*, Dec. 15, 1789.

[111] See *Stockbridge Western Star*, Dec. 7, 1790, and *Gazette of the United States*, Aug. 18, 1790.

[112] See *Archives des Affaires étrangères, Etats-Unis*, Vol. XXXV, p. 647.

[113] Concerning the parties in the United States at this period, see *Political Parties and Party Problems in the United States*, by Y. A. Woodburn, pp. 1-10.

[114] See *Journal of Maclay*, pp. 18-22.

[115] Concerning the American Senate, see *Archives des Affaires*

étrangères, Etats-Unis, Vol. XXXIV, p. 354; Vol. XXXV, pp. 66 and 301-303. See also the *Journal of Maclay, passim*, and in particular pp. 89, 233, etc.

[116] See *Journal of Maclay*, pp. 249 and 349-350, and *Writings of Thomas Jefferson*, Vol. I, p. 279, etc.

[117] See Chapter Three, Note 114, and *Writings of Thomas Jefferson*, Vol. I, pp. 270-283 and 417 *et seq.*

[118] See *Archives des Affaires étrangères, Etats-Unis*, Vol. XXXV, p. 375, etc.

[119] For the attitude of the Senate, see *Journal of Maclay*, who was himself a senator and whose testimony cannot be doubted, since it is borne out by a series of facts; see pp. 74, 379 and 412 (concerning the consular convention with France), 381, 382 (concerning the question of tonnage and the Senate's desire to break the alliance with France), and finally, 386 and 397, which are irrefutable documents; etc.

[120] See *Archives des Affaires étrangères, Etats-Unis*, Vol. XXXV, p. 301.

[121] Concerning Fenno, see *Life and Correspondence of Rufus King*, Vol. I, pp. 400-430, 501-503, etc. For much information on Fenno, I am indebted to Miss Frances Ward of Evanston, Ill., who possesses a remarkable collection of papers and documents concerning this period of American history and who is preparing a study on Fenno. Concerning Freneau as a journalist, see, in *Johns Hopkins University Studies, The Political Activities of Philip Freneau*, by Samuel E. Forman, *passim*, and *Writings of Thomas Jefferson*, Vol. I, p. 353; Vol. IX, p. 77; *Writings of Madison*, Vol. VI, p. 24, etc.

[122] For a better example of the Republican polemic, see Freneau's *National Gazette* (1791-1792), and, for the Federalist side, *The Gazette of the United States* (same years). See also the *Diary or Loudon's Register* of New York, which published in June, 1792, Paine's *Rights of Man*.

[123] Concerning the Jefferson-Adams quarrel, see *Writings of J. Q. Adams*, Vol. I, pp. 65-110, and *Writings of Thomas Jefferson*, Vol. VIII, p. 243.

[124] See *Life and Writings of Thomas Paine*, Vol. III, pp. 101-109.

[125] See *The Political Writings of Joel Barlow* (New York, 1796), p. 92 *et seq.*

[126] See *Recueil de Documents pour l'Histoire du Club des Jacobins de Paris*, by F. A. Aulard, Vol. III, pp. 350-351.

[127] See, in the *Massachusetts Historical Society*, the manuscript journal of Castorland.

[128] See, for example, *Description topographique de six cent mille Acres de Terre dans l'Amérique septentrionale* (prospectus, 1792) and *Plan de Vente de trois cent mille Acres de Terre situées dans le Comté de Northumberland et d'Huntington* (1794). Concerning La Fayette, see *Correspondance inédite de Lafayette*, p. 193. On B. Constant, see *La Jeunesse de B. Constant*, by M. Rudler, p. 483. Concerning Mme. de la Tour du Pin, see *Journal d'une Femme de cinquante Ans* (published by A. de Liedekerke, Beaufort, 1913), *passim.* Concerning Madame de Genlis, see *Mémoires inédits de Madame la Comtesse de Genlis*, Vol. IV, p. 129. Concerning the Sulpicians, see *The Sulpicians in the United States*, by Charles G. Herbermann, pp. 15-23.

[129] See, for example, *Mercure de France*, March 3, 1793; *Journal encyclopédique*, Jan. 30, 1793, and pamphlets such as *Les Aventures politiques du Pére Nicaise* (Paris, 1793), p. 21, etc.

[130] See *Adresse aux Anglais, par un Représentant de la Nation française* (Paris, 1791), pp. 7-8.

[131] See *Recueil de Documents pour l'Histoire du Club des Jacobins de Paris*, by F. A. Aulard, Vol. III, pp. 290 and 307, and *Annales patriotiques*, Feb. 7, 1792.

[132] See *Courrier des quatre-vingt trois Départements*, March 6, 1792.

[133] See *Annales patriotiques*, Feb. 7, 1792.

[134] See *Courrier des quatre-vingt trois Départements*, April 20, 1792.

[135] See on this subject the very curious testimony of Genet himself in *Life and Writings of Thomas Paine*, Vol. IV, p. 12.

[136] See *La Trompette du Père Duchêne*, No. 92, Aug. 18, 1792.

[137] See, for example, *Lettre d'un Quaker américain à un Républicain français* (Paris, 1792).

[138] See *Archives des Affaires étrangères, Etats-Unis*, Vol. XXXVI, pp. 480-500.

[139] Michel-Ange-Bernard Mangourit was a revolutionist from the beginning. He was sent to the United States as Consul at Charleston; from there he went to Valais, and then to Italy. Concerning his activities in America, see "The West in Diplomacy," by F. J. Turner, in the *American Historical Review* (1898), Vol. III, *passim*, and in particular pp. 570-580, 629, etc.

[140] Similar celebrations took place in many other large cities. For those of Boston and New York, see *Boston American Apollo*, Jan. 3, 1793, and *Boston Columbian Sentinel*, Jan. 26, 1793.

[141] All this is taken from *Reminiscences of Charleston*, by Charles Fraser (Charleston, 1854), pp. 39 and 40 *et seq.*

[142] See *Archives des Affaires étrangères, Etats-Unis*, Vol. XXXVII, p. 295 *et seq.*

[143] See *id.*, same pages and pp. 393-395.

[144] See *National Gazette*, April 20, 1793; *Massachusetts Historical Society*, Vol. II, Series 5; *Belknap Papers*, Vol. II, p. 325; *Writings of Madison*, Vol. I, pp. 251-253, etc.

[145] This fact is related by La Rochefoucauld Liancourt in *Voyages dans les Etats-Unis d'Amérique* (Paris, Year VIII), Vol. VI, p. 8.

[146] See, for example, *The Boston American Apollo*, Jan. 11, 1793.

[147] Concerning the enthusiasm in America in 1793, see *Writings of James Monroe*, Vol. I, pp. 251-254, 271, 277, etc. See especially *Massachusetts Centinel*, June 23, 1793; *Stockbridge Western Star*, Jan. 15 and April 16 and 23, 1793; *Pennsylvania Gazette*, July 10, 1793; *Gazette of the United States*, May 25, 1793; *General Advertiser*, April 26 and May 31, 1793.

[148] See Turner, *The West in Diplomacy*, p. 639.

[149] See *Archives des Affaires étrangères, Etats-Unis*, Vol. XXXVII, p. 434 *et seq.*

[150] *Id.*, Vol. XXXVIII, pp. 35 and 80-94.

[151] *Id.*, pp. 112, 158, and 402-406.

[152] *Id.*, Vol. XXXIX, pp. 137-140.

[153] See *Notes on the Life of Noah Webster*, compiled by Emily E. F. Ford, edited by Emily E. F. Skeel, Vol. I, pp. 366-369.

[154] See Morse, *Federalist Party in Massachusetts*, p. 101 *et seq.*, and *Life and Correspondence of Rufus King*, Vol. I, pp. 460-470.

[155] See *Diary of Gouverneur Morris*, Vol. II, pp. 45-55 and 50-60; and *Archives des Affaires étrangères*, *Etats-Unis*, Vol. XXXIX, p. 159; *Annales patriotiques*, Nov. 20, 1793.

[156] See, for example, *The West in Diplomacy*, by F. Turner, pp. 639-640.

[157] See *Diary of Ezra Stiles*, Vol. III, pp. 491 and 496; *Mr. Mellen's Thanksgiving Sermon*, Nov. 20, 1794; *A Discourse on the Fall of Papacy*, by R. Fleming (Boston, 1794), etc.

[158] See *Reminiscences of Charleston*, by Charles Fraser, p. 40; *Pennsylvania Gazette*, July 10, 1793; *New York Daily Advertiser*, July 12, 1793, etc.

[159] Noah Webster, lexicographer, pamphleteer and journalist (1758-1843).

[160] William Willcox, a lawyer from New York, famous for his sensational attacks on France from 1792 to 1798. He had begun by being a warm defender of France. See his article in the *Federal Gazette*, June 13, 1793.

[161] Webster was led to found a Federalist newspaper in 1793 in order to defend the policy of his party and criticize France. Wolcott prompted him and helped him. Concerning this enterprise, see *Notes on the Life of Noah Webster*, by E. E. F. Ford, Vol. I, pp. 364-370.

[162] See *Writings of James Monroe*, Vol. I, p. 251. See in particular the series of articles signed "A Republican" in the *Philadelphia Independent Gazetteer* (1794), etc.

[163] See *Le Défenseur de la Constitution*, by Maximilien Robespierre (1792), pp. 328-329.

[164] On the religious unity of all the revolutionary doctrines, see *Les Origines des Cultes Révolutionnaires*, by A. Mathiez, pp. 9 and 21; on the Girondists, *id.*, p. 75.

[165] See *Recueil de Documents pour l'Histoire du Club des Jacobins de Paris*, by F. A. Aulard, Vol. IV, p. 273 *et seq.*

[166] In *Nouveau Voyage dans les Etats-Unis de l'Amérique septentrionale*, by J. P. Brissot, Vol. I, p. xxiv, we read: "The prosperity of a society is always in proportion to the degree of liberty, which in turn is in inverse ratio to the extent of the powers of the government."

[167] Concerning this mysterious affair, see the account of Paine himself, whom there is no reason for doubting, since all the documents that can be found confirm his statements and prove the bad faith of Gouverneur Morris. See *Life and Letters of Thomas Paine*, Vol. III, pp. 150-215. The letter from Gouverneur Morris in the *Archives des Affaires étrangères, Etats-Unis*, Vol. IV, p. 91, shows that, far from seeking to aid him, Morris tried only to harm him. See also *id., Mémoires et Documents, Etats-Unis*, Vol. X, p. 162.

[168] See *Recueil de Documents pour l'Histoire du Club des Jacobins de Paris*, by F. A. Aulard, Vol. IV, p. 411 *et seq.*

[169] See *Feuille villageoise*, Jan. 3, 1793.

[170] See *Républicain français*, 2 Fructidor, Year II.

[171] *Alphabet des Sans-culottes* (Paris, Year II), p. 11.

[172] *Entretiens d'un Citoyen de Philadelphie*, by Citizen Maurin, employee in the Ministry of Foreign Affairs.

[173] See *Le Chansonnier de la Montagne* (Paris, Year III), pp. 37 and 69; *La Lyre républicaine* (Paris, Year III), pp. 163 and 171.

[174] Concerning Robespierre's intentions with regard to America, see *Archives des Affaires étrangères, Etats-Unis*, Vol. XXXIX, pp. 159, 255-260 and 284.

[175] *Id.*, Vol. XL, pp. 298-302; Vol. XLVII, pp. 407-412.

[176] *Id.*, Vol. XL, pp. 264, 290-295, and 299-302; Vol. XLI, p. 17.

[177] See the description of the situation in which Fauchet found himself, in his dispatches and those of his colleagues, *id.*, Vol. XLI, pp. 387 and 375-377; Vol. XLII, p. 322; Vol. XLIII, pp. 147-152 and 151-153; Vol. XLVII, pp. 410-418.

[178] *Id.*, Vol. XLI, p. 99; Vol. XLIV, pp. 476-527; and Vol. II (Supplement 1), pp. 136-150.

[179] See *id.*, Supplement 1, Vol. II, pp. 135-150, and Vol. XLIV, pp. 263-268 and 487-515.

[180] See *Diary of Ezra Stiles*, Vol. III, pp. 497 and 518.

[181] See *The order of the Exercises of Commencement*, July 20, 1791 [at Harvard]; *The Harvard Advocate*, 1913-1914, pp. 76-79 (very curious article by Mr. Baldensperger on Nancrède); *Providence Gazette*, July 8, 1792.

[182] See *A History of Columbia University* (1904), p. 75; *The Teaching of Modern Languages in the United States*, by Charles H. Handschin, p. 22.

[183] See *The Teaching of Modern Languages in the United States*, pp. 13-14.

[184] Concerning Quesnay de Beaurepaire and his works, see *Avis impartial aux Citoyens, adressé aux honorables Membres du Comité de Subsistance de Paris*, Aug. 19, 1789; *Second Avis impartial aux Citoyens ou Contrepoison* (no date); *Troisième Avis impartial aux Citoyens* (no date); *Quatrième Avis impartial aux Citoyens* (no date). All these pamphlets are signed by Quesnay and contain details on his life and attitude. He announced this series as a periodical, but no subsequent numbers have been found.

[185] See *Writings of Thomas Jefferson*, Vol. IX, pp. 291 and 297; *Life and Works of John Adams*, Vol. VIII, pp. 516-517, etc.

[186] See *The American Museum: A Letter to a Young Lady* (October, 1792); *Study on the Education of Youth* (November, 1792), by Noah Webster, pp. 282-284. For teachers of dancing and French, see, for example, *New York Daily Advertiser*, Oct. 20, 1790, and Nov. 9, 1791; *New York Journal*, Aug. 28, 1791, etc.

[187] Concerning the importation of French books at this period, see the curious information contained in *Mathew Carey, Author, Editor and Publisher*, by Earl Bradsher (1912). The catalogues of books consulted furnish supporting evidence; see in particular those of the New York Society Library for 1791, 1792, 1793,

and the catalogues of Carey in the *American Mercury* for 1791 and 1792 (there is one for each month). These are the most typical, for New York and Philadelphia were then the two principal centers of the book trade in the New World.

[188] See, for example, *Columbian Magazine*, February, 1790, pp. 82-87; November and December, 1791, pp. 293 and 381; April, 1792, pp. 225-228, etc. *Charlotte, a Tale of Truth*, by Mrs. Rowson (Philadelphia, 1794), *The Power of Sympathy* (Boston, 1789).

[189] See *Modern Language Notes*, Vol. XXXV, pp. 10-18, the article by Prof. Schinz on Nancrède and his *Abeille française*. The Harvard Library possesses a copy of *L'Abeille*.

[190] See, for example, *Voyage dans les Etats-Unis d'Amérique*, by La Rochefoucauld Liancourt, Vol. I, pp. 148-152 and 316-320, etc.

[191] See, for example, the collection, *Miscellaneous Works, Prose and Poetical, by a Young Gentleman of New York* (1795), by J. B. Linn, in which there are real lyric qualities and a romanticism that is sometimes delightful. See further *A Family Tablet* (Boston, 1796), by Abiel Holmes, and *Poems on Several Occasions by John Swanick, Esq.* (Philadelphia, 1796), especially pp. 38, 45 and 120, etc.

[192] See *Transactions of the American Philosophical Society*, the list of members at the beginning.

[193] Concerning the theater, see *New York Daily Advertiser*, Jan. 1 and Feb. 4 and 22, 1791, etc.; *Boston American Apollo*, Nov. 9, 16, and 23, and Dec. 7, 1792.

[194] See in particular the archives of the French Benevolent Society of Philadelphia, founded Jan. 1, 1793, in which we find picturesque information concerning the Société des Grivois founded in the same city in 1794 by Frenchmen.

[195] See in the collection of the Pennsylvania Historical Society the papers relative to the two French lodges from Santo Domingo, established at Philadelphia between 1792 and 1794, the Amenity and the Lodge of Saint John of Jerusalem. Concerning the conflicts between the French Masons and the American lodges in the United States, see, for example, *Proceedings of the M. W.*

Grand Lodge of Ancient York Masons of the State of Virginia, by John Dove (Richmond, 1874), pp. 151 *et seq.*, 181, etc.

[196] See Boston *Herald of Freedom*, April 22, 1791; *State Gazette of North Carolina*, Feb. 5, 1789; *Argus*, Aug. 21 and Sept. 4, 1792, etc.; *Nouveau Voyage de Brissot*, Vol. I, p. 121.

[197] See *The Sulpicians in the United States*, by C. G. Herberman, pp. 38-51.

[198] See *Salem Gazette*, July 22, 1794; *Stockbridge Western Star*, Feb. 28, 1794; *Northampton Hampshire Gazette*, Jan. 16, 1790; letter from John Fenno to Col. J. Ward (collection belonging to Miss Frances Ward of Evanston, Ill.). See the very typical sermon by Samuel Stillman: *Thoughts on the French Revolution, A Sermon*, Nov. 20, 1794 (Boston).

[199] Tanguy de la Boissière, after having been a notary at Santo Domingo, emigrated to the United States. There he wrote articles and pamphlets; later he returned to France. The only known copy of his *Niveau de l'Europe et de l'Amérique septentrionale* is at the Bibliothèque Nationale. See *Archives des Affaires étrangères, Etats-Unis*, Vol. XLV, pp. 80-84.

[200] See *The Poems of Philip Freneau*, edited by F. L. Pattee (Princeton, 1902), Vol. III, p. 102.

[201] See, for an example of the Federalist pamphlets, John Quincy Adams, *Publicola* (*Writings of J. Q. Adams*, Vol. I, pp. 65-110), and *Columbus* (*id.*, Vol. I, pp. 149-176); for an example of the Republican pamphlets, see in particular Madison, *Helvidius* (*Writings of J. Madison*, Vol. VI, p. 138 *et seq.*).

[202] In addition to the sermons of Stillman and Mellen cited above, see that of J. Morse, *The Present Situation of the Other Nations, A Sermon*, Feb. 19, 1795, and that of S. West, *A Sermon*, Feb. 19, 1795.

[203] See *Writings of Samuel Adams*, Vol. IV, pp. 353-358, 368, etc.

[204] Concerning the attitude of the Federalist leaders, the responsibility of Hamilton, Jay, and Washington, see *Jay's Treaty*, by Samuel Flagg Bemis (New York, 1923), and especially pp. 70-76, 198-205, etc.

[205] See *Writings of James Monroe*, Vol. I, pp. 285, 293-296; Vol. II, pp. 1-10 (his instructions).

[206] *Id.*, Vol. II, pp.1-30, etc.

[207] *Id.*, Vol. II, pp. 34-51.

CHAPTER V

[1] See *Correspondence and Public Papers of John Jay*, Vol. II, pp. 352, 354, 452 *et seq.;* Vol. III, p. 54; *Archives des Affaires étrangères, Etats-Unis*, Vol. XXV, 64-70.

[2] See *Archives des Affaires étrangères, Etats-Unis*, Vol. XXXI complete, in which Otto, the French chargé-d'affaires, explains his negotiations with Jay in Vol. XXXII, p. 186; Vol. XLIV, pp. 465-470. Concerning Jay's views in 1787, see *id.*, Vol. XXXIII, p. 33 *et seq.*

[3] See *Writings of Washington*, Vol. XII, pp. 340, 418 *et seq.*, 403, etc.

[4] See *Correspondence and Public Papers of John Jay*, Vol. II, pp. 351 and 452; Vol. III, p. 119 *et seq.*, and especially Vol. IV, p. 199 *et seq.* and 208. See *Writings of Madison*, Vol. VI, pp. 130-135, and *The Life of John Jay*, Vol. I, pp. 297-300.

[5] Concerning Jay's treaty, see the book by Samuel Flagg Bemis, *Jay's Treaty* (New York, 1923), in which the rôle of Jay is analyzed with the greatest clearness and a perfect impartiality. See especially Mr. Bemis' opinion concerning the negotiations as a whole and their results, pp. 260-270.

[6] See *Correspondence and Public Papers of John Jay*, Vol. IV, p. 144.

[7] See *Writings of Washington*, Vol. XIII, pp. 76-78. See also the newspapers of the time; for example, *The Boston Independent Chronicle* for April, 1795, and following months. See also *Reminiscences of Charleston*, by Fraser, p. 45.

[8] See *Writings of Washington*, Vol. XIII, p. 76.

[9] The *Philadelphia General Advertiser*, better known under its other name, *The Aurora*, was founded in 1790 by Franklin Bache, grandson of Franklin. From its beginning this newspaper distin-

guished itself among the other publications by its interest, the abundance of news that it contained, and the value of its articles. In the first number Bache defines the policy of the newspaper thus: "The Liberty of the press is the stronghold of Liberty."

The Aurora was to have divisions on: (1) internal politics, (2) external politics, (3) agriculture, (4) commerce, (5) industry, (6) the arts, (7) the sciences, (8) intellectual works, (9) anecdotes, (10) poetry.

The Aurora was faithful to this program until 1798. In that year, Bache, who, in spite of the epidemic of yellow fever, had not been willing to leave his post, succumbed to the disease. Duane succeeded him with no less vehemence but less talent. *The Aurora* was the unofficial organ of the French legation.

[10] See *Writings of Samuel Adams*, Vol. IV, pp. 365-375. Concerning Dickinson, see in particular *Writings of Dickinson* (1801), Vol. II, which contains his *Letters of Fabius* complete.

[11] See *Philadelphia General Advertiser*, November and July 7, 1795; *New York Daily Advertiser*, Feb. 14 and May 14, 1795; *Providence Gazette*, April 18, 1795, etc.; and also in *The History of Philadelphia*, by Sharf and Westcott, the descriptions of the last months of 1795 and the first months of 1796.

[12] See *Poems of Freneau*, Vol. III, pp. 129, 132, and 134.

[13] See *Works of Alexander Hamilton*, Vol. V, pp. 190-491.

[14] See *Archives des Affaires étrangères*, *Etats-Unis*, Vol. XLIV, pp. 508-517, and Vol. XLVIII, pp. 259-263, etc.

[15] William Cobbett (1766-1835), English publicist, who was anti-revolutionary during his stay in America and was very active in serving the Federalists and the Minister of England there. Returning to England in 1804, he became a radical. See *Mathew Carey, Editor . . .* , by Earl L. Bradsher, up to p. 20, for the life of Cobbett.

[16] See *The Dangers Which Threaten Europe, from the French of Mallet du Pan*, by James Rivington (New York, 1795), and *The Democrat, or Intrigues and Adventures of Jean le Noir* (New York, Rivington, 1795). See also *Stockbridge Western Star*, Sept. 15, 1795; *Gazette of the United States*, May 27, 1796; *Porcupine's Gazette*, March 13, 1797, etc.

[17] *Charleston City Gazette*, Nov. 9, 1795.

[18] See, for example, *Gazette of the United States* for the years 1795, 1796, and 1797, under the dates of Jan. 10, Feb. 16, March 12, April 18, and July 9, 1795; Feb. 19, March 5, and May 18, 1796, etc. See also *Porcupine's Gazette.*

[19] See *Boston Columbian Sentinel*, *Salem Gazette*, and *Stockbridge Western Star* for 1795-1796. These are the most typical organs of Federalism in Massachusetts. In them one can follow day by day the campaign against French Jacobinism. See the analysis of this campaign in *The Boston Independent Chronicle*, March 30, 1795.

[20] See *The Federalist Party in Massachusetts*, p. 101. On the United States as the chosen people, see *A Sermon on the Freedom and Happiness of America*, Feb. 19, 1795, by Abiel Holmes, and also *A Sermon Delivered on the Ninth of May*, 1798, by Jeremy Belknap, and *A Discourse by Eliphalet Porter* (Boston, 1798), etc.

[21] See Chapter IV, and Notes 156-159.

[22] See *The Revolution in France Considered in Respect to its Progress and Effects, by an American* (New York, 1794).

[23] See *Answer to Paine's Rights of Man, by H. Mackensie, Esquire, To which is added a Letter from P. Porcupine* (Philadelphia, 1796), and *The Federalist Party in Massachusetts*, pp. 107-109, as well as *Dissertation on the Character, Death and Resurrection of Jesus Christ*, by Jeremy Belknap (Boston, 1795).

[24] See *Federalist Party in Massachusetts*, pp. 85-95, and *New England and the Bavarian Illuminati*, by Vernon Stauffer, *passim*, for the whole book is devoted to the study of the spread of Barruel's book and ideas. Abbé Augustin Barruel (1741-1820), writer and pamphleteer, who published his great anti-revolutionary work at London in 1797: *Mémoires pour servir à l'Histoire du Jacobinisme*, five volumes.

[25] See *The Wonderful Works of God, A Sermon*, by David Osgood (Boston, 1794). *A Discourse Delivered Feb.* 29, 1795, by David Osgood (Boston, 1795), and *The Present Situation of the Nations of the World Contrasted with Our Own. A Sermon Delivered, Feb.* 19, 1795 (Boston, 1795), by Jedediah Morse.

[26] See *The Altar of Baal Thrown Down, or the French Nation Defended Against the Pulpit Slander of David Osgood*, by Citoyen de Novion (Boston, 1795).

[27] See the list contained in *The Federalist Party in Massachusetts*, pp. 101-106.

[28] See in particular *The Forester, an American Tale*, by Belknap (1796), pp. 100-108. *Observations on the Dispute Between the United States and France*, by R. Goodloe Harper (Philadelphia, 1797). See in the newspapers Hamilton's *Horatius* (*Writings of Alexander Hamilton*, Vol. V, pp. 180-184) and his *Camillus* (*Writings of Alexander Hamilton*, Vol. V, pp. 190-250), and the very good *résumé* of the results that the publications of Genet's instructions brought about, in Vol. II of Supplement 1, of *Correspondance politique* (*Etats-Unis*), *Archives des Affaires étrangères*, pp. 130-140.

[29] See *Archives des Affaires étrangères*, *Etats-Unis*, Vol. XLI, p. 126.

[30] *Id.*, Vol. XXXIX, pp. 255-260 and 466-470; Vol. XL, pp. 298-302; Vol. XLI, p. 17; Vol. XLIV, pp. 487-527.

[31] *Id.*, Vol. XLIV, pp. 502-527.

[32] *Id.*, Vol. XLIV, pp. 263-268.

[33] *Id.*, the pages cited above seem to exculpate Fauchet. Vol. XLIV, pp. 508-512, confirms this impression, which Adet's statement in his dispatch of the first of Vendémiaire, Year VI, renders almost a certainty. (*Id.*, Vol. XLVIII, pp. 259-263.)

[34] See *id.*, Vol. XLIII, pp. 323, 371, 411, 425, and 473; Vol. XLIV, pp. 5 and 487-510.

[35] See *id.*, Supplement 1, Vol. II, pp. 130-140, and regular series, Vol. XLIV, pp. 57, 73, 219, and 508-510; Vol. XLVI, pp. 342-343.

[36] See *id.*, Vol. XLV, pp. 82-83 and 252. Adet's remark concerning Jefferson is taken from Vol. XLVI, p. 502.

[37] See *id.*, Vol. XLV, pp. 16-18.

[38] See *id.*, Vol. XLV, pp. 41, 52, and 141; Vol. XLVI, pp. 130, 131, and 342. Concerning his proclamation, see Vol. XLVI, pp. 383, 393, and 400.

[39] See the account of the fluctuation of public opinion from

day to day by Liancourt in *Voyages dans les Etats-Unis d'Amérique* (Paris, Year VIII), Vol. V, *passim*, and particularly, pp. 113, 150-152, 183, 233-234, 236-237, and 238; Vol. VI, pp. 89-90 and 327; Vol. VII, pp. 68-72, etc. Concerning the democratic spirit in the West, see *The Lexington* (Kentucky) *Gazette* for 1796 and 1797, and especially Sept. 6, 1797; *The Rights of Men* (Paris, Ky.); *The Washington Mirror*, etc. To form an idea of the opposition press, see *The Philadelphia Aurora*, edited by Bache; *The Boston Independent Chronicle*, *The Charleston City Gazette*, and Greenleaf's *New York Argus* for the years 1796-1797. Concerning Baltimore see the entire file of *The Maryland Journal* for the years 1795-1796 and the *Gazette française*, 27 Thermidor, Year II. On South Carolina, see *Charleston City Gazette* and *Reminiscences of Charleston*, by Charles Fraser (Charleston, 1854), pp. 42-49. Concerning Tammany and other associations, see *New York Argus*, July 5, 1796, etc.

[40] See *The Political Writings of John Dickinson* (Wilmington, 1801), pp. 167-286.

[41] H. H. Brackenridge, born in Scotland in 1748, came to the United States in 1753, studied at Princeton, where he made the acquaintance of Freneau, and later studied law. He settled in the West and became an intelligent, democratic, and moderate judge. He published *Modern Chivalry*, mentioned in this work, in 1796.

[42] See in particular pp. 147-149 of *Modern Chivalry*, where these ideas are expressed.

[43] For this point of view clearly and honestly expressed, see Monroe's address to the Convention, *Writings of James Monroe*, Vol. II, p. 11.

[44] *Id.*, Vol. II, pp. 108 *et seq.*, 162, 167 *et seq.*, and 194-205.

[45] See *id.*, Vol. II, pp. 227-230, 236-255, and 310-314.

[46] See *id.*, Vol. II, pp. 162, 347-359, and 407-410; concerning his relations with the French government and the stratagems of the latter, see *id.*, Vol. II, pp. 432-440, 440-447, 460-462, 484-488, etc.

[47] Concerning Monroe's patience, see *id.*, Vol. III, pp. 8-10, 48, 54, 62, 19 *et seq.*, etc.

[48] See *id.*, Vol. III, p. 48 *et seq.* See also *Archives des Affaires étrangères, Etats-Unis*, Vol. XLV, pp. 150, and 182-190; Vol. XLVI, pp. 100-110.

[49] See *id.*, Vol. XLIV, pp. 524-527; Vol. XLV, pp. 141, 172, 348-350, 381, and 411; Vol. XLVI, pp. 144, and 425; Vol. XLVII, pp. 32, 247, etc.

[50] Concerning the life of Paine at this period, see the impartial information furnished by Monroe (*Writings of Monroe*, Vol. II, pp. 440-447; Vol. III, pp. 150-170, etc.). We cannot place great confidence in what Conway says about Paine.

[51] *Writings of Thomas Paine*, Vol. III, pp. 256-285, 328-344, 286, 312, 345-367, etc.

[52] See *Archives des Affaires étrangères, Etats-Unis*, Vol. XLVI, pp. 130 and 425; Vol. XLVII, p. 32.

[53] See *Paris pendant la Réaction thermidorienne et sous le Directoire*, by A. Aulard (Paris, 1898), Vol. III, pp. 299, 571, 595, 672, and 700; Vol. IV, pp. 23, 44, 57, 75, 84-86, 104, 162, etc. The account of the confusion between John and Samuel Adams occurs on p. 700, Vol. III.

[54] See, for example, *La Gazette Nationale*, (Aug. 31, Sept. 9, Oct. 2, and Dec. 13, 1795, and Jan. 31 and March 29, 1796), which blames Jay's treaty but praises the American people and sets forth the necessity for an understanding. See also *Mercure français* for 15 Vendémiaire, 4 and 20 Messidor, Year III; *Gazette de France* for 19 Germinal, Year III; 25 Fructidor, Year III; and *L'Historie* for 15 Pluviôse, Year IV, etc.

[55] See *Paris pendant l'Année* 1796, No. 5; *Tableau de Paris*, June 24 and July 9, 1796; *Courrier Républicain* for 21 Vendémiaire, Year III. See also *Mémoires du Comte de M.* (Paris)—the memoirs of the Comte de Moré de Pontgibaud—pp. 248-249. See the opinions that Chateaubriand held and wrote at this time: *Œuvres complètes de Chateaubriand* (Paris, 1834), Vol. I, pp. 15 and 155.

[56] See especially *Les Mémoires du Comte de M.*, pp. 224-225, 226-227, and 228-257, and *Journal d'une Femme de cinquante Ans* (*Journal de le Marquise de la Tour du Pin de Gouvernet*), pp. 5-25; Vol. II, pp. 69-72.

[57] See *Journal d'une Femme de cinquante Ans*, pp. 1-4; Vol. II, pp. 85-87.

[58] *Id.*, *passim*, and especially Vol. I, pp. 333-341, and Vol. II, pp. 1-89.

[59] *Œuvres complètes de Chateaubriand* (1834), Vol. I, p. 153.

[60] *Id.*, p. 154.

[61] *Id.*, pp. 153-156. The criticism of the Quakers is contained in Note 3, p. 151.

[62] *Id.*, Vol. II, pp. 110-124 and 252-262.

[63] See *Lettres écrites des Rives de l'Ohio*, by Claude-François-Adrien de Lezay Marnésia (Paris, Year IX), pp. 1-8 and 113-144.

[64] See Note 55 of this chapter.

[65] See Rozengarten, *French Colonists and Exiles in the United States*, the chapters devoted to Gallipolis and the Asylum.

[66] Jean Gabriel Peltier, a famous royalist pamphleteer, editor of *Les Actes des Apôtres*. Died in 1825.

[67] See *Tableau de la Situation actuelle des Etats-Unis d'Amérique* (Paris, Year III, 1795), Vol. I, pp. 118 and 36-38.

[68] Charles Pictet de Rochemont (1755-1824), after having served in the French army (1775-1783), returned to Geneva, where he exercised certain public functions and was appointed Counselor of State. He endeavored to develop agriculture in his country and exerted a real influence, as much by his example as by the works that he published. In 1814 he represented the Geneva government at Paris. Later he was sent to the Congress of Vienna. On his return, he was appointed commander of the armed forces of Geneva. The quotations concerning the United States are taken from pp. 26-37 and 116-119 of his *Tableau de la Situation actuelle des Etats-Unis de l'Amérique.*

[69] See *Des Prisons de Philadelphie, par un Européen* (*le Citoyen La Rochefoucauld Liancourt*). There were at least three editions of this pamphlet. See also *Un Philanthrope d'Autrefois, La Rochefoucauld Liancourt*, by F. Dreyfus, pp. 108-128.

[70] Adrien de Lezay Marnésia (1770-1814), son of Claude-François-Adrien, Marquis de Lezay Marnésia, was a pamphleteer of the opposition under the Directory and a friend of

Roederer. He later became reconciled with the Empire and was appointed prefect.

[71] Comte Pierre-Louis Roederer (1754-1835). See his pamphlet, *Du Gouvernement* (no date), p. 53.

[72] Jean-François de Laharpe (1739-1803), noted literary critic, monarchist in 1795. See his pamphlet, *Oui ou Non* (no date).

[73] Jean-Jacques, Comte Lenoir Laroche (1749-1825), a moderate monarchist, who, after having tried to defend Louis XVI and escaped from the Terror, enjoyed a certain prominence under the Directory. He was Minister of Police and a member of the Conseil des Anciens. Later he was reconciled with the Empire and, at the time of the Restoration, to the Bourbons, who made him a peer of France.

[74] See *Des Moyens de régénérer la France*, by Citizen Delacroix (Paris, Year V), pp. 302-306.

[75] Joseph-Marie, Comte de Maistre (1754-1821), gentleman of Savoy. See his pamphlet, *Considerations sur la France* (London, 1797), p. 65.

[76] See *Actes des Apôtres*, July 2, 1797; *La Quotidienne*, Feb. 14, 1797; *Paris pendant* 1797, Jan. 14, 1797; *L'Historien*, 15 Nivose, 23 Nivose, and 20 Germinal, Year V; *Courrier universel*, 3 Floréal and 18 Messidor, Year V; *Mercure universel*, 10 Germinal, Year V; *Journal de Paris*, 29 Floréal, Year V, etc.

[77] See in particular *Nouvelles politiques*, April 25 and May 17, 1797.

[78] Claude-Emmanuel-Joseph-Pierre, Marquis de Pastoret (1756-1840). At first a violent revolutionist, he became a conservative in 1792 and emigrated. Under the Directory he was a member of the Five Hundred and was outlawed as a royalist. Senator under the Empire, he was made a peer by the Bourbons. See his speech in the newspapers of the time, all of which published it; see, in particular, *Paris pendant* 1797 under the date of June 30, 1797.

[79] Pierre-Samuel Dupont de Nemours (1739-1817), a noted economist, friend of Turgot, and one of the principal writers of that school. He also held official positions under Louis XVI and during the Revolution. Under the Directory, he was a member

of the Conseil des Anciens and edited *L'Historien*, a conservative and philosophic newspaper. He emigrated to America and died there.

[80] Concerning the attitude of the conservatives, see the articles by Ségur cited above, which are very typical. On the attitude of the Directory, see the responses of the unofficial and Jacobin papers. The most typical seems to me to be that contained in the issue of *Le Journal des Hommes libres* for 7-8 Messidor, Year V, in which the whole situation is discussed and the Directory cleared of blame.

[81] See in particular Fauchet's complete report to the Directory, *Archives des Affaires étrangères*, *Etats-Unis*, Vol. XLIV, pp. 460-520.

[82] See *id.*, Vol. XLIV, pp. 460-462.

[83] See *id.*, Vol. XLV, p. 41.

[84] See *Voyage aux Etats-Unis de l'Amérique*, 1793-1798, by Moreau de Saint-Méry, *passim*, and especially pp. 38, 41-44, 60-65, 99-107, 115-118, 134-136, 143, 213, 222-225, 263, 287-294, 304, 305, 308, etc.

[85] Note the extraordinary analogy between p. 299 of the *Voyage de Moreau de Saint-Méry* and p. 101 of the *Mémoires de l'Institut National des Sciences et Arts*, *Sciences morales et politiques*, Vol. II (Paris, Year III), which contains Talleyrand's memorandum concerning commercial relations of the United States with England. Concerning Talleyrand's reception in the United States, see *Journal d'une Femme de cinquante Ans*, Vol. II, pp. 18-20, 25-35, 63-64, and 69-70; *Mémoires du Comte de M.*, pp. 230-235, 236-246, etc. See also *Voyage de Moreau de Saint-Méry*, which contains many opinions that derive from Talleyrand or at least from the intimacy between Talleyrand and Moreau.

[86] See *Mémoires de l'Institut National des Sciences et des Arts*, *Sciences morales et politiques*, Vol. II, pp. 101-102.

[87] *Id.*, p. 106.

[88] See, for example, *Nouvelles politiques*, April 17, 1797; *Journal d'Economie politique*, 30 Germinal, Year V; *L'Historien*, 18 Germinal, Year V, etc.

[89] See *Décade philosophique*, 30 Pluviôse, 10 Ventose, 30 Germinal, Year IV; 20 Pluviôse, 30 Germinal, 30 Floréal (letter from Marsillac), 20 Messidor, Year V; La Sentinelle, 16 Nivose, 5 Messidor (letter from M. de Bulow), Year V; *Le Républicain français*, 10 Frimaire, Year VI; *Writings of Thomas Paine*, Vol. III, p. 368; *Writings of Jefferson*, Vol. IX, p. 355; *Gazette française de New York*, May 8, 1797.

[90] Ferdinand-Marie Bayard, born in the Orne in 1768, was a writer and an officer of the regular army, but this book seems to be the only permanent monument that he left. *Voyage dans l'Intérieur des Etats-Unis*, by Ferdinand Bayard (Paris, Year V, 1797).

[91] See, for example, *Annales patriotiques*, March 17, 28, and 29, May 23, and Nov. 12, 1796; March 24 and April 9, 1797; *Le Républicain français*, 22 Vendémiaire, 8 Brumaire, 17 Nivose, 2 Pluviôse, Year V; 2 Vendémiaire, Year VI; Louvet's *Sentinelle*, 4 Vendémiaire, 30 Vendémiaire, 19 Brumaire, 24 Floréal, 16 Prairial, 8 Thermidor, Year IV, etc.

[92] See *Mémoires de Barras*, Vol. II, p. 85; *Mémoires de La Réveillère-Lépaux*, Vol. II, pp. 257-267; *Mémoires historiques et diplomatiques de Barthélemy*, by Soulavie, p. 60; *Writings of J. Q. Adams*, Vol. II, pp. 27, 71, 168, 175, and 185; *Writings of James Monroe*, Vol. II, pp. 130-135, 460, 456, 463, and 484; Vol. III, p. 624; *Writings of Thomas Paine*, Vol. III, p. 268. The testimony of La Réveillère-Lépaux, although it is the most precise and most detailed, cannot be accepted without some reservations, since it does not agree with contemporary documents and accords too glorious a rôle to its author.

[93] See *Works and Writings of John Adams*, Vol. III, pp. 537, 540, 554, 557, and 558; Vol. X, pp. 114-116 *et seq.*

[94] See the account of these transactions in the remarkable book by Albert Beveridge, *The Life of John Marshall*, Vol. I, pp. 24-357.

[95] Concerning Talleyrand's attitude see, in addition to his communication to the Institute, which is very typical, his *Mémoires* (published by the Duc de Broglie), pp. 236-239 and 240, and

Mémoires, Lettres inédites et Papiers secrets (Paris, 1891), pp. 125 and 129.

[96] See *Works and Writings of John Adams*, Vol. VIII, pp. 570 *et seq.*, 617, 624, and 677-692; Vol. IX, pp. 11 *et seq.*, 29, 33, etc.

[97] Letombe was French Consul at Boston for a long while. He was a personal friend of John Adams and enjoyed great esteem in the United States. Concerning Letombe and Adams, see *Works and Writings of John Adams*, Vol. IX, pp. 12-14.

[98] Alexandre-Maurice Blanc de la Naulte, Comte d'Hauterive, Counselor of State (1751-1830). Consul at New York in 1792. After his dismissal from this post, he remained in America, where he later served as a secret agent for France. He was very close to Talleyrand, who took him into the Ministry of External Relations. He played an important part under the Empire and was in favor with the Restoration. Concerning his secret activities and his friendship with Talleyrand, see *Papiers de Barthélemy*, Vol. VI, p. 251, and *Archives des Affaires étrangères, Etats-Unis*, Vol. XLVII, pp. 393-397; Vol. XLVIII, pp. 16, 141, 265, 310-320, 369-370, etc. Concerning General Collot's mission, see *Works and Writings of John Adams*, Vol. IX, pp. 12-15, and Marc de Villiers du Terrage, *Les dernières Années de la Louisiane française*, p. 365 *et seq.* Concerning the other propagandists, see *Archives des Affaires étrangères*, Vol. XLVII, pp. 198 and 268-276; Vol. XL, pp. 285 and 286; Vol. XLI, pp. 13-20; *Voyage de Moreau de Saint-Méry*, pp. 247-250, 252-253, etc.

[99] See *Gazette française de New-York*, Feb. 8, 1797, and *New York Herald*, Jan. 7, 1797.

[100] See *Annals of Congress*, Vol. VI, pp. 1340 *et seq.*, 2362, 2714, 1778, etc. See also Gordy, *Political History of the United States*, Vol. I, pp. 296-297, which quote the passage from Gallatin transcribed here.

[101] The newspapers which give the most accurate idea of the violence of the struggle and in which we find all the characteristics here mentioned are *The Gazette of the United States*, *Porcupine's Gazette*, on the Federalist side, and *The Aurora* and *The Boston Independent Chronicle*, on the Republican side.

[102] See in particular the protest that Volney felt obliged to publish on the subject of this rumor, *Aurora*, Feb. 8, 1796.

[103] See *The Russels of Birmingham*, by J. Jeyes, pp. 251-255 and 270-280; *Writings of Thomas Jefferson*, Vol. X, p. 35; *The Nature and Danger of Infidel Philosophy*, by the Reverend Timothy Dwight (New Haven, 1798); *Porcupine's Gazette*, June 7, 1798, etc.

[104] See *Poems of Philip Freneau*, Vol. III, pp. 135, 139, 151, etc., and *Writings of James Monroe*, Vol. III, pp. 383-457.

[105] For examples of these rumors, see *Columbian Centinel* (Boston), Jan. 24, 1798.

[106] See *Voyage de Moreau de Saint-Méry*, p. 263.

[107] See concerning the situation at this time, *Archives des Affaires étrangères*, Vol. XLIX, p. 333 *et seq.*

[108] *Writings of Thomas Jefferson*, Vol. XII, p. 347.

[109] See *Porcupine's Gazette* for February, 1798.

[110] See *Writings of Thomas Jefferson*, Vol. X, pp. 63, 219, etc. Concerning the South, see, for example, the files of the *Lexington (Kentucky) Gazette* for 1798.

[111] See *Works and Writings of John Adams*, Vol. VIII, pp. 570-620.

[112] See *Writings of Thomas Jefferson*, Vol. X, pp. 51, 58, 63, and 77, and Gordy, *Political History of the United States*, Vol. I, p. 319.

[113] See *The Aurora* for April and May, 1798. There was a whole campaign in this direction during these months. See especially the series of articles signed *Sydney.*

[114] See the praises of Souvaroff and Nelson in *The Gazette of the United States*, April-July, 1799; *Porcupine's Gazette*, Jan. 29, 1799, and the following weeks; the *Columbian Centinel* (Boston) for June, 1799, and the number of Sept. 25, 1799.

[115] See this caricature in the *Archives des Affaires étrangères, Etats-Unis*, Vol. L, p. 39.

[116] See *id.*, Vol. L, pp. 285-286; Vol. LI, p. 13; *Voyage de Moreau de Saint-Méry*, pp. 251-253.

[117] See in *The Lexington (Kentucky) Gazette*, November and December, 1798, the series of articles signed "Timoleon."

[118] See *What Is Our Situation and What Are Our Prospects?* (May, 1798), by Joseph Hopkinson; *An Address to the People of Maryland* (Philadelphia, 1798), by John Dennis; *Mr. Harper's Speech on the Foreign Intercourse Bill* (1798).

[119] See *Works of Alexander Hamilton*, Vol. VI, pp. 259-318.

[120] See in particular *The Gazette of the United States* (Philadelphia), April, 1798, to December, 1799; *The Columbian Centinel* (Boston), *The Commercial Advertiser* (New York), *The United States Chronicle* (Providence), same dates.

[121] No newspaper gives a more exact and complete idea of the way the Federalist polemic was carried on than *The Gazette of the United States* for the years 1799-1800. On July 5, 1799, it printed an article on France which contained the declaration that the war then in progress was a war of religion, "a bloody promulgation of a new faith, as was that of Mohammed in the seventh century."

[122] See Vernon Stauffer's book on this question, *New England and the Bavarian Illuminati*. Although it is somewhat confused, it contains very complete information on the entire campaign of the Congregationalist clergy.

[123] See *The American Geography*, by Jedediah Morse (1789). See the praises of France in *The Present Situation of the Other Nations of the World Contrasted with Our Own. A Sermon*, by Jedediah Morse (1795).

[124] See the speech by Thayer reported in *The Newport Mercury*, Oct. 16, 1798, and in *The Hartford Courant*, Aug. 6, 1798. As examples of anti-French sermons, see *A Discourse on the National Sin*, by William Linn (1798); *The Duty of Americans*, by the Reverend Timothy Dwight; *The Devil Let Loose* (Boston, 1799); *A Discourse by Eliphalet Porter* (1798), etc. Note the gibes of the Republicans on this alliance of all the churches against France, *Boston Independent Chronicle*, Sept. 30, 1799.

[125] All this is only a *résumé* of *New England and the Bavarian Illuminati*, by Vernon Stauffer.

[126] There is not a single American newspaper, but, from August, 1798, on, frequently printed articles, discussions, or literary or historical extracts on this subject. But the newspapers of

New England were the most ardent. See in particular *The Massachusetts Mercury* of Boston.

[127] See *An Impartial Review of the Causes and Principles of the French Revolution, by an American* (Boston, 1798), pp. 1-35 and *passim.*

[128] *Letters on Various Interesting and Important Subjects,* by Robert Slender (Philadelphia, 1799).

[129] See *Poems of Freneau,* Vol. IV, p. 202.

[130] See *The Second Warning* (Paris, 1798) and *Letters from Paris to the Citizens of the United States,* by Joel Barlow (London, 1801).

[131] See in *The Aurora* of Philadelphia, March 19, 1799, the very curious article signed "A Republican" against the dangerous union of Federalist politicians and the clergy and against the tendency of the American President to act as a pope.

[132] See *New England and the Bavarian Illuminati,* by V. Stauffer, pp. 250-300. See also *American Mercury,* Sept. 26 and Nov. 1 and 14, 1799; *The Bee,* Dec. 20 and 27, 1799; *Aurora,* Nov. 16 and 25 and Dec. 6 and 9, 1799; *Connecticut Courant,* Nov. 30, 1799; *Massachusetts Mercury,* Dec. 27, 1799, etc.

[133] See *A View of the New England Illuminati* (Philadelphia, 1799), and *Voyage de La Rochefoucauld Liancourt,* Vol. III, p. 260.

[134] See *Works and Writings of John Adams,* Vol. VIII, p. 624; Vol. IX, pp. 11, 24, 29, 33, 35, etc. See also Notes on the *Life of Noah Webster,* compiled by E. E. F. Ford, edited by E. E. F. Skeel, Vol. I, pp. 504-505.

[135] See *Archives des Affaires étrangères, Etats-Unis,* Vol. XLIX, pp. 333 and 393-404; Vol. LI, pp. 40-50. The phrases quoted are from Vol. XLIX, pp. 393-404.

[136] See *Paris pendant le Révolution thermidorienne et sous le Directoire,* Vol. IV, pp. 767 and 791; Vol. V, p. 21, etc.

[137] See *Décade philosophique,* 30 Prairial, Year VI, p. 570 *et seq.; Journal des Hommes libres,* 22 Prairial, Year VI; *La Chronique universelle,* 22 and 23 Prairial, Year VI; *Paris pendant* 1798, May 30, 1798; *Le Spectateur du Nord,* 3 Complé-

mentaire, Year VI; *Patriote français*, December, 1798, pp. 441-463, etc.

[138] See *Archives des Affaires étrangères, Etats-Unis*, Vol. L, pp. 118-124 and 270-285; Vol. LI, pp. 40-50, and *The Life and Letters of H. G. Otis*, by Morison, pp. 168-170.

[139] See *Archives des Affaires étrangères, Etats-Unis*, Vol. XLIX, pp. 999-1007.

[140] See *id.*, pp. 51, 131 *et seq.*

[141] See in particular *id.*, Vol. L, pp. 270-285; Vol. XLIX, pp. 99-107; *Chronique universelle*, 22-23 Prairial, Year VI; *Décade philosophique*, 20 Thermidor, Year VI; *Courrier universel*, 1 Vendémiaire, Year VII; *Journal des Débats*, 25 Pluviôse, Year VII.

[142] See *Eclaircissements donnés par le Citoyen Talleyrand à ses Concitoyens* (Paris, Year VII).

[143] See *Archives des Affaires étrangères, Etats-Unis*, Vol. LI, pp. 49-51.

[144] See *id.*, Vol. LI, pp. 311, 330, and 380-397.

[145] See in particular *L. Hauteval, Citoyen français au Gouvernement et au Peuple américain, Nouveau Tableau spéculatif de l'Europe*, by General Dumouriez (1798); *Pacification de l'Europe*, by the Citizen Flassan (Paris, Year VIII), especially pp. 65-67; *Nécéssité de la Paix*, by J. T. Bruguière (Paris, Year VIII), etc.

[146] See *La Clef du Cabinet*, 13 Pluviôse, Year VIII, and *Paris sous le Consulat*, by A. Aulard, Vol. I, p. 133.

[147] See a typical example of this concept of Washington's character in *L'Historien*, 10 Pluviôse, Year IV.

[148] See, as example of Washington's unpopularity, Paine's pamphlet against him, *Letter to Washington*, in *Writings of Thomas Paine*, Vol. III, pp. 213-252.

[149] See *Mémoires de M. de Bourrienne*, Vol. II, pp. 183-185.

[150] Félix Faulcon (Deputy to the States-General, in the Council of the Five Hundred, and after the 18 Brumaire, in the Corps Législatif) always showed himself to be a moderate monarchist, and under the Directory came out clearly against the government. For his speech and his motion, see *Gazette de France*, 20

Pluviôse, Year VIII; *Journal des Hommes libres*, 14 Pluviôse, Year VIII, etc.

[151] See *Archives des Affaires étrangères*, Vol. LI, pp. 311-320.

[152] See *Mémoires de M. de Bourrienne*, Vol. II, pp. 183-185; *Paris sous le Consulat*, by A. Aulard, Vol. I, pp. 149 and 267.

[153] On Elisa Bonaparte's relations with Fontanes, see *Biographie des Contemporains* (Paris, 1836), Vol. II, under the name of Fontanes, p. 1713.

[154] See *Eloge funèbre de Washington* (delivered in the Temple of Mars by Louis Fontanes, Year VIII), pp. 28-29.

[155] See *Journal des Débats*, 14 Pluviôse, Year VIII.

[156] See *Gazette de France*, 20 Pluviôse, Year VIII; *Journal de Paris*, 9 Fructidor, Year VIII.

[157] See *Paris sous le Consulat*, by A. Aulard, Vol. I, p. 284; *Clef du Cabinet*, 8 Ventose, Year VIII, etc. See also *Eloge de Washington*, by G. F. Dubroca (Paris, Year VIII). Dubroca, born in 1757, was a bookseller and writer. He had a mystic and religious temperament and assisted in founding the Theophilanthropic Church.

[158] See *Archives des Affaires étrangères*, *Etats-Unis*, Vol. LI, pp. 380-397. Concerning Otto's attitude, see *id.*, Vol. II, Supplement 1, pp. 130-152. For the attitude of Hauterive, see his book, *De l'Etat de la France*, pp. 91, 144, 145, etc.

[159] Concerning this celebration, see Albert-Firmin Didot's *Souvenir de Jean-Etienne Despréaux* (1894), p. 48, and *Napoléon et Marie-Louise, Souvenirs historiques de M. le baron de Méneval* (Paris, 1844), Vol. I, pp. 33-39; *Journal du Comte Roederer* (Paris, 1909), pp. 21-23; *Journal de Paris*, 10 Vendémiaire, Year IX, etc.

[160] See in *Napoléon inconnu*, by F. Masson, the notes that Napoleon took on the United States and the documents that he copied from the newspapers when he was a young man, pp. 461, 471, 500, and 503.

[161] See, for example, what Jefferson himself said on this subject: *Writings of Jefferson*, Vol. X, pp. 311-313 and 315.

[162] Concerning this campaign against Jefferson, see *Writings of Thomas Jefferson*, Vol. X, p. 77; *Life and Correspondence*

of *Rufus King*, Vol. III, p. 299. See also, as a typical example of what was being written at the time, the long series of articles published from June to September in *The Columbian Centinel* (Boston) under the title "Jeffersoniad" and signed "Demos." All the newspapers of the period discussed this question, but those of New England were the most relentless.

[163] This attitude on the part of the American democrats is well defined by Jefferson; see *Writings of Thomas Jefferson*, Vol. X, p. 145; Vol. XIII, pp. 236-238.

[164] Concerning Volney, see *Writings of Thomas Jefferson*, Vol. X, p. 35; *The Russels of Birmingham*, by J. Jeyes, p. 270 *et seq.;* Volney's book entitled *Tableau du climat et du sol des Etats-Unis d'Amérique* (Paris, 1803). See the preface, pp. i-xvi, which contains his judgment on the United States.

[165] Concerning the Duc de La Rochefoucauld Liancourt and his travels in America, see *Journal d'une Femme de cinquante Ans*, Vol. II, pp. 60-62, and Liancourt's own book, *Voyage dans les Etats-Unis d'Amérique*, especially Vol. I, p. 87; Vol. III, pp. 49, 113, 119, 146, 71, 94, and 260; Vol. IV, p. 275; Vol. V, pp. 28, 175, and 235; Vol. VI, pp. 206 and 207; Vol. VII, p. 109. See further *Voyage de Moreau de Saint-Méry*, pp. 243-246.

[166] See *Writings of Thomas Paine*, Vol. IV, pp. 236-246, 304-355, etc.; *Paris sous la Réaction thermidorienne et sous le Directoire*, by A. Aulard, Vol. I, pp. 159, 163, and 176-178; *Paris sous le Consulat*, by A. Aulard, Vol. I, p. 295; *Journal de Paris*, 13 Ventose, Year VIII. For the extracts from the works of Franklin or articles concerning him, see, for example, *Journal du Bonhomme Richard*, Year III and IV, *passim* (in particular 3 Complémentaire, Year III). *Décade philosophique*, 10 Prairial, Year V, p. 483; 20 Prairial, Year VI; 10 Vendémiaire, Year VII; *Journal d'Economie politique*, 10 Ventose, Year V, pp. 25-38, 10 Fructidor, Year V, p. 36; *Messager du Soir*, 1 Vendémiaire, Year V; *Journal de Paris*, 2 Nivose, Year IV; *Gazette nationale*, 29 Messidor, Year VI, etc.

[167] See preceding note, and for the citation, *Journal du Bonhomme Richard*, 3 Complémentaire, Year VIII.

[168] See *Mémoires du Duc de Montpensier*, preface, pp. xi-xv,

and pp. 210-215; Antoine-Philippe d'Orléans, Duc de Montpensier (1755-1807). He distinguished himself at Valmy, was imprisoned at Marseilles, and emigrated to America and later to England. His brother, the Comte de Charolais, and his other brother, Louis Philippe, Duc d'Orléans (1773-1850), accompanied him to America.

[169] Abbé J. L. Bonnet de Fréjus emigrated during the Revolution. He was naturalized as an American citizen, but returned to France under the Consulate. He published various works in favor of Bonaparte and the Bourbons, of whom he believed him to be a partisan.

[170] See *Œuvres complètes de M. le Vicomte de Chateaubriand* (1834), Vol. VII, pp. 22-26.

[171] See *id.*, pp. 279 *et seq.* and 290-291.

[172] See *Voyages dans la haute Pennsylvanie*, by an adopted member of the Oneida Nation (Paris, Year IX)—in reality by Crèvecœur—Vol. II, pp. 183-184.

[173] See *Œuvres complètes de M. le Vicomte de Chateaubriand* (1834), Vol. X, p. 139, and *id.*, Vol. X, pp. 5-6.

[174] See *The Teaching of Modern Languages in the United States*, by Charles Hart Handschin, pp. 19-20; for the discontinuing of the announcements of French professors in the American papers, see *Porcupine's Gazette*, in which the only advertisements of French professors or translators are accompanied by the assurance that said Frenchman is not a democrat (for example, May 24 and 25, 1797). For attacks against French professors and the ways in which they were intimidated, see *The Gazette of the United States* during December, 1799. See, further, *Harvard Records of the College Faculty* under the dates June 22 and 23, 1798, Nov. 9, 1798, etc.

[175] See *The Russels of Birmingham*, by J. Jeyes, pp. 270-272; *Tableau du Climat et du Sol des Etats-Unis*, by C. F. Volney, pp. x-xii; *An Oration*, by Leonard Woods; *Life and Letters of Simeon Baldwin*, p. 418.

[176] See *Porcupine's Gazette*, Aug. 1, 1798, and *Education, a Poem, Spoken at Cambridge, July* 18, 1799, *at the Request of the Phi Beta Kappa*, by William Bigelow, p. 12.

[177] See *Harvard Records of the College Faculty*, dated June 23, 1798, and *The Teaching of Modern Languages in the United States*, by Charles Hart Handschin, pp. 19-22.

[178] See *id.*, p. 20.

[179] See in *History of the Harvard Law School*, by C. Warren, the very faithful picture of the conditions under which law was studied from 1770 to 1800 in the United States (Chapters VI, VIII, and IX-XIII). Concerning the study of medicine, see Theodore Harrington, *Harvard Medical School, a History*, *passim*, and in particular pp. 340-380 and 431.

[180] See *Early Proceedings of the American Philosophical Society* under the dates of April 15, 1796; Jan. 20, 1797, and April 18, 1800.

[181] See *Mémoires du Comte de M.* (Moré de Pontgibaud), pp. 236-240.

[182] See *Journal of the Friends' Historical Society* (1919), Vol. XVI, pp. 18-22 and 81-90, and Marsillac's manuscripts in the Library of the Friends at London. See also *Journal of Eliza Drinker* (edited by H. D. Biddle), under the dates of May 4, 1797, and June 19, 1798. See what the American newspapers hostile to France said of this affair: *Porcupine's Gazette*, June 7, 1798.

[183] Concerning the Tilly-Bingham scandal, see:

Printed sources: *Journal of Eliza Drinker*, April 27, 1799; *Philadelphia a Century ago*, by K. M. Rowland (*Lippincott's Magazine*, Vol. LXII, pp. 804-808); *The Life and Letters of H. G. Otis*, by S. E. Morison, Vol. I, pp. 125-145.

Manuscript sources: Brief of the Tilly-Bingham case in the archives of the Philadelphia Historical Society. This is the most fruitful source, and I am very grateful to the administration of the Philadelphia Historical Society for having allowed me to see and make use of these unpublished manuscripts.

[184] See, for example, the description of this contrast in the letters of Mrs. B. Stoddert, which K. M. Rowland quotes in *Philadelphia a Century ago*.

[185] See the catalogues of the Library Company of Charleston (1770, 1772, 1811); *A Supplementary Catalogue of the Books*

Belonging to the New York Society Library, Which Have Been Added Since the Year 1793 (New York, 1800); *Catalogue of the Library of the Late J. Buckminster* (Boston, 1812). The catalogues of the booksellers are also very interesting. Those of M. Carey, the principal importer of French books, appeared frequently in *The Aurora.* The catalogues of Nancrède, the French bookseller at Boston, appeared in the newspapers of that city and also in *Porcupine's Gazette*, which published one on Feb. 20, 1799. Concerning Carey and his trade in French books, see *Mathew Carey, Editor, Author, and Publisher*, by Earl I. Bradsher, *passim*, and especially pp. 17-21. Concerning Nancrède, see *Federal Gazette* (Boston), Jan. 2, 1798; the article by Mr. Baldensperger in *The Harvard Advocate*, Dec. 5, 1913; that of Professor Schinz in *Modern Language Notes*, Vol. XXXV, pp. 10-18. Moreau de Saint-Méry was also an active importer and printer of French books; Professor Schinz has published an article on him, *La Librarie française en Amérique au Temps de Washington*, in *La Revue d'Histoire littéraire de la France*, Vol. XXIV, pp. 568-584.

[186] See this fact in Chapter II.

[187] See *History of the American Theatre*, by William Dunlap (London, 1833), pp. 65, 105 *et seq.*, and 163.

[188] See *Voyage de Moreau de Saint-Méry*, pp. 267-270; *Charleston City Gazette*, Feb. 6, 1798; Dunlap, *History of the American Theatre*, under the date Nov. 20, 1793. See also *South Carolina State Gazette*, Oct. 17, 1794, and *passim* for 1795.

[189] Alexandre Duval (1767-1842) was a sailor, soldier, engineer, architect, secretary to the States of Brittany, and actor. He wrote many plays which enjoyed success at the time. Concerning Dunlap, see *Tell Truth, A Comedy* (New York, 1797), and *The Wife of two Husbands*, by W. Dunlap, etc.

[190] See *Female Patriotism, or the Death of Jean d'Arc, an Historic Play in Five Acts*, by John Burk (New York, 1798). The verses quoted are from Act IV.

[191] Charles Brockden Brown (1771-1810), novelist and publicist. To form an idea of the productions of the time and the imitations of the French, see *The Nightingale, or a Mélange of*

Literature, edited by John Lathrop, Jr. (Boston), especially May, June, and July, 1796, in which months extracts from Bernardin de Saint-Pierre, Marmontel, and Descartes were published regularly. See also *The American Universal Magazine*, 1797-1798, and *The New York Magazine*, especially July, September, and December, 1797.

[192] See *Poems of Philip Freneau*, Vol. IV, pp. 202-250. The verses on Washington quoted here are taken from this volume, pp. 234-237.

[193] Freneau was often inspired by Rousseau; the 1786 edition of his poems contains one entitled "Saint-Preux to Eloisa."

For little verses imitated from the French, see, for example, *Poems on Several Occasions*, by John Swanick (Philadelphia, 1797), pp. 17, 38, 45, and 120; and *Miscellaneous Works of D. Humphreys* (New York), p. 222, etc.

[194] See *Writings of Jefferson*, Vol. VIII, p. 234.

[195] From this point of view, the correspondence of Jefferson that has been published cannot afford an exact idea of his relations with France. It would be necessary to make a calendar of his papers, as has been done for Franklin. But my studies at the Virginia Historical Society and in the Archives of the State of Virginia, which contain an enormous collection of the letters of Jefferson, permitted me to acquaint myself with the general contents of these files.

[196] See "Popular Churches after the Revolution," by J. S. Bassett, in *Massachusetts Historical Society Proceedings*, Vol. XLVIII, pp. 254-268.

[197] See *The Temple of Reason*, Nov. 8, 1800.

[198] See *The Sulpicians in the United States*, by Charles G. Herbermann, pp. 39-75.

[199] I owe this information to Prof. Barrett Wendell, who, a few months before his death, was kind enough to go through his family papers with me and show me letters dated from the beginning of the nineteenth century. He even told me that he would like to make a study of the influence of French Catholicism on the cultured society of Boston from 1800 to 1815. I have done nothing here save to take over the ideas which he voiced at

that time and supported with a bulk of local manuscript documentation. I cannot pass over this opportunity of mentioning the inexhaustible kindness of Prof. Wendell to any student who applied to him, and the personal gratitude that I owe him.

[200] See "Popular Churches," by J. S. Bassett, same pages as those cited above.

BIBLIOGRAPHY

PERIODICALS IN ENGLISH

American Advertiser (Richmond), 1783-1786.
American Antiquarian Society Proceedings (Worcester), 1913 and 1920.
American Historical Review (New York and Chicago), 1898 and 1921.
American Magazine (New York), 1787-1788.
American Museum (Philadelphia), 1787-1792, 1797-1798.
American Surgical Association Proceedings, 1904.
American Universal Magazine (Philadelphia), 1797-1798.
Argus (New York), 1791-1797.
Aurora (called at first *General Advertiser;* Philadelphia), 1790-1800.
The Bee (New London), 1797-1800.
Boston Continental Journal (Boston), 1778-1787.
Boston Evening Post (Boston), 1771-1782.
Boston Gazette (Boston), 1770-1800.
Boston Independent Chronicle (Boston), 1777-1800.
Boston Post Boy (Boston), 1770-1775.
City Gazette (Charleston), 1789-1800.
Columbian Centinel (Boston), 1793-1800.
Columbian Magazine (Philadelphia), 1787-1792.
Commercial Advertiser (New York), 1797-1800.
Connecticut Courant (Hartford), 1774-1800.
Diary or Loudon's Register (New York), 1792-1797.
Freeman's Journal (Philadelphia), 1781-1788.
Gazette of the United States (New York and later Philadelphia), 1789-1900.
Georgia State Gazette (Augusta), 1785-1789.
The Harvard Advocate (Cambridge), 1913-1914.
Herald of Freedom (Boston), 1788-1791.
Independent Gazetteer (Philadelphia), 1795-1797.
The Journal of the Friends' Historical Society (London), 1905, 1910, 1918, 1919.

Lexington Kentucky Gazette (Lexington, Ky.), 1787-1800.
Lippincott's Magazine.
Magazine of American History (New York and Chicago), 1881.
Maryland Journal (Baltimore), 1773-1797.
Massachusetts Sentinel (Boston), 1788-1800.
Massachusetts Historical Society Proceedings (Boston), 1915-1916.
Massachusetts Mercury (Boston), 1799.
Massachusetts Spy (Boston), 1770-1789.
Mississippi Valley Historical Review, Vol. I and II.
Modern Language Notes (Baltimore), 1920.
Modern Philology, 1917.
National Gazette (Philadelphia), 1791-1793.
New London Connecticut Gazette (New London), 1770-1800.
Newport Mercury (Newport), 1772-1800.
New York Daily Advertiser (New York), 1785-1800.
New York Gazette (New York), 1770-1772.
New York Gazetteer (New York), 1784-1787.
New York Journal (New York), 1770-1776, 1791.
New York Magazine (New York), 1795-1797.
New York Packet (New York), 1776.
New York Weekly Mercury (New York), 1770-1783.
New York Weekly Museum (New York), 1788-1800.
The Nightingale (Boston), 1796.
Norfolk and Portsmouth Journal (Norfolk, Va.), 1787-1789.
Northampton Hampshire Gazette (Northampton), 1786-1795.
Ohio Company Series (Marietta, Ohio), 1915.
Pennsylvania Chronicle (Philadelphia), 1770-1773.
Pennsylvania Gazette (Philadelphia), 1770-1799.
Pennsylvania Journal (Philadelphia), 1770-1793.
Pennsylvania Ledger (Philadelphia), 1775-1778.
Philadelphia Independent Gazetteer (Philadelphia), 1782-1792.
Porcupine's Gazette (Philadelphia), 1796-1799.
Providence Gazette (Providence), 1774-1800.
Rights of Men (Paris, Ky.), 1797-1798.
Rivington's Gazette (New York), 1773-1783.
Salem Gazette (Salem), 1789-1800.
South Atlantic Quarterly (Durham, N. C.), 1914.
South Carolina Gazette (Charleston, S. C.), 1772-1775.
Stockbridge Western Star (Stockbridge, Mass.), 1789-1797.
The Temple of Reason (New York), 1800.

Transactions of the American Philosophical Society (Philadelphia), 1789.
The United States Chronicle (Providence), 1798-1800.
Virginia Gazette (edited by Dixon), 1771-1796.
Virginia Gazette (edited by Purdie), 1776-1777.
Virginia Gazette (edited by Pinkney), 1772-1786.
Virginia Independent Chronicle (Richmond), 1785-1789.
Washington Mirror (Washington), 1797-1798.
William and Mary Quarterly (Williamsburg), 1905-1906.
Yale Review (New Haven), 1894.

BOOKS AND PAMPHLETS IN ENGLISH

A History of Columbia University (New York, 1904).
An Impartial Review of the Causes and Principles of the French Revolution (Boston, 1798).
A View of the New England Illuminati (Philadelphia, 1799).
Catalogue of the Library Company of Charleston, 1770-1772, 1811.
Catalogue of the Library of Harvard University, 1773.
Catalogue of the Library of the late J. Buckminster (Boston, 1812).
Catalogue of the Philadelphia Society Library, 1789.
Catalogue of the Society Library of New York, 1770, 1791, 1792, 1793, 1800.
Debates and Proceedings in the Congress of the United States (Washington, 1832-1862). The ten first volumes.
Early Proceedings of the American Philosophical Society (Philadelphia, 1884).
Historical Catalogue of Brown University (Providence, 1914).
Journal of the Continental Congress (Ford and Hunt edition, Washington).
Old Family Letters, 2 vol. (not dated).
Salisbury Family Memorial (not dated).
The Charter, Bye-Laws of the New York Society Library (New York, 1789).
The Democrat, or Intrigues and Adventures of Jean le Noir (New York, 1795).
The Devil Let Loose (Boston, 1799).
The Motley Assembly, A Farce (Boston, 1779).

The Order of the Exercises of Commencement (Cambridge, Mass., 1791).
The Revolution in France, Considered in Respect to its Progress (New York, 1794).

ADAIR, JOHN, *The History of the American Indians* (London, 1775).
ADAMS, HENRY, *The Life of Albert Gallatin* (Philadelphia and London, 1886).
ADAMS, JOHN, *Works*, edited by C. F. Adams (Boston, 1855), 10 vol.
ADAMS, J. Q., *Writings*, edited by P. L. Ford (New York, 1914), Vol. I and II.
ADAMS, R. G., *Political Ideas of the American Revolution* (Durham, 1922).
ADAMS, SAMUEL, *Writings*, edited by H. A. Cushing (New York, 1906), 4 vol.
ADAMS, ZABDIEL, *A Sermon Preached at Lexington* (Boston, 1783).
ALLEN, ETHAN, *Reason the Only Oracle of Men* (Bennington, 1784).
ALSOP, RICHARD, *The Political Greenhouse for the Year* 1798 (Hartford, 1799).
BAIRD, *American Philosophy, Early Schools.*
BALDWIN, S. F., *Life and Letters of Simeon Baldwin* (New Haven, no date).
BARLOW, JOEL, *Letters from Paris* (London, 1801).
——, *The Political Writings* (New York, 1796).
——, *The Second Warning* (Paris, 1798).
——, *The Vision of Columbus* (Hartford and London, 1787).
——, *Columbiad* (Philadelphia, 1807).
BASSETT, J. S., *Popular Churches after the Revolution, Mass. Hist. Soc. Proceedings*, 1914, 1915.
BAYLAY, R. A., *History of National Loans* (Washington, 1881).
BELKNAP, JEREMY. *A Sermon Delivered on the 19th of May*, 1798.
——, *Dissertation on the Character, Death and Resurrection of Jesus Christ* (Boston, 1795).
——, *The Foresters, an American Tale* (Boston, 1791).
BELOTE, *The Scioto Speculation* (Cincinnati).

——, *Selection of the Gallipolis Papers* (Hist. and Phil. Society of Ohio, 1907), 2 vol.
BEMIS, S. F., *Jay's Treaty* (Macmillan, 1923).
BEVERIDGE, ALBERT, *The Life of John Marshall* (Boston and New York, 1916-1919), 4 vol.
BIGELOW, WILLIAM, *Education, a Poem* (Salem, no date).
BRACKENRIDGE, H. H., *Modern Chivalry*, 1796.
BRADSHER, EARL S., *Matthew Carey, Author, Editor, and Publisher* (New York, 1912).
BROWN, C. B., *The Novels* (Boston, 1827), 7 vol.
BUCKLEY, J., *A History of the Methodists* (New York, 1896).
BURK, J. D., *Female Patriotism* (New York, 1798).
BYARS, *Life of Saugrain* (St. Louis, no date).
CAMPAN, MADAME, *Memoirs on Marie-Antoinette and her Court* (Millet, 1909).
CANDIDUS, *Plain Truth* (Philadelphia, 1771).
CARROLL, H. K., *The Religious Forces of the United States* (New York, 1893).
CLAIRAC, CHEVALIER DE, *L'Ingénieur de Campagne* (Philadelphia, 1776).
COOMBE, THEODORE, *The Harmony between the Old and New Testament* (Philadelphia, 1774).
CREVECŒUR, HECTOR SAINT-JOHN DE, *Letters of an American Farmer* (Philadelphia, Carey, 1793).
DEANE, S., *Deane Papers* (published by C. Isham, New York, 1886-1890), 5 vol.
DENNIS, JOHN, *An Address to the People of Maryland* (Philadelphia, 1798).
DEUX-PONTS, G. DE, *My Campaigns in America* (Boston, 1868).
DICKINSON, J., *Writings*, edited by P. L. Ford (Philadelphia, 1895), and also the edition of 1801 (Wilmington), 2 vol.
DOVE, JOHN, *Proceedings of the M. W. Grand Lodge of Ancient York Masons of the State of Virginia* (Richmond, 1784).
DRINKER, ELIZABETH, *Journal of Eliz. Drinker*, edited by H. L. D. Biddle (Philadelphia, 1889).
DUNBAR, L. B., *A Study of the "Monarchical" Tendencies in the United States . . . Univ. of Illinois Studies*, Vol. X.
DUNLAP, W., *History of the American Theatre* (London, 1833).
——, *Tell Truth, a Comedy* (New York, 1798).
——, *The Wife of Two Husbands* (no date).

DWIGHT, REV. TIMOTHY, *The Duty of Americans* (New Haven, 1798).

EDDY, G. S., *A Project of Peace by P. A. Gargaz* (New York, 1922).

ELLIOTT, JONATHAN, *Debates in the Several State Conventions* (Philadelphia, 1881), 5 vol.

FILSON, JOHN, *Beginnings of Kentucky* (Lane, 1910).

FLEMING, R., *A Discourse on the Fall of Papacy* (Boston, 1794).

FORD, P. L., *Bibliography of Benjamin Franklin* (Brooklyn, 1889).

——, *Pamphlets on the Constitution of the United States* (Brooklyn, 1888).

FORD, E. F., *Notes on the Life of Noah Webster* (New York, 1912), 2 vol.

FORMAN, S. E., *The Political Activities of Philip Freneau* (Baltimore, 1902).

FRANKLIN, B., *Works*, edited by A. H. Smyth (New York, 1907), 10 vol.

——, *The Way to Wealth* (Paris, 1795).

FRASER, CHARLES, *Reminiscences of Charleston* (Charleston, 1854).

FRENEAU, PHILIP, *The Poems*, edited by Fred Lewis Pattee (Princeton, 1902), Vol. I-III (see also under R. Slender, a pseudonym of Freneau).

FROST, JOHN, *Lives of American Merchants* (New York, 1844).

GALLOWAY, J., *A Candid Examination of the Mutual Claims of Great Britain and the Colonies* (New York, 1775).

——, *The Churches' Flight into the Wilderness* (New York, 1774).

GORDY, *Political History of the United States* (New York, 1904), 2 vol.

GUILDAY, REV. PETER, *Life and Times of John Carroll* (New York, 1922).

HALE, *Franklin in France* (Boston, 1888), 2 vol.

HAMILTON, A., *Works*, edited by H. C. Lodge (New York, 1904), 12 vol.

HANDSCHIN, C. H., *The Teaching of Modern Languages in the United States* (Washington, 1913).

HARPER, R. C., *Observations on the Dispute between the United States and France* (Philadelphia, 1797).

——, *Speech on the Foreign Intercourse Bill* (1798).

HARRINGTON, THEODORE, *Harvard Medical School. A History* (New York, 1905).
HAYES, I. M., *Calendar of the Papers of Benjamin Franklin* (Philadelphia, 1908), 5 vol.
HAZEN, C. D., *Contemporary American Opinion of the French Revolution* (Baltimore, 1897).
HEALD, D., *The Harvard Medical School in* 1788-1789 (Boston, 1910).
HERBERMANN, G., *The Sulpicians in the United States* (New York, 1916).
HITCHCOCK, GAD., *A Discourse on the Man of Sin* (Boston, 1799).
HOLMES, ABIEL, *A Family Tablet* (Boston, 1796).
——, *A Sermon on the Freedom and Happiness of America* (1795).
HOPKINSON, JOSEPH, *What Is Our Situation?* (no date).
HUMPHREYS, DAVID, *Miscellaneous Works* (New York, 1804).
——, *The Anarchiad* (New Haven, 1861), in collaboration with J. Barlow, J. Trumbull, L. Hopkins.
INGLIS, CHARLES, *The Letters of Papinian* (New York, 1779).
IZARD, R., *Correspondence* (New York, 1844), Vol. I and II.
JAY, JOHN, *Correspondence and Public Papers*, edited by H. P. Johnston (New York, 1890), 4 vol.
JEFFERSON, THOMAS, *Notes on the State of Virginia.*
——, *Writings*, Monticello edition (Washington, 1924), 20 vol.
JELLINEK, G., *Declaration of the Rights of Man and of Citizens* (Holt, 1910).
JEYES, J., *The Russels of Birmingham* (London, 1911).
JUSSERAND, J. J., *Rochambeau in America* (Washington, 1912).
KAPP, FRIEDRICH, *Life of Johann Kalb* (New York, 1881).
KING, RUFUS, *Life and Correspondence* (New York, 1894), 3 vol.
LAMONT, DE, *The Art of War* (Philadelphia, 1778).
LEE, R. H., *Memoirs of the Life of R. H. Lee* (Philadelphia, 1825).
LEONARD, D., *Massachussettensis* (Boston, 1776).
LINN, J. B., *Miscellaneous Works* (New York, 1795).
LINN, WILLIAM, *Discourse on the National Sin* (New York, 1798).
MACLAY, WILLIAM, *Journal* (New York, 1890).
MACKENZIE, H., *Answer to Paine's Rights of Man* (Philadelphia, 1796).

Madison, James, *Notes on the Proceedings of the Federal Conventions* (Washington, 1897).
——, *Writings*, edited by Gaillard Hunt (New York and London, 1900-1902), 6 vol.
Pan, Mallet du, *The Dangers Which Threaten Europe* (New York, 1795).
Mather, S., *The Dying Legacy* (Boston, 1783).
Mayhew, J., *Papist Idolatry* (Boston, 1765).
Meade, Bishop, *Old Churches and Families of Virginia* (Philadelphia, 1861), 2 vol.
Miller, S., *A Brief Retrospect of the Eighteenth Century* (New York, 1803).
Minot, G. R., *History of the Insurrections in Massachusetts* (Worcester, 1788).
Mitchell, J. P., *Saint Jean de Crèvecœur* (New York, 1916).
Monroe, J., *Writings*, edited by E. M. Hamilton (New York, 1903), Vol. I-III.
Moore, Frank, *Songs and Ballads of the American Revolution* (New York, 1856).
Morison, S. E., *The Life and Letters of H. G. Otis* (Boston and New York, 1913), 2 vol.
Morris, Gouverneur, *Diary and Letters* (1888), 2 vol.
Morse, A. E., *The Federalist Party in Massachusetts* (Princeton, 1909).
Morse, Jedediah, *The American Geography* (1789).
——, *The Present Situation of Other Nations of the World Contrasted with Our Own* (Boston, 1795).
——, *A Sermon Preached at Charlestown* (Boston, 1798).
——, *A Sermon* (Hartford, 1799).
Morton, Mrs. S. W. A., *The Power of Sympathy* (Boston, 1789).
Newman, A. H., *A History of the Baptist Church in the United States* (New York, 1894).
Ogden, J. C., *A View of the New England Illuminati* (Philadelphia, 1794).
Osgood, David, *A Discourse Delivered* (Boston, 1795).
——, *The Wonderful Works of God* (Boston, 1794).
Paine, Thomas, *Complete Works of Thomas Paine* (Chicago, Belford, 1885).
Pellew, G., *John Jay* (Cambridge, 1898).

PERKINS, J. B., *France in the American Revolution* (Boston, 1911).

PHILLIPS, PAUL, *The West in the Diplomacy of the American Revolution. University of Illinois Studies* (1913).

PORCUPINE, PETER, *The Political Censor* (Philadelphia, 1796).

PORTER, ELIPHALET, *A Discourse* (Boston, 1798).

——, *A Sermon Delivered in the First Religious Society in Roxbury* (Boston, 1784).

RAMSAY, D., *History of the American Revolution* (Philadelphia, Aitken, 1789).

——, *Life of George Washington* (New York, 1807).

RAYNAL, ABBE, *Philosophical and Political History of the Settlements and Trade of the Europeans in the East and West Indies*, translated by J. O. Justamond (London, 1776).

——, *The American Revolution* (Philadelphia, Bell, 1782).

——, *Sentiments of a Foreigner on the Disputes of Great Britain with America* (Philadelphia, 1775).

ROTCH, WILLIAM, *Memorandum* (Boston, 1916).

ROWSON, MRS., *Charlotte, a Tale of Truth* (Philadelphia, 1794).

ROZENGARTEN, J. G., *The Early French Members of the American Philosophical Society* (Philadelphia, 1907).

——, *French Colonists and Exiles in the United States* (Philadelphia, 1907).

SEDGWICK, THEODORE, *A Memoir of the Life of William Livingston* (New York, 1833).

SHARF, T., and WESTCOTT, T., *The History of Philadelphia* (Philadelphia, 1884), Vol. I-III.

SHEA, J. G., *History of the Catholic Church in the United States* (New York, 1892), Vol. I, II.

SHERWOOD, SAMUEL, *An Address* (New York, 1776).

SLENDER, ROBERT, *Letters on Various Interesting Subjects* (Philadelphia, 1799).

SMITH, COL. JAMES, *Account of the Remarkable Occurrences in the Life and Travels of Col. James Smith During his Captivity with the Indians* (1790), 2 vol.

STANSBURY, J., *The Loyal Verses of John Stansbury and S. Jonathan Odell* (Albany, 1860).

STAUFFER, VERNON, *New England and the Bavarian Illuminati* (New York, 1918).

STILES, EZRA, *The Literary Diary*, edited by F. B. Dexter (New York, 1901), 3 vol.

STILLMANN, SAMUEL, *Thoughts on the French Revolution. A Sermon* (Boston, 1794).
SULLIVAN, *The Altar of Baal Thrown Down, or the French Nation Defended Against the Pulpit Slander of David Osgood* (Boston, 1795).
——, *An Impartial Review . . . of the French Revolution* (Boston, 1798).
SWANICK, JOHN, *Poems on Several Occasions* (Philadelphia, 1797).
TOCQUEVILLE, COMTE DE, *Democracy in America* (Cambridge, 1862).
TURNER, F. J., *The West in Diplomacy, American Hist. Rev.*, Vol. III, 1898.
TRUMBULL, JOHN, *Autobiography* (New York and London, 1841).
WARREN, C., *History of the Harvard Law School* (New York, 1908).
——, *Warren-Adams Letters. Mass. Hist. Soc. Collections*, 1917.
WASHINGTON, *Writings, Collected by W. C. Ford* (New York, 1889-1893).
WEBSTER, NOAH, *A Collection of Essays* (Boston, 1790).
WEBSTER, PELATIAH, *Essays on the Free Trade* (Philadelphia, 1779).
WEST, S., *A Sermon* (Boston, 1795).
WITHERSPOON, JOHN, *The Works* (Edinburgh, 1804), 9 vol.
WOODS, LEONARD, *An Oration* (New York, 1798).

PERIODICALS IN FRENCH

Actes des Apôtres (Paris), 1789-1790, 1796-1797.
Affaires de l'Angleterre et de l'Amérique (Paris), 1776-1780.
Affiches de Province (Paris), 1777.
L'Ami du Peuple (Paris), 1790.
Les Annales patriotiques (Paris), 1789-1797.
L'Année littéraire (Paris), 1770-1789.
Bibliothèque britannique (Geneva), 1796-1800.
La Bouche de Fer (Paris), 1790-1791.
Le Carnet de la Sabretache (Paris), 1896.
Chronique de Paris (Paris), 1789-1793.
Chronique universelle (Paris), Year VI.

La Clef du Cabinet (Paris), Year V-Year IX.
Le Conservateur (Paris), Year V.
Courrier d'Avignon (Avignon), 1770-1789.
Le Courrier de l'Amérique (Philadelphia), 1784.
Le Courrier de l'Europe (London), 1776-1792.
Le Courrier de Provence (Paris), 1789-1791.
Le Courrier des Départements (Paris), 1791-1792.
Le Courrier de Versailles à Paris (Versailles and Paris), 1789-1793.
Le Courrier français (Paris), 1789-1795.
Le Courrier français (Philadelphia), 1797.
Le Courrier républicain (Paris), Year III-Year V.
Le Courrier universel (Paris), Year I-Year VIII.
La Décade philosophique (Paris), Year III-Year IX.
Les Ephémérides du Citoyen (Paris), 1770-1776.
L'Esprit des Journaux (Paris), 1770-1800.
La Feuille du Jour (Paris), 1790-1792.
Feuille hebdomadaire de la Généralité de Limoges (Limoges), 1777-1782.
La Feuille villageoise (Paris), 1790-1793.
Les Folies d'un Mois (Paris), 1790-1792.
Le Fouet national (Paris), 1789-1790.
La Gazette de France (Paris), 1770-1800.
La Gazette de Leyde (known also as *Nouvelles extraordinaires de Leydes*) (Leyden), 1770-1793.
La Gazette de Paris (Paris), 1789-1792.
La Gazette française (New York), 1797.
La Gazette nationale (Paris), 1789-1890.
Gazette ou Journal politique des Deux Ponts (Deux Ponts), 1770-1789.
L'Historien (Paris), Years III-IV.
Journal d'Agriculture (Paris), 1770-1783.
Journal d'Economie politique (Paris), Years IV-V.
Journal général de France (Paris), 1785-1790.
Journal de la Cour et de la Ville (Paris), 1790.
Journal de Lyon (Lyons), 1784-1788.
Journal de Paris (Paris), 1777-1800.
Journal de Politique et de Littérature de Bruxelles (Brussels), 1776-1778.
Journal des Débats (Paris), 1789-1800.
Journal des Hommes libres (Paris), Years II-VIII.

Journal des Savants (Paris), 1770-1789.
Journal des Sciences et des Beaux-Arts (Paris), 1770-1783.
Journal du Soir (Paris), 1790-1800.
Journal encyclopédique de Bouillon (Bouillon), 1770-1793.
Journal général de la Cour et de la Ville (Paris), 1790-1791.
Journal historique et politique de Genève (Geneva), 1770-1792.
Journal universel (Paris), 1789-1795.
Le Logographe (Paris), 1789-1792.
Mélanges publiés par la Société des Bibliophiles (Paris), 1903.
Mémoires de l'Institut National des Sciences et Arts (Paris), Year III.
Mercure de France (Paris), 1770-1800.
Mercure universel (Paris), 1791-1800.
Le Messager du Soir (Paris), Years II-VI.
Le Niveau de l'Europe et de l'Amérique septentrionale (Philadelphia), 1794-1796.
Nouvelles de la République des Lettres (Paris), 1777-1786.
Nouvelles éphémérides économiques (Paris), 1776-1786.
Nouvelles politiques (Paris), 1797.
Observations sur la Physique (Paris), 1770-1790.
Paris pendant 1796, *Paris pendant* 1797, *Paris pendant*, 1798 (London).
Le Patriote français (Paris), 1789-1793, Years VI-VII.
Le Père Duchène (edited by Hébert; Paris), 1789-1793.
Le Père Duchène (edited by Lemaire), 1790-1792.
Le Postillon (Paris), 1790.
La Quotidienne (Paris), 1792-1797.
Le Rédacteur (Paris), 1798-1800.
Le Républicain français (Paris), 1792-1798.
Revue d'Histoire littéraire de la France, 1917.
Revue de Paris, 1898-1923.
Revue des Etudes historiques (Paris), 1923.
La Revue rétrospective (Paris), 1889.
La Sentinelle (Paris), 1792-1797.
Le Spectateur du Nord (Hamburg), 1798-1800.
La Suisse universitaire, 1901.
Le Tableau de Paris (Paris), 1796.
Tribut de la Société nationale des neuf Sœurs (Paris), 1790-91.
L'Union (Paris), 1790.

BOOKS AND PAMPHLETS IN FRENCH

Adresse aux Anglais par un Représentant de la Nation française (Paris), 1791.
Alphabet des Sans Culottes (Paris), Year II.
Amélie, Anecdote anglaise (no date).
L'Américain aux Anglais (Philadelphia), 1781.
A Monsieur le Comte de Lally Tollendal, en Réponse à sa Lettre à ses Commettants (no date).
L'Apocalypse britannique (London, 1782).
Articles de Confédération et d'Union perpétuelle des Colonies anglaises de l'Amérique (1776).
Au Peuple français sur les Assignats, par un Citoyen des Etats-Unis (Paris, 1790).
Aux Emigrés de toutes les Contrées de l'Europe (Philadelphia, 1784).
Les Aventures politiques du Père Nicaise (Paris, 1793).
Biographie des Contemporains (Paris, 1836), 5 vol.
Calendrier de Philadelphie (Paris, 1778).
La Cassette verte de M. de Sartines (The Hague, 1774).
Catalogue des Noms de Villes, Villages, Rivières . . . contenus dans la Carte de l'Amérique septentrionale. . . . Chez le Rouge (1777).
Le Chansonnier de la Montagne (Paris, Year III.)
Le Comte de Vergennes cause des Etats généraux (Paris, 1788).
Conseil des Cinq Cents. Opinion de Boulay Paty. Session of 3 Prairial, Year VI.
Considérations sur le Mémoire adressé à L. L. H. H. P. P., by John Adams (no date).
Considérations sur les Fonds publics, le Climat des Etats-Unis, d'Amérique (Paris, 1793).
Considérations sur les Fonds publics des Etats-Unis (Paris, 1793).
Convention entre la République française et les Etats-Unis de l'Amérique, 8 Vendémiaire, Year IX (Paris, no date).
Correspondance qui dévoile la Trahison du Sénateur américain, W. Blount (Philadelphia, no date).
Correspondance du Lord Georges Germaine (Berne, 1782).
Correspondance secrète publiée par M. de Lescure (Paris, 1866), 2 vol.

Déclaration des Droits du Roi et de la Nation française (no date).
Décret du 7 Juillet, 1791 (Paris, no date).
De l'Amérique et des Américains (Berlin, 1771).
De la République et de la Monarchie (Paris, 1789).
Description topographique de 600,000 Acres de Terres (Paris, 1792).
Le Despotisme des Parlements (no date).
Deux Français aux Etats-Unis. Mélanges publiés par la Société des Bibliophiles français. Series 2, Document 6.
Dictionnaire social et patriotique.
Discours composé en 1788, qui a remporté le Prix à l'Académie française en 1792 (Paris, 1792).
Dissertation sur les Suites de la Découverte de l'Amérique. . . . Par un Citoyen, ancien Syndic de la Chambre de Commerce de Lyon (1787).
Entretiens de Guillaume de Nassau, Prince d'Orange et du Général Montgomery (London and Paris, 1780).
Etablissements français dans les Etats-Unis d'Amérique (Paris, no date).
Etrennes à la Nation (Paris, no date).
Extraits des Gazettes américaines (Paris, 1786).
Extrait du Journal de la Société de 1789 (Paris, 1799). This is La Rochefoucauld's speech on Franklin.
Le Financier philosophe et patriote, by M. C. J. B. (Paris, 1790).
Frankliniana. . . . Par un Américain (Paris, 1800).
Histoire de la Guerre d'Amérique (London, 1783).
Histoire d'un Pou français (Paris, 1781).
L'Indépendance absolue des Américains des Etats-Unis prouvée (Paris, 1798).
L'Intérêt de la France à une Constitution monarchique (Berlin, 1790).
Je crains la Banqueroute (no date).
Journal d'un Voyage dans l'Amérique septentrionale, traduit de l'Anglais (Paris, 1793), 2 vol.
Journal d'un Officier de l'Escadre de M. le Comte d'Estaing (Paris, 1782).
Lettre adressée à l'Abbé Raynal (Paris, 1791).
Lettre circulaire du Congrès des Etats-Unis d'Amérique (Paris, Year III).

Lettre de M. Bergasse à ses Commettants (no date).
Lettre de M. de V. à M. le C. D. M. (Paris, 1790).
Lettre de M. R. esquire au Lord Comte de D. (Amsterdam, 1779).
Lettres du Comte d'Albany au Lord Bute (1780).
Lettre d'un Correcteur des Comptes à M. le Marquis de La Fayette (1788).
Lettres d'un Membre du Congrès américain (Paris, 1779).
Lettre d'un Quaker américain à un Républicain français (Paris, 1792).
La Lyre républicaine (Paris, Year III).
Les Négociants armateurs et marins de la Commune de Nantes au Conseil des Cinq Cents (Year VIII).
Notes sur les Défrichements en Amérique à l'Usage des Européens (no date).
Le Nouveau Mississippi (Paris, 1790).
Observations sur le Scioto (no date).
Pamphlet programatique (Geneva, 1780).
Le Parlement de Paris établi au Scioto (Paris, 1790).
Paul Jones ou Prophéties sur l'Amérique (no date).
Pétition respectueuse des Amis de la Société chrétienne, appelés Quakers, prononcée à l'Assemblée Nationale, le Jeudi 10 *Février* 1791 (no date).
Plan de Vente de 300,000 *Acres de Terres situées dans les Comtés de Nortumberland et de Huntington* (Philadelphia, 1794).
Premiers Mouvements de Bretagne (1789).
Le Procès des trois Rois (London, 1780).
Réclamation du tiers Etat (1788).
Recueil Clairembaut Maurepas, Raunié edition (Paris), 10 vol.
Recueil des Lois constitutives des Colonies anglaises confédérées sous la Dénomination d'Etats-Unis (Philadelphia and Paris), 1778.
Recueil d'Estampes représentant différents Evénements de la Guerre qui a procuré l'Independance aux Etats-Unis (Paris, no date).
Réflexions impartiales sur les Conséquences qui doivent résulter pour la Grande-Bretagne de l'Indépendance des Américains (London, 1780).
Réflexions impartiales sur l'Amérique (Amsterdam and Paris, 1781).
Réflexions sur la Dette publique exigible (no date).

Réponse à la Déclaration du Congrès américain (London, 1777).
Réponse de l'Amérique septentrionale à la Lettre écrite du Palais Royal (Philadelphia and Paris, 1785).
Rêveries d'un Suisse (London, 1781).
Roman politique sur l'Etat présent des Affaires de l'Amérique (Amsterdam and Paris, 1779).
Songe d'un Habitant du Scioto (Paris, 1790).
Tableau de la Situation actuelle des Etats-Unis de l'Amérique (Paris, 1795).
Théorie des Etats Généraux (Paris, 1789).
Traité d'Amitié et de Commerce conclu entre le Roi et les Etats-Unis (Paris, 1778).
La Trompette du Père Duchène (Paris, 1792).
Vie privée et politique de J. L. R. Hébert (Paris, Year II).
Vie privée, impartiale, du Marquis de La Fayette (Paris, 1790).
Le Vœu de toutes les Nations (1778).

ALEMBERT, D', *Œuvres* (Paris, 1822), 5 vol.
ALLONVILLE, COMTE D', *Mémoires secrets* (Paris, 1836), 6 vol.
AMABLE, LOUIS, *Une Loge maçonnique d'avant* 1789 (Paris, 1897).
ARNAULT, *Œuvres de M. Arnauld* (Paris, 1803), 11 vol.
AUBURNET, *Voyages dans les Parties intérieures de l'Amérique septentrionale* (Paris, 1790), 2 vol.
AULARD, *Recueil de Documents pour l'Histoire des Jacobins* (Paris, 1889-1897), 6 vol.
——, *Paris pendant la Réaction thermidorienne et sous le Directoire* (Paris, 1898), 5 vol.
——, *Paris sous le Consulat* (Paris, 1903-1909), 4 vol.
——, *Histoire politique de la Révolution Française* (Paris, 1909).
AUTREY, FABRY D', *Les Quakers à leur Frère Voltaire* (1768).
BACHAUMONT, *Mémoires secrets* (Paris, 1771-1787), 36 vol.
BARBIER LE JEUNE, H. S. LE, *Asgill* (Paris, 1785).
BARERE, *Mémoires* (Paris, 1842), Vol. I-III.
BARRAS, *Mémoires* (Paris, 1895), Vol. I-IV.
BARRON, *Histoire de la Fondation des Colonies des anciennes Républiques* (Utrecht, 1778).
BARRUEL, ABBE, *Mémoires pour servir à l'Histoire du Jacobinisme* (Hamburg, 1797).
BARTRAM, W., *Voyage dans les Parties sud de l'Amérique septentrionale* (Paris, Year VIII), 2 vol.

Bayard, F. M., *Voyage dans l'Intérieur des Etats-Unis* (Paris, Year VI).
Beaumarchais, *Observations sur le Mémoire justificatif de la Cour de Londres* (London and Philadelphia, 1779).
——, *Œuvres complètes* (Paris, 1835).
Berger, Eugene, *Le Vicomte de Mirabeau* (Paris, 1904).
Bernardin de Saint-Pierre, *Œuvres complètes* (Paris, 1830), 12 vol.
Besnard, Yves, *Souvenirs d'un Nonagénaire* (Paris, 1880).
Blackfort, D. de, *Précis de l'Etat de l'Amérique* (Milan, 1771).
Blin, M., *Lettre à Monsieur Mounier* (Paris, 1789).
Bonnet de Frejus, J., *Réponses aux principales Questions qui peuvent être faites sur les Etats-Unis* (Lausanne, 1795), 2 vol.
——, *Etats-Unis de l'Amérique à la Fin du* XVIIIe *siècle* (Paris, no date), 2 vol.
Bossu, *Nouveaux Voyages dans l'Amérique septentrionale* (Amsterdam, 1778).
Bostel Dumont, *Voyage à la Louisiane* (Paris, 1802).
Bouille, Marquis de, *Mémoires* (Paris, 1821).
Bourdon, L. C., *Voyage d'Amérique* (London and Paris, 1786).
Bourrienne, de, *Mémoires* (Paris, no date).
Brion de la Tour, *Almanach intéressant* (Paris, 1780).
Brissot, J. P., *Mémoires publiés par Claude Perroud* (Paris, 1910), 2 vol.
——, *Correspondance, publiée par Claude Perroud* (Paris, 1912).
Brissot de Warville, J. P., *Bibliothèque philosophique de Jurisprudence* (1782-1786), 10 vol.
——, *Examen critique des Voyages de M. le Marquis de Chastellux* (London, 1786).
——, *Nouveau Voyage dans les Etats-Unis* (Paris, 1791), 3 vol.
——, *Testament politique de l'Angleterre* (1780).
Brissot de Warville et Claviere, J. P., *De la France et des Etats-Unis* (London, 1787).
Brugiere, J. P., *Nécessité de la Paix* (Paris, Year VIII).
Buffenoir, Hippolyte, *La Comtesse d'Houdetot* (Paris, 1901).
Buffon, *Œuvres complètes* (Paris, 1846), 3 vol.
Burnaby, A., *Voyage dans les Colonies du Milieu de l'Amérique septentrionale* (Lausanne, 1778).
Burk, W., *Histoire des Colonies européennes dans l'Amérique* (Paris, 1767).

CAMPAN, MADAME, *Mémoires sur la Vie privée de Marie-Antoinette* (Paris, 1822), 3 vol.

CARLI, J. R., *Lettres américaines* (Boston and Paris, 1788), 2 vol.

CARVER, J., *Voyage dans les Parties intérieures de l'Amérique septentrionale* (Paris, 1784).

CERISIER, *Le Destin de l'Amérique* (London, 1780).

CERUTTI, *Lettre à M. le Vicomte de Noailles* (Paris, 1789).

——, *Idées simples et précises sur le Papier Monnaie* (Paris, 1791).

CHAS, *Histoire philosophique et politique des Révolutions de l'Angleterre.*

CHAS ET LEBRUN, *Histoire philosophique et politique de la Révolution de l'Amérique* (Paris, Year IX).

CHASTELLUX (?), *Discours sur les Avantages et les Désavantages qui résultent pour l'Europe de la Découverte de l'Amérique* (Paris, 1787).

CHASTELLUX, CHEVALIER DE, *Voyage de Newport à Philadelphie*, Imprimerie de l'Escadre (no date).

——, *Voyage de M. le Chevalier de Chastellux en Amérique* (Cassel, 1785).

CHASTELLUX, MARQUIS DE, *Voyage dans l'Amérique septentrionale* (Paris, 1786).

CHATEAUBRIAND, VICOMTE DE, *Mémoires d'Outre-tombe* (Paris, 1898-1901, Edition Biré), 6 vol.

——, *Œuvres complètes* (Paris, 1831), 31 vol.

CHENIER, A., *Œuvres* (Edition Dimoff, Paris, no date), 3 vol.

CHAVANNE DE LA GIRAUDIERE, *L'Amérique délivrée* (Amsterdam, 1783), 2 vol.

CHINARD, G., *L'Amérique et le Rêve exotique* (Paris, 1913).

——, *L'Exotisme américain dans l'Œuvre de Chateaubriand* (Paris, 1918).

COMBEROUSSE, MICHEL DE, (sometimes written Decomberousse), *Asgill* (Paris, Year IX).

CONDORCET, MARQUIS DE, *Eloge de Franklin*, Paris, 1791.

——, *Lettres d'un Citoyen des Etats-Unis à un Français* (Philadelphia, 1788).

——, *Œuvres, publiées par Condorcet O'Connor* (Paris, 1847-1849), 12 vol.

COOPER, THOMAS, *Renseignements sur l'Amérique* (Hamburg, 1795).

COSTE, J. F., *De antiqua Medico-Philosophia orbi novo adaptanda* (Lyons, 1783).
CREVECŒUR, HECTOR SAINT JOHN DE, *Lettres d'un Cultivateur américain* (Paris, 1784 and 1787), 3 vol.
——, *Voyage dans la Haute Pennsylvanie* (Paris, Year IX), 3 vol.
CROY, DUC DE, *Journal inédit* (Paris, 1907), 4 vol.
DAYMON, F., *Le Règlement militaire* (Philadelphia, 1776).
DELACROIX, *Constitutions des principaux Etats de l'Europe et des Etats-Unis de l'Amérique* (Paris, 1791), 4 vol. Numerous other editions. There is one in 6 vol. (1801).
——, *Des Moyens de régénérer la France* (Paris, Year V).
DEMEUSNIER, *L'Amérique Indépendante* (Ghent, 1790), 3 vol.
——, *Essais sur les Etats-Unis* (Paris, 1786).
DESLANDES, *Discours sur la Grandeur et l'Importance de la Révolution qui vient de s'opérer dans l'Amérique* (Paris and Frankfort), 1785.
DIDOT, *Précis sur la Révolution et le Caractère français, adressé aux Citoyens des Etats-Unis d'Amérique* (Year II).
DIDOT, ALBERT FIRMIN, *Souvenirs de J. E. Despréaux* (Paris, Year VIII).
DONIOL, HENRY, *Le Comte de Vergennes et P. M. Hennin.*
——, *Histoire de la Participation de la France à l'Etablissement des Etats-Unis* (Paris, 1899), 5 vol.
DREYFUS, F., *Un Philosophe d'autrefois* (Paris, 1903).
DUBROCA, Y. F., *Eloge de Washington* (Paris, Year VIII).
DUBUISSON, *Abrégé de la Révolution de l'Amérique anglaise* (Paris, 1778).
DUCHER, *Nouvelle Alliance à proposer entre les Républiques française et américaine* (no date).
DUCRAY DUMINIL, *Lolotte et Fanfan* (Paris, 1788).
DEFFANT, MARQUISE DU, *Correspondance complète* (Paris, 1767), 3 vol.
——, *Lettres à H. Walpole* (Paris, 1824), 4 vol.
DUMAS, COMTE M., *Souvenirs* (Paris, 1839), 3 vol.
DUMONT, ETIENNE, *Souvenirs sur Mirabeau* (Paris, 1832).
DUMOURIEZ, GENERAL, *Nouveau Tableau spéculatif de l'Europe* (1798).
——, *Suite des Mémoires* (Paris, 1848).
DURAND, ABBE, *Le Franklinisme réfuté* (Paris, 1788).

DUTENS, *Mémoires d'un Voyageur qui se repose* (Paris, 1806), 3 vol.

DUVAL, A., *Œuvres complètes* (Paris, 1822), 2 vol.

DUVAL, GEORGES, *Souvenirs de la Terreur* (Paris, 1841).

EPINAY, MADAME D', *Mémoires et Correspondance* (Paris, 1818), 3 vol.

EUSTACE, JEAN SKEY, *Traité d'Amitié et de Commerce entre S. M. Britannique et les Etats-Unis* (Paris, Year IV).

——, *Le Citoyen des Etats-Unis, Jean Skey Eustace à ses Frères d'Armes* (Paris, 1793).

FAUCHET, CLAUDE, *Coup d'Œil sur la Situation des Affaires entre la France et les Etats-Unis* (Paris, 1798).

FAUCHET, ABBE, *Eloge civique de B. Franklin* (Paris, 1790).

FERSEN, COMTE DE, *Le Comte de Fersen et la Cour de France* (Paris, 1877), published by M. de Klinkowstrom, 2 vol.

FEUGERE, A., *Bibliographie critique de l'Abbé Raynal* (Angoulême, 1922).

——, *Un Précurseur de la Révolution, l'Abbé Raynal* (Angoulême, 1922).

FLASSAN, *Pacification de l'Europe* (Paris, Year VIII).

FRANQUEVILLE, COMTE DE, *Le premier Siècle de l'Institut* (Paris, 1913).

FREVILLE, *Les Droits de la Grande-Bretagne établis contre les Prétentions des Américains* (The Hague, 1776).

FONTANES, *Eloge funèbre de Washington* (Paris, Year VIII).

GALIANI, ABBE, *Correspondance inédite* (Paris, Year VIII).

——, *Lettres* (Paris, 1881), 2 vol.

GARAT, *Mémoire sur Suard et le* XVIIIe *siècle* (Paris, 1820), 2 vol.

GENLIS, COMTESSE DE, *Mémoires inédits* (Paris, 1825), 10 vol.

GENTY, ABBE, *Influence de la Découverte de l'Amérique sur le Bonheur du Genre humain* (Paris, 1787).

GEORGEL, J. F., *Mémoires* (Paris, 1817-1818), 6 vol.

GIRAUD, *Nouvelles Etudes sur Chateaubriand* (Paris, 1912).

GODARD, P. S., *Influence de la Révolution de l'Amérique septentrionale sur les Opinions et la Législation de l'Europe.* (In reality by Condorcet. No date.)

GORGY, *Les Torts apparents* (Paris, 1787).

GRASSET SAINT-SAUVEUR, *Description des principaux Peuples de l'Amérique* (Paris, Year VI).

——, *Tableau cosmographique de l'Europe, de l'Asie, de l'Afrique et de l'Amérique* (Paris, 1787).

GRIMM, *Correspondance* (*Edition Tourneux*, Paris, 1877), 16 vol.

GUILLARD DE BEAURIEU, *L'Elève de la Nature* (Lille, 1783), 3 vol.

GUSTAVE III, *Lettres à la Comtesse de Boufflers* (Bordeaux, 1900).

HAUSSET DU, *Mémoires* (Paris, 1825).

HAUTERIVE, COMTE D', *De l'Etat de la France* (Paris, Year IX).

HAUTEVAL, L., *Hauteval Citoyen français au Gouvernement et au Peuple américain.*

HILLIARD D'AUBERTEUIL, *Essais historiques et politiques sur les Anglo-Américains* (Bruxelles, 1782), 2 vol.

——, *Essais historiques et politiques sur la Révolution de l'Amérique septentrionale* (Paris, 1783), 3 vol.

——, *Histoire de l'Administration du Lord North* (Paris, 1784).

——, *Miss Mac Rae* (Philadelphia, 1784).

HOLBACH, D', *Le Système de la Nature* (1770), 2 vol.

HORNOT, *Anecdotes américaines* (Paris, 1776).

ISNARD, *Observations sur le Principe qui a produit les Révolutions de France, de Genève et d'Amérique* (Evreux, 1789).

JEFFERSON, T., *Observations sur la Virginie* (Paris, 1786).

JELLINECK, G., *La Déclaration des Droits de l'Homme* (Paris, 1901).

JUMELIN, J. B., *Lettre écrite au Bonhomme Richard concernant les Assignats* (no date).

KAGENECK, M. DE, *Lettres* (Paris, 1874).

LA CHAISE, M. P. DE, *Lettre d'un Américain aux Citoyens français sur la Représentation* (Paris, 1789).

LA CHANONIE, G. DE, *Mémoires politiques et militaires du Général Tercier* (Paris, 1902).

LACOMBE, BERNARD DE, *La Vie privée de Talleyrand* (Paris, 1910).

LA CREPINIERE, A. DE, *Lettre écrite du Palais Royal aux quatre Parties du Monde* (Paris, 1785).

LA FAYETTE, MARQUIS DE, *Mémoires, Correspondance et Manuscrits du Général Lafayette* (London, 1837), 6 vol.

——, *Correspondance, éditée par Jules Thomas* (Paris, 1903).

LA HARPE, J. F., *Oui on Non* (no date).

LAMBERT, BARONNE (*née* PANNELLIER D'ARSONVAL), *Souvenirs* (Paris, 1902).

LAMETH, TH. DE, *Mémoires* (Paris, 1913).

LA REVEILLERE LEPAUX, *Mémoires* (Paris), 3 vol.

LA ROCHEFOUCAULD LIANCOURT, *Des Prisons de Philadelphie* (Paris, Year VIII).

——, *Extrait du Journal de la Société de* 1789 (no date).

——, *Voyage dans les Etats-Unis d'Amérique* (Paris, Year VII), 8 vol.

LA ROCHEJACQUELIN, MARQUISE DE, *Mémoires* (Paris, 1826), 2 vol.

LA ROCHETILHAC, P. DE, *Almanach américain* (Paris, 1783).

LAUREAU, *L'Amérique découverte* (Autun, 1782).

LAUZUN, DUC DE, *Mémoires* (Paris, 1880), 2 vol.

LAVISSE, *Histoire de France* (Paris, 1910), Vol. IX.

LEBOUCHER, ODET JULIEN, *Histoire de la dernière Guerre* (Paris, 1787).

LENOIR LAROCHE, *De l'Esprit de la Constitution qui convient à la France* (Paris, Year III).

LE ROY, *Seconde Lettre à M. Benjamin Franklin* (no date).

——, *Suite de la Lettre adressée à M. Benjamin Franklin* (Rouen, 1787).

LETOMBE, *Mémoire et Projet concernant les Agences, la Résidence et la Navigation des Français dans les Ports des Etats-Unis* (no date).

LEZAY MARNESIA, MARQUIS C. F. ADRIEN DE, *Lettres écrites des Rives de L'Ohio* (Paris, Year IX).

LEZAY MARNESIA, COMTE ADRIEN DE, *Considérations sur les Etats de Massachusetts et de Pennsylvanie* (no date).

LEVIS, MARQUIS DE, *Souvenirs et Portraits* (Paris, 1813).

LINT, DE, *Réponse à la Déclaration du Congrès américain* (London, 1777).

LIVINGSTON, WILLIAM, *Examen du Gouvernement d'Angleterre* (London and Paris, 1789).

LOCKROY, EDWARD, *Journal d'une Bourgeoise pendant la Révolution* (Paris, 1881).

LOMENIE, DE, *Beaumarchais et son Temps* (Paris, 1856), 2 vol.

LONGCHAMPS, ABBE PIERRE DE, *Histoire impartiale des Evénements politiques et militaires de la dernière Guerre* (Amsterdam, 1785).

LOUVET DU COUVRAY, *Les Amours du Chevalier de Faublas* (Paris, 1789), 2 vol.

MABLY, ABBE DE, *Observations sur le Gouvernement et les Lois des Etats-Unis* (Amsterdam, 1784).

MAILHE, *Discours qui a remporté le Prix à l'Académie des Jeux floraux* (Toulouse, 1784).

MAISTRE, COMTE JOSEPH DE, *Considérations sur la France* (London, 1797).

MALOUET, *Mémoires* (Paris, 1868), 2 vol.

MANDRILLON, *Recherches philosophiques sur la Découverte de l'Amérique* (Amsterdam, 1784).

——, *Le Spectateur américain* (Amsterdam, 1784).

——, *Le Voyageur américain* (Amsterdam, 1782).

MARIE-ANTOINETTE, *Correspondance secrète de Marie-Antoinette et de Mercy* (Paris, 1874).

MARSILLAC, JEAN DE, *Le Principe ou la Règle de Vie des premiers Chrétiens* (Amsterdam, 1791).

——, *La Vie de Guillaume Penn* (Paris, 1781).

MARSOLLIER, J. B., *Asgill* (Paris, 1793).

MASSON, F., *Napoléon inconnu* (Paris, 1895).

MATHIEZ, ALBERT, *Les Origines des Cultes révolutionnaires* (Paris, 1904).

MAURIN, *Les Entretiens d'un Citoyen de Philadelphie* (no date).

MAYER, DE, *Asgill* (Amsterdam and Paris, 1784).

MAZZEI, *Recherches historiques et politiques sur les Etats-Unis* (Paris, 1788), 4 vol.

MENEVAL, BARON DE, *Napoléon et Marie-Louise* (Paris, 1844).

METRA, *Correspondance secrète* (Neuwied, 1774-1793), 19 vol.

MIRABEAU, *Considérations sur l'Ordre de Cincinnatus* (London, 1784).

——, *Mémoires biographiques* (Paris, 1834), 8 vol.

MONTBARREY, PRINCE DE, *Mémoires autographes* (Paris, 1826), 3 vol.

MONTPENSIER, DUC DE, *Mémoires* (Paris, 1837).

MOREAU, J. N., *Mes Souvenirs* (Paris, 1898), 2 vol.

MOREAU DE SAINT-MERY, *Voyage aux Etats-Unis* (New Haven, 1913).

——, *Extraits d'un Ouvrage manuscrit* (no date).

MORELLET, ABBE, *Avis aux Faiseurs de Constitution* (Paris, 1789).

——, *Lettre écrite à l'Occasion de l'Ouvrage intitulé, "Examen du Gouvernement de l'Angleterre"* (no date).
——, *Mémoires sur le* XVIII e *siècle et la Révolution* (Paris, 1821), 2 vol.
MORELLY, *Le Code de la Nature* (1755).
MOUNIER, *Considérations sur les Gouvernements* (Paris, 1789).
——, *Adolphe* (London, 1795).
——, *Recherches sur les Causes qui ont empêché la France de devenir libre* (Geneva, 1792).
MULOT, ABBE, *Journal intime* (Paris, 1902).
NANCREDE, *L'Abeille française* (Boston, 1792).
NECKER, *Du Pouvoir exécutif dans les grands Etats* (1792).
NOEL, *Journal d'un Voyage fait dans l'Intérieur de l'Amérique* (Paris, 1793), 2 vol.
PAUW, DE, *Recherches philosophiques sur les Américains* (Berlin, 1770 and 1771), 3 vol.
PERNETTY, DOM, *Dissertation sur l'Amérique et les Américains* (Berlin, 1770).
PHILADELPHE, CHARLES, *Pamphlet programatique* (Geneva, 1780).
PICTET, C., *Tableau de la Situation actuelle des Etats-Unis d'Amérique* (Paris, 1795).
PINTO, ISAAC, *Lettre de M. S. B. au Sujet des Troubles qui agitent actuellement toute l'Amérique septentrionale* (The Hague, 1776).
——, *Réponse de M. I. de Pinto aux Observations d'un Homme impartial* (The Hague, 1776).
——, *Seconde Lettre de M. de Pinto à l'Occasion des Troubles des Colonies* (The Hague, 1776).
POISSONNIER, *Discours sur la Naissance de Mgr. le Dauphin* (Paris, 1782).
PONTGIBAUD, COMTE DE MORE DE, *Mémoires* (Paris, 1828).
POWNALL, THEODORE, *Pensées sur la Révolution de l'Amérique* (Amsterdam, no date).
——, *Mémoire adressé aux Souverains de l'Europe* (London and Brussels, 1781).
QUERARD, *La France littéraire* (Paris, 1833), 11 vol.
QUESNAY DE BEAUREPAIRE, *Mémoire sur l'Académie des Sciences et des Beaux-Arts des Etats-Unis* (Paris, 1788).
RABAUT SAINT-ETIENNE, *Adresse aux Anglais* (Paris, 1791).
RACINE, ABBE, *Discours sur la Paix* (Toulouse, 1784).

RAMSAY, D., *Histoire de la Révolution de l'Amérique* (Paris, 1787), 2 vol.

——, *Vie de George Washington* (Paris, 1811).

RAYNAL, G. T., *Considérations sur la Paix de* 1783 (Berlin, 1783).

——, *Histoire philosophique et politique des Etablissements et du Commerce des Européens dans les deux Indes* (Amsterdam, 1770), 6 vol. (For the other editions, see Chapter I.)

——, *Révolution de l'Amérique* (Dublin, 1781).

——, *Tableau et Révolution des Colonies anglaises de l'Amérique septentrionale* (Amsterdam, 1781), 2 vol.

ROBERT, F., *Le Républicanisme adapté à la France* (Paris, 1790).

ROBERTSON, G., *Histoire de l'Amérique* (Maestricht, 1777), 4 vol.

ROBESPIERRE, MAXIMILIEN, *Le Défenseur de la Constitution* (Paris, 1792).

——, *Œuvres complètes* (Paris, 1912), 3 vol.

ROBIN, ABBE, *Nouveau Voyage dans l'Amérique septentrionale* (Philadelphia and Paris, 1782).

ROCHAMBEAU, MARQUIS DE, *Mémoires* (Paris, 1809), 2 vol.

ROEDERER, *Du Gouvernement* (no date).

ROLAND, MADAME, *Lettres publiées par Claude Perroud* (Paris, 1900), 2 vol.

——, *Lettres Nouvelle Série* (Paris, 1913), 2 vol.

——, *Lettres aux Demoiselles Cannet* (Paris, 1867), 2 vol.

ROMAIN, COMTE DE, *Souvenirs d'un Officier royaliste* (Paris, 1824), 3 vol.

ROUBAUD, ABBE, *Histoire générale de l'Asie, de l'Afrique et de l'Amérique* (Paris, 1770-1775), 14 vol.

ROYER, ABBE, *Discours prononcé dans l'Eglise N. D. de Provins* (Paris, 1775).

RUDLER, *La Jeunesse de Benjamin Constant* (Paris, 1908).

SAINTE-BEUVE, *Causeries du Lundi* (Paris, no date), third edition, Vol. VII.

SAINTE-CROIX, BARON DE, *Observations sur le Traité de Paix conclu à Paris le* 10 *Février* 1763 (Amsterdam, 1780).

SALADIN, CHARLES, *Coup d'Oeil politique sur le Continent* (1800).

SAURIN, B. J., *L'Anglomane* (Paris, 1772), comedy in one act.

SAUVIGNY, B. DE, *Washington ou la Liberté du Nouveau Monde* (Paris, no date).

SEGUR, COMTE DE, *Mémoires ou Souvenirs et Anecdotes* (Paris, 1824-1826), 3 vol.

SERVAN, *Projet de Déclaration des Droits de l'Homme et du Citoyen* (1789).

SOULAVIE, *Mémoires historiques et diplomatiques de Barthélemy.*

——, *Mémoires sur le Règne de Louis XVI* (Paris, 1801), 6 vol.

SOULES, F., *Histoire des Troubles de l'Amérique* (Paris, 1787), 4 vol.

STAEL, MADAME DE, *Considérations sur la Révolution française* (1818), 3 vol.

SWAN, COLONEL, *Causes qui se sont opposées au Progrès du Commerce entre la France et les Etats-Unis* (Paris, 1790).

TALLEYRAND PERIGORD, MAURICE DE, *Eclaircissements donnés par le Citoyen Talleyrand* (Paris, Year VII).

——, *Mémoires, Lettres inédites et Papiers secrets, publiés par le Duc de Broglie* (Paris, 1891).

——, *Mémoires sur les Relations commerciales des Etats-Unis avec l'Angleterre* (Paris, 1799).

TANGUY LA BOISSIERE, *Mémoire sur la Situation commerciale de la France avec les Etats-Unis* (no date).

——, *Observations sur la Dépêche écrite le 16 Janvier 1797, par M. Pickering* (Philadelphia, 1797).

TOCQUEVILLE, COMTE DE, *La Démocratie en Amérique* (Paris, 1880), 3 vol.

TOUR DU PIN DE GOUVERNET, MARQUISE DE LA, *Mémoires d'une Femme de cinquante Ans* (Paris, 1913), 2 vol.

TOURON, PERE, *Histoire de l'Amérique* (Paris, 1768), 4 vol.

TUCKER, *Cui bono?* (London, 1782).

VASSE, BARONNE DE, *Mémoires pour servir à l'Histoire de la Révolution de l'Amérique* (1787 [?]).

VERGENNES (?), *Mémoire historique et politique sur la Louisiane* (Paris, 1802).

VERRIER, *Atlas ou Recueil de Cartes détaillées des Provinces de l'Amérique septentrionale* (Paris, 1784).

VICQ D'AZYR, *Œuvres* (Paris, 1805), 6 vol.

VILLIERS DU TERRAGE, MARC DE, *Les dernières Années de la Louisiane Française* (Paris, 1903).

VINCENT, *Lettres d'un Membre du Congrès américain* (Paris, 1779).

VOLNEY, CHASSEBŒUF DE, *Tableau du Climat et du Sol des Etats-Unis* (Paris, 1803), 2 vol.

VOLTAIRE, *Œuvres* (1877-1882), 50 vol.

INDEX